AUTODESK® INVENTOR® 2010

NO EXPERIENCE REQUIRED

Thom Tremblay

WILEY

Wiley Publishing, Inc.

Senior Acquisitions Editor: Willem Knibbe
Development Editor: David Clark
Technical Editor: Dan Hunsucker
Production Editor: Christine O'Connor
Copy Editor: Tiffany Taylor
Editorial Manager: Pete Gaughan
Production Manager: Tim Tate
Vice President and Executive Group Publisher: Richard Swadley
Vice President and Publisher: Neil Edde
Book Designer: Franz Baumhackl
Compositor: James D. Kramer, Happenstance Type-O-Rama
Proofreader: Nancy Bell
Indexer: Robert Swanson
Project Coordinator, Cover: Lynsey Stanford
Cover Designer: Ryan Sneed
Cover Image: Thom Tremblay

Library of Congress Cataloging-in-Publication Data

Tremblay, Thom, 1967-
  Autodesk Inventor 2010 : no experience required / Thom Tremblay.
     p. cm.
  ISBN 978-0-470-48169-1 (paper/website)
  1. Engineering graphics. 2. Engineering models—Data processing. 3. Autodesk Inventor (Electronic resource) I. Title.
  T353.T7656 2009
  620'.00420285536—dc22
                              2009023122

10 9 8 7 6 5 4 3 2 1

Dear Reader,

Thank you for choosing *Autodesk Inventor 2010: No Experience Required*. This book is part of a family of premium-quality Sybex books, all of which are written by outstanding authors who combine practical experience with a gift for teaching.

Sybex was founded in 1976. More than 30 years later, we're still committed to producing consistently exceptional books. With each of our titles, we're working hard to set a new standard for the industry. From the paper we print on, to the authors we work with, our goal is to bring you the best books available.

I hope you see all that reflected in these pages. I'd be very interested to hear your comments and get your feedback on how we're doing. Feel free to let me know what you think about this or any other Sybex book by sending me an email at nedde@wiley.com. If you think you've found a technical error in this book, please visit http://sybex.custhelp.com. Customer feedback is critical to our efforts at Sybex.

Best regards,

NEIL EDDE
Vice President and Publisher
Sybex, an Imprint of Wiley

To Thomas Cecil Tremblay. I doubt that I will ever meet
a harder working, more devoted man in my lifetime.
He's a modest man of many talents who sacrificed
so my mother, Joan, could always be there
for my sister Angela and me.

ACKNOWLEDGMENTS

I would first and foremost like to thank my wife Nancy and our children: Chris, Kyle, Logan, and Sydney for putting up with another book. Her support has been invaluable.

I'd like to thank tech editor Dan Hunsucker for all his hard work, expertise, and extraordinary ability to decipher what I was writing.

Thanks to Willem Knibbe, David Clark, Pete Gaughan, Christine O'Connor, Tiffany Taylor, and the others whose names I don't know but who worked very hard to try to make me look smart.

I also want to extend my sincere thanks to Lynn Allen, Alan Jacobs, Joe Astroth, Denise Harvey, and all of the Autodesk family who supported and encouraged me during this effort.

ABOUT THE AUTHOR

Thom Tremblay is a Subject Matter Expert on the Autodesk Strategic Universities team. He's been working with Inventor for 10 years and is an Inventor Certified Professional. He has used it to design everything from cabinets and castings to ships and video monitors. He has close ties to the Inventor community; is a frequent speaker at colleges, universities, and training centers; and presents annually at Autodesk University.

Contents at a Glance

Introduction   *xvii*

CHAPTER 1   Finding Your Way in the Inventor Interface   1

CHAPTER 2   Building the Foundation of the Design   51

CHAPTER 3   Moving into the Assembly World   111

CHAPTER 4   Working with Solid Models and Weldments   155

CHAPTER 5   Working with the Frame Generator   217

CHAPTER 6   Working with Purchased and Multipurpose Parts   257

CHAPTER 7   Functional Design Using Design Accelerators   309

CHAPTER 8   Creating Contoured and Plastic Parts   365

CHAPTER 9   Communicating Your Design   429

APPENDIX A   Keyboard Shortcut Guide   485

APPENDIX B   Import and Export File Formats   493

Index   *497*

CONTENTS

Introduction   *xvii*

CHAPTER 1   **Finding Your Way in the Inventor Interface**   **1**

Inventor's User Interface 2
     Application Menu 3
     Quick Access Toolbar 4
Learning the Basics of Tabs 5
     Get Started Tab 5
     Ribbon Appearance 7
Learning to Use the Dialog Boxes 9
     Buttons 9
     Dialog Box Tabs 9
     Context Menus 10
The Open Dialog Box 10
     Shortcuts and the File List 11
     Navigation Controls 12
     File Display Options 13
     Other Controls 14
     Opening a File 15
The New File Dialog Box 16
More of the Inventor Interface 17
     The Browser Bar 17
     The Design Window 18
     The Status Bar 19
     Revisiting the Quick Access Tools 19
Working in the Design Window 21
     View Tab 22
     The ViewCube and the Navigation Bar 28
     Document Tabs 29
Make Yourself at Home: Customizing Inventor 30
     Application Options 30
     The General Tab 32
     The Colors Tab 32
     The Display Tab 34

The Hardware Tab 35
The Drawing Tab 36
The Sketch Tab 36
The Part Tab 37
The Assembly Tab 38
Creating a New Work Environment 38
Project Files 41
Project File Manager Buttons 44
Creating a Project File 44
Using the Help System and Infocenter 49
Are You Experienced? 50
Now you can 50

CHAPTER 2   Building the Foundation of the Design   51

It's About the Design 52
Creating the Sheet Metal Housing 52
Sketching Tools 52
Sketch Constraints 58
Sketch Dimensions 62
Inventor's Sheet Metal Tools 73
Sheet Metal Defaults 73
The Sheet Metal Defaults Dialog Box 73
Creating a New Sheet Metal Rule 74
The Style and Standard Editor 75
The Contour Flange Tool 81
The Flange Tool 83
The Mirror Tool 88
The Hole Feature 96
The Punch Tool 99
Are You Experienced? 109
Now you can 109

CHAPTER 3   Moving into the Assembly World   111

So, What's Next? 112
Developing a More Challenging Part 112
The Lofted Flange Tool 116
Output Options 117
The Face Tool 122

The Corner Round Tool 125

The Rip Tool 127

The Assembly Modeling Concept 135

Creating Assembly Constraints 137

The Constraint Tool 138

Working with Standard Parts 150

Are You Experienced? 153

Now you can 153

CHAPTER 4 **Working with Solid Models and Weldments** **155**

Keep It Simple, Make It Work 156

Making Parts 156

The Extrude Tool 157

Building the Bearing Plate 159

Work Features 161

The Chamfer Tool 166

Weldments 171

Drawing Views 175

Beginning a New Drawing from a Template 175

Creating a New Template 181

Creating Base Views 182

Defining the Base View 184

Creating a Projected View 187

Creating Section Views 192

Detail Views 193

Creating a Detail View 194

Detailing Tools 196

The Center Mark Tool 196

Placing Dimensions in Inventor 199

The General Dimension Tool 200

The Baseline Dimension Tool 204

Hole/Thread Notes 205

Dimension Editing Tools 207

Associativity 212

Drawing View Associativity 212

Adding Another Sheet 214

Are You Experienced? 216

Now you can 216

CHAPTER 5 **Working with the Frame Generator** **217**

Leveraging the Assembly 218
  Building the Foundation of a Metal Frame. 218
Restructuring an Assembly 222
  Demoting a Component in the Assembly 222
Frame Generator. 224
  Building a Frame 226
  Editing the Frame 229
  Adding the Bearing Supports 232
Bolted Connections. 234
  Adding a Bolted Connection 234
Representations. 248
  View 249
  Position. 249
  Level of Detail. 249
  Creating a View Representation. 250
Selection Filters 251
  Enhanced Highlighting. 252
Are You Experienced?. 255
  Now you can. 255

CHAPTER 6 **Working with Purchased and Multipurpose Parts** **257**

Reusing Your Own Parts. 258
  iMates 258
Creating a Cast Part 262
  Defining the Basic Shape. 262
  Adding Draft. 266
  The Fillet Tool 268
Derived Parts. 277
  Creating a Machined Handle 277
The Split Tool 280
  Method 280
  Faces. 280
  Remove 281
Supplier Content Center. 286
  Using Supplier Content 288
  Modifying Supplier Content 295

Assembly Sketches 296
Creating the 2D Layout 297
Using the Named Parameter 304
Are You Experienced? 308
Now you can. 308

CHAPTER 7   Functional Design Using Design Accelerators   309

Design Accelerators. 310
The Bearing Generator 310
The Shaft Component Generator 316
The V-Belts Component Generator 322
The Sweep Tool 335
Type. 335
Orientation. 336
The Rule Fillet. 340
Parallel Key Connection Generator 344
The Copy Object Tool 352
The Thicken/Offset Tool 353
The Unfold and Refold Tools. 358
Are You Experienced? 364
Now you can. 364

CHAPTER 8   Creating Contoured and Plastic Parts   365

Working with Plastic Parts. 366
The Multibody Part 366
Building the Basic Part 366
The Shell Tool 369
The Shell Tab 370
The More Tab 371
Plastic Part Features 375
Making Components 381
The Replace Tool 383
The Loft Tool. 385
The Curves Tab. 386
The Conditions Tab 386
The Transition Tab 388
The Revolve Tool 396
The Circular Pattern Tool 400

The Rib and Web Tools 404
The Decal Tool 408
The Sculpt Tool 411
    Sculpting the Power Knob 411
    Adding the Text 413
    Adding the Power Knob 416
The Grill Tool 417
    The Boundary Tab 417
    The Island Tab 418
    The Rib Tab 418
    The Spar Tab 418
    The Draft Tab 419
    Editing the Sketch 419
    Adding the Grill 421
    Adding Grills to the Assembly 423
Are You Experienced? 428
    Now you can 428

CHAPTER 9   **Communicating Your Design**   **429**

3D Is Just the Beginning 430
Advanced Drawing Views 430
    Sketch-Derived Views 430
    The Break-Out View 432
    The Break View 438
Presentation Files 441
    Creating an Exploded View 442
    Editing the Presentation 445
    Editing the View of the Animation 447
    Creating an *.AVI* File 450
    Creating an Exploded-View Drawing 451
Assembly Annotations 452
    Parts List 452
    Balloon/Auto Balloon 454
    Bill of Materials 458
    DWF 460
Inventor Studio Overview 462
    Getting Started 463
    The General Tab 463

The Output Tab 465
The Style Tab (Realistic Rendering) 465
The Style Tab (Illustration Rendering) 467
Creating a Quick Rendering 468
Creating an Illustration Rendering. 471
Scene Styles 472
Surface Styles. 476
Working with Animation 479
Are You Experienced?. 484
Now you can. 484

APPENDIX A   **Keyboard Shortcut Guide**   **485**

APPENDIX B   **Import and Export File Formats**   **493**

Import File Formats 494
Export File Formats 495

Index   *497*

INTRODUCTION

This year, Autodesk Inventor will have been available to the public for 10 years! The acceleration that we feel as we age is compounded when you work in the world of CAD.

If you had asked me five years ago what Inventor 2010 would be able to do, my guess would've probably come up shy of what was available in Inventor 2008. The power, flexibility, and ease of use contained in the 2010 release of Inventor is far beyond anything I could've honestly believed possible.

With that come a few questions. How do you learn it all? Can someone know everything about every tool? Most important, does anyone really need to know them all? In 11 years of working with commercial users and 2 years of working with those in academia, some things have become readily apparent.

First, most users use only a fraction of the tools available to them, and those are typically the tools they learned first. Sometimes that's all they need. Sometimes, though, a far better and easier option is a mouse click away—but the realities of deadlines and the ability to hammer something into shape using the tool they know makes it scary to explore new tools.

In writing this book, I wanted to use the process of developing the parts of a product to explore many different tools. In fact, you won't try the most commonly used tools until well after you've explored others. This should be a learning experience. It should also be easy. The irony of people sticking to the basics is that the basic tools are the most tedious and difficult to use. The advanced tools do more of the work for you and are easier to learn.

I genuinely enjoy using Autodesk Inventor, and I wholly believe that as amazing as it is today; the future will be just as surprising as anything I've seen to this point.

Who Should Buy This Book

This book isn't intended as a text on creating engineering drawings or to teach engineering or design philosophy. This book assumes that you are:

- ▶ A working professional with design and drafting experience

- ▶ Familiar with basic Microsoft Windows functions

- ▶ Familiar with drafting and design terminology

For example, this book will discuss how to create orthographic projections in a drawing but will not discuss what an orthographic projection is.

Given that, I don't assume you have 3D solid modeling experience or even experience with a computer-aided design (CAD) program. If this book encourages people who've never used 3D or even CAD to try Inventor, then I will consider it an unqualified success.

The exercises in this book will focus on how you can use Autodesk Inventor and Autodesk Inventor LT as tools to carry out design work for a production environment.

System Requirements

The basic system requirements for Autodesk Inventor Suite and LT 2010 are as follows:

Operating systems

- ▶ Windows XP Professional (SP2 and SP3), XP Professional x64 (SP2)
- ▶ Windows Vista (SP1), Home Basic, Home Premium, Business, Enterprise, Ultimate (32-bit or 64-bit)

Hardware

- ▶ Intel Pentium 4, Core, or AMD Athlon 64, AMD Opteron or later; 2GHz or faster processor
- ▶ 2GB of RAM (minimum)
- ▶ >1.5GB free disk space for Inventor LT and >3GB for Inventor Suite with Content Center
- ▶ Direct3D 9 or 10, or OpenGL graphics support with >64MB of RAM
- ▶ DVD ROM drive
- ▶ Internet Explorer 6 or 7
- ▶ Microsoft Excel 2003 or 2007 for iComponents, thread customization, and table-driven parts

What's Inside

Here is a preview of each chapter.

Chapter 1: Finding Your Way in the Inventor interface   This chapter presents the interface and working environment of Autodesk Inventor.

Chapter 2: Building the Foundation of the Design   This chapter discusses how to use Sheet Metal tools to build the base component of the assembly.

Chapter 3: Moving into the Assembly World   After building another amazing sheet metal part, you combine the two to start forming the product.

Chapter 4: Working with Solid Models and Weldments   Developing solid models, subassemblies, and weldments is easy with Autodesk Inventor. You'll also explore Inventor's powerful 2D drawing tools.

Chapter 5: Working with the Frame Generator   Purchased components have fixed sizes. You can leverage Inventor's steel shapes library to quickly build a complex frame.

Chapter 6: Working with Purchased and Multipurpose Parts   Why draw the components you use when suppliers make them available to you? You'll also learn the workflow for cast parts.

Chapter 7: Functional Design Using Design Accelerators   Accessing the standard content that you frequently use is a great advantage. But using engineering tools to validate the components you'll use based on calculations is a powerful, unique feature of Inventor.

Chapter 8: Creating Contoured and Plastic Parts   More and more components are made of plastic. Inventor has specialized tools for developing plastic features. You'll also work with multibody parts and tools for creating advanced shapes.

Chapter 9: Communicating Your Design   Advance assembly views, exploded assemblies, and assembly instruction animations help you communicate. Inventor Studio is an environment within Inventor that allows you to create photo-realistic renderings and animations from 3D models.

You'll need to download data for some exercises from **www.sybex.com/go/ inventor2010ner**. The files are contained in a zip file, and downloading the data beforehand will save time.

How to Contact the Author

I appreciate your interest in this book and in Inventor. If you'd like to share your feedback or stories about how this book may have helped you, I'd love to hear from you.

You can reach me at **thom.tremblay@yahoo.com**.

Sybex strives to keep you supplied with the latest tools and information you need for your work. Please check the website at **www.sybex.com**, where we'll post additional content and updates that supplement this book should the need arise. Enter **Autodesk Inventor 2010: No Experience Required** in the Search box (or type the book's ISBN: **978-0-470-48169-1**), and click Search to get to the book's update page.

Now, let's begin exploring Inventor. I hope you'll have some fun along the way.

CHAPTER 1

Finding Your Way in the Inventor Interface

▶ Understanding Inventor's interface behavior

▶ Opening existing files

▶ Creating new files

▶ Modifying the look and feel of Inventor

▶ Managing file locations

▶ Accessing the Help system

Inventor's User Interface

When you're learning a new software application, it can sometimes seem as though finding a tool is more difficult than learning to use it.

When Inventor first launches, you're greeted with an opportunity to participate in the Customer Involvement Program (Figure 1.1). This program will help Autodesk improve the product in the future. I highly recommend lending a hand — your input may influence the future of the software you're learning today.

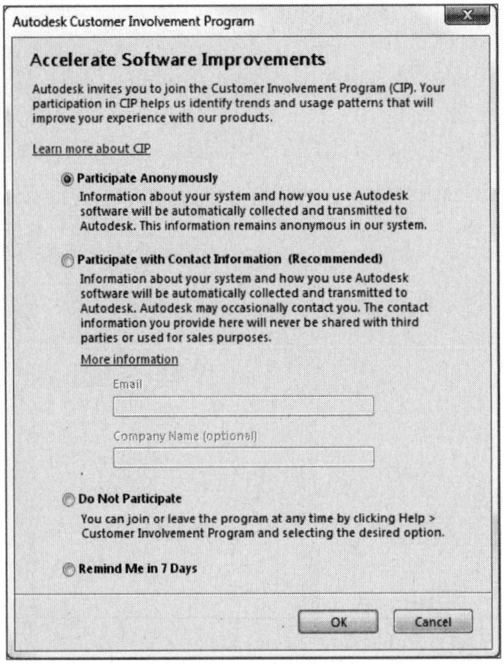

FIGURE 1.1 Autodesk Customer Involvement Program sign-up dialog

After you've signed up for the Customer Involvement Program, you'll be able to view the Inventor interface. With no file loaded, you can immediately see its simplicity. Let's start by becoming familiar with the component of Inventor that you'll use every time you start the program: the graphical user interface (GUI). Figure 1.2 shows the main components that we'll review and expand on in this chapter.

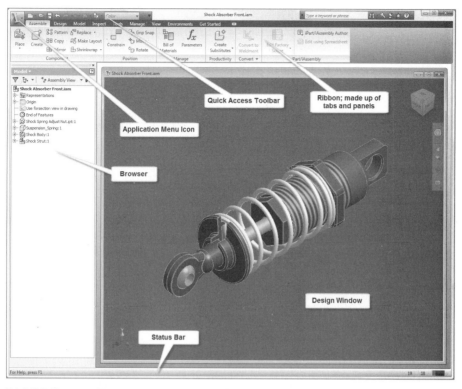

FIGURE 1.2 The parts of the Inventor GUI

If you're used to the look and feel of Microsoft Word or Excel 2007, you should find a lot of similarities with the standard tools in Inventor. If you're experienced with recent versions of AutoCAD, you'll find similarities with the drawing and sketching tool icons in Inventor.

Application Menu

Across the top of the Inventor application is the title bar. It tells you the name of the file you're currently editing; or, if you're just starting out, it reminds you that you're using Autodesk Inventor and which version.

In the upper-left corner is a large icon with an *I* on it. This is Inventor's version of the Microsoft Office 2007 Office button; clicking it opens the Application menu (Figure 1.3). The menu contains the primary file-modification tools, a printing option, and a list of recent documents.

The Application menu offers a lot great features, including being able to see the names or images of recently opened files and being able to click the thumb-tack icon to keep a file on the list no matter how long it's been since you opened it. You can also access the options for Autodesk Inventor that control its appearance and some aspects of its behavior.

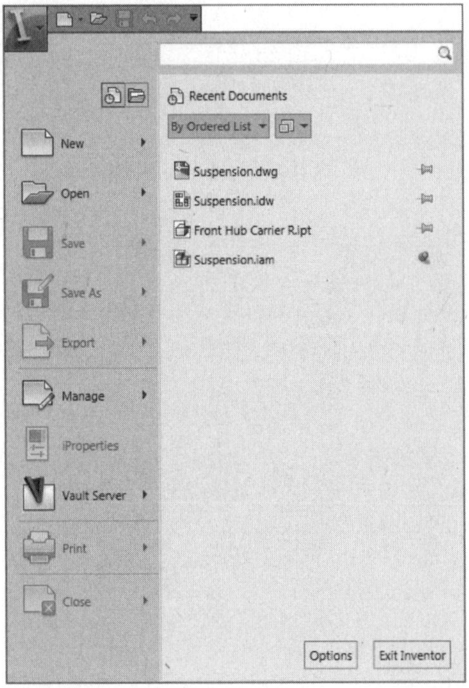

FIGURE 1.3 The Application menu (expanded) and Quick Access Toolbar (discussed in the next section)

Quick Access Toolbar

The Quick Access Toolbar — also shown in Figure 1.3, just to the right of the Application Menu button — is a dynamic toolbar that displays shortcuts to many common file tools. Tools for creating a new file and opening a file are on the Application menu, but shortcuts to these commonly used tools also appear on the Quick Access Toolbar by default. Other commonly used tools, like Undo and Redo, are also on this toolbar. As you open different types of files, other tools will appear, such as Print or the ability to select a part color from a pull-down.

You can Add frequently used tools to the Quick Access Toolbar to save time and eliminate the need to search for a tool that you use frequently.

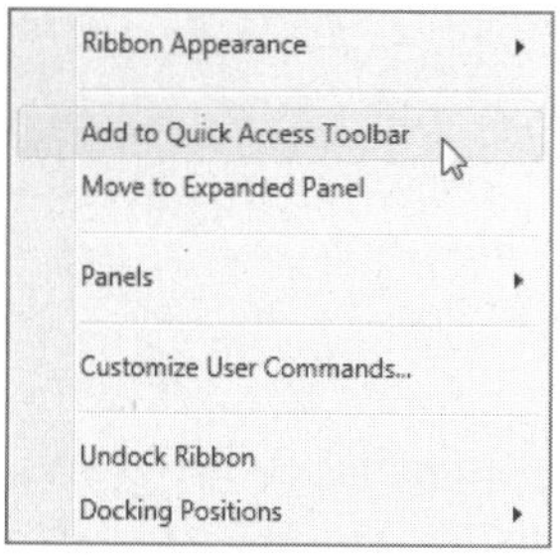

Ribbon Appearance	▸
Add to Quick Access Toolbar	
Move to Expanded Panel	
Panels	▸
Customize User Commands...	
Undock Ribbon	
Docking Positions	▸

To add a tool, right-click the desired tool shown in the Ribbon below the title bar, and select Add to Quick Access Toolbar from the context menu.

While we're discussing fundamentals, let's take a little time to review some of the basic functions of the interface in general.

Learning the Basics of Tabs

The Autodesk Inventor 2010 interface is frequently referred to as a *Ribbon interface* because of the large ribbon of tools that is displayed horizontally across the top of the screen. Depending on the type of file you're editing, multiple tabs may appear on the Ribbon. In each tab there are additional groupings of tools called *panels* that offer even more precise organization.

In this book's exercises, I'll refer to the location of a tool by the tab and panel on which it's located. This should make it easier to locate new tools as they're introduced. When tools are reused, the specific location may not be given to encourage learning their location.

Depending on your screen resolution, some panels will switch to a narrower, expandable version to allow the primary tool to be displayed on the Ribbon.

Get Started Tab

Inventor is set up to open by default with no file or dialog boxes open. The interface displays only the Get Started tab (Figure 1.4) and behind it another tab called Tools.

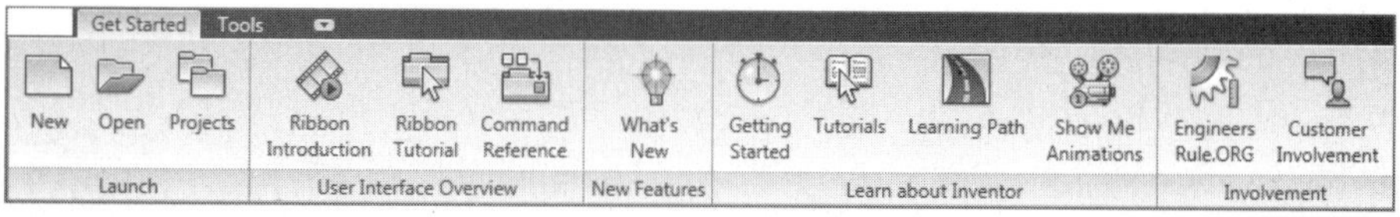

FIGURE 1.4 The Get Started tab gives you access to the basic tools as well as learning materials.

On the Get Started tab are the basic New, Open, and Projects tools. (We'll talk more about Projects later in this chapter.) These tools are in the Launch panel. The Learn about Inventor panel and User Interface Overview panel contain tutorials that go into some of the concepts of the interface and provide easy access to information about this version of Inventor and Inventor's tools in general.

For an added touch, the Involvement panel offers quick access to the Autodesk Education Community where students and teachers can access free software and curricula. This panel also provides an important link to the Autodesk Customer Involvement program, where you can participate in programs and tell Autodesk what you like about Inventor or where you would like improvements made.

Inventor has a tradition of a dynamic interface. Inventor automatically offers different tools based on the type of file you're in or what you're doing in that file. For example, when you create a new Part file, Inventor begins the new file in a sketch by default; therefore, the Sketch tab is active (Figure 1.5).

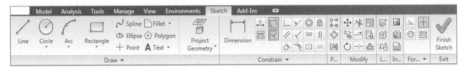

FIGURE 1.5 Tabs that are automatically selected by Inventor are also highlighted.

Because Inventor is now primarily focused on these sketching tools, the dynamically selected tab is highlighted in color; the bottoms of the tab's panels also appear in color. If you need to use a tool on another tab, the dynamically selected tab's highlight makes it easier to return to. To use a tab that Inventor didn't select, you only have to click the name of the tab.

Over the course of the following chapters and exercises, you'll see that frequently, Inventor presents the tab that you need most when you need it. You'll also notice in Figure 1.5 that not all tools are the same size, which makes it easier to find the most commonly used tools. Some panels have a downward-pointing arrow next to the panel name to show that you can access additional tools by clicking the arrow and expanding the panel.

Ribbon Appearance   ▸

Add to Quick Access Toolbar

Move to Expanded Panel

Panels   ▸

Customize User Commands...

Undock Ribbon

Docking Positions   ▸

If you find that you rarely use one of the tools, you can move it to the hidden portion of the panel by right-clicking the tool and selecting Move to Expanded Panel.

You can also rearrange panels by clicking an individual panel's title bar and dragging it to a new location in the tab.

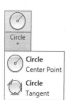

Some individual tools have options. For example, there is more than one type of circle; so, next to the default circle you see a downward-pointing arrow. Clicking this arrow expands the available options.

All of these tools have tooltips as well. Some of these are referred to as *progressive tooltips*; they give you basic information if you pause over the tool and then provide illustrations or more in-depth information if you pause a little longer.

Ribbon Appearance

The Ribbon can also appear in different ways. The default appearance is referred to as Normal (shown earlier, in Figure 1.5). To modify the overall appearance of the Ribbon, right-click any part of the Ribbon and hover over the words Ribbon Appearance until the list of options is displayed. You can also click the words

Ribbon Appearance if you're in a hurry. Figures 1.6–1.8 show the Sketch tab in different modes.

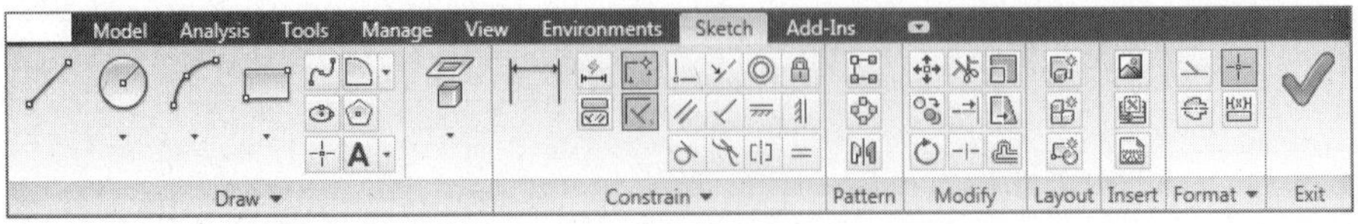

FIGURE 1.6 The Sketch tab in Text Off mode

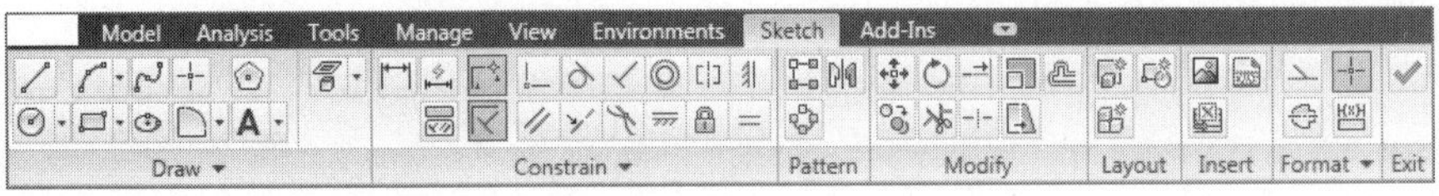

FIGURE 1.7 The Sketch tab in Small mode

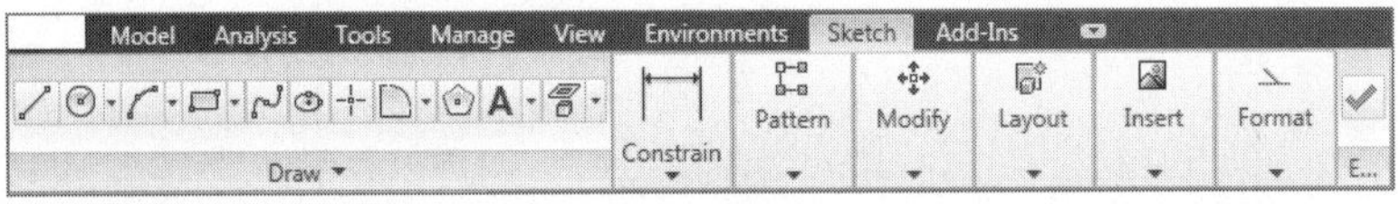

FIGURE 1.8 The Sketch tab in Compact mode

The Ribbon itself can also be reduced in size to maximize screen space.

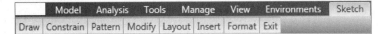

A small icon appears next to the tab names. Click it once, and the Ribbon is reduced to showing only the panel names of the selected tab; a second click removes the panels, leaving only the list of tabs. A third click of the button restores the Ribbon to its full display in whatever mode you had selected.

Hovering over or clicking the collapsed panel name causes the panel to expand, revealing the tools. If the panel name is concealed, click the tab name; the Ribbon appears for a short time or until you select a tool or click another part of the screen.

Selecting a tool on the Ribbon often causes a dialog box to appear on the screen. Let's review some of the things you need to know about dialog boxes.

Learning to Use the Dialog Boxes

One thing that makes Inventor easy to use is a kind of "graphical language" common to all the dialog boxes. These are items that behave consistently wherever they appear. As you use Inventor, working with these items will become second nature. As you're getting started, knowing what to look for will make it easy to understand what Inventor needs from you in order to accomplish your task.

Buttons

The following buttons and button states have the same effect no matter where you encounter them in Inventor's interface:

A button with a red arrow indicates that Inventor needs you to select something. Text may appear next to the arrow, identifying the type of input that Inventor is looking for.

A button with a white arrow means that Inventor has been given the information it needs.

The OK button is grayed out until Inventor has the necessary user input to execute an operation. Clicking OK initiates the command or function and closes the dialog box.

The Apply button is also grayed out until Inventor has the necessary user input to execute an operation. Clicking Apply initiates the command or function but doesn't close the dialog box. This allows you to execute the function and start using it again immediately.

The Cancel button closes the dialog box without executing any operation.

The More button exposes additional options for a dialog box. After those options become visible, the arrows then point to the left so you can hide the options again.

Any button with an ellipsis after the name launches another dialog box or selection window when clicked.

Dialog Box Tabs

Another element of the common graphical language is the way dialog boxes are organized. Many dialog boxes have tabs across the top, with each tab offering additional options. Although most common functions are contained on the first tab, when you begin working with a new dialog box, it's worth taking a few moments to explore the options on the other tabs. For example, in the Extrude dialog box illustrated here, the Shape tab offers the basic options to select the shape and define the distance it will be extruded, whereas the More tab offers options to apply taper or draft to the shape.

Context Menus

You can access a large number of Inventor's tools by clicking your secondary mouse button — typically the right button — at different places on your screen. As in other Windows software, right-clicking displays a *context menu* of options that are relevant to what you're doing at the time. In the exercises and examples in this book, I'll often instruct you to right-click and select the next operation from a context menu.

To make it easier to get a feel for Inventor's interface, let's open a file to see the changes that occur to the interface and get your first glimpse at its dynamic nature.

The Open Dialog Box

The tool to launch the Open dialog is available in several locations, as you probably noticed in the earlier parts of the chapter.

As in any contemporary software, this dialog box allows you to select a file or files to open in Inventor, as shown in Figure 1.9. If you're accustomed to Microsoft Windows Explorer and some of its viewing options, this dialog box will seem familiar. Using it should be comfortable for you right away. The dialog box includes several components, and it's important to understand what these parts are and what they will do for you.

Inventor LT users see a slightly different Open dialog box. Inventor LT doesn't have assembly capabilities, so it doesn't need some elements. It will still be beneficial for LT users to understand the capabilities of Inventor Suite or Professional 2010 in case you use it in the future.

 N O T E   It's possible to resize many dialog boxes by clicking and dragging the corners, in order to allow easy viewing of the information displayed.

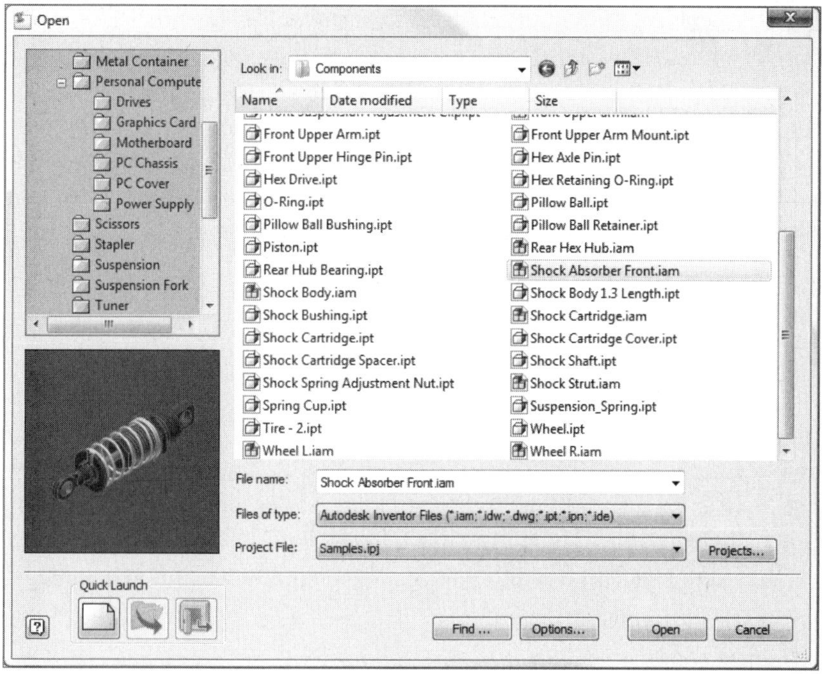

FIGURE 1.9 File list displaying large icons

Shortcuts and the File List

At upper left in the Open dialog box is an area with a list of shortcuts to Frequently Used Subfolders (Figure 1.10). You can customize this pane to create shortcuts to folders that you'd like to access quickly. You can even set up subreferences and have a structure that replicates the folder structure on your hard drive.

FIGURE 1.10 Frequently Used Subfolders list

Centered in the dialog box and making up the bulk of it is the file list, where the files are displayed. The File of Type option, described shortly, controls what files are listed. You can open a file (or files) from here by selecting the filename(s) and clicking OK or by double-clicking the filename.

At the top of the dialog box is the Look In field. This displays the name of the folder whose files are currently displayed below it in the file list. The arrow to the right allows you cascade the folder structure or to begin browsing for other folders.

Look in: Components   ▼

Navigation Controls

To the right of the Look In field are four icons that allow you to navigate easily and to control how you view the files you're looking for.

These tools share icons and functions with many standard Windows icons and tools:

Go To Last Folder Visited   The first button has an arrow pointing left. This button allows you to navigate back to the previous folder(s) you were browsing in. It works on the same principle as the Back button in a web browser. When you've just begun a session, the arrow is grayed out, because you don't have any browsing history to recall.

Up One Level   The next icon looks like a folder with a green arrow pointing up. This takes you up a level in your folder structure from wherever you're currently browsing.

Create New Folder   The third icon allows you to create a new folder in the folder that you're currently browsing in.

The View Menu   The icon on the right is a fly-out tool that lets you change the way the files you're browsing are displayed. Depending on the operating system you're using, you see different options ranging from a detailed listing of dates and file size to thumbnail previews of the files in the display area. In Figure 1.11, you can see the same folder as in Figure 1.9 being browsed with the Thumbnail display option.

You'll find commonality in the controls between Inventor and many Microsoft applications. This is done so that you don't have to learn every aspect of the user interface from scratch.

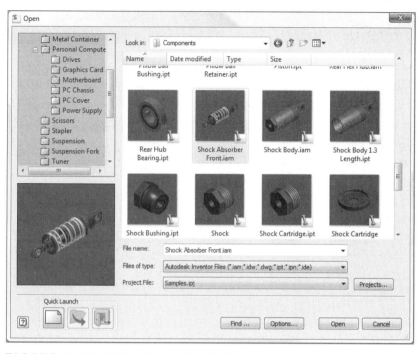

FIGURE 1.11 File list showing Thumbnail view

File Display Options

Immediately below the file list are three selection pull-down lists that control the file display options:

File name:	Engine MKII.iam
Files of type:	Autodesk Inventor Files (*.iam;*.dwg;*.idw;*.ipt;*.ipn;*.ide)
Project File:	Samples.ipj

File Name   This pull-down displays the full name of the selected file(s). If you click the arrow to the right, and it opens a list of recently open files.

Files of Type   This option is very important. Clicking the arrow to the right lets you choose from a list of file types that Inventor can open. It's important to filter the file types displayed because of the broad array of types.

Project File   This fly-out allows you to select from a list of project files that have been used in the past. The active or current project file is shown any time the Open dialog box is brought up. To the right of the pull-down is a button marked Projects, which launches the Project File editor, which in turn allows you to select project files that have not been used previously, edit existing project files, or create a new project file. We'll look at the Project File dialog box later in this chapter in the "Project Files" section.

To the left of File Display Options is the File Preview pane. As you select a file in the file list, a preview of that file appears in this area. Not all files have a preview to display.

At lower left in the Open dialog box are three icons under the heading Quick Launch. At least one of these icons won't be available at any given time. If you're in the Open dialog box, the first icon is available; it switches you from Open to the New dialog box. The middle icon switches you back to Open from New. The third icon is for opening files from the Vault, a great data-management system that I highly recommend installing. (The Vault comes with Inventor, so there's no additional cost; it offers great benefits that I'll talk about briefly in Appendix C.) This icon is available only if the project file that is active has the Vault enabled.

At lower right is the Find button. Clicking it displays a Find File dialog box (Figure 1.12) that can execute simple or complex searches. You can search for file properties, creation dates, or strings of text, and you can even save your searches to be reused in the future.

Other Controls

Three more options complete the Open dialog box:

Options   Available only when you import, export, or open a file that can have additional settings applied to it. For example, if you want to export a DWG file for use with AutoCAD, you can select which version of AutoCAD can open the file, back to AutoCAD 2000.

Open   Executes the opening of the selected file or files. You can open multiple files at the same time by holding the Ctrl key to select multiple individual files or by holding Shift to click a range of files. You can also open multiple files by dragging a file or files from Windows Explorer onto the title bar of Autodesk Inventor.

Cancel   Exits the attempt to open a file, and returns you to Inventor.

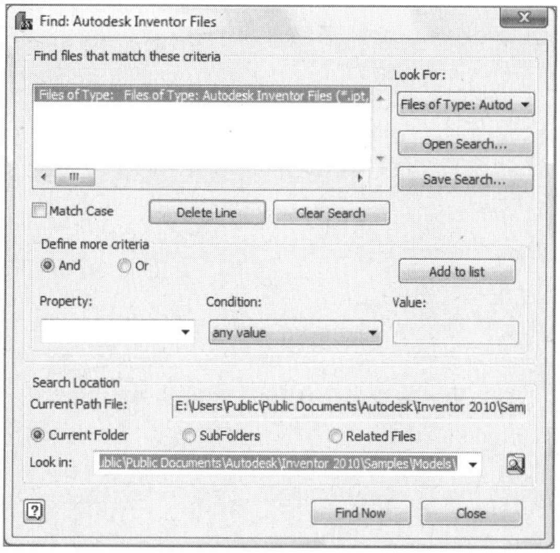

FIGURE 1.12 The Find File dialog box

Opening a File

Now that you've had an overview of the parts and functions of the Open dialog box, let's put what you've learned to use. (Some options won't be available to Inventor LT users; again, LT can't work with assemblies.) Follow these steps:

1. Click the Open icon on the Get Started tab to access the Open dialog box. If the Samples project isn't displayed as the active project, use the pull-down list to select it. It should be on the short list of project files. If it doesn't appear on the list, open the Project File dialog box by clicking the Projects button next to the pull-down, select Samples from the list, and click Open. This should set that project to be active and return you to the Open dialog box. Use the Frequently Used Subfolders list to find the Assemblies\Suspension\Components\ Shock Absorber Front.iam assembly file.

2. When you've found the file, you can select it with a single mouse click and click OK, or you can double-click the file in the window. Once the file is open, you should see something like Figure 1.13.

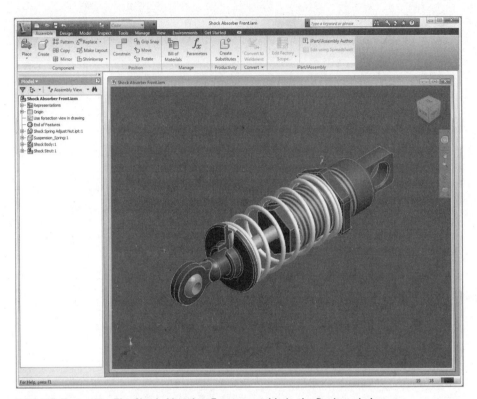

FIGURE 1.13 The Shock Absorber Front assembly in the Design window

If you're not opening an existing file to edit it, then chances are you're creating a new one.

The New File Dialog Box

The New File dialog box (Figure 1.14) is much simpler than the Open dialog box. Like the Open dialog box, it has a Quick Launch section that allows you to switch to the Open dialog box and where you can set the active project file.

Every new drawing you create in Inventor is based on a template, which provides information such as borders, title blocks, layer colors, and the standard dimension style. You can customize these templates, and Inventor comes with a sizable selection to give you a head start. It's also possible to convert existing AutoCAD drawings to Inventor templates.

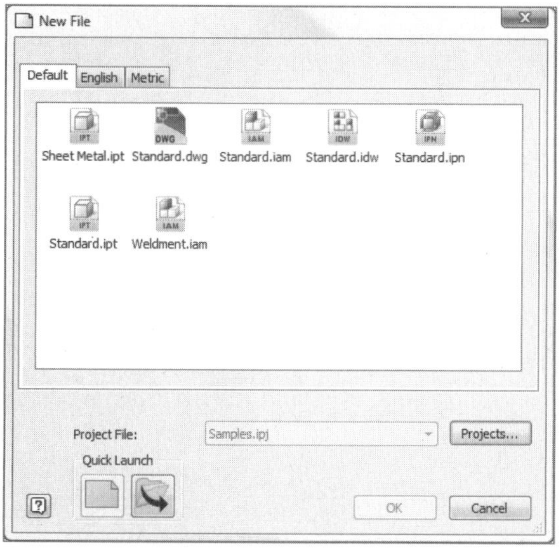

FIGURE 1.14 The New File dialog box showing the Default templates

In the New File dialog box, Inventor's collection of built-in templates is categorized in tabs across the top. There are templates for Default, English, and Metric measurements.

More of the Inventor Interface

Because you have the assembly loaded, let's use it to explore how you'll interact with Inventor and take a closer look at some of the elements of the interface that we just touched on.

The Browser Bar

In the default display, the Browser bar (Figure 1.15) is positioned on the left edge of the screen. The Browser bar displays a list of features or components and the relationships that reflect how the file you're working in was built. Regardless of the type of Inventor file, you can easily review critical information about how it was constructed. This is particularly important when you're working on a file that you didn't create or last edit.

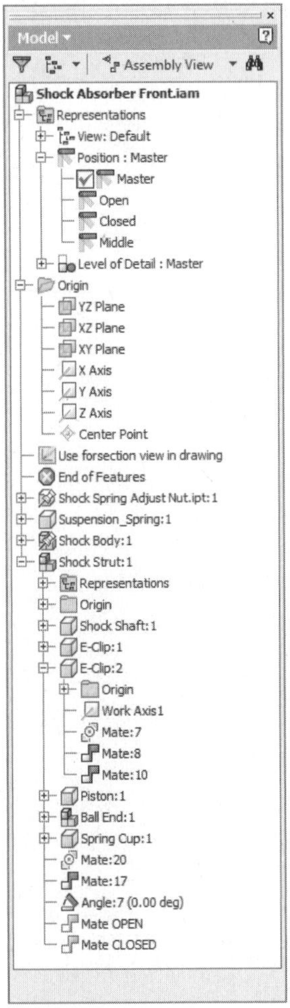

FIGURE 1.15 The Browser bar displays the contents and structure of the file you're editing.

As you create and edit 3D and 2D files in later chapters, you'll do quite a bit of work with the Browser, and you'll see some capabilities that any user can take advantage of.

The Design Window

The Design window displays the file you're editing. Along with the display of drawings and geometry, this window has a couple of special elements worth noting that appear by default. The 3D indicator shows the part or assembly file's orientation to the X, Y, and Z axes. As shown earlier in Figure 1.13 the X axis is red, the Y axis is green, and the Z axis is blue. Although it isn't always critical to orient parts in a particular direction, doing so can be useful for understanding how a part is constructed and for sketching a horizontal or vertical relationship between points.

The Status Bar

The final major screen element I'd like to review before you begin working in Inventor is the status bar. This term refers to the display along the bottom edge of the Inventor window. It has multiple functions, but most of them are for delivering information.

 N O T E   If you're an AutoCAD user, you probably noticed that there is no "command line" in Inventor. However, when you're in a command, if you become unsure of what is expected, you can look at the lower-left corner of the Inventor window: on the status bar will be a prompt describing what is expected of you.

While you're creating geometry, the right side of the status bar displays feedback about that geometry. For example, while you're drawing a line, the status bar tells you the position of your endpoint, along with the line's length and direction. This helps you to approximate the size of the geometry you're creating.

The status bar has a couple of other important capabilities. At the far right, you'll find two numbers. The first of the two numbers represents Total Occurrences in Active Document, which is the number of parts being shown on screen. The second number represents the Open Documents in Session, which is the number of files being accessed by Inventor.

For example, an assembly that has five copies of one part file in it may display the numbers 5 and 2 because you're displaying five components on screen that reside in two files — one part file and an assembly file. The Shock Absorber Front.iam that you loaded shows that there are 19 total occurrences and 18 active files in Inventor.

Revisiting the Quick Access Tools

With the Assembly file loaded, some new items appear on the Quick Access Toolbar.

Two icons you need to be familiar with are our old friends Undo and Redo. If you make a mistake, Inventor allows up to 30 steps of Undo and Redo. A great feature in Inventor is that changes to the model view (zooming, panning, and so on) don't use Undo steps. You can even undo the creation or opening of a file.

Just to the right of Redo is the Return button. You'll use the Return button frequently, although its importance has been reduced in Inventor 2010 compared to previous releases. This tool moves you from one editing state to the one above it. Right now, that may not make sense; but its importance will become clear as you start working in Inventor.

Some tools aren't always available, even though they're visible in a faded state. If Inventor is unsure that what it's displaying is the most current information, the Update button becomes available and lets you update the data that is on the screen.

Next is the Filters pull-down list. *Filters* are tools for focusing or streamlining selections. They can limit or enhance the selection of certain types of entities in parts, assemblies, or drawings. The use of filters is a great thing to learn and explore. Many experienced Inventor users are missing out by not becoming more comfortable with them.

A different type of pull-down takes up quite a bit of space on the Quick Access Toolbar. It allows you to choose a different color for a selected part or parts. With no parts selected, it lets you access data about the physical properties or materials used in Inventor. Materials are different than colors — if you tell a part it's made of lead, it will have a different mass than a part with a Material value of Aluminum. On the other hand, you can make a piece of aluminum look like it's wood by changing its color.

The final icon is Recover, which normally appears faded or dimmed. When it's red, this indicates an error that Inventor's Design Doctor wants to assist you with.

The Design Doctor (Figure 1.16) lists any errors and allows you to select which one you want to fix first in the Select screen. On the Examine screen, it offers a solution; and the Treat screen lets you select what treatment method you want to use.

Another important thing to know about the Design Doctor is that you don't have to respond immediately. You can do most things in Inventor while a problem remains unresolved. In fact, you may do something that you know will cause a problem, and when you're finished, the problem will resolve itself. This is the kind of flexibility that has made Inventor popular.

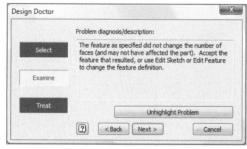

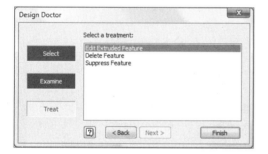

FIGURE 1.16 The Design Doctor screens

Working in the Design Window

Because you have the assembly loaded, let's use it to explore how you'll interact with Inventor and take a closer look at some of the tools that help you manipulate the model on the screen.

View Tab

The View tab (Figure 1.17) contains tools that aren't necessarily used every time you work with Inventor but can establish some of your preferences. It also contains some other useful tools for presenting your designs. Let's review them.

FIGURE 1.17 The View tab

Appearance Panel

The Appearance panel includes several tool sets. The first tool, Slice Graphics, is available only when you're editing a sketch. It allows you to section the part or the assembly to make the sketch easy to see and edit.

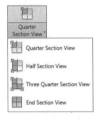

Next is a group of four tools you use to create sections of 3D parts and assemblies using planes or faces to define what portions are removed. The default tool is the Quarter Section View; it works much like Slice Graphics, but it removes roughly a quarter of the assembly depending on the planes selected.

To the right is a pair of options that control whether the model is viewed in a perspective or orthographic view. You can even alter the lens length of the perspective view to give a different effect by holding the Ctrl key and pressing the Shift key while rolling the mouse wheel.

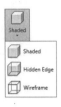

The first of these options lets you display the 3D model as a shaded display, hidden edge display, or wireframe display. Figure 1.18 illustrates the three modes.

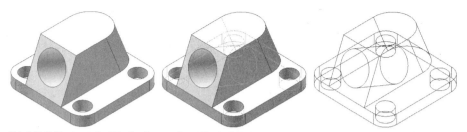

FIGURE 1.18 3D display modes. Shaded (left) is the most realistic; Hidden Edge (middle) shows the edges on the back of the shaded model; and Wireframe (right) allows you to see all of a part's features.

As you can see in Figure 1.19, displaying a shadow of the model can sometimes help you keep your orientation. The display of the two types of shadow is controlled by the fly-out above and to the right of the Orthographic/Perspective button. Ground Shadow casts a shadow of the overall shape of the part or assembly as though there were a light above it, and X-Ray Shadow shows more of the internal characteristics of a part and casts individual shadows for the parts of an assembly.

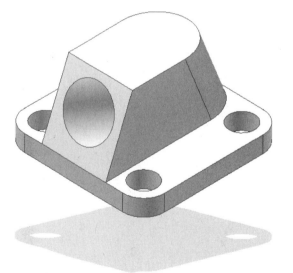

FIGURE 1.19 Displaying a shadow can help maintain orientation.

The button below that controls whether inactive parts of an assembly dim or change appearance when you activate a part in the assembly to edit it. It isn't available to Inventor LT users.

With Transparency On set (the default), only the component being edited in the context of an assembly is a solid color. All the other parts change in some way. I highly recommend working in this mode because it helps you keep track of whether you're in the assembly or editing a part in the assembly. Transparency Off keeps components in their normal appearance even though you're in effect editing only one component.

To demonstrate this, hover over the gray part (Shock Strut) on the left of the assembly, and notice that it highlights. When it has become highlighted, double-click it quickly. After it has been made "active," your display should look something like Figure 1.20.

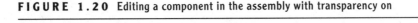

FIGURE 1.20 Editing a component in the assembly with transparency on

Navigate Panel

The Navigate panel contains tools for altering your view of the model or drawing. Most of these tools are also presented in a more heads-up fashion directly in the Design window next to your model. We'll cover the tools in the context of this panel, but I suspect you'll use them like I do: either through the window toolbar or using the mouse and keyboard shortcuts that accompany them.

The Navigation Wheels (plural because there are a few different versions) allow heads-up access to the Zoom, Orbit, and Pan tools as well as several other features. Navigation Wheels can be found not only in Inventor but in other Autodesk products as well, such as AutoCAD. Because of this, some of the tools aren't specifically built for Inventor. Walk, Look, and Up/Down may be useful for showing someone how to navigate through a large assembly, but I suspect that other tools will be more useful to you.

One key is to position the function you want to select on the wheel over the point you want it centered on, before you pick the point. The point where you pick the tool is picked up as the center for Zoom or the pivot point for Orbit, for example.

Clicking over the downward arrow at lower right lets you select a different size wheel set or control the options of the Navigation Wheels. Selecting the X at upper right closes the Navigation Wheels.

One tool on the Navigation Wheels that you may find useful but not try otherwise is the Rewind tool (Figure 1.21). As I mentioned earlier, the Undo function doesn't record or affect changes to Zoom.

FIGURE 1.21 The Rewind tool

Rewind shows you a film reel–style list of previous views; as you move through them, you see the model move back to previous points of view. This is a double benefit because the film reel allows you to move quickly to an approximate view that you want to recall, but the onscreen display gives you the full view immediately so you can be sure you're getting what you want. In case you're wondering, you can also press the F5 key to recall previous views, but it doesn't offer the film reel view. If you press F5 again, it goes back again. Holding the F5 key automatically cycles back through previous views until you release it.

The Pan tool is presented with a hand icon. *Panning* means sliding the image on the plane of the screen without changing its size or your point of view of it. You can use Pan as a click-and-drag tool. And you can release and restart panning while staying in the command. Pan is also available by pressing the F2 key or by pressing and holding the wheel or the middle mouse button.

N O T E   Keyboard shortcuts appear in brackets on the Inventor menus. For a complete listing of keyboard shortcuts, refer to Appendix A.

A tool that I use very often is the View Face tool. View Face is a bit of a misnomer because after you've selected the tool, it highlights not only faces but also edges as you move your cursor over the model. If you select an edge, it rotates the view of the model so that the edge you selected is centered and horizontal. If you select a face, it rotates the view so that you're looking directly at the face, and it centers the face in the view as well. This is a great tool to get yourself reoriented if you become confused about what you're looking at. You can also access the tool through the PgUp key.

Previous view has a fly-out option of Next view if you've already restored a previous view. Like the Rewind tool, you can use F5 for Previous as well.

The next tool has multiple options. The default is the Zoom Window tool.

The first icon is Zoom All. No matter what your point of view, clicking this icon frames your model evenly in the Design window, which is where you're currently seeing the Shock Absorber assembly.

Click the Zoom icon. You'll notice that the onscreen pointer changes its shape to two arrows: a small arrow pointing up and a large arrow pointing down. Click and drag anywhere in the Design window: note that as you drag up, the model gets smaller; and as you drag down, the model gets larger. If you drag as far as you can in the Design window but want to continue to zoom, release the mouse button, move the cursor, and click to start zooming again. To stop the Zoom command, press your Esc key or right-click the screen and select Done [Esc]. You can also access the Zoom command by pressing and holding the F3 key. Releasing the key ends the command. If you're not convinced that it's easy enough to access the Zoom command, there's one more option. If you have a wheel mouse, try rolling it. If you roll the mouse away from you, the model gets smaller. If you roll the wheel toward you, it gets larger.

N O T E   In AutoCAD, you get the exact opposite zooming with a wheel mouse. This is because AutoCAD's zoom is based on the idea of moving a camera, and Inventor's is based on moving the object that you're looking at. If you absolutely need to have Inventor zoom in the AutoCAD fashion, you can change a setting in the application options, which we'll review later in this chapter.

Zoom Window allows you to zoom in on a specific area by creating a "window" frame around the area that you want larger. To create the frame, you select the tool, click where you want one corner, and, while continuing to hold down the button, drag the size of the frame. When you've encompassed the area you want to make larger, release the mouse button. Figure 1.22 shows the zoom area being framed, and Figure 1.23 shows the result. Try enlarging your view of a portion of the assembly using the Zoom Window tool. You can also access Zoom Window by pressing the Z key on your keyboard.

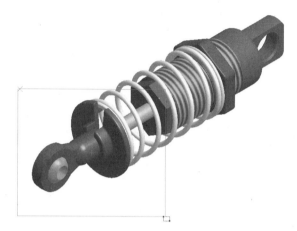

FIGURE 1.22 Framing the area to zoom in on

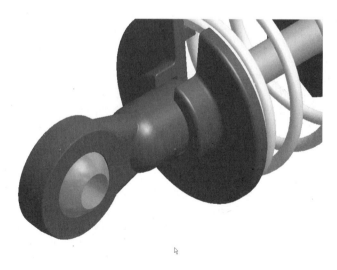

FIGURE 1.23 The result of zooming

Zoom Selected centers and enlarges any face of any part that you select. After you've started the command, you can move your screen pointer over any part of an assembly or any face of a part. As you do so, you'll also notice that yellow or green dots appear as you move over points. If you select one of the points, the view doesn't enlarge but centers on the selected point.

Next is the Orbit tool. Until the introduction of the ViewCube (see the next section, "The ViewCube and the Navigation Bar"), it was the primary way users could quickly rotate a model to view it from other directions. It's valuable to learn about the Orbit tool, but I expect most new users to become as dependent on the ViewCube as I have in the short time that I've been using it.

When you start the Orbit tool by selecting it or pressing the F4 key, a circle with four rays appears. This is known as the *Reticle.* The horizontal and vertical lines represent the X and Y axes of the screen. As you near them, the cursor changes to an arrow in a loop. Clicking and dragging at that time rotates the object about the axis of the screen. When you move your mouse outside the circle and away from the axes, the cursor changes to an arrow in a circle. Clicking and dragging at that time causes the model to rotate about the Z axis of the screen. If you move away from the center of the screen, you see yet another cursor: this one takes the shape of the arrow on an Enter key. Clicking with this arrow displayed is a shortcut out of the Orbit tool.

Now, move the cursor inside the circle, where it looks similar to the toolbar button you selected in the first place. Clicking and dragging inside the Reticle causes the model to tumble about the center point of the screen. You can change what portion of the model is centered on the screen by hovering over a point and clicking the primary mouse button, which relocates the pivot point. This causes the model to shift position similar to clicking a point using the Zoom Selected tool.

The Constrained Orbit tool lies in the fly-out menu under the Orbit tool. It's basically the same as Orbit but is designed to pivot around the axes of the model.

The ViewCube and the Navigation Bar

Whenever you open a 3D model in Inventor, the ViewCube appears in the upper-right corner of the Design window. The ViewCube allows you to click the named faces of the cube and have the part orient itself to match the cube's new orientation. You can also rotate the part about its center by clicking the cube and dragging it while holding down the mouse button. Other features include the ability to select corners and edges of the cube to rotate the part.

When you're looking directly at a standard view, two curved arrows appear. These arrows let you spin the part about the axis of the screen. It's the same effect as if you pressed a finger into the center of a piece of paper and rotated the sheet under your finger.

As you near the ViewCube, another icon appears at the upper left; it looks like a house. Clicking this returns your model to the Home view. You can also return to the Home view at any time by pressing the F6 key.

You'll work with the ViewCube throughout this book. If you prefer to not use the View Cube, you can select the downward arrow and place it into the heads-up toolbar in the Design window.

These are just the basic tools for navigating within Inventor. Let's explore some modifications you may wish to make to give Inventor a look and feel that will be more hospitable to you in the future.

By default, a shortcut toolbar for the tools found in the Navigation panel is also displayed on the screen below the ViewCube. You can customize this toolbar to show the various viewing tools and relocate it to different parts of the screen along with the ViewCube.

Although I use the Navigate panel constantly in Inventor, I have decided to remove it from my screen to maximize image-capture space. I want to make sure that you don't mistake my omitting it from screen captures in this book for thinking that I don't use or value this great feature of the user interface.

Document Tabs

The Document tabs appear at the bottom of the Design window when you have more than one file open in Inventor. Several tools are associated with these tabs. The first three items let you cascade the files on the screen, arrange them to fill the Design window, or select an open file to display from the fly-out.

Each open file displays a tab, and these tabs appear across the bottom in a row next to the buttons with the file name in the tab. The tab for the active file also displays an X that you can select to close the individual file.

If you hover over a tab, a preview of that file (including the file's path) appears as a specialized tooltip. This makes it much easier to find the file you want without having to cycle through each one.

Make Yourself at Home: Customizing Inventor

Now that you have a basic feel for some of the tools you'll use most frequently, it's time for you to make yourself at home. You may have noticed that the background of the Design window changed colors in the previous images. I made this change for clarity in the printed images; you can also make changes to tailor Inventor to your needs. Inventor can be customized at several levels. In this section, I'll detail a few of the options and even show you how to save the way you've configured Inventor for future use.

Changing the coloring of Inventor's work environment and sketching elements can make it easy to see what you're working on. Some users like to reposition or resize the tools to give themselves more room to work or to make the tools easier to find. You'll experiment with most of these settings once or twice, but when you're comfortable you may not want to change them again.

Some of the options in these exercises are unique to assemblies and drawings of assemblies, so they won't appear in Inventor LT.

Application Options

Let's start with the Application Options dialog box (Figure 1.24). This is the central repository for your personal settings. These are the settings that control how Inventor looks to you and what options you want to use. These tools don't affect settings that are local to models and drawings. To access the Application Options dialog box, choose the Tools tab, and select Application Options. Or, pick the Options button at the bottom of the Applications Menu fly-out.

Notice the Import and Export buttons at the bottom of the window. These two tools allow you to save the settings that you prefer or even transfer them to other users or other systems where you'll be using Inventor. Your settings are saved as XML files.

The AutoCAD_Related_Options.xml file changes the Help system to AutoCAD-related settings, reverses the mouse-wheel zoom direction, and changes the background to black. If you installed Inventor with AutoCAD preferences, you may have some of the same settings already active. The Inventor_Default_Options.xml file restores Inventor's default settings.

As with other dialog boxes, a Help button appears at lower left with specific help for the tool you're working with. Clicking Help lists the specific portions of the tab that you have active.

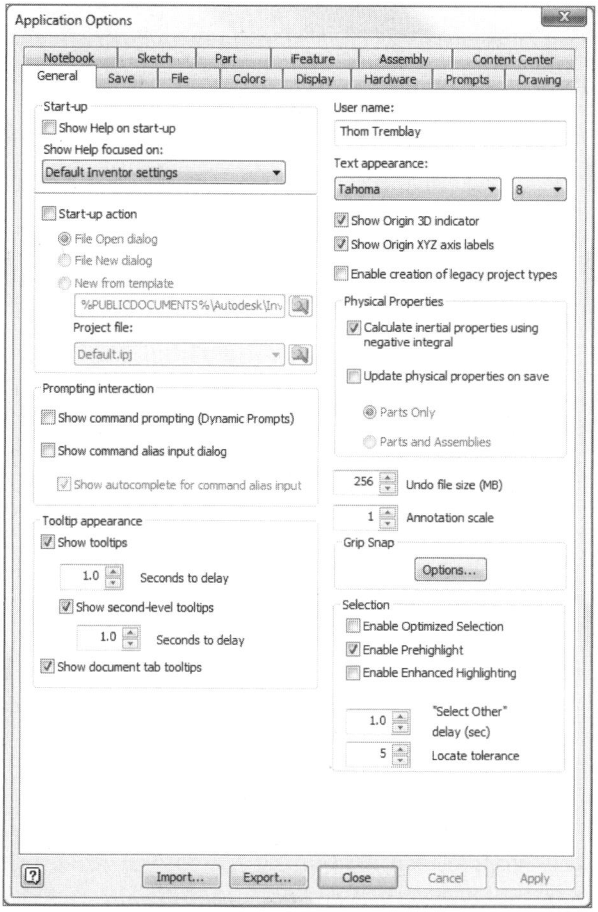

FIGURE 1.24 The Application Options dialog box, with the General tab displayed

Let's walk through the dialog box tab by tab. We won't cover absolutely everything, but some items can make major changes to Inventor's look, feel, and behavior. Some items won't be covered at this time; I'll discuss them when they become more relevant later in the book.

Each tab has several subsections with borders around groups of check boxes, radio buttons, and pull-downs lists. Each section has a header that makes it easy to figure out what all those devices will affect. The following comments are organized by tab and subsection to make navigation as painless as possible.

The General Tab

Tools on the General tab (see Figure 1.24) tell Inventor how you want the program to start, what name you want recorded as the author for files that you create, and other basics:

Start-up   The Show Help on Start-up option lets you bring up the Help system every time you open Inventor. If you want to use this, and you're an experienced AutoCAD user, you may want to consider switching the focus of the Help system to the one for AutoCAD users.

Start-up Action   Inventor 2010 has no start-up action by default, but you may choose to enable this option. As discussed earlier, the Open dialog box allows you to switch to the New dialog box, but in this section you can change whether Inventor starts with Open or New. You can also have Inventor begin a new file based on a specific template.

Tooltip Appearance   This is an interesting set of options. The first option lets you disable or change the wait time for the initial tooltip. Below that, you can disable the second-tier progressive tooltip. Finally, you can disable the preview of the documents displayed when you hover over the Document tab at the bottom of the Design window.

Selection   The Enable Optimized Selection option may be useful if you're using Inventor on a system with limited graphics performance. It sets the selection and highlighting to initially highlight only the parts that are closest to the front in the display. Enable Enhanced Highlighting displays the geometry selected to create an assembly constraint if you hover over the constraint in the browser. This is a fantastic aid in navigating an assembly that someone else built.

The Colors Tab

To change the overall look of Inventor, the Colors tab (see Figure 1.25) has the tools for the job. Many users simply change the color scheme, but several other options can be useful:

Color Scheme   Inventor has several standard color schemes that control the color of the graphics window background, highlighted elements, and sketch elements.

Background   Inventor can use a single color, a gradient of colors, or any standard raster image as a background for the graphics window. It comes with a library already installed.

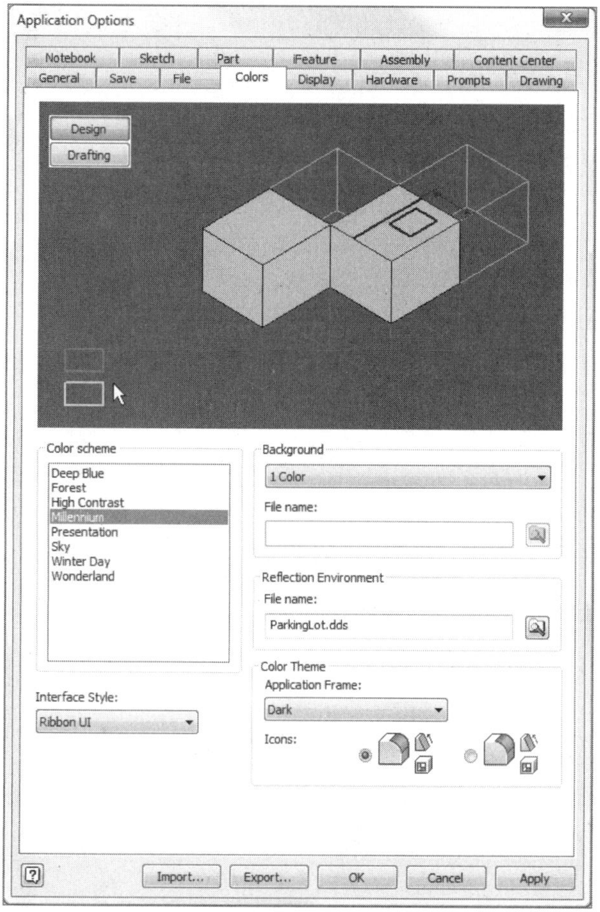

FIGURE 1.25 The Colors tab in the Application Options dialog box

Reflection Environment   Inventor comes with several image files that surround the model you're working on, so that if you have reflective colors on parts such as chrome, you'll see this image "reflected" on those parts.

Color Theme   To further adjust your environment, you can select whether the backgrounds of the Ribbon tab names and your Quick Access Toolbar are light or dark by selecting the Application Frame pull-down option. You can also set the color of your tool icons to be a subdued Blue or the bolder Amber theme.

The Display Tab

This is the tab where Inventor users can do the most tailoring of how Inventor displays your models. Looking at Figure 1.26, you can see just how many options there are. Many of them can have a noticeable effect on how Inventor looks:

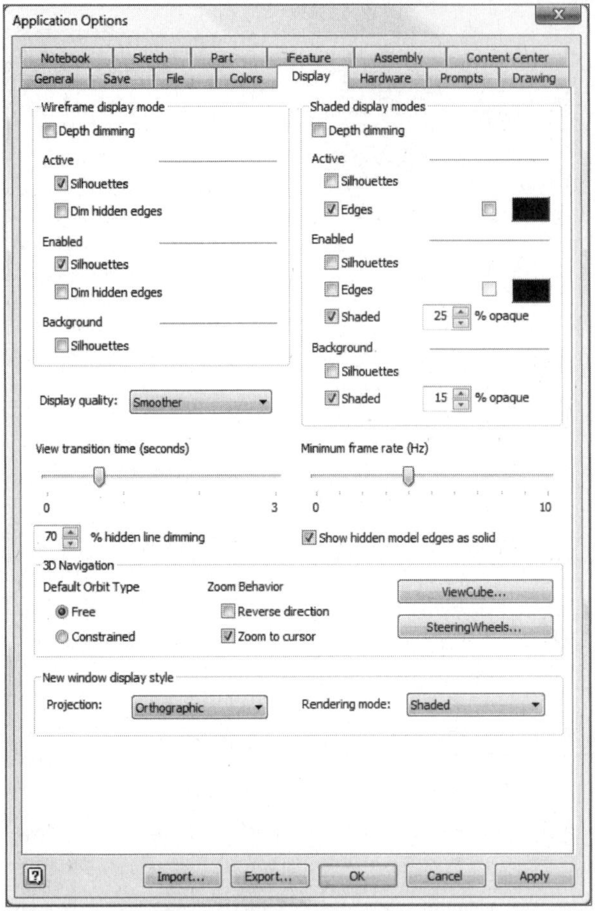

FIGURE 1.26 The Display tab in the Application Options dialog box

Wireframe Display Mode   When you're in Wireframe mode, choosing Active ➤ Dim Hidden Edges enables the model edges in the background to appear with less intensity than edges in the foreground. The amount of dimming is controlled by the % Hidden Line Dimming value near the bottom of the Display tab.

Shaded Display Modes   There are a lot of interesting ways to work with these options. Experiment — you can't hurt anything. In an exercise later in this chapter, you'll change a couple of the settings and see an effect in which rather than parts fading when you activate a single component, the parts that you aren't editing go to wireframe display.

Enabled   This setting can be a little confusing because it affects the display of parts that will be *inactive* in the assembly when you've activated another part. For example, when you double-clicked the Shock Absorber earlier in the chapter, you activated that part. The other parts appeared dimmed but still shaded. If you had Shaded deselected in this tab, those inactive parts would appear as wireframe.

Background   This value controls the visibility of components that aren't enabled in the assembly. Not having a component enabled gives it the appearance controlled here and disables the ability to select it in the assembly.

Minimum Frame Rate (Hz)   When you have limited graphic or system-memory capacity, Inventor may degrade the quality of the model image while rotating or zooming. The higher this value is, the more quickly Inventor will degrade the detail of the assembly in order to display it at the selected frame rate. This can be a great setting to explore when you're working with extremely large assemblies.

Show Hidden Model Edges as Solid   Deselecting this check box changes the display of hidden edges in the wireframe view from solid lines to hidden lines.

3D Navigation   The Reverse Direction option under Zoom Behavior controls the direction of the wheel-button zoom. This option was added for AutoCAD users who prefer the effect of moving the camera, as mentioned earlier. You can also set your default values for the ViewCube or Navigation Wheels here.

The Hardware Tab

If you're using Windows 2000 or XP, you can use this tab to select whether the graphics engine in Inventor is based on OpenGL or Direct3D. Vista users will see that there is no OpenGL option.

Notice the Use Software Graphics option. If you experience frequent crashes, try running with this setting for a while. Your performance will be greatly limited; but if you find that your system is more stable that way, it means you need to find an approved driver for your graphics card or update your graphic hardware. You can find more information about graphics drivers under the Help flyout menu under the heading Additional Resources.

The Drawing Tab

Notable here is the Default Drawing File Type option. Beginning with Inventor 2008, you can create 2D drawings as native DWG files, which are compatible with AutoCAD. The original IDW file format of Autodesk Inventor is still a valid and reliable file, but the strength of having fully native 2D data that can be shared with AutoCAD is very useful.

The Sketch Tab

Figure 1.27 shows the Sketch tab. The settings on this tab tend to be personal. Grid lines and axes are often set differently from user to user in a company, which is why the options are available:

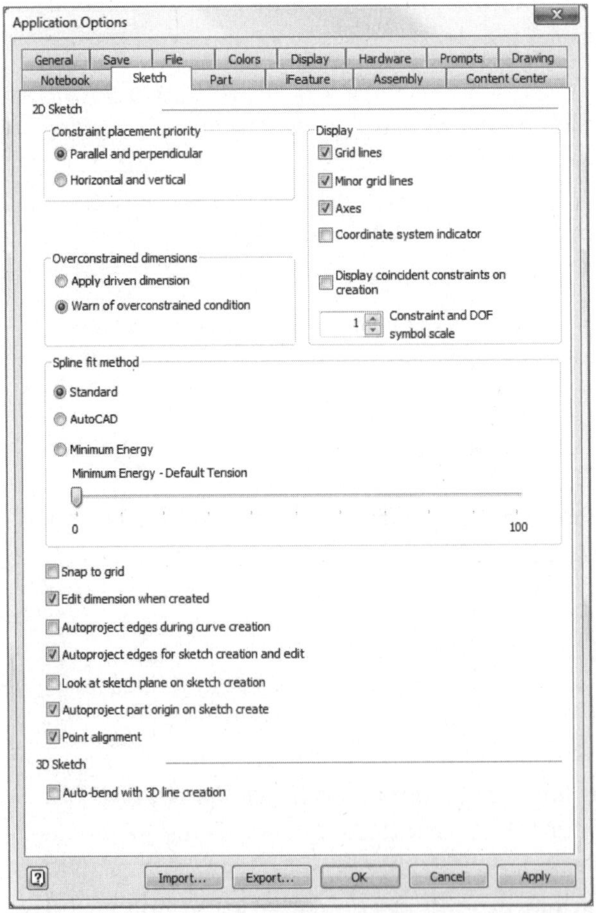

FIGURE 1.27 The Sketch tab in the Application Options dialog box

Overconstrained Dimensions   When we discuss applying dimensions and constraints to sketches in future exercises, you'll learn that Inventor won't allow a sketch to be "overconstrained." *Constraining* a sketch means that you apply controls to the movement of points in a sketch and to the size of a sketch. When Inventor detects a redundant or unnecessary constraint, this option defines whether Inventor automatically places a reference dimension or prompts you for what to do.

Display   When beginning a new sketch, you may or may not want to see grid lines. Some users feel the grid helps them keep the proportions of the sketch more accurately. Minor gridlines are smaller gridlines that appear between the primary ones. The axes are thicker lines that cross through the center of the sketch on the X and Y axes.

Edit Dimension When Created   Selecting this check box causes Inventor to prompt you for the value of a dimension as soon as it's placed it in a sketch. This can be helpful for remembering to apply the values for the dimension as you place them.

Autoproject Edges for Sketch Creation and Edit   When you create a new sketch on a part or assembly face with this option selected, the edges that are coplanar with that sketch are copied into the sketch. This can be handy for locating new features, but I find that many of these projected edges aren't used as a reference and can also cause errors downstream. Autodesk has improved the robustness of this feature, but it's an option that I often remove.

Look at Sketch Plane on Sketch Creation   When you create a new sketch on a face in an isometric view of a part, Inventor's default isn't to change your view orientation. With this option selected, the display behaves like the Look At zooming tool and brings your focus perpendicular to your new sketching plane.

Autoproject Part Origin on Sketch Create   This option causes Inventor to project the location of the center point of the part into every new sketch. Having this geometry projected doesn't mean you have to use the geometry or constrain geometry to it. This can be very useful if you design turned or other components that are frequently symmetrical.

The Part Tab

The option you may want to customize here is Sketch on New Part Creation. This allows you to choose your default sketching plane. It's a purely subjective preference, but many people find that they think about parts they are designing in either a profile or an overhead view. This option lets you choose how a part is oriented when it's first created.

The Assembly Tab

The noteworthy option here is Constraint Audio Notification. By default, when you place a constraint in Inventor, the sound of a cowbell is played. When you're starting out, this is a handy feature for confirming that a constraint was placed. After you hear the cowbell a couple of hundred times per day, you can come here to disable the audio cue.

Creating a New Work Environment

I know that some of this can be hard to digest, so let's do some hands-on work. Let's create a new work environment. We'll keep the changes limited to the visual elements for now. After you're finished, you can make other changes at any time.

Some steps won't be applicable to Inventor LT users. LT users can also use the file you previously opened or choose another file.

Follow these steps:

1. If you still have gray Shock Strut components active from the previous action, you're all set. If not, double-click the Shock Strut (gray parts) in the Design window to activate them. Another alternative is to double-click Shock Strut:1 in the Browser or to right-click the Shock Strut and select Edit.

2. Open the Application Options dialog box by selecting the Tools tab and picking Application Options.

3. Select the Colors tab.

4. Under Color Scheme, choose Wonderland, and watch the preview change at the top. Note that most of the screen elements change. Click the Apply button at lower right, and you'll see the change take effect in the Design window in the background.

5. At upper left in the preview pane are Design and Drafting buttons that show the effect of the color scheme in the 3D and 2D environments. Click the Drafting button, and then click the Design button.

6. In the Background area, change the style from 1 Color to Gradient, and note the effect.

7. Select the Presentation Color scheme, and click Apply.

8. Change the Background option to Background Image. Although there is a file that is the default for each color scheme, after you make this change you can select any BMP, JPG, PNG, GIF, or TIF for use as a

background. After switching to Background Image, click Apply again to see the effect.

9. Switch the Background option back to Gradient. A gradient background offers better performance than a background image for lower-powered systems. However, the 1 Color setting provides the best performance.

10. Set your Color Theme to Light Application Frame and select the Amber Icon color. Click Apply to see the changes.

 N O T E   For clarity in print, screen images captured for this book are created with the Presentation color scheme and the 1 Color option. This is a great setup if you need to create printable images from your models.

11. Switch to the Display tab.

12. Under Wireframe Display Mode, select Dim Hidden Edges under the Active group.

13. Under Shaded Display Modes, in the Active group, deselect Edges and select Silhouettes.

14. Under Shaded Display Modes, in the Enabled group, deselect Shaded and select Silhouettes.

15. Deselect the Show Hidden Model Edges as Solid option.

16. Update your display by clicking Apply. Shock Strut should be the only shaded component on the screen.

17. Switch to the Sketch tab.

18. Make sure the check box next to Autoproject Part Origin on Sketch Create is selected.

19. Deselect Edit Dimension When Created.

20. Deselect Autoproject Edges for Sketch Creation and Edit.

21. Deselect Look at Sketch Plane on Sketch Creation.

22. Switch to the Drawing tab, and change the Default Drawing File Type to Inventor Drawing (*.dwg), using the pull-down.

 N O T E   Many users prefer to work without the grid lines, minor grid lines, and axes. In the images in this book, none of these options are on, for clarity.

23. Let's save it all. Click the Export button at the bottom of the dialog box. The Export dialog box opens to the default location for the profile, but you can save your settings to any location. Name your file `NER Interface Settings.xml`.

24. Click OK to save the file. Your screen should look something like Figure 1.28.

25. Click the Return button to return to the assembly environment.

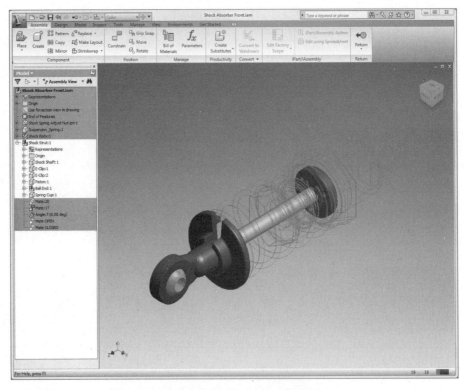

FIGURE 1.28 The interface after using Application Options

You've done it. You've made Inventor look and behave differently than it did when it was installed. For your own use, you may choose different settings, but it's important that you're comfortable with making changes to Inventor so that it suits you and the interface isn't a distraction from working. Combining these options with the Ribbon display options can give you a work environment that you'll enjoy.

Project Files

Inventor is normally a breeze to work with. There are only a handful of ways to make it difficult. One common bad habit is not properly controlling where files are kept. Inventor keeps track of where things are supposed to be using a *project file*.

As an old friend of mine so perfectly put it, "A project file is a text file that tells Inventor where to put stuff" — and that's all there is to it. The project file allows you to control where Inventor looks for templates, what styles are available, and where Inve]ntor stores files, including standard parts like bolts. This opens up a lot of possibilities, such as using different project files to switch templates with different title blocks when you work on jobs for multiple customers. Over time, more and more Inventor users establish one project file and sort jobs as folders under that project file. In an earlier example, in the Open File dialog box, you used the Frequently Used Subfolders list to find the assembly of the Shock Absorber. The Samples.ipj project file you selected is a great example of a project file that is used to organize many different datasets with many different types of design. Figure 1.29 shows what Samples.ipj looks like if you open it in the Project File editor.

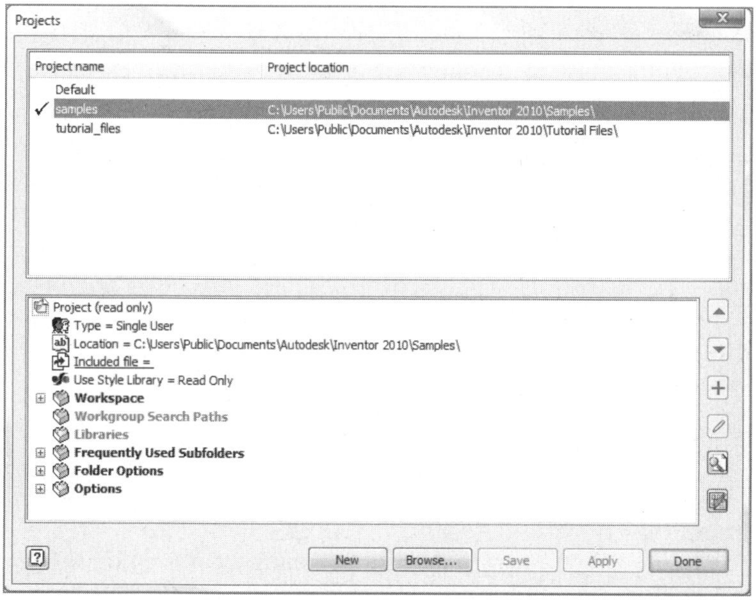

FIGURE 1.29 The Project File editor

The Project File editor is a fairly simple tool. It has a list of project files that have been used at the top in the Select Project pane, a display of the paths and properties of the highlighted project file in the bottom in the Edit Project pane, and a handful of tools on the right for modifying the project file. You must follow a few rules for project files:

▶ You can't change the active project file when a file is open.

▶ You can't add a Frequently Used Subfolders shortcut to a folder that isn't "under" the location of the project file.

▶ To edit a project file, you must have read/write access to the file or to the folder it's in.

As you select different options, the buttons on the right change to show that they are available or unavailable. As you read through the descriptions of what the sections of the project file do, try selecting them, and note which buttons become available. As you explore, continue to use the Samples.ipj project file that you made active previously. Here are some of the elements of the project file:

Type   You'll work with two primary types of project file. The Type option allows you to select between them:

> **Single User**   For the stand-alone user who won't be sharing data with other users simultaneously.
>
> **Vault**   Only available if you've installed the Vault, Autodesk's file-management tool that comes with Inventor. It enables simultaneous sharing with multiple users.

 N O T E   Two other types of project file let multiple users access data — but I can't recommend strongly enough that you use the Vault if you intend to share data in a network environment. The Vault is free and provides additional tools to make your work easier.

Location   This setting tells Inventor where the file is installed and also establishes a relative path that other search paths use to shorten their own searches for files. The project file may be in C:\Users\Public\Documents\Autodesk\Inventor 2010\Samples\, but during its search Inventor will skip all the previous directories and begin searching for files under the \Samples folder. This may not seem important, but it can greatly improve performance.

Use Style Library   Only users with the proper permissions can control the value of this setting. It controls whether a user can edit, use, or even access style libraries.

Libraries   In addition to the Content Center libraries that ship with Autodesk Inventor, you can declare that files in specific folders be treated as library files. These files can't be edited while you're using a project file that defines them as a library. It's also important that you not allow these files to be edited by people who don't consider them a library.

Frequently Used Subfolders   As you saw earlier in this chapter, you can define shortcuts that take you to folders that are relevant to the work you need to get done. Creating a path to a folder and another path to another folder under it replicates the structure on the disk. These shortcuts can be given any name, and you should name them in a way that is clear to you. For example, a disk path of `C:\Users\Public\Public Documents\Autodesk\Inventor 2010\Samples\Models\Assemblies\Suspension\Components` could have a shortcut of Brackets.

Folder Options   This area lets you establish paths to styles and templates that are in locations other than the ones that Inventor uses when it's installed. This is important in a network environment where you may want to have everyone accessing the same templates from a central source. The Content Center Files path tells Inventor where to put the local copies of standard content used by the files that you're working with. This too is an important consideration for a network environment so that you don't, for example, have multiple people keeping individual copies of the same standard bolt on their own computers.

Options   The group contains a couple of interesting items, but most of them are less frequently modified than other parts of the project file. The Old Versions to Keep on Save value controls the number of versions of the file that are saved to an `Oldversions` directory in the file path. You can restore these older files as new files or over the current versions of the files. It's important to note that if you restore over a current version, all changes made since the old version was saved are lost.

 N O T E   The `Oldversions` **directory can hold multiple versions of a file, created each time the file is saved. It's like having multiple BAK files that can be restored.**

Project File Manager Buttons

The buttons on the right side of the editor not only help you edit the file but also, by being available or being grayed out, offer visual cues for whether you can make certain changes.

The arrow buttons are available where there are lists of folders that you may want to sort for priority or convenience.

The Add button appears when you've selected a category where a path or other information can be added.

Edit is active when a value can be edited.

Clicking this button expands options for the project workspace or for establishing a workgroup. Note that workgroups aren't used with single-user or Vault-oriented project files. When this (or any other) dialog is expanded, the arrows point to the left to show that the dialog can also be collapsed.

Clicking this button generates a list of duplicate files in the project. You can use the list to compare files and choose how to treat them. If two unique parts have the same name, you can modify one of them to avoid confusion downstream. If you have two instances of an identical file, you should remove one of them and allow Inventor to seek out the remaining instance so there is no risk of having the incorrect version of a part in the assembly.

The Content Center can have many types of standard content (nuts, bolts, and so on), and you may not use all of them in a project. This button allows you to limit the standards that are used by the project.

Creating a Project File

Now that you have a basic overview of the project file, it's time to make one of your own that you'll use for future exercises:

1. Close any files that you have open in Inventor. Don't save changes to the Shock Absorber Front.iam file if you're prompted to do so.

2. On the Get Started tab, choose Projects.

3. Click the New button at the bottom of the dialog box. Doing so opens a wizard that will help you step through creating a new project file.

If you have Autodesk Vault installed, you have the option to choose to create a new Vault project or a new single-user project, as shown in Figure 1.30. If you don't have Vault installed, you aren't offered the Vault project option.

4. Select the radio button next to New Single User Project, and click the Next button at the bottom.

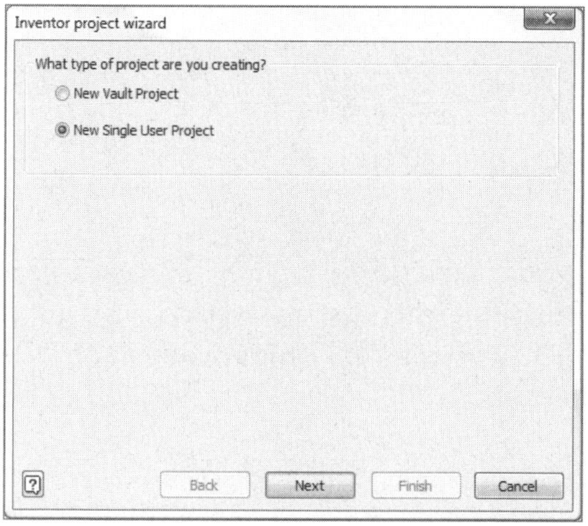

FIGURE 1.30 Defining the type of new project

On the next screen, you can name the file and set up its location. Keep in mind that you are not only establishing the location of a file but also establishing the root folder for the models that you'll be creating.

5. Type **NER Inventor 2010** in the Name text box.

6. The Project (Workspace) Folder line lists the default path that Inventor uses. Click the ellipsis icon to the right to begin browsing to a different folder. Figure 1.31 shows the Browse For Folder dialog box. In this case, you want to create a new folder. Don't create the folder in the location initially offered. Instead, scroll to your C drive, select the root of the C drive, and click the Make New Folder button. This creates a new folder on the C drive and allows you to rename it. Name the new folder **Data**, and click OK to close the Browse For Folder dialog box.

FIGURE 1.31 Creating a new folder

7. When you return to the Inventor Project Wizard, you should see the path C:\Data under Project (Workspace) Folder and a text string showing C:\Data\NER Inventor 2010.ipj under Project File To Be Created (Figure 1.32).

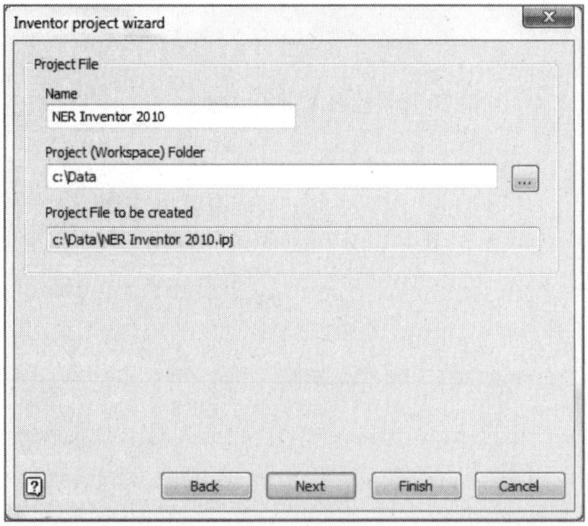

FIGURE 1.32 The new project name and path

8. Click Finish.

9. When you return to the Projects dialog box (Figure 1.33), your new project file doesn't automatically become the active project file. Do *not* change the active project file at this time. When you do wish to make your new project active, you must highlight it and click the Apply button or double-click the filename in the Select Project pane.

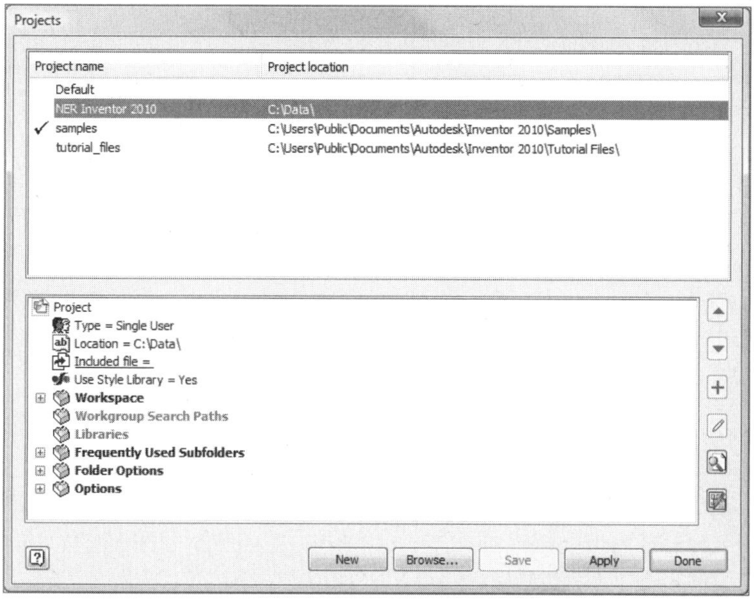

FIGURE 1.33 NER Inventor 2010 project file added to the list of project files

10. You'll see that the Frequently Used Subfolders line is dimmed. This is because no shortcuts are currently listed. In some cases, you'll add a new shortcut that leads to an existing path. You'll create a shortcut and the path it leads to in one sequence.

11. Select the Frequently Used Subfolders line in the Edit Project pane. When you do so, the Add button becomes available. Click that button, and two boxes appear. The first is for the name of the shortcut you want to add; the second is for the path. Next to the Path button is a folder search icon that you can click to select an existing folder or create a new one.

12. Change the Shortcut name to **Parts**.

13. In this case, you're adding a new folder to the path, so you can add a Parts folder after Data in the path and press Enter.

14. Add to the project file another Frequently Used Subfolder nicknamed Assemblies with the path C:\Data\Assemblies.

   If you click the folder search icon, a file dialog box titled Choose or Add a Path for the Project File appears. It has one important difference: clicking the Make New Folder button automatically creates a new folder under the workspace folder you defined when you created the new project file. Inventor should create a new folder and highlight the name for renaming. If Inventor doesn't offer you a chance to rename the folder to Parts, you can do so using Windows Explorer.

15. For a final modification let's establish the ability to modify the standards Inventor uses to define your drawings, sheet-metal parts and other elements. Right-click the Use Style Library value, and select Yes from the list of options that appears.

16. After you've added the paths and write permissions for the style library, save the change by clicking the Save button at the bottom of the dialog box. The completed project file should look like Figure 1.34

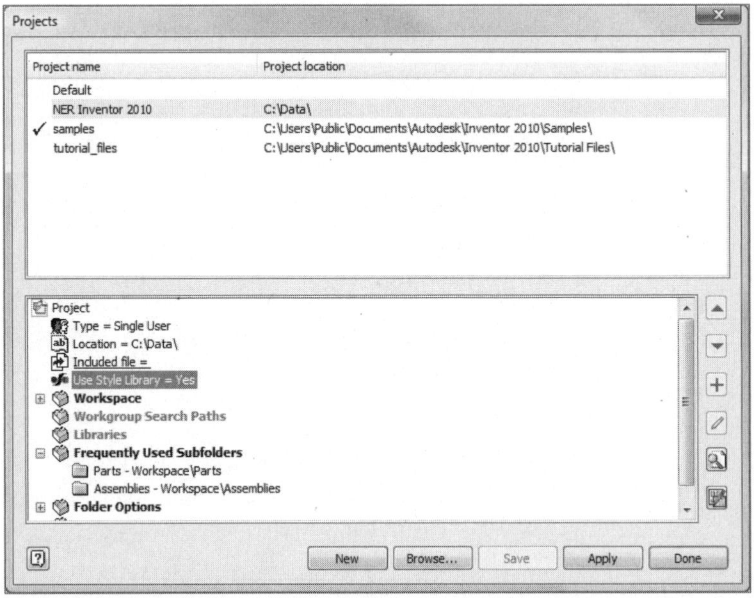

FIGURE 1.34 Completed project file with a shortcut to the Parts folder

17. Double-click on the *NER Inventor 2010* project to make it the active Project File.

Defining a project file isn't a difficult process, but it's an important one. It's a good idea to decide how you want to share data with others and review how you currently sort your design data to help define how your project file should be arranged. It's possible to change your file structure after the fact if necessary, and Inventor can help you find the files it needs — but it's worth some extra time to think about how you want to sort your data.

Inventor must know where files are to work effectively. Failing to control your file locations can inhibit the program's performance — and having to tell Inventor where to find files will cause you undue stress.

Using the Help System and Infocenter

Although any software can be improved, I find the Help system in Inventor to be very good. It even comes in different flavors. One type of help is oriented toward existing Inventor users and those who have used other 3D design programs. Or, if you're an experienced AutoCAD user, you can have the Help system compare Inventor to AutoCAD to help you relate a little more easily. Regardless of how you use it, I encourage you to take advantage of the Help system as an additional resource.

To access the primary Help system, type a keyword or words for search in the space in the Infocenter at the right end of the title bar where it says Type a Keyword or Phrase. Click the search icon (binoculars), and both topics local to Inventor Help and online resources will be listed.

Next to the search icon are links to Autodesk Subscription Center, Communications center, and Favorites that will let you set up information feeds from Autodesk and a listing of your favorite searches and their results.

The last icon expands to offer shortcuts to a number of the Inventor help and learning tools. Clicking it opens the Inventor Help window where you can search or browse to the answer you're seeking.

Are You Experienced?

Now you can...

☑ recognize and control the elements of the interface

☑ open files in Autodesk Inventor 2010

☑ navigate in the Design Window

☑ customize your working environment

☑ create a project file

☑ access the Help system

CHAPTER 2

Building the Foundation of the Design

▶ Learning the essential sketching tools

▶ Learning the basics of parametric dimensions

▶ Understanding sketch constraints

▶ Developing sheet metal styles

▶ Using sheet metal tools to define the foundation

▶ Developing flat patterns of components

▶ Creating drawings of components

It's About the Design

When people use Autodesk Inventor, they don't use it for the sake of using Inventor. It's used as a means to create the products that they and their employer will build. In this way, the design software is simply a tool. Traditionally, books about a software package have focused on the software's tools rather than how they're used as part of the process creating a product.

In this book, I want to introduce tools that are needed to build components as you need them. Because of the type of product you'll be building, I'll introduce a number of tools a little later that most books would teach first. Other tools are often used at the beginning of a part, but I'll instead use them to add detail.

When defining your assembly, the first component you place in the assembly should be the component you would typically grab off the shelf and attach things to. This component is referred to as the *base component*. It's possible to change the base component of an assembly, but more often than not your choice of the base component will be from your experience and therefore correct. If you keep a realistic assembly process in mind, the functions that Inventor uses to define the relationships between parts will be easier to understand and perform more reliably as you edit the assembly. Sometimes, using planes or axes that run through the part is the easiest way to properly locate an object. This is particularly useful if you're using a technique referred to as *middle-out* to define a component that connects two or more parts you've already placed in the assembly.

Most users don't create individual parts; they create assemblies of parts. That is why Autodesk Inventor was written with the assembly in mind. The size and complexity of assemblies may vary, but at their core they're collections of components that are fastened, welded, or in some other way stuck together.

With this brief introduction, let's begin the process of building your first component and developing a design in Inventor.

Creating the Sheet Metal Housing

Most books and tutorial about Inventor start with parts that are created using Extrude or Revolve features. Because this book's intent is to follow a more reasonable workflow, you'll begin with the type of component that is best for your design.

First, you need to define how the feature will be created.

Sketching Tools

Just as assemblies are made up of components, components are made up of features. There are two types of features: *sketched* and *placed*. A sketched feature is the first feature you place in a part. It's generally made up of a 2D sketch on a face or plane that you convert into a 3D shape. Examples of sketched feature tools include Extrude, Revolve, and Rib.

Placed features are placed onto other features. Examples of placed feature tools include Fillet, Chamfer, and Face Draft. Features that are placed or that use the faces of other features as a foundation are said to be *children* of the features they're built on, which are called *parent* features.

Your first component (and pretty much any part) will start by using a sketch to define its basic shape. This sketch is different than the type of sketch you may be used to creating in a 2D CAD package. The lines, arcs, and circles that make up these sketches can be modified by changing a dimension value. They can also be related to one another to limit their size or location.

By default, when you create a new Part file, Inventor assumes that you want to create a sketch. Figure 2.1 shows the Sketch toolbar as it appears when you start a new part. In this case, it's a sheet metal part.

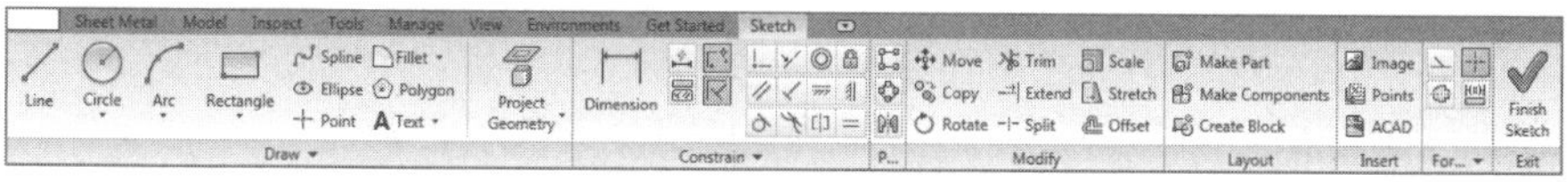

FIGURE 2.1 Sketch tools displayed in the Ribbon

Most of the tools in the various panels of the Ribbon will be familiar. As you build the various components of your product, you'll use a lot of these tools. Because Inventor has a very consistent workflow from tool to tool, you should easily be able to incorporate any of the tools you don't use into future work. Let's dive right in and start using these tools. I think you'll find that it's a simple process, so relax and get ready to enjoy using Inventor.

In this exercise, you'll create a sketch that defines the basic shape of the housing for a fan. When you're creating a sketch for a feature, it's best to try to define as much of the feature or component in one simple sketch as possible. Follow these steps:

1. Close any files you have open in Inventor.

2. Make sure NER Inventor 2010 is the active project file.

3. Select the New File icon under the large I icon of the Application menu at upper left in the Inventor interface.

4. Select the English tab in the New File dialog.

5. Click the Sheet Metal (in).ipt template and click the OK button, or double-click the icon of the template file to create a new sheet metal part.

A new file opens in Inventor. The differences between a standard part and a sheet metal part are subtle but important. Behind the scenes in a sheet metal part, Inventor creates a number of named values that control the thickness of the material, the size and shape of reliefs where the material is bent, and the radius of the bend. The sheet metal part also presents a different set of tools; they will be offered on the Sheet Metal tab when you're finished sketching.

For learning purposes, you aren't going to draw your first sketch as well as possible. Although it's important to draw your sketch nearly perfectly, not doing so can be fixed as well:

6. In the Draw panel of the Sketch tab, select the Line tool.

7. A message at lower left in the status bar prompts you to "Select start of line, drag off endpoint for tangent arc". Inventor is asking you to pick a place to start your line. Near lower right in the design window, click and release the mouse button to start the Line tool.

8. Drag your cursor to the left. As you do so, Inventor displays a glyph of a horizontal line when your line is horizontal, as shown in Figure 2.2.

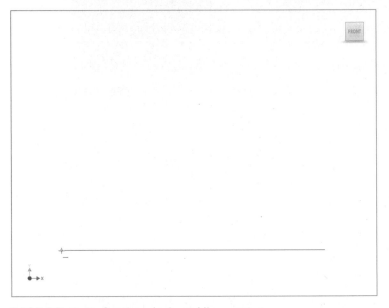

FIGURE 2.2 Creating a horizontal line segment

9. When your line looks similar to Figure 2.2 and is horizontal, click again to create the first segment.

When you create a line segment that has a glyph showing whether it's vertical, horizontal, perpendicular, or parallel to another object, that segment will keep that property. This is known as a *constraint*. Inventor's sketching environment includes a number of constraints that make life a lot easier when you need to modify your part.

10. Even though you've created a line segment, Inventor continues using the Line tool. Move your cursor toward the top of the screen, with the Perpendicular glyph displayed. See Figure 2.3. Note that if you move left or right far enough, the glyph disappears; it reappears as you near vertical. Click to place this line in the sketch.

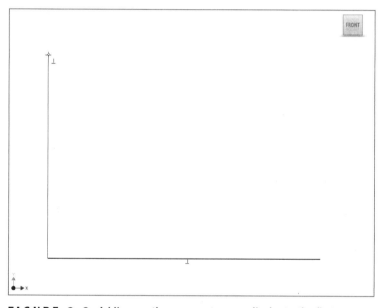

FIGURE 2.3 Adding another segment perpendicular to the first

11. Move your cursor to the right. You'll notice a glyph displaying two parallel lines not only near your cursor but in the center of your first line segment. This shows that Inventor is trying to create a relationship between the segments that will keep them parallel to each other. Don't click your mouse yet.

12. Move your cursor over the second line you created, and move the cursor up and down without clicking.

13. Move the cursor back to the right. Inventor now wants to create a relationship to your second line rather than the first (Figure 2.4). This is called *scrubbing* or *gesturing* on a sketch element; it allows you to change the way the sketch is constrained.

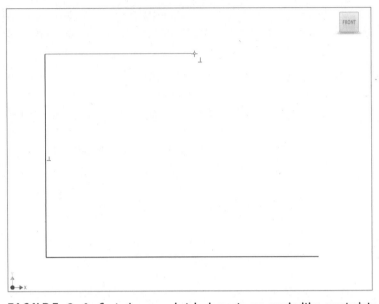

FIGURE 2.4 Gesturing over sketch elements can reprioritize constraints.

14. Move the cursor slowly so that your new segment preview is still perpendicular to the last segment. As your new line nears the same length as the first, you should see a dotted line indicating that the endpoints are aligned. When you see this (see Figure 2.5), click to place the new segment.

Now you're going to make a "mistake." The last segment won't create a rectangle — which is kind of correct, because your first part doesn't need a closed shape. But you'll make other errors that you'll correct, including the fact that presently, the sketch is nowhere close to the proper size — something you won't normally want.

15. Move your cursor near the first point, but place the endpoint above and to the right of the beginning, as shown in Figure 2.6.

16. After you've selected the endpoint for the fourth segment, Inventor is still ready to create more. You can right-click your mouse and select Done [Esc] from the context menu that appears on your screen, or you can simply press the Esc key to end the Line tool.

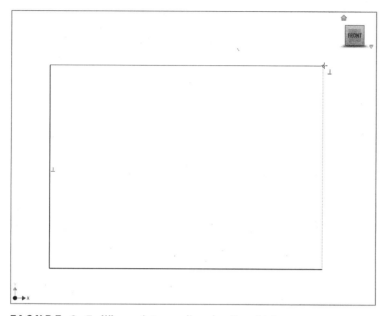

FIGURE 2.5 When points are aligned, a line of inference appears on the screen.

FIGURE 2.6 The initial completed sketch

17. For now, you're finished sketching. At the right end of the Sketch tab is the Exit panel, and in it is the Finish Sketch icon. Click this to end your sketch.

As soon as you select the Finish Sketch icon, Inventor's Ribbon interface changes, as explained in Chapter 1. Now, you see the tools that are available to create sheet metal components. Take a moment to notice that the placed features like Flange, Cut, and Corner Round are grayed or dimmed and aren't selectable. As discussed earlier in this chapter, these tools depend on having an existing feature to build on — and right now, all you have is a sketch.

18. Find the Save icon on the Quick Access Toolbar at upper left on the screen. Click it, and save the new file as Housing.ipt in the Parts folder of your Workspace (Figure 2.7).

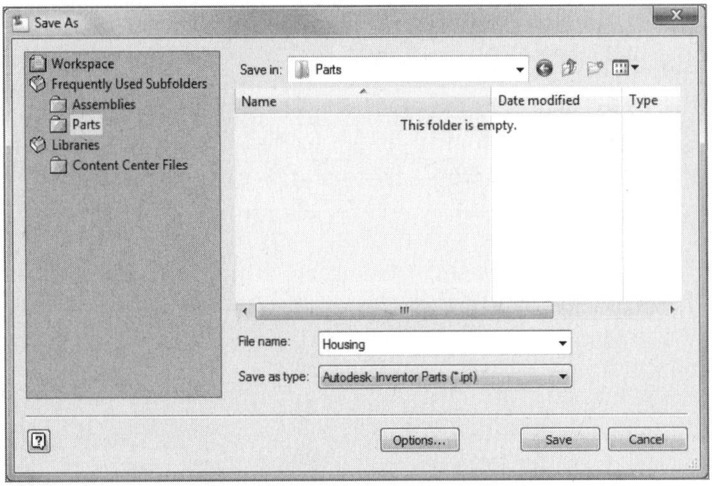

FIGURE 2.7 Save your part file to c:\Data\parts.

The constraints that are placed on the sketch while you're using tools like Line are just the beginning. Understanding these tools and being able to control them is the key to creating components that can be edited and behave predictably. Let's take a little time to review the tools that are available for constraining the sketch.

Sketch Constraints

You can place a number of types of constraint in a sketch. Figure 2.8 shows the constraints available for sketching, as displayed in the Constrain panel on the Sketch tab. It's worth taking a little time to review them:

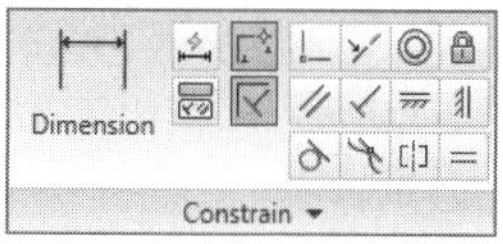

FIGURE 2.8 The Sketch tab's Constrain panel

Coincident   This constraint is by far the most common. It can be placed between endpoints, between midpoints, and even between a point and a curve or line. If you want a point to maintain a relationship with just about anything, Coincident will do it.

Collinear   This simply tells lines to be aligned with one another.

Concentric   For a Concentric relationship to be placed, you need to have at least one arc and one circle. Two arcs or two circles will also work. This is essentially a specialized Coincident constraint used only for the centerpoint of a radius. Because an ellipse also has a centerpoint, it will work with that shape as well.

Fix   The Fix constraint enables you to hold a position on a point. It can be useful for positioning critical points while others are allowed to move freely around them. Fixing a point is sometimes referred to as *grounding* the point. You can also use Fix on lines, arcs, circles, and so on.

Parallel   This constraint is also commonly applied while sketching. Like all constraints, it's maintained until it's removed. If one of the members of the constraint relationship changes direction, the other does as well.

Perpendicular   This constraint creates a relationship between line segments that keeps them at 90 degrees. It's commonly placed automatically while sketching.

Horizontal and Vertical   These two constraints can occasionally catch you off guard. It's important to remember the orientation to the coordinate system. Vertical relates to the Y axis of the active sketch, and Horizontal relates to the X axis. These constraints are used for far more than keeping lines oriented. You can constrain a point to be vertical or horizontal to another point. This can aid in aligning critical points as you develop around them. A keyboard shortcut is available for the Vertical constraint: while in a sketch, pressing the I key starts the constraint placement.

Tangent   You can create this condition between lines and arcs, arcs and splines, and circles and other circles.

Smooth   This constraint is similar to Tangent but with a deeper mathematical meaning. Rather than a simple relationship that affects the points where two entities meet, Smooth causes splines to change downstream from the connection point to maintain the continuity of the curve. This constraint isn't placed automatically in a sketch.

Symmetric   This constraint is often overlooked but is very powerful when you're working on symmetrical sketches whose size is in flux. As with Parallel, any change made to one member affects the mirrored or symmetrical member of the constraint.

Equal   Using the Equal constraint can create a lot of interesting relationships. You can keep any two (or more) like entities at the same value. Two lines can maintain the same length, and two (or more) arcs can maintain the same radius. This helps reduce the number of redundant dimensions that may be placed in a sketch otherwise. The = key is the keyboard shortcut for this constraint.

Two additional options control how or whether constraints are placed automatically in the sketch. The default is to have both options turned on so they appear as engaged buttons:

Constraint Inference   This controls whether Inventor recognizes conditions such as Parallel or Perpendicular in the sketch. With the option off, tools such as Line still appear to follow horizontal or vertical, but no glyph is displayed. If you build a shape, any Coincident constraints are automatically added to the sketch.

Constraint Persistence   Turning this off prevents Inventor from capturing any conditions in the sketch. With Constraint Inference on and Constraint Persistence off, you can draw using parallelism and so forth; but when you finish your sketch, no actual constraints (other than coincidence) will be included in the sketch. You can't have a condition where Constraint Inference is off and Constraint Persistence is on. Shutting off Constraint Inference automatically disables Constraint Persistence.

You can tell Inventor to ignore inference and persistence momentarily by holding the Ctrl key while sketching. Coincidence is still captured, but everything else is ignored.

To review the constraints that exist in an entire sketch, right-click in the Design window and select Show All Constraints from the menu or press the F8 key. If you want to review the constraints placed on an individual geometry piece, select the geometry segment, right-click, and select Show Constraints.

N O T E AutoCAD's osnap options appear to be similar to many of Inventor's sketch constraints, with one critical difference. If you tell AutoCAD that a line is attached to the endpoint of another line by using an osnap, AutoCAD creates the new line with an endpoint that's precisely in the same position as the other point. It doesn't create a relationship between the points. If the first line is moved, the new line won't follow. In Inventor, the relationship is maintained until it's deliberately removed or Inventor is told that the relationship shouldn't be created.

Viewing the Constraints in a Sketch

Now that you've created your basic sketch, let's review the constraints that were placed. This can be useful for recalling how you constructed a sketch, and it can be a life saver if you're modifying parts created by others:

1. Continue working in Housing.ipt, or reopen the file.

2. In the Browser panel at left on the screen, locate Sketch1 and double-click the icon with a pencil and square. Doing so returns you to editing the sketch and changes the Inventor Ribbon to display the Sketch tab.

3. When you're ready to begin editing the sketch, press the F8 key to display the existing sketch constraints. See Figure 2.9.

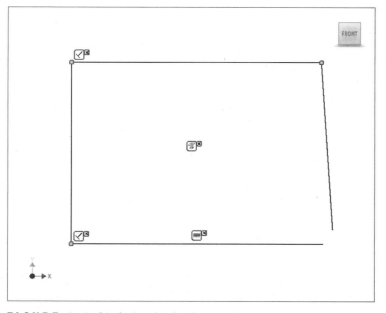

FIGURE 2.9 Displaying the sketch constraints

4. On the screen, you see small, yellow squares where segments meet. Hover over one of them; after a moment, the icons for the Coincidence constraints appear. There are two, to denote that two elements are affected by the constraint. Move your mouse back and forth between the two, and you'll see that the different lines highlight.

5. Position your mouse over the Perpendicular icon at lower left. Both segments highlight simultaneously.

6. If you used the same settings for your Application Options as I have, from the exercise in Chapter 1, you see an additional icon in the center of the screen: This is for the projected center of the sketch. Right-click the icon, and select Hide to turn off the icon's visibility.

7. Right-click the Perpendicular icon at upper left. Select the Delete option from the context menu that appears on the screen. Doing this not only removes the icon but also eliminates the relationship between the entities.

8. Click and drag the right endpoint of the top horizontal line, and see that it moves. Release the mouse button; the sketch remains as it was previewed, as shown in Figure 2.10.

9. Press the F9 key to turn off the display of the sketch constraints.

You can display another tool temporarily on the screen to better understand the state of the sketch constraints: The Degrees of Freedom (DOF) of the sketch shows which elements are still flexible in their movement and how. You'll use this powerful yet simple addition in the next exercise to make the effects of sketch dimensions easier to understand.

Sketch Dimensions

Sketch constraints create specific relationships between parts of the geometry. When you need to be able to define a relationship based on a size, that's when you need a *sketch dimension*.

Sketch dimensions have slightly fewer options than the dimensions you place on drawing views but follow the same basic rules. Unlike many 2D CAD tools, only one Dimension tool is used for defining a sketch in Inventor. You can use this Dimension tool to place different types of dimension simply by gesturing on the geometry that you want to control. You also have some context-menu options; but for the most part, picking the sketch elements will do the trick.

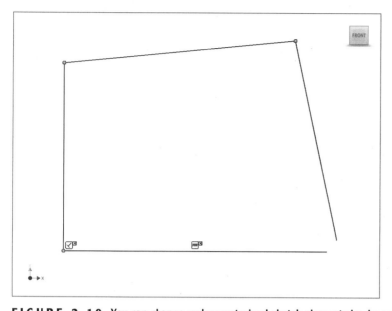

FIGURE 2.10 You can change underconstrained sketch elements by dragging them with the mouse.

Inventor's sketch dimensions can also simplify creating geometry with different units. If you're working in inches but need to size something based on a known metric measurement, you can input the value and the units. If you don't specify the units, Inventor uses the default units of the template from which you started the part. Inventor does the calculations for you and maintains the units that you specified in the background.

One school of thought says you should dimension part sketches so that the dimensions can be reused. I believe you should dimension your sketches in whatever fashion allows you to change your part in a predictable way; if they happen to be reusable for detail dimensions later on in the drawing, great. If they can't be reused, then it's easy to create new dimensions in the drawing.

Some companies don't allow sketch dimensions to be reused in a drawing. Inventor is installed by default with the ability to update a 3D part by modifying a sketch dimension's value in the 2D drawing. This option can be set during installation; but rather than risk a mistake, many companies discourage or bar the practice of reusing sketch dimensions in drawings.

Controlling a Sketch Using Dimensions

In the previous exercise, you reviewed the constraints that were added automatically to the geometry of the sketch. In this exercise, you'll use both dimensions and constraints to complete the sketch for the first feature of your part:

1. Press F8 to make the sketch constraints visible again.

2. Right-click away from any sketch geometry, and select Show All Degrees of Freedom from the Context menu.

In addition to the constraint icons, you should now see a collection of arrows. The line segments have some restricted movement. The lines constrained to be horizontal can only move vertically. The opposite is true for vertical lines. And the points in the corners can move in any direction on the sketch plane. See Figure 2.11 for a reference.

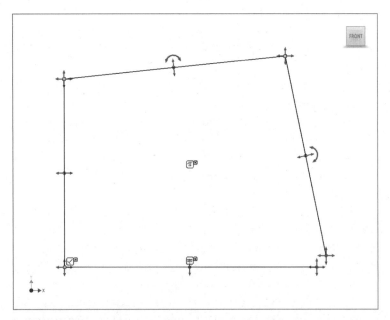

FIGURE 2.11 DOF symbols help you understand how geometric constraints limit sketch flexibility.

When you create a new component or assembly, Inventor automatically inserts the XY, XZ, and YZ planes as well as the X, Y, and Z axes. I have the intersection of those axes automatically projected in to my sketch. The fan blade is the center of the design. This blade will turn on about the Z axis. To make it easier to maintain spacing, you'll use the Origin planes as a reference when placing components in the assembly. Although I don't always use the origin as a common reference, you'll do this for nearly all the parts in this design. You'll become familiar with me asking you to add Horizontal and Vertical constraints to sketch elements (and I hope you won't become frustrated by how many times I ask you to do this).

The shape you presently have needs to become a square with a small gap in one corner. It also needs to be much larger than it currently is. Going forward, I'll ask you to approximate the correct part size when creating your sketch. Now, you'll use some tools to correct this deliberate mistake and end up with what you need:

3. Select the Horizontal constraint icon in the Constrain panel.

4. Move to the double-ended arrow in the middle of the vertical line on the left. As you near it, the midpoint of the line highlights. Select it when it does.

5. Select the centerpoint of the sketch, in the middle of the Design window.

Depending on where you started your sketch and how long the segments are, the sketch will shift to align the midpoint horizontally to the centerpoint. Placing a Horizontal constraint limits vertical movement. It seems a little strange at first — the way to think about it is that the midpoint is limited to moving horizontally.

On the right end of the status bar, Inventor now displays "7 dimensions needed". When you're working with parametrics, it's desirable but not mandatory that every DOF be removed from the sketch. When this is done the sketch is *fully constrained*. Another thing to be aware of is that you really don't need seven dimensions per se. Adding a geometric constraint can eliminate one or more of the needed dimensions. This is one of those things in life that you need to know but that you don't need to think much about in most cases.

Now, let's limit center the bottom line using a Vertical constraint:

6. Press the Esc key to end the use of the Horizontal constraint tool.

7. Select the Vertical constraint from the Constrain panel, or press the I key to start the tool.

8. This time, select the sketch centerpoint and the midpoint of the bottom horizontal line. This line shifts into alignment as well.

   OK. You've set the foundation, and you have something to build on. I know it hasn't been too exciting yet, but now the changes will start to be more apparent:

9. Select the Parallel constraint, and pick the top and bottom lines. The curved arrow on the top line disappears because the top line is now held parallel to the bottom line that is also constrained to be horizontal. See Figure 2.12.

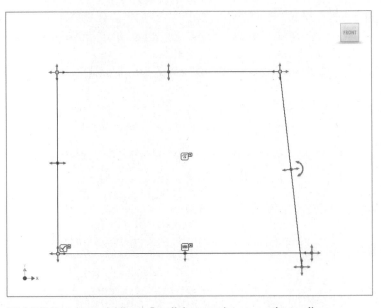

FIGURE 2.12 Adding a Parallel constraint moves the top line.

10. Let's change gears. Select the Dimension tool from the Constrain panel.

11. Move over the vertical line on the left. The entire line highlights. When it does, click to begin placing a dimension that previews the length of the line. Click again to the left of the line to place the dimension in the sketch. See Figure 2.13.

    Adding the dimension to the sketch limits your ability to change the line's length by dragging, so the icons on either end change. If you were prompted by a dialog box appearing to enter a value for the dimension when you placed it, click the X button on the dialog box to close the dialog.

    After you complete step 12, close the dialog; go into Application Options, and on the Sketch tab, deselect Edit Dimension When Created.

12. The Dimension tool is still running. Select the top horizontal line. Then, move to the angled line on the right. The glyph changes to an angular dimension when you're over the line. See Figure 2.14.

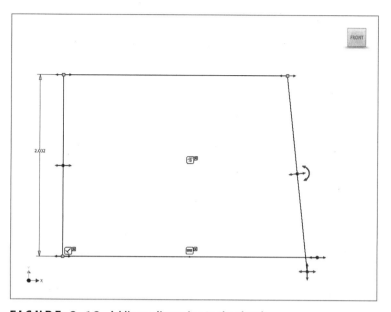

FIGURE 2.13 Adding a dimension to the sketch

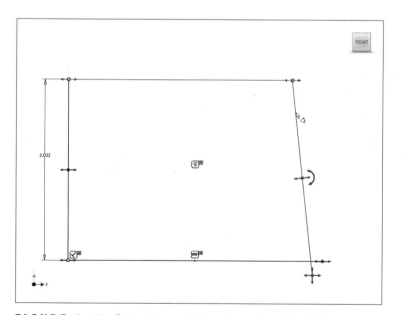

FIGURE 2.14 Gesturing over different geometry offers different dimensioning options.

13. Place the angular dimension inside the perimeter of the sketch, as shown in Figure 2.15.

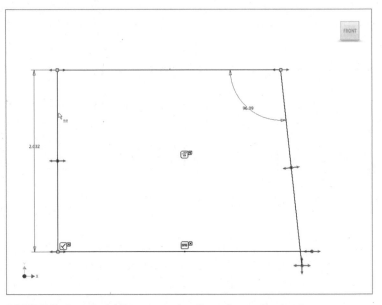

FIGURE 2.15 Adding an angular dimension to the sketch

14. With the Dimension tool still active, click the numerical value of the first dimension to edit its value. See Figure 2.16.

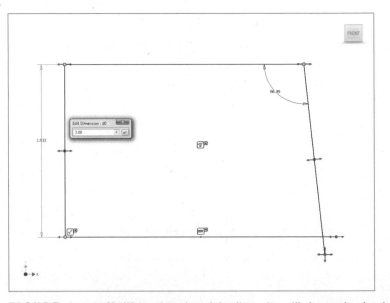

FIGURE 2.16 Modifying the value of the dimension will change the sketch.

15. Set the value in the dialog box to 3, and click the green check mark to accept the new value. Doing so changes the sketch. You may need to zoom out to see the complete sketch, as shown in Figure 2.17.

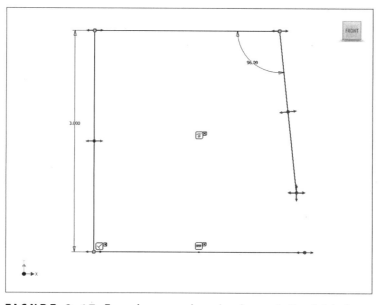

FIGURE 2.17 Even when you make major changes to the sketch, the constraint relationships remain intact.

16. Select the Equal constraint, or press the = key on your keyboard.

17. When the constraint highlights, pick the bottom line. Then, pick the vertical line on the left.

18. Pick the top line and the vertical line on the left.

The top, bottom, and left lines are now all the same length and will all be affected by any change to the 3.000 dimension.

The other dimension in the sketch is the angular dimension. You can modify its value to be 90 degrees to make the last line vertical. Sometimes you may want to place a dimension to see a value but not use it to control the geometry. When Inventor places parametric dimensions, it's possible to convert them into driven dimensions. This function is part of a series of overrides that exist in the sketch. Over the coming exercises, you'll use all of them at least once and some of them many times. Let's review these options, which reside in the Format panel on the Sketch tab:

Construction   When you draw in Inventor, the geometry is *normal* geometry by default. Normal geometry is intended to build shapes from which to make 3D features. Construction geometry is ignored by 3D modeling tools but can be used to define the shape and location of the 2D sketch geometry.

Center Point   Any geometry placed in a sketch has points included. You can select these points for different functions. When the Center Point override is selected, points that are placed in a sketch are automatically selected as a place to put a hole feature. This option is typically switched on.

Centerline   This option can convert any normal or construction geometry to take on special properties as a centerline. Centerlines can be selected automatically for creating round or turned shapes using the Revolve tool. They can also change the behavior of dimensions, causing them to recognize a sectional profile as having its size based on a diameter rather than a linear dimension.

 Driven Dimension   The dimensions you placed on the sketch in the previous exercise are referred to as *parametric* dimensions. Their value changes the size of sketch geometry. There are times where you want a dimension to simply show what size something is but not be able to change the geometry. A *driven dimension* allows this. It even displays itself in the sketch in parentheses as a reference dimension would be displayed.

N O T E   Since Release 9, AutoCAD has had associative dimensions that have the ability to change their values when the geometry they're attached to changes. This is essentially how driven dimensions behave.

Now you'll finish the sketch so you're ready to create the first feature of your component. Let's start with a little experiment using a sketch override. Then, you'll go back to the dimensions and constraints you're getting used to:

1. Use the Esc key to clear any tools that are active.

2. Click the angular dimension at upper right, and then select the Driven Dimension override from the Format panel on the Sketch tab. See Figure 2.18.

   You'll see that there is more freedom on the angled line. Now, fully constrain the sketch:

3. Start the Vertical constraint, and select the angled line. Note that the driven dimension responds to the change and the angular DOF is removed.

4. Place a dimension between the right endpoint of the bottom line and the end lowest point of the line that you just made vertical. Edit its value to .125in, as shown in Figure 2.19.

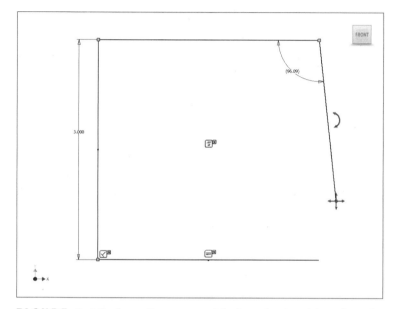

FIGURE 2.18 Converting a parametric dimension to a driven dimension makes it associative.

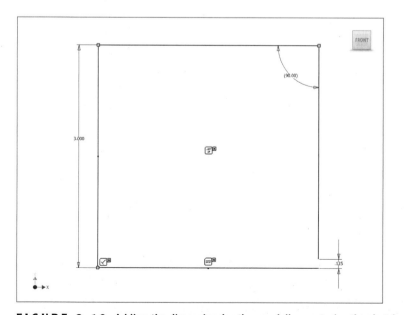

FIGURE 2.19 Adding the dimension for the gap fully constrains the sketch.

Even though the sketch is fully constrained, there is still a major problem: it's too small. Let's fix it:

5. Edit the 3.000 dimension to read 36, and pick the green checkmark or press the Enter key to accept the new value.

6. Double-click your middle mouse button or select Zoom All from the Navigate panel in your Design window. Your completed sketch should look like Figure 2.20.

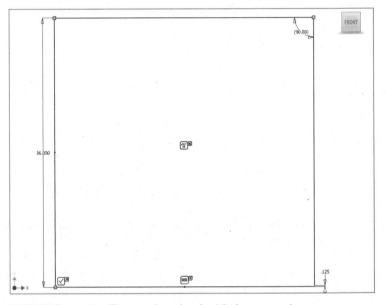

FIGURE 2.20 The complete sketch with the proper size

7. Click the Finish Sketch tool to exit the sketching environment and begin using the sheet metal tools.

8. Save your work.

Sketching in Inventor is normally a straightforward situation. More often than not, the sketches are simple; but even when they're complex, the control provided through dimensions and constraints makes them easy to modify.

Inventor's Sheet Metal Tools

Producing a sheet metal component must be done with an understanding of the limitations of the production methods available and the materials that a company typically uses.

Most people build sheet metal parts from readily available sheets that have predefined thickness and material properties. Based on the tooling, you can even predict how the material will stretch as it's processed. For years, engineers and designers have developed tables that they use to calculate what shape and size they need to cut into the sheet to be able to bend the part into the proper finished size. Now they can let the computer do the work for them by creating their parts using Inventor.

Sheet Metal Defaults

Sheet metal defaults are essentially styles in the vein of the layer styles or dimension styles you'll learn about later in this book. They're meant to be established within the templates and standards used in the part. A *sheet metal rule* is a name given to a set of properties for the sheet metal that will be used for a part. It consists of three elements: a thickness, a material, and an unfolding method. You define a style through the Sheet Metal Defaults and Style and Standard Editor dialog boxes. After a sheet metal default is defined, it can be shared through the style libraries.

The Sheet Metal Defaults Dialog Box

The Sheet Metal Defaults dialog box (Figure 2.21) works a little differently than most dialog boxes in Inventor. Instead of being the source of the feature that will be created, or the place where edits are performed, it's a front-end for either selecting what rules will be applied to your new component or overriding the Thickness, Material, or Unfold value of the rules you've already created. It lets you define a new set of conditions unique to the current Part file.

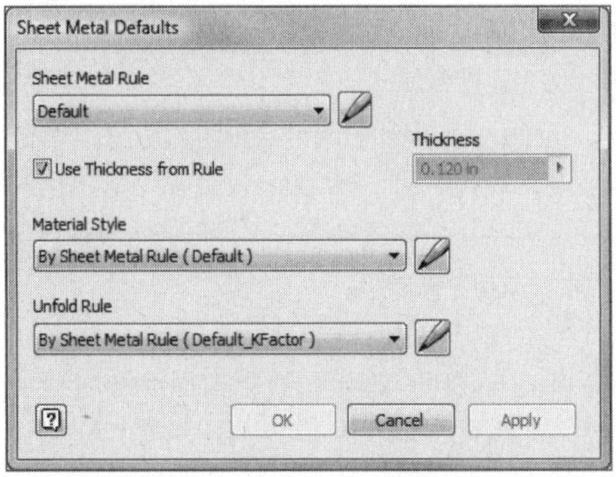

FIGURE 2.21   The Sheet Metal Defaults dialog box

You don't establish the rules of your sheet metal components here (you do that in the Style and Standard Editor); you select which rule will be used and, if you like, choose to override portions of the rule. Here's an overview:

Sheet Metal Rule   This fly-out lets you select which existing sheet metal rule you want to use.

Use Thickness from Rule   Deselect this check box, and you'll be able to override the default thickness of the selected sheet metal rule.

Material Style   This pull-down shows a list of the materials available in the standard and allows you to select one that is different from the material specified in the sheet metal rule.

Unfold Rule   As with the Material Style pull-down, Unfolding Rule is an override option to the active rule and lets you switch the unfold method from the default.

Creating a New Sheet Metal Rule

In this exercise, I'll introduce you to the tool that will define the rules you'll use for future exercises:

1. Select the Sheet Metal Defaults tool in the Setup panel on the Sheet Metal tab. Doing so opens the Sheet Metal Default dialog shown in Figure 2.21.

    In the next stage of the exercise, you'll use the Style and Standard Editor to define new values for the rule. First, let's examine this tool.

2. Select the Edit Sheet Metal Rule to open the Style and Standard Editor.

The Style and Standard Editor

On the right side of the Style and Standard Editor dialog (Figure 2.22) are three tabs, which establish the conditions for the active rule and let you create the rule's properties.

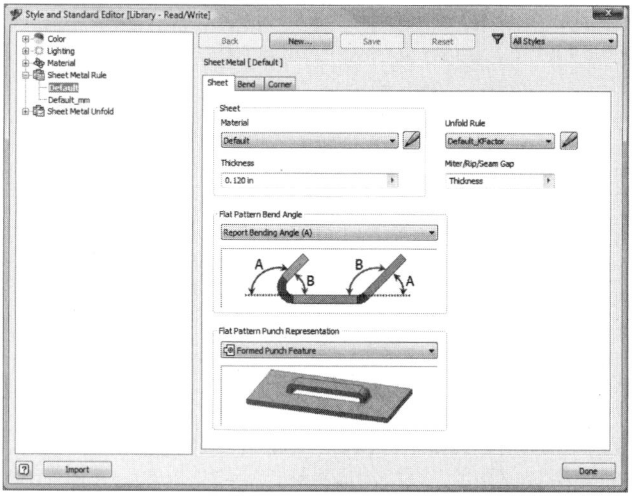

FIGURE 2.22 Style and Standard Editor showing sheet metal rules

The Sheet Tab

The Sheet tab (Figure 2.22) controls the properties of the raw material and how it deforms when you begin to bend it.

Sheet

The Sheet group is used to establish the material that is used in the part:

Material   Use this pull-down list to select the default material for the rule.

Thickness   Enter the value of the material for the rule here. For production use, I suggest checking with your suppliers and perhaps your Manufacturing department to verify the thickness of the material that you use for a particular gauge.

Unfold Rule

One of the most important things to discuss with Manufacturing is the method they use to calculate the flat pattern. Based on that method, you may need to modify the formulas for calculating a K Factor unfold or establish some different bend tables for your material. Working with Manufacturing may get you access to existing data that they use, which will make things go more smoothly when it's time to get the parts produced.

After you've established the range of options for calculating the flat pattern, you can use the Unfold Rule pull-down to set the default method for this rule.

Flat Pattern Punch Representation

This is another area where it's beneficial to work with Manufacturing if you haven't been previously responsible for generating flat patterns.

Depending on your organization, you may have to include detailed representations of features that will be punched into your part, or only a simple center mark for where the punch should strike, or something in between.

Inventor offers four methods, and selecting the appropriate one is very important:

Formed Punch Feature   Even though the part will be flat, the punched features continue to display in 3D with this option, and a center mark is displayed at the placement origin for the punch feature.

2D Sketch Representation   When you define a punch tool (as discussed later in this chapter), Inventor lets you specify a 2D sketch to use as a representation. This sketch may be the perimeter of the feature, or it can be a symbol that an automated programming system uses for tool selection.

2D Sketch Rep and Center Mark   This displays the 2D sketch and a center mark for where the strike is programmed to occur.

Center Mark Only   If you plan to use a table to list what punches are used, you can show where the punches need to be placed on the flat part.

The Bend Tab

The Bend tab (Figure 2.23) controls the default radius of bends that are applied and specifies how to treat bends that are less than the full width of another face.

Bend Relief

Before you create a bend, it's sometimes necessary to cut a notch into the metal to limit the distortion of the unbent portion. This is called a *bend relief*.

Relief Shape

This pull-down list lets you select the default relief shape for the rule. The standard shapes are as follows:

Straight   Straight creates a rectangular shape.

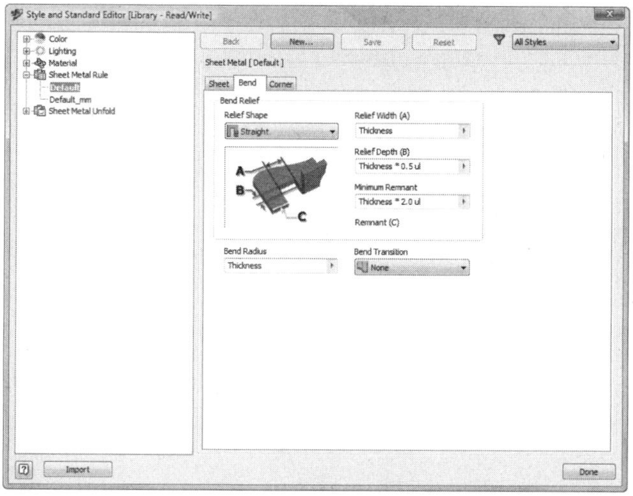

FIGURE 2.23 The Bend tab of the Style and Standard Editor

Round   With this option enabled, the interior edge of the relief is rounded.

Tear   With this option enabled, there is no predefined relief, and the metal is allowed to shear during the bending process.

Along with the shape selection is a preview of the bend shape; you can enter dimension values on the right to size the default bend relief.

Bend Radius

The default radius can be an absolute value or a factor such as the thickness of the material divided by 2.

Bend Transition

When a bend occurs that doesn't require a relief, but the edges don't align, you can use this pull-down list to establish the shape of the material at the edge of the bend. The differences between the options are easiest to see in the flat pattern.

The Corner Tab

The Corner tab (Figure 2.24) tells Inventor how you want the edges of bends to relate when they're next to one another in a corner.

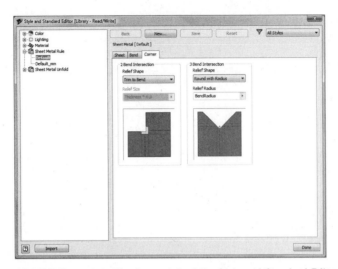

FIGURE 2.24 The Corner tab of the Style and Standard Editor

2 Bend Intersection

There are six methods for defining how a two-bend intersection is calculated. Two of them (Round and Square) also offer a size for the intersection. The others calculate the intersection based on the size of the bends included in the corner and the process that is used in manufacturing.

The method you choose is reflected in the 3D model and the flat pattern.

3 Bend Intersection

A corner where three bends meet is extraordinarily difficult to calculate. In reality, as long as the faces and major bends are correct, the geometry of the corner is relevant only in the flat pattern from which the part is formed.

For this reason, the value you select for the 3 Bend Intersection option only modifies the way the corner is calculated in the flat pattern. If you look at the folded part, it shows a notch in the corner and displays the gaps between the edges. The corner will construct properly when the physical part is made from the accurate flat pattern — and that is far more important.

Creating New Sheet Metal Rules

Now that you've had an overview of the Style and Standard Editor as it pertains to sheet metal rules, let's create a couple of rules:

1. Click the New button at the top of the Style and Standard Editor.

New...

2. In the New Style Name dialog, enter **Steel - 16 ga** for the value, and click OK.

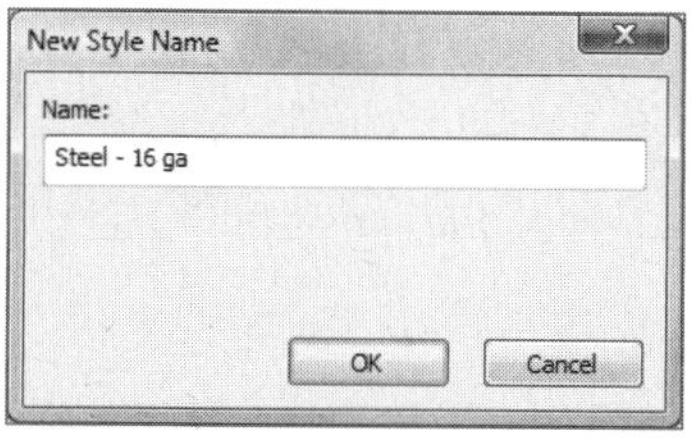

The new rule appears on the list in the left column under Sheet Metal Rule but isn't automatically made the active rule for editing.

3. Double-click Steel - 16 ga to make it the active rule.

4. On the Sheet tab, select Steel, Mild from the Material pull-down.

5. Set the Thickness to .06in.

6. Select 2D Sketch Rep and Center Mark from the Flat Pattern Punch Representation option. See Figure 2.25.

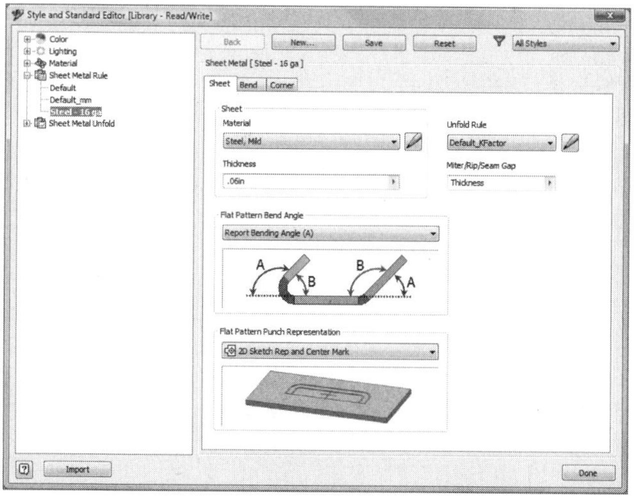

FIGURE 2.25 Sheet tab values for the new sheet metal rule

7. Switch to the Bend tab, and change the Relief Shape to Round.

8. On the Corner tab, set the Relief Shape to Arc Weld.

9. Save the new rule by clicking the Save button at the top of the dialog box.

10. With the Steel - 16 ga rule active, click the New button again to create a copy of that style.

11. In the New Style Name dialog, enter **Aluminum - .13** and then click OK.

12. Activate the new style.

13. Change its Material to Aluminum - 6061 and its Thickness to .13in. Leave all other settings the same.

14. Save the new style.

15. Set the Steel - 16 ga style as your active style again.

The work you've done in the Style and Standard Editor up to this point has only affected the part you're currently working in. If you work with sheet metal, you'll want to establish these rules and be able to use them in other parts. To do this, you publish them to the Style Library. This is a very simple process, as you'll see in the next few steps:

16. Right-click the Steel - 16 ga rule in the left column, and select Save to Style Library from the context menu.

17. Do the same for the Aluminum - .13 rule. It isn't necessary to make that rule active to save it to the library.

18. Click the Done button in the dialog box to close it.

19. When the dialog closes, you see the Sheet Metal Defaults dialog again. Select the down arrow next to the rules to see that your two new rules are available for use.

20. Click Cancel to return to your component and save your work.

When creating rules, it's good to use the tribal knowledge that exists in your company to make sure they're done correctly the first time. You may even limit the ability of most users to create rules so that only a standards manager has the ability to create or edit this important data.

Now, finally, let's make something 3D! The first 3D tool you'll use is the Contour Flange.

The Contour Flange Tool

Sometimes, you need to create a part with a lot of bends that are all the same width. Think of a drainage gutter: It's cut to consistent length, but it has bends that flip from one side to the other. If you were to sketch the basic shape, thicken it, and have it extend to a length, the part would be done. That is the inspiration for the Contour Flange tool; its dialog box is shown in Figure 2.26.

Creating a Base Feature with Contour Flange

Now that our sketch has been prepared, it's time to create our first 3D geometry.

1. In the Design window, press the F6 key or select the Home View icon to put your sketch into a non-plan view.

2. Pick the Contour Flange tool in the Create panel of the Sheet Metal tab.

3. The Profile button in the dialog expects you to pick a sketch. Select your sketch, and set the Distance value at the bottom of the dialog to 12 in. Use the Distance Mid-plane option (see Figure 2.27) to divide the distance value in each direction.

4. Click OK to create the feature.

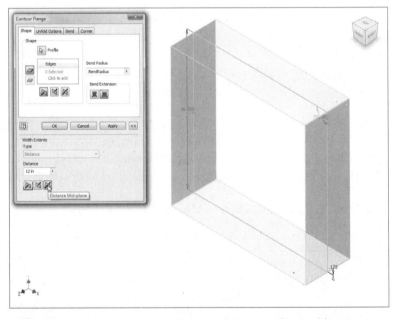

FIGURE 2.26 The Contour Flange dialog box

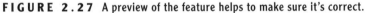

FIGURE 2.27 A preview of the feature helps to make sure it's correct.

In the browser, the icon for Sketch1 was replaced by Contour Flange 1. This has a small plus sign in a box. Click the box to expand the feature: The sketch was "consumed" by the feature, but it's still accessible if you want to edit it.

Congratulations — you've made your first 3D feature in Autodesk Inventor. I know it took a while, but the things you've learned up to this point will be very important going forward are the foundation of everything else. But wasn't it easy to make this? Now you'll do something more complex, but it will be easy too.

Next, you'll use the Flange tool, which is one of the most commonly used sheet metal tools. Let's take a moment to get familiar with its dialog box so that you can recognize the functions of some of the buttons that commonly appear in the sheet metal tools.

The Flange Tool

After you create a base feature in sheet metal, chances are you'll use the Flange tool next. Figure 2.28 shows its dialog box.

FIGURE 2.28 The Flange dialog box

A flange is a placed feature with a lot of options. The Flange tool and the Face tool have the same tabs that allow individual override, so we'll focus on the Shape tab.

The Shape Tab

You place a flange by selecting an edge to which you want to add a bend and adjacent face. The upper-left portion of the Shape tab (Figure 2.28) is where you select those edges. The Edges list displays the number of edges that have been selected.

You can select edges in two ways:

 Edge Select Mode   This option lets you select individual edges to place flanges on. You can select multiple edges, but you have to select them with individual clicks of the mouse.

Loop Select Mode   This option lets you select all the perimeter edges of a face with a single click.

These selection options also work with the Contour Flange tool when it's placed after the initial feature is placed.

Additional options on the Shape tab are as follows:

Flange Angle   This option establishes the angle at which the flange will be developed once you've located it by selecting the edge.

Height Extents   You can set the height of a flange by value using Distance or until it meets a face using the To option. You select these options from a pull-down list.

You can also flip the direction of the flange by clicking the Flip Direction button.

Height Datum   The three buttons illustrate the options that you can use to define whether the height of a flange is measured aligned to the length of the flange or orthogonal to the face plane.

Bend Position   Four modes are available to define how the bend is started from the selected edge. The icons illustrate clearly how the bend is developed.

More (>>)   Expanding the dialog box exposes an option to create flanges that are narrower than the selected edge using different types of selections. There is also an option for using an older definition methodology limited to the Height Datum and Bend Position options.

Many of the dialog boxes have Unfold Options, Bend, and Corner tabs. These tabs provide access to override tools for the individual feature. The tabs contain the same properties as the sheet metal rule definition tabs, but changes affect only the current feature, not the active rule. This gives you the ability to take one feature and give it a special bend radius or change the bend relief. You can even go back and change a feature after it has been placed, using Edit Feature.

Let's add flanges to your component and see how advanced and intelligent some of these features can be.

Adding Flanges to the Part

For this exercise, I considered having you add the flanges one at time. But the spirit of this book is to use a design-oriented approach, so instead you'll use the tools that add efficiency to the process. We'll also take a look at a few other options along the way.

In some of the images, you'll notice that I have turned on the edges of the active part in the Application options. This can make it easier to sort out edges on a sheet metal part. Follow these steps:

1. In the Browser right-click the icon next to Housing.ipt, and select iProperties from the Context menu.

2. Doing so brings up the file properties for this component. Select the Physical tab (Figure 2.29), and click the Update button to see the physical properties of the part as it currently is, including the mass. Click the Close button when you're finished reviewing the values.

FIGURE 2.29 The physical properties of a component are constantly monitored.

3. On the Quick Access Toolbar is a pull-down that allows you to change the color of the part. Select the color of your choice. For the record, I selected Blue Pastel for clarity in the images.

4. Start the Flange tool, and zoom into the lower-left corner of the part.

5. Select the inside edge of the bottom, as shown in Figure 2.30. A preview of the flange as specified appears.

6. Select the inside edge of the left side, as shown in Figure 2.31.

 When the second edge is selected, a corner treatment is applied automatically. An icon appears at the corner along with one in the center of each new flange. Selecting these icons brings up dialogs that let you edit their placement properties on the fly.

7. Select the inside edges of the remaining two sides. The result should preview as show in Figure 2.32.

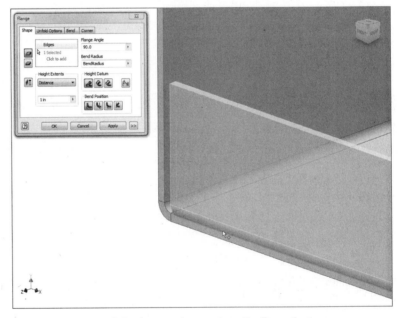

FIGURE 2.30 Selecting an edge previews the flange feature.

8. Click OK to place the four flanges. They appear as a single feature in the Browser: Flange1. The component should look like Figure 2.33.

9. Save the file.

You could repeat the process for the opposite side; but instead, let's use another tool.

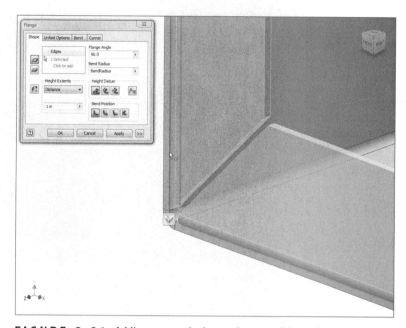

FIGURE 2.31 Adding a second edge to the same flange also adds a corner treatment.

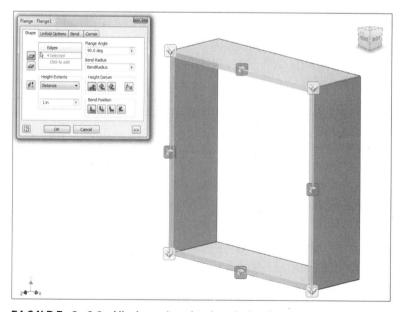

FIGURE 2.32 All edges mitered and ready for placement at once

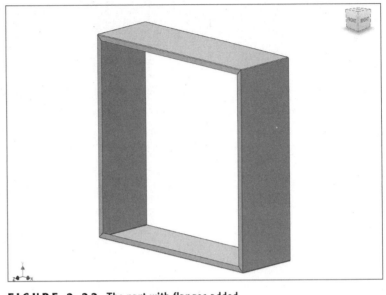

FIGURE 2.33 The part with flanges added

The Mirror Tool

This tool does what it says. If you're familiar with the Mirror command in AutoCAD, then you're more than half way to understanding how this tool works — although I think you'll find it's considerably more powerful.

When the tool starts, you see the dialog shown in Figure 2.34. One of the things users appreciate about Autodesk Inventor is consistency in the dialogs. You'll notice the red arrows as discussed in Chapter 1; but there are several other icons we'll discuss.

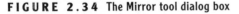

FIGURE 2.34 The Mirror tool dialog box

In placed features that create patterns, you can affect individual features using this option. This prompts you to select the features that you want to replicate and then asks for a plane or edges to pattern them by.

The other option replicates the entire existing solid body based upon a plane or axis.

Optimized

By expanding the More button at lower right, you can choose different options for calculating the pattern. The Optimized option is useful when you're creating very large patterns. It ignores the parametric values of the original feature and replicates it based purely on its geometry.

Now, let's use the Mirror tool to create more flanges:

1. Start the Mirror tool in the Pattern panel of the Sheet Metal tab.

2. As you move near the flanges you just created, they highlight. Select the Flange feature either in the Design window or by picking Flange 1 in the Browser.

3. When the Mirror tool is set to use individual features, it allows you to pick as many as you want. Pick the button next to Mirror Plane to select a plane to mirror about.

4. Move to the Browser, and select the plus sign next to the Origin folder icon. This expands your base planes and axes. Select the XY Plane for your Mirror Plane.

5. Doing so generates a preview of the new feature, as shown in Figure 2.35. Click OK to create the new flanges.

   Now, you'll use the Flange tool again with a slightly different approach.

6. Rotate the model so that you can see the gap near the corner of the part from the inside.

7. Select the Flange tool from the Create panel.

8. Select the interior edge at the bottom of the right side.

9. Pick the More button in the dialog box, change the Type to Width, and set the Width value to 11. See Figure 2.36.

10. Click OK to accept the new flange if the preview is like Figure 2.36. If it isn't, reevaluate the edge you selected.

11. In the Flat Pattern panel of the Sheet Metal tab, select the Create Flat Pattern tool.

    This causes Inventor to create the all-important flat pattern of your part (Figure 2.37), including the bend lines that will be needed in order for Manufacturing to properly shape the finished part.

The flat pattern isn't a separate file. Instead, it resides as a parallel state in the Browser. The folded model is also maintained in the Browser, but it's grayed out and therefore inactive.

12. Double-click the folded model in the browser. Doing so restores the visibility of the folded part.

13. Restore the home view.

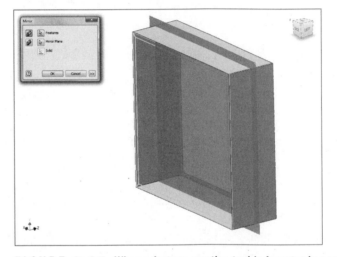

FIGURE 2.35 When a feature-creation tool in Inventor has enough information to create geometry, it usually offers a preview.

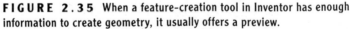
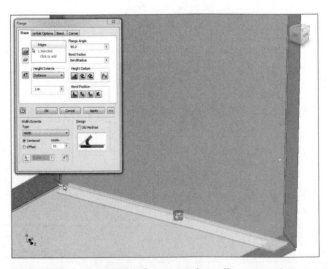

FIGURE 2.36 Width Extents options allow you make common modifications quickly.

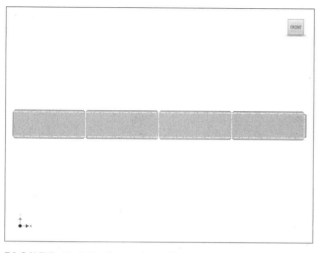

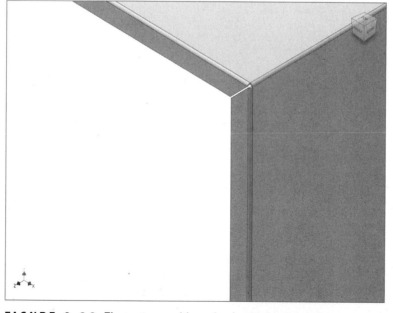

FIGURE 2.37 Generating a flat pattern is critical to production.

14. Zoom in to the front, upper-right corner of your part so that it resembles Figure 2.38.

15. Save your work.

FIGURE 2.38 The next area of focus for developing the part

The flat pattern also has a function in the folded part. If you need to know how a feature will appear in the flat pattern, you can project a preview of the flat pattern into a sketch and use it as reference geometry. In this example, you'll create a notch on the edge of your folded part that points to the speed indicator for your fan:

1. Pick the Create 2D Sketch tool from the Sketch panel, and select the right, exterior face of the part as highlighted in Figure 2.39.

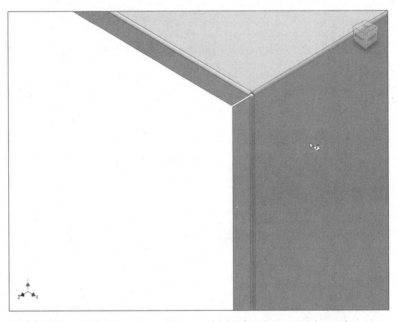

FIGURE 2.39 The edges of the face highlight when you select a face to sketch on.

The Sketch tab again appears and is active. The Browser also changes by graying the existing features and adding a new sketch to the tree.

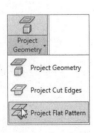

2. In the Draw panel, pick the down arrow next to the words Project Geometry. Doing so expands the Projection Options. Pick the Project Flat Pattern option.

3. Pick the front face of the flange, shown in Figure 2.40. This projects that flange into the sketch as if it were unfolded, as shown in Figure 2.41.

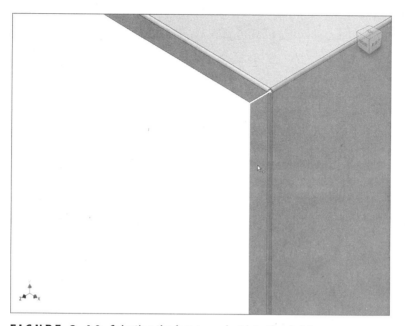

FIGURE 2.40 Selecting the face to project into the sketch

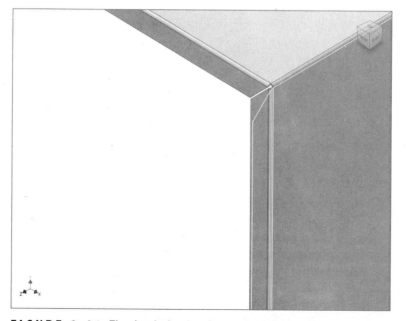

FIGURE 2.41 The sketch showing the projected flat pattern

4. Set the view in your Design window to approximate Figure 2.42.

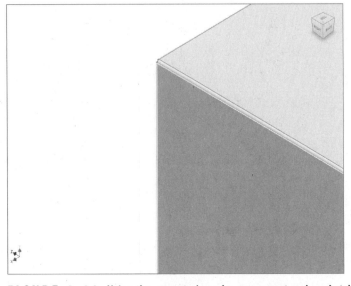

FIGURE 2.42 Using the correct view of a component makes sketching a lot easier.

5. Start the Rectangle tool in the Draw panel, and create a rectangle similar to the one in Figure 2.43.

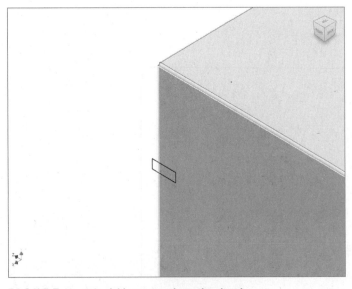

FIGURE 2.43 Add a rectangle to the sketch.

6. Dimension the rectangle as shown in Figure 2.44.

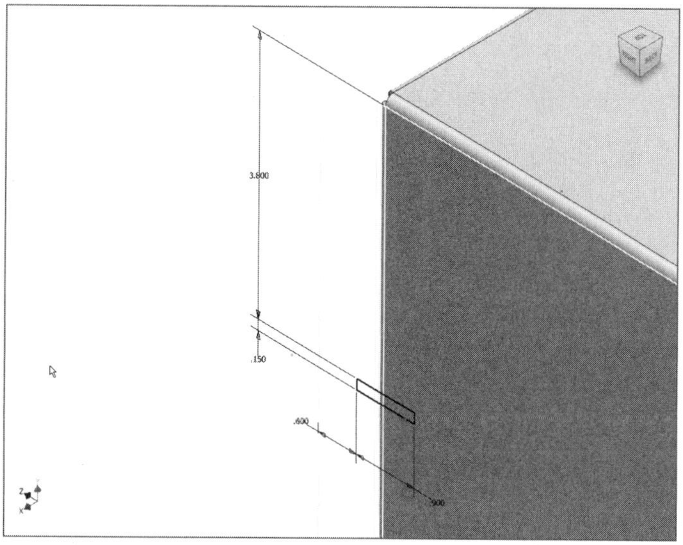

FIGURE 2.44 Use parametric dimensions to size and locate the rectangle.

7. Finish the sketch.

8. Now that the rectangle has been positioned, set your view so that you can see the front flange again.

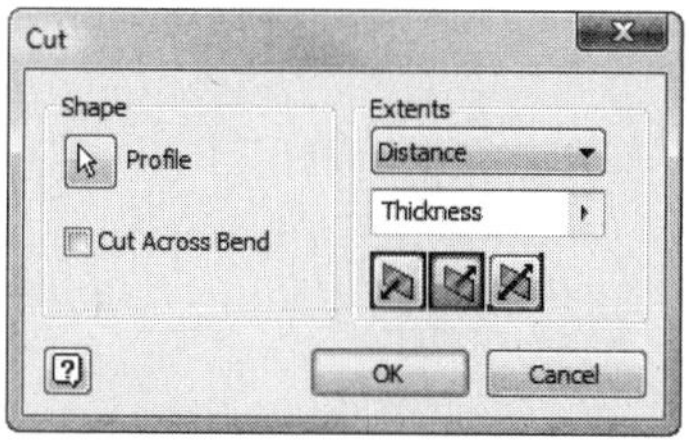

9. Pick the Cut tool from the Modify panel.

   The rectangle should automatically be selected, and the Extents value of Thickness should be shown. Thickness is one of the values or parameters automatically included and linked to the Thickness of the sheet metal rule.

10. Pick the Cut Across Bend option in the dialog box. You should see a preview of how the rectangle wraps around the front flange as it's cut into the material. See Figure 2.45.

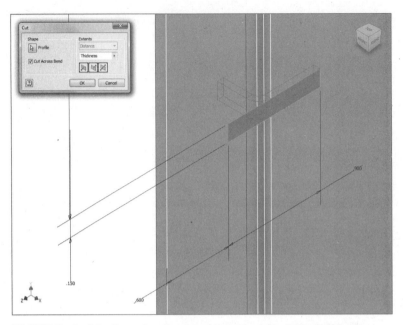

FIGURE 2.45 Even when the cut goes across a bend, it maintains the distance in the flat pattern.

11. Click OK to create the feature.

12. Save your work.

Up to this point, you've used sheet metal features. If you look at the Ribbon, the Model tab is still available. You can also use regular solid modeling tools for some purposes while working in a sheet metal component.

One feature that is common to both environments is the Hole feature. Not only are holes common, but they're also created using a broad variety of techniques. Therefore the Hole dialog has a lot of options.

The Hole Feature

The Hole dialog box, shown in Figure 2.46, is a great example of how many capabilities can be stuffed into a small, easy-to-navigate interface.

Four groups of options in this dialog box walk you through placing holes on your model.

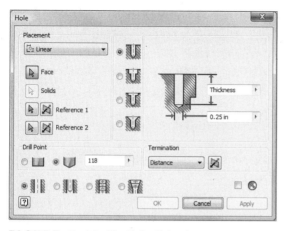

FIGURE 2.46 The Hole dialog box

The options in the first group, Placement, reflect which type of placement you select from the fly-out menu:

Linear   This is the default placement. To use it, select the face on which you want to place the hole, and select two edges from which you want to position it. When you select an edge, a dimension is placed showing the hole's current distance from the edge. You have to click both edges before you can change the dimension value for placing the hole. The edges don't have to be perpendicular to each other, but they can't be parallel. The Reference buttons allow you to flip the hole to the other side of the edge that you're dimensioning from.

From Sketch   This placement option asks you to select points on an existing sketch to place holes on. In your sketch, if you've specified that a point is a hole center (by using the sketching override buttons on the Inventor standard toolbar or by using the Center Point tool in a 2D sketch), it's automatically selected for placing a hole. If a point that you don't want to use is automatically selected, you can deselect it by holding the Ctrl key and clicking the point.

Concentric   This is a common way of placing holes. You select a plane to place the hole on and then select an arc, a circle, or a face with a radius on which to center the hole.

On Point   The last option is similar to From Sketch, but the hole center has to be placed on a special point called a *work point*. You can select a direction vector for the hole based on a model edge, or a *work axis*.

Select the type of hole you want to create by using one of the four icons just to the right of the Placement group. To the right of the area where you select the type of hole you want to place, a graphic displays the contour of the hole and the hole's dimensional values. You can change those values directly in the graphic when they're made available:

Drilled   This hole has one diameter from the beginning edge to the bottom of the hole.

Counterbore   This uses a drilled hole for the middle portion but creates a cylindrical relief beginning from the same plane.

Spotface   Spotface is geometrically similar to a counterbore hole — the two could be mistaken for each other — but they're typically used for different real-world applications. A spotface is usually used when the surface it's being placed on is unsuitable for a bolt or fitting to be tightened to. In a spotface hole, the depth and diameter of the upper cylinder are controlled just like a counterbore, but the depth of the drilled portion begins at the bottom of the spotface instead of the same plane, as in the counterbore. You can see this easily by clicking back and forth between the two and watching the dimension in the graphic change.

Countersink   Countersink uses a conical relief to seat screws so their heads are flush or nearly flush with the surface the hole is placed in.

Drill Point allows you to specify whether a hole is pointed or flat at its bottom. The pointed option even allows for the use of custom drill point angles for special applications.

The Termination group options control how and where the end of the hole occurs:

Distance   Distance uses a dimension in the graphic above it to set a value.

Through All   Through All passes the hole through any feature that it encounters and theoretically makes an infinitely deep hole.

To   This option allows you to define a stopping face where the drill will pass through but not continue beyond.

At lower-left are four more options that control what class of hole is created. In this area, you can save a lot of work looking up standards:

Simple Hole   Simple Hole creates a basic, cylindrical hole that is sized in the graphic in the dialog box.

Clearance Hole   This is a personal favorite of mine. After years of keeping a handbook or wall chart handy to be able to properly size the counterbore for a hex head bolt, I enjoy being able to have the hole sized for me by simply selecting the fastener type and size.

Tapped Hole   Tapped Hole is also a simple option to use. All you do is select the thread you need, and Inventor sizes the hole based on the standard. Tapped holes don't have actual helical threads placed in the model, but they do appear threaded; Inventor uses a bitmap on the surface of the hole, and in drawings it displays the major and minor diameter of the thread.

Taper Tapped   Taper Tapped is the same as Tapped Hole but uses the tapered standards like NPT and ISO Taper. Because of industrial standards, you aren't allowed to place a taper tapped hole at the bottom of a counterbore.

Both types of threaded hole also let you control the depth of the threaded portion of the hole, with an option to fully thread the hole by selecting Full Depth. You can also choose whether the threads are Right Hand or Left Hand.

Let's use the Hole tool with a sheet metal twist to place the next feature:

1. Start the Hole tool from the Modify panel.

2. Using the Linear Placement method, pick the face on which you sketched the rectangle to begin placing the hole.

3. You need to select two edges from which to position the hole. Pick the edges shown in Figure 2.47. After you pick the second, set the values to those shown in the figure.

4. Set the Diameter to .397, and note that the depth of the hole is automatically set to Thickness.

5. Click OK to create the hole.

6. Save your work.

The Punch Tool

The Punch tool is a specialized feature that creates deformations or custom-shaped holes in the part. The location points of these features can be extracted for detailing in the drawing or for programming production machinery. Figure 2.48 shows the PunchTool dialog box.

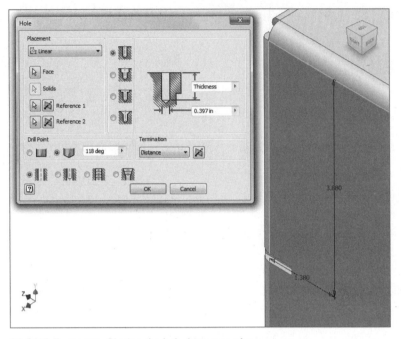

FIGURE 2.47 Placing the hole from two edges

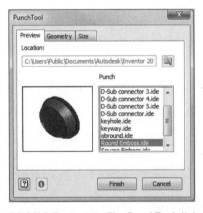

FIGURE 2.48 The PunchTool dialog box

When you open the tool, you're shown a list of included sample punch tools. There is also a dialog box in which you can access special geometry or size the tool if it has optional sizes.

The Geometry Tab

The Geometry tab (Figure 2.49) lets you select placement points for the Punch tool and set its placement angle.

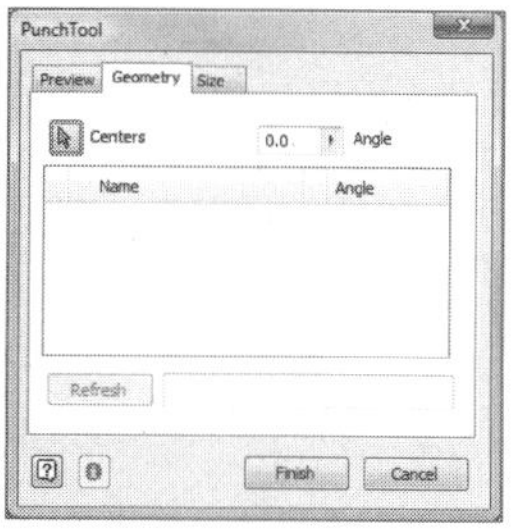

FIGURE 2.49 The PunchTool dialog box's Geometry tab

The Size Tab

When an iFeature or Punch tool is defined, its size values can be set to unlimited, within a range, or with only certain sizes selectable from a list. Use the Size tab (Figure 2.50) to set those size values by entering a value or selecting it from the Name pull-down next to Value.

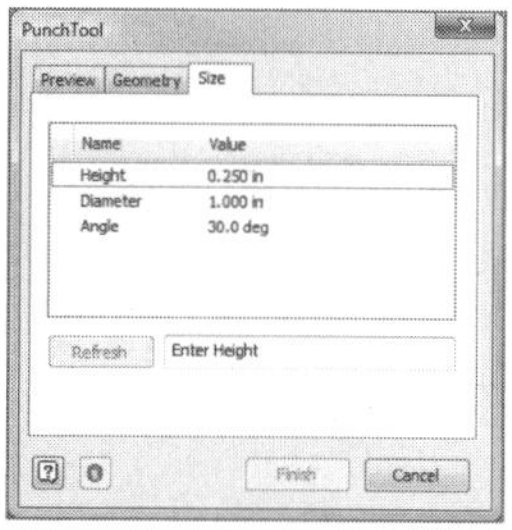

FIGURE 2.50 The PunchTool dialog box's Size tab

Before you can add punch tools, you need to create points on which to place the punches:

1. Rotate your part so that you can see its bottom.

2. Create a sketch on the bottom exterior face of the part.

3. Select the Construction linetype override from the Format panel.

4. Draw a rectangle similar to that shown in Figure 2.51.

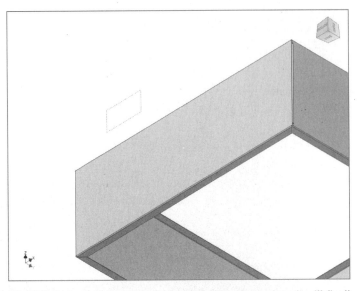

FIGURE 2.51 A sketch can be made away from where it will finally be placed.

5. Use Esc to end the Rectangle tool.

6. Drag your mouse around the rectangle to select it. See Figure 2.52.

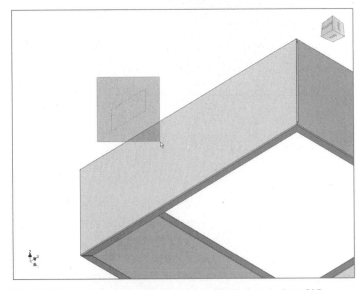

FIGURE 2.52 Drag selection works like it does in AutoCAD.

7. With your rectangle selected in the sketch, click the Centerpoint override. This places special hole centers on the corners of the rectangle.

8. Pick and drag the corners of the rectangle into the approximate position shown in Figure 2.53.

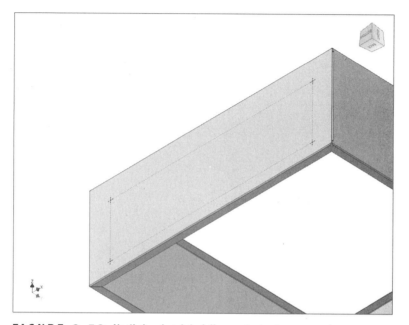

FIGURE 2.53 Until the sketch is fully constrained, you can drag underconstrained sketch elements around the sketch.

9. Use Vertical and Horizontal constraints to center the rectangle on the sketch center like you did with your first sketch.

10. Place the dimensions on the sketch as shown in Figure 2.54.

11. Finish the sketch, and return to the sheet metal tools.

12. Save your work.

Before you place your punch tool features, let's take a moment to discuss why you would make the changes to the original rectangle. In many of the upcoming exercises, you'll use construction lines to control where regular sketch lines are placed. For this particular feature, it wasn't necessary to change the lines to construction lines. However, I like the practice of converting sketch elements, especially when they're closed profiles like rectangles or circles, to construction elements so you know they're not intended to build features.

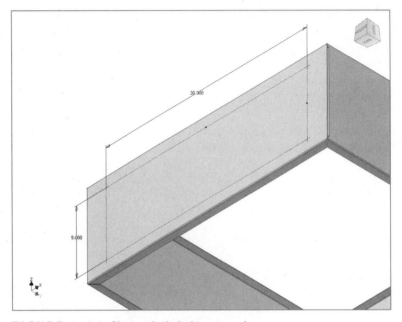

FIGURE 2.54 Placing the hole from two edges

The second step of converting the endpoints of the line segments to center-points will be evident in the next portion of the exercise. Any time you have a sketch that includes centerpoints, Inventor automatically places features like holes or Punch tools on those centerpoints. You can hold the Crtl key and dese-lect them if you don't want to use a point, but it's a great way to pick multiple hole locations at once.

13. Start the Punch tool from the Modify panel.

14. A PunchTool Directory dialog appears, in which you can select where your punch tools are located. Double-click the Round Emboss.ide file.

15. Immediately, the four points are replaced by either a wireframe preview of the Punch tool or a preview of the tool's footprint, as shown in Figure 2.55.

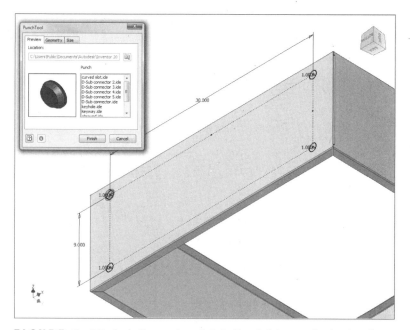

FIGURE 2.55 Including centerpoints in the sketch saves having to select point for Punch tool placement.

16. On the Size tab, use the pull-down selector to pick the 1.500 in tool diameter. Note that the preview doesn't update.

17. Click the Finish button. See Figure 2.56.

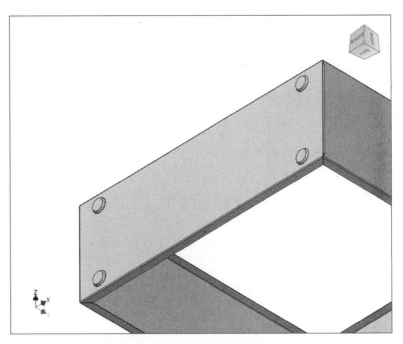

FIGURE 2.56 The completed Punch tool feature has added feet to the housing.

18. Return to the home view.

19. View the flat pattern. The cut and the hole feature are visible, but the Punch tool features aren't. This is because the sheet metal rule says that this type of feature is displayed in the drawing as an outline and center mark so it isn't left as a 3D feature in the flat pattern.

20. Zoom in on the cut feature.

21. Switch to the Tools tab, and start the Distance measurement tool.

22. Click the horizontal edge beneath the cut. A value appears in the Measure Distance dialog. This is the length of the selected edge.

23. Move near one of the bottom corners of the rectangular cut. A small circle appears around the corner. When it does, pick again.

   The dialog box that shows the length of the edge now displays the minimum distance between the entities. You'll see that the distance is 0.6 in (Figure 2.57), which is what you dimensioned it to be while previewing the flat pattern.

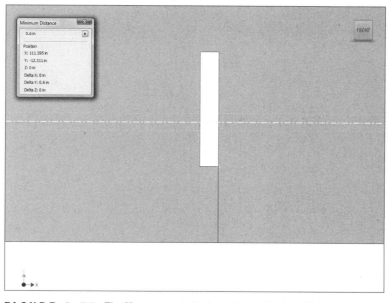

FIGURE 2.57 The Measure tool displays the results in a dialog and shows what was measured on the model.

24. Close the dialog by selecting the X icon at upper right, and return to the folded model.

25. In the Browser, right-click the Housing.ipt folder again, and check the Physical Properties. Compare them to Figure 2.58.

26. Close the dialog, and save your work one more time.

In this chapter, you've built a not-so-simple part using only a handful of features and a few sketches. As we progress, you'll continue to reuse the same basic techniques to define many kinds of parts. The first sketch you created may not have seemed difficult, but a sketch like that is one of the most difficult things you can do in Inventor.

Take a moment to look over your work (See Figure 2.59) and be proud. Using older systems, a part like this would've been difficult to define with the proper consistency. The corners might not have been represented properly, and you most certainly could not have developed a flat pattern that included the allowance for the stretching of the material without extensive manual calculations.

This is just the first part. By the time you're finished with the entire project, you'll have enhanced this part and others.

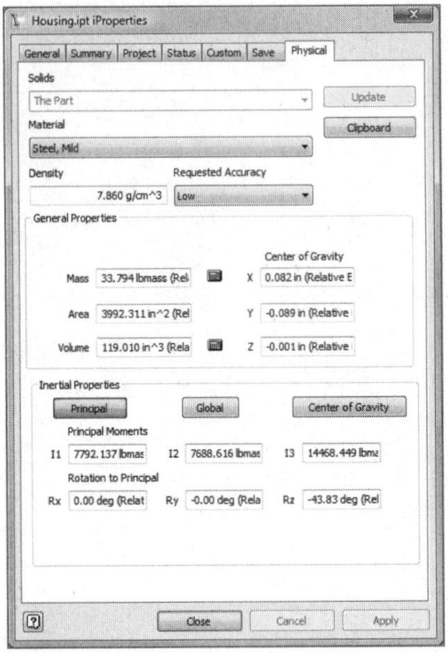

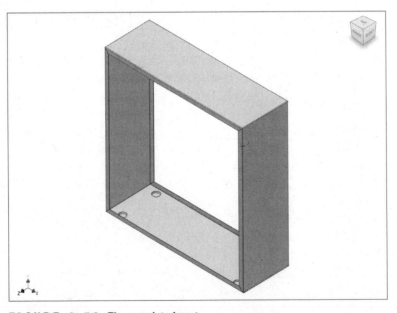

FIGURE 2.58 The updated Physical Properties of the component

FIGURE 2.59 The completed part

Are You Experienced?

Now you can...

- ☑ define sketches using dimensions and constraints
- ☑ create complex sheet metal components
- ☑ extract a flat pattern for constructing the part
- ☑ define the location for Punch tools
- ☑ measure the distance between part edges

CHAPTER 3

Moving into the Assembly World

▶ Using additional tools to construct different
sheet metal parts

▶ Developing a flat pattern

▶ Beginning the assembly of your product

▶ Taking advantage of included standard parts

So, What's Next?

Starting out with a sheet metal component is unusual for a book on Autodesk Inventor. Now, just to make sure nobody thinks it was an accident, you'll make another sheet metal component. Of course, the real reason you're going to create another sheet metal part is that it's the next logical component to build. For this component, you'll use Sheet Metal tools that are advanced in their capability to create geometry, but easy to learn and use.

In this chapter, we'll also begin to explore Inventor's assembly capabilities and the interactions between the components in an assembly. I think you'll find that assemblies are logical; if you struggle, the solution is most likely found in thinking about the pure geometric aspects of building things. Just like the Sheet Metal tools, you'll learn the assembly tools as you go and in context, rather than by my piling a bunch of functions on you.

Developing a More Challenging Part

The Sheet Metal tools were added to Autodesk Inventor way back in the year 2000. Over the years, these capabilities have steadily expanded; but until Inventor 2010, you were limited to Bend/Break operations. There was no capability to cause deformation or to transition from one shape to another. Having these tools included opens up tremendous possibilities.

The first feature-creation tool you'll use is lofted flange. A lofted flange is a sketched feature, so to use it you must have a sketch. Actually, because this tool is made for transitioning between sketches, you'll need to make two sketches:

1. Create a new file using the Sheet Metal (in).ipt template.

2. In the Draw panel, find the Polygon tool and start it.

   If you want a square, and you always want it to be a square, the Polygon tool can be a quick way to make one — especially if you want the square to be located based on the center of the sketch. Of course, it's great for making any regular polygon.

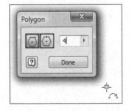

3. Enter 4 in the dialog to set the number of sides, and move your cursor to the point that is automatically projected for the center of the sketch. A point on point glyph appears.

4. Click the sketch center to start creating a square.

5. Drag your mouse so the square takes up most of the Design window, and click again to place your polygon. Don't be alarmed if it's tilted.

6. Start the Horizontal constraint from the Constrain panel, and select the top edge of your shape.

    If you didn't exit the Polygon tool before started the Horizontal constraint, it's cancelled when you start the new tool. This is typically the way Inventor works.

7. Add a dimension to the left side of the square, and set its value to 33.7. See Figure 3.1.

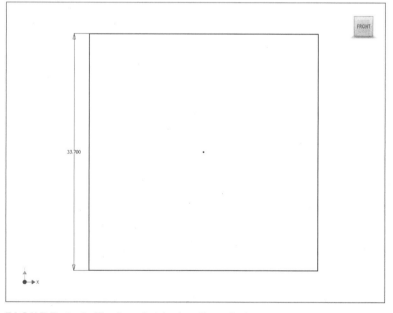

FIGURE 3.1 The first sketch after dimensioning

Because you created this part from an Inch template, it isn't necessary to add **in.** to the end of the value. That is necessary only when you want a unit of measure that is different from the current one.

8. Finish the sketch.

9. Save the new file into the `Parts` folder as `Duct.ipt`.

10. Restore the home view so that the sketch is positioned in an isometric view.

11. In the Browser, expand the `Origin` folder, right-click XY plane, and select Visibility from the context menu.

Doing so makes the XY plane of the part visible. You need to create another sketch that is parallel to your first sketch but set away from it in the Z axis. Presently, the component has no geometry on which you can create that sketch, so you'll need to create a plane.

On the Sheet Metal (and Model) tab is a Work Features panel. That panel contains tools for creating your own planes, axes, and points on which to base other geometry. To create a new work plane, all you need to do is start the Work Plane tool, pick and drag from an existing plane, and specify the distance between them.

Because work planes are frequently created in order that sketches can be placed on them, Inventor includes a special function that you'll use now.

12. Press the S key on your keyboard.

This is a keyboard shortcut for creating sketches. You can also edit a sketch by pressing S and then picking geometry belonging to the sketch you want to edit.

13. Pick and drag from the edge of the origin XY plane on the screen to the left until the Offset dialog reads 12.000. Then, release the mouse. If the dialog shows something other than 12.000, type 12 to move the plane into position. See Figure 3.2.

You've simultaneously created a work plane and a new, active sketch on it.

14. Start the Circle tool from the Draw panel.

15. Click the sketch center. Using the display on the status bar at lower right, click the screen again when the Radius is roughly 15in.

16. Using the same Dimension tool, click the circle. The tool automatically offers you a diameter for the circle. Click again to place the dimension; then, click the value and set it to 30 in the dialog.

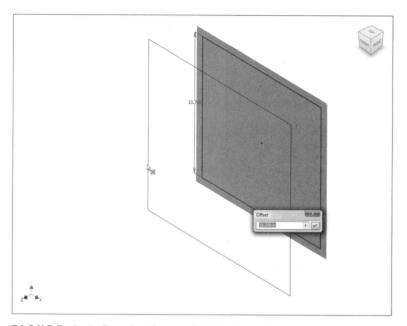

FIGURE 3.2 Dragging the new sketch into location

17. Finish the sketch.

18. Hold down your Ctrl key, and pick Work Plane 1 and XY Plane in the Browser.

19. Right-click, and deselect Visibility from the context menu to hide both planes.

20. Click the Front face of the ViewCube so your Design window looks like Figure 3.3.

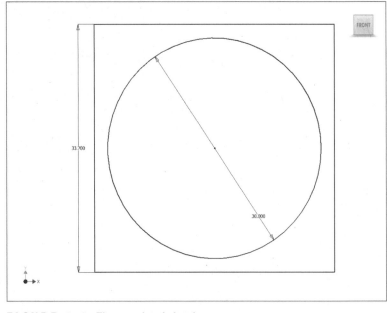
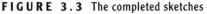

FIGURE 3.3 The completed sketches

21. Save your work.

You've created two sketches of different shapes and sizes. It's time to let Inventor do some very complex math and turn this into a part from which you can generate a flat pattern.

The Lofted Flange Tool

If you've ever seen the way a duct transitions from a round shape to a rectangular shape, you've seen the inspiration for this tool. Although the tool has a few different uses, creating ducts is its primary function.

The Lofted Flange dialog box (Figure 3.4) displays many of the same characteristics as other dialog boxes, but it also includes some unique features that we need to review and some that you've already seen but that we haven't discussed yet.

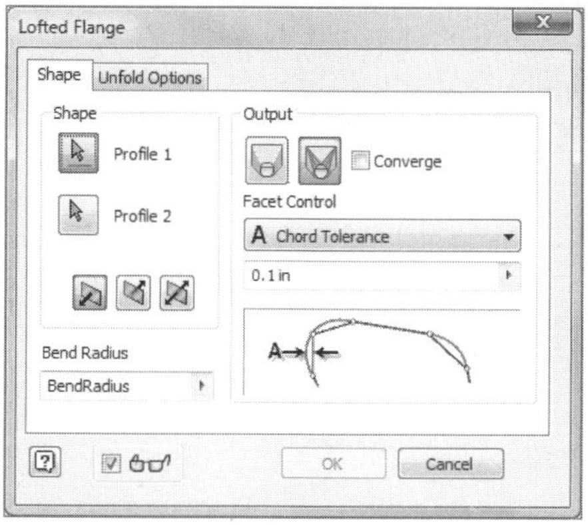

FIGURE 3.4 The Lofted Flange dialog

When you created a contour flange and a regular flange, you may have noticed three icons with arrows in the dialog boxes. Selecting one of these icons will define which side of the sketch or selected edge your material is added to or whether the material's thickness is divided equally on each side. You'll also see these options on many of the tools on the Model tab. It's important to verify that your material is being added to the side that you want, or your overall component size may be affected.

Output Options

The Output group in the dialog contains two primary options. You need to know how this part will be manufactured, to select the option properly:

Die Formed   Selecting this option creates a transition where the bent portions are created as a single bend. This requires a more specialized manufacturing process, but the result is a smoother part. Selecting this option also disables the Facet Control options.

Press Break   If the part will be manufactured using a press break, and if having the transition formed in steps or facets is acceptable, then you should use this option. Picking the Converge check box lets Inventor blend the facet edges together at the end where they meet.

Facet Control   Three options define how large and how many facets make up the bent portions of a transition. They're called out by a letter and name. The dialog also displays an illustration that offers a graphical description of the selected option:

A - Chord Tolerance   This option calculates the number and size of facets based on a tolerance for how far the flat face can deviate from the ideal curve.

B - Facet Angle   This is a limit on how much the facet can deviate from the adjacent facet, measured in degrees.

C - Facet Distance   Use this option if you want to limit the maximum width of the facets.

Bend Radius   Instead of having a Bend tab in the dialog, the opportunity to override the default bend radius of the active sheet metal rule appears on the Shape tab.

Preview   Many dialogs include a pair of glasses. When this option is checked, Inventor previews the geometry as you saw it do in Chapter 2. When you're doing complex assembly functions or creating difficult features on a system with limited memory or graphics capability, you may want to disable this option to improve performance.

Now, let's put it to the test and see how it does with your sketches:

1. Restore the home view.

2. Start the Lofted Flange tool, found on the Create panel.

3. Without changing any options, select the Square Sketch for Profile 1.

4. The program dialog is ready for Profile 2. Pick the circle. The preview shows the faceted transition.

5. Change the value of Chord Tolerance from 0.1in to 0.5in. See Figure 3.5.

6. Switch the Output value to Die Formed.

7. Click OK to create the lofted flange.

8. Orbit around your part to see how it's assembled.

9. Select the Back face on the ViewCube. Use the rotation arrows to properly show the word Back if need be.

10. Right-click the ViewCube, and select Set Current View as Front, as shown in Figure 3.6.

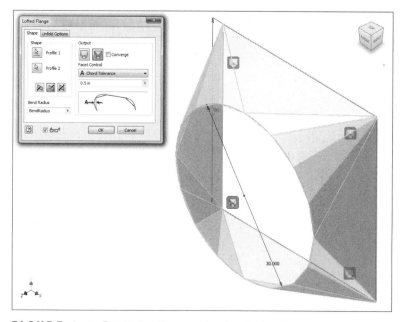

FIGURE 3.5 Previewing the press-break output option

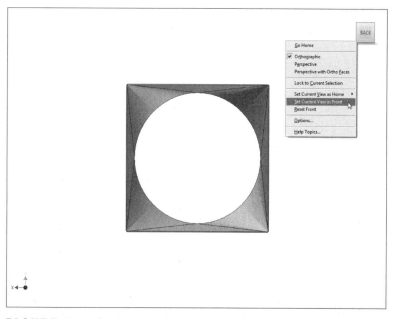

FIGURE 3.6 Setting a new front view

11. Select the XY plane in the Browser, and then either click the Create 2D Sketch tool or press the S key.

In Inventor, you can either start the Sketch tool and then select the face or select the face and start a new sketch on it. For the next step, you could use Horizontal and Vertical constraints to center the rectangle in the sketch; but the steps use dimensioning techniques so you can see another option.

12. Draw a rectangle above the part, as shown in Figure 3.7.

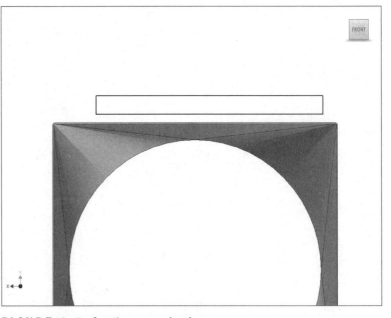

FIGURE 3.7 Creating a new sketch

13. Dimension the width of the rectangle to be 32.

14. Dimension the height of the rectangle to be .5.

15. Create a dimension between the sketch center and the top of the rectangle. Set its value to **35.8/2**, as shown in Figure 3.8.

N O T E   Inventor does the math for you if you need to calculate a value. You can even use parentheses to build algebraic equations. For angles, you can input degrees or even radians, using RAD for the unit.

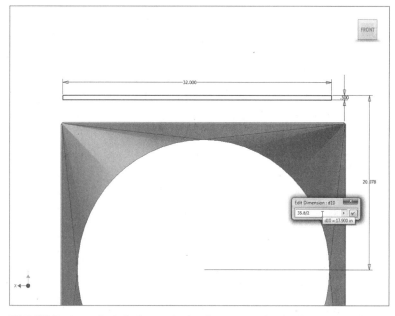

FIGURE 3.8 Include factors in the dimension value, and Inventor will calculate the value.

16. Create a dimension from the left edge of the rectangle to the sketch center. Edit the value; when the value appears, click the 32.000 dimension.

   Doing so enters the dimension name of the 32.000 dimension into the dialog. Inventor gives every dimension a name automatically. You can rename any dimension using the Parameters tool on the Manage tab, or you can enter a new value on the fly. Dimension names can't have spaces or special characters.

17. In the Edit Dimension window, put the cursor before the dimension name that was assigned when you selected the 32.00 dimension, and type half_width=.

18. Type /2 after the dimension name, as shown in Figure 3.9.

19. Click the green check mark to accept the new value. Change the dimension name from the automatic name to *half_width*.

20. Finish the sketch, and save your work.

Now, you'll use a new feature to convert this rectangle into a flange of sorts.

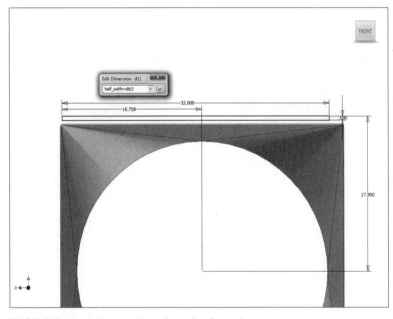

FIGURE 3.9 Using a formula in the dimension

The Face Tool

The Face tool is like an Extrude tool, but you don't have to set a distance. The distance is determined by the thickness of the material. The only other rule is that you have to have at least one closed loop in the sketch. Figure 3.10 shows the dialog box; it's extremely useful if you need to add a flange to a part but the flange will have an irregular shape. Very often, the Face tool is used to define the base feature of a sheet metal part.

In addition to having the usual option tabs and sketch-selection tools, the Face tool can select edges to blend the face to. After an edge is selected, a pre-view of how the bend will occur between the new face and the existing body appears.

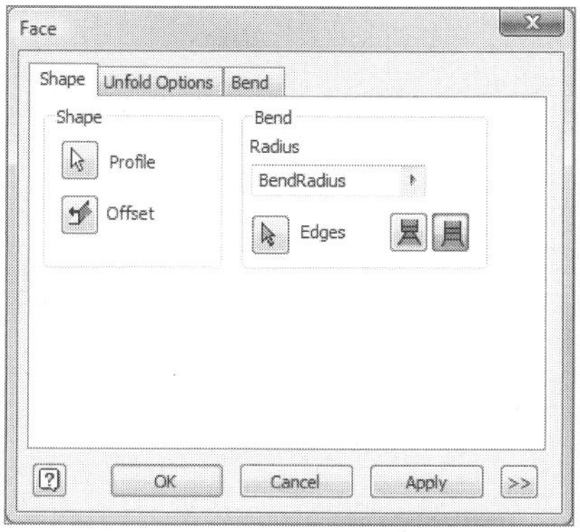

FIGURE 3.10 The Face dialog box

Often, you'd use a flange to create this type of geometry; but with your lofted flange, it would be difficult to properly input the angle that lets this feature be parallel with the XY plane. So, you'll create this as a Face feature and use the Blend option:

1. Start the Face tool. Because you only have one profile in your sketch, Inventor assumes you want to use your rectangle to create the face.

2. Click the arrow button next to Edges.

3. Select the outside edge of the lofted flange, as shown in Figure 3.11.

4. Click OK to create the new Face feature.
   Look closely at your component. Note that the bend relief next to the new face/flange has a square bottom, and observe the thickness of the part.

5. Click the Sheet Metal Defaults tool.

6. Select Aluminum - .13 from the Sheet Metal Rule pull-down, and click OK to accept it as the rule that will now govern your part.
   Note the change to the bend-relief shape and the slight change in material thickness and color. It looks good; but for this part, you want the bend that was added to the face to have a smaller bend radius.

7. Double-click the icon next to Face1 in the Browser.
   As with all Inventor tools, this will launch the same dialog you saw when you created the feature.

8. Change the Bend Radius value to .05.

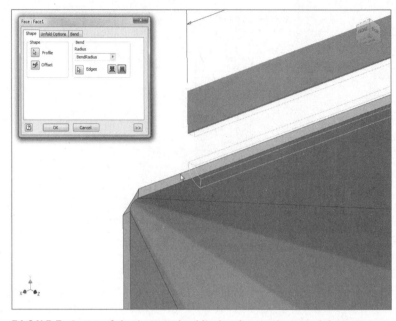

FIGURE 3.11 Selecting an edge blends a face to the rest of the part.

9. Click OK. Your part should look like the one in Figure 3.12.

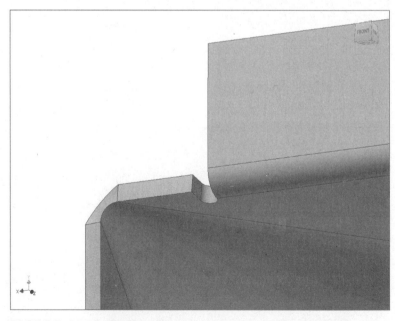

FIGURE 3.12 Modifying the active rule and overriding parts of the rule keep the user in control.

The Corner Round Tool

This tool is very simple. It places rounds on only the edges that can be rounded while cutting the flat pattern. The Fillet tool in the Model tab puts a rounded edge on just about anything; but this is a sheet metal–specific tool. It has two modes. Corner mode allows you to select individual edges — although not all edges are acceptable, as mentioned. You can deselect an edge by holding Ctrl and picking again. Feature mode rounds any edge on a selected feature. Let's use this tool:

1. Select the Corner Round tool from the Modify panel.

2. Switch the Mode to Feature, and leave the Radius set to .25.

3. Move over the face you created. It highlights. Pick it when it does; the open corners preview, showing that they will be rounded, and the dialog indicates that two edges are selected.

4. Click OK to add the rounds to the corner. See Figure 3.13.

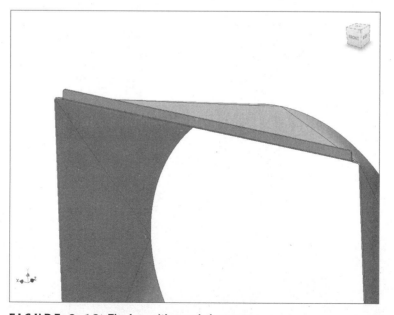

FIGURE 3.13 The face with rounded corners

For your design, you need four of these flanges. You could draw them individually, or you can replicate them as you did in Chapter 2 . In Chapter 2, you
used the Mirror tool, and I said that it's very similar to the Pattern tools. Let's
see if I was right:

1. Click the Circular (pattern) tool in the Pattern panel.

2. Instead of picking the features you want from the screen, pick Face1
   and Corner Round1 in the Browser.

3. Click the arrow button next to Rotation Axis, and pick the Z axis in
   the Browser.

4. A preview appears, showing a total of six faces. Change the value
   under the word *Placement* in the dialog to 4, and click OK.

5. Inspect the new faces, and make sure they all have rounded corners
   and bend reliefs. Then, save your work. See Figure 3.14.

At this point, you still aren't prepared to create a flat pattern of your part. In
order to do so, you need to create a gap in the part. This is where the Rip tool
comes in.

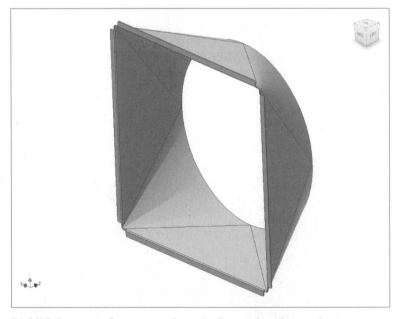

FIGURE 3.14 Patterns can dramatically speed up the creation process.

The Rip Tool

In cases where you use a lofted flange or a solid-modeling technique to create a sheet metal part, and you need an opening to enable proper flat-pattern creation, the Rip tool gives you three options. Depending on the option you choose, it works as either a sketched or a placed feature (see Figure 3.15):

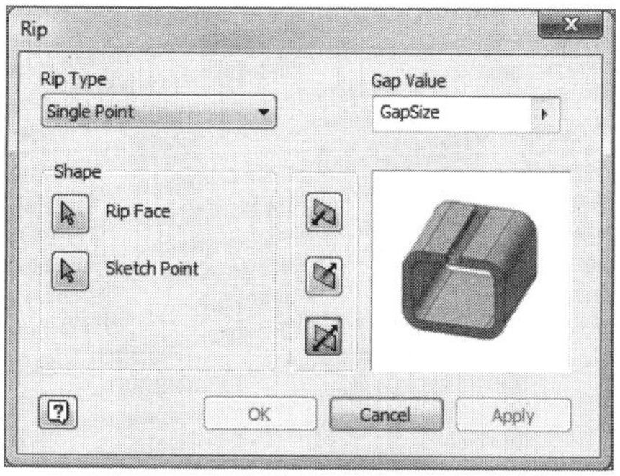

FIGURE 3.15 The Rip tool dialog box

Single Point   Creating a sketch on a face allows you to rip the face by selecting only a single point.

Point to Point   This option also relies on a sketch being present but gives you the added control of picking a beginning and an end point to cut between. This option even allows spiral cuts along a curved surface.

Face Extents   Acting as a placed feature, this removes the face you select and the material normal to it to create the gap.

For this model, you want complete control over the placement of the rip:

1. Set your view so that you can see the Top, Left, and Front faces of the ViewCube, and zoom in on the bottom of the duct as shown in Figure 3.16.

2. Create a new sketch on the triangular face that makes up the inside surface of the bottom of the part.

3. Use the Project Geometry tool from the Draw panel, and select the edge of the triangular face highlighted in Figure 3.17.

4. Finish the sketch.

5. Start the Rip tool from the Modify tab.

6. Set the Rip Type to Point to Point.

7. Select the triangular face for the Rip Face.

8. Select the two ends of the projected line in the sketch for the Start Point and End Point.

9. Set the Gap value to .06.

10. Click OK to create the rip.

11. Click the Create Flat Pattern tool. See Figure 3.18.

12. Pick the Go to Folded Part icon at the end of the Flat Pattern tab.

13. Save your work.

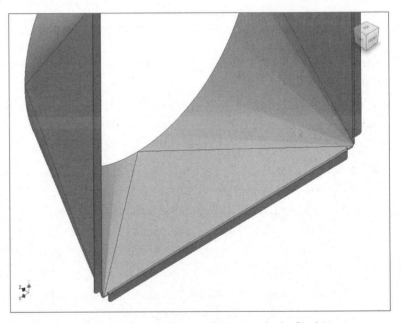

FIGURE 3.16 Locating the face to which to apply the Rip feature

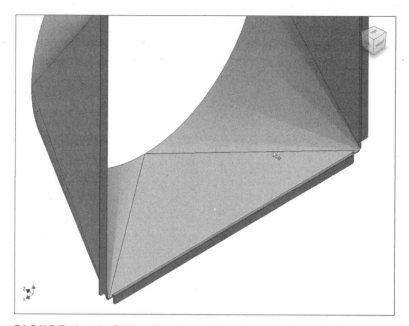

FIGURE 3.17 Picking the edge provides the two points to rip between.

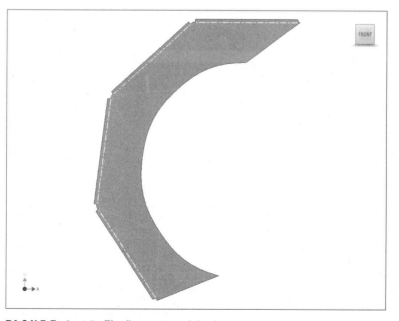

FIGURE 3.18 The flat pattern of the duct

The last thing you need to add to this component for the time being is a way to mount it to your housing. Eventually, it will be held in place by being sandwiched between the housing and the grill; but for now, you need to make it possible for Manufacturing to hold it in place during assembly and to take some of the load off the fasteners that will be holding the grill:

1. Create a new sketch on the XY plane.

2. Set your view to be the front view.

3. Pick the Construction linetype override in the Format panel.

4. Draw a horizontal line near the top of the open space inside the part (see Figure 3.19). After you've picked the second point of the line segment, right-click, and select Restart form the context menu.

   Now that the tool has been restarted, you can move your cursor to the middle of the first line, and the midpoint will highlight. You could pick the midpoint this way (which is how I usually do), but I want you to be aware of another option.

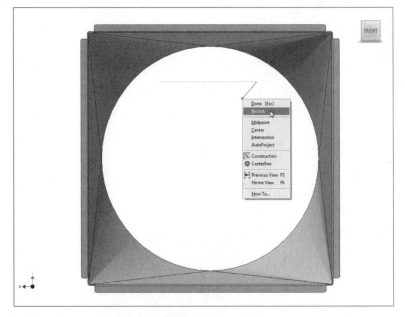

FIGURE 3.19 Using a sketch to position holes

5. Right-click in an open part of the screen.

   The context menu offers you the ability to change the linetype override. You can also limit the type of points the tools will seek out.

6. Pick Midpoint from the list, and move near the horizontal line. The midpoint is highlighted no matter where you are on the line.

7. When the midpoint appears, click to place the first point of the line.

8. Create the line perpendicular to the first one, pointing down.

9. Create a Coincidence constraint between the midpoint of the second line and the sketch center, as shown in Figure 3.20.

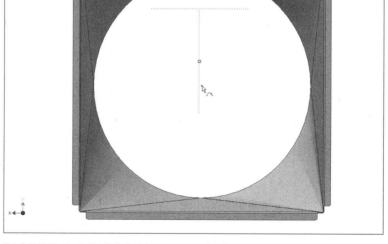

FIGURE 3.20 A Coincidence constraint between a midpoint and the sketch center can create symmetry quickly.

10. Dimension the top of the T to be .5in. from the top edge of the face and the width of the top of the T to be 18in., as shown in Figure 3.21.

11. Finish the sketch.

12. Start the Hole tool. Notice that no points are selected automatically, because you didn't define them as hole centers.

13. Pick the three endpoints, as shown in the preview in Figure 3.22.

14. Make the hole a Countersink type, set Termination to Through All, select the Direction option next to Termination to reverse the direction, and make it a Clearance Hole for a 100° flat-head machine screw, as shown in Figure 3.22.

All the characteristics of the hole are automatically entered into the dialog box based on the standard you select. That's a lot easier than looking everything up on a hole chart.

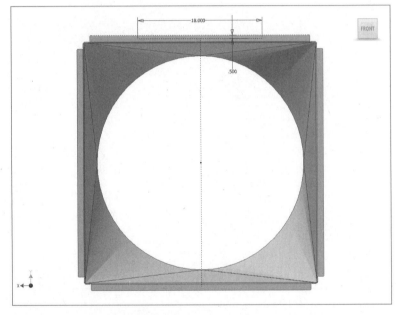

FIGURE 3.21 The finished sketch

15. Click OK to place the three holes.

16. Switch to the flat pattern to see that the holes have been added. Then, return to the folded model.

17. Save your work.

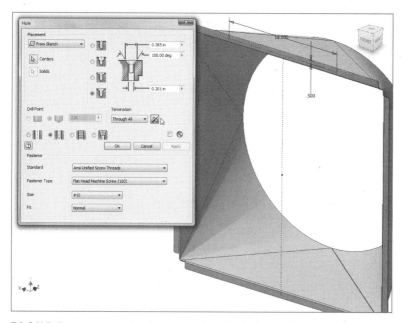

FIGURE 3.22 Placing the mounting holes in the duct

So far, the instructions for the exercises have had you build parts correctly. (The same will be true for most of this book.) In this exercise, I deliberately had you construct the primary feature, the lofted flange, using an incorrect size. When you created the sketch and work plane for the circle, you did so at a distance of 12in. This is the same width as the housing, which doesn't leave a lot of room for a fan blade or anything else. Let's correct this error now:

1. Locate Work Plane 1 in the Browser.

2. Double-click the icon. A dialog appears, showing the distance the plane was defined by. The plane also highlights.

3. Set the value for the plane to 8in., and use the check mark to accept the new value. See Figure 3.23.

4. This type of modification doesn't cause the model to update. Instead, the Update icon appears on the Quick Access Toolbar.

5. Click the Update tool. The model then recalculates. See Figure 3.24 to compare your result.

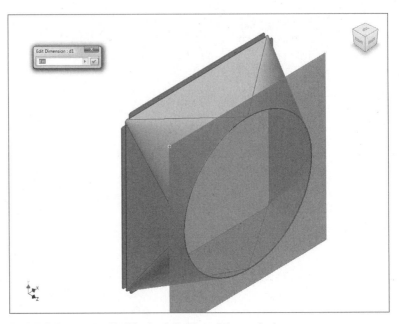

FIGURE 3.23 Modify the definition of the work plane.

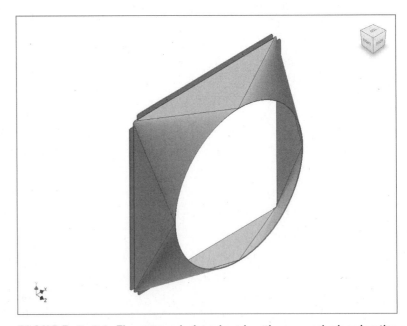

FIGURE 3.24 The part recalculates based on the new work-plane location.

6. Let's change the appearance of your component. In the Quick Access Toolbar, select Aluminum (Polished).

7. Save your work.

You're finished with this component for now, but you need to start moving toward the bigger picture. So far, you've created two components more or less in a vacuum. In a couple of chapters, you'll see some truly remarkable tools called *design accelerators* that work only in the Assembly environment. Between now and then, I hope to show you that working with assemblies offers some other benefits.

The Assembly Modeling Concept

The Assembly environment is essentially a container holding all the components that you need to stick to each other in one way or another. I have always found that in Inventor, creating an assembly is a much more direct process than building its parts. You can create a part using a broad variety of tools and techniques based on how you want to edit it. By contrast, the way you build an assembly model is based largely on how you'd build the assembly in the real world. You can also use the assembly model to experiment with different ways of structuring the real assembly and perhaps discover a better way of doing things.

You can also use an assembly model to build variations on a particular design. The ability to swap out parts for alternatives and check fits or test a mechanism's range of motion makes it much easier to detect flaws in a system before spending money on the real thing.

To build an assembly, designers traditionally stack 3D parts, creating constraints to hold the parts together as they would be in the real world. If you try to create an assembly without using constraints, the parts won't maintain their relationships as they change. Constraints in assembly modeling are different from those in 2D sketching, but the principle of an enduring relationship that limits unexpected behavior is the same.

Let's start your assembly by bringing the components you've built so far into the same space:

1. Create a new assembly file using the Standard (in).iam template.

2. Starting a new type of file presents another new tab for the Ribbon. The first tool is Place in the Component panel. Click this tool.

3. The Place Component dialog is similar to the Open File dialog. Find Housing.ipt using the Frequently Used Subfolders on the left. Select it in the File window, and click Open to begin placing the part in the assembly.

Doing so places an instance of the housing at the center of the assembly. The assembly has the same origin planes, axes, and so on as a part file. The first part placed automatically aligns its origins with those of the assembly. Each copy of a part that is placed is referred to as an *instance* of the component. For this assembly, you need only one housing part.

4. Inventor places the first instance and offers you the opportunity to place others. Because you need only one, press the Esc key to stop placing components.

5. Open Windows Explorer or a My Computer window.

6. Navigate to the C:\Data\Parts folder.

7. Pick and drag Duct.ipt into the Design window from Explorer. See Figure 3.25.

   The first component is the base component and is grounded by default, so it doesn't move. The duct isn't grounded, so you can pick and drag the component to a different position.

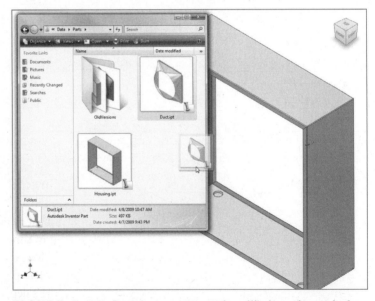

FIGURE 3.25 Dragging a component from Windows also works for an assembly.

8. Pick and drag the duct away from the housing, as shown in Figure 3.26.

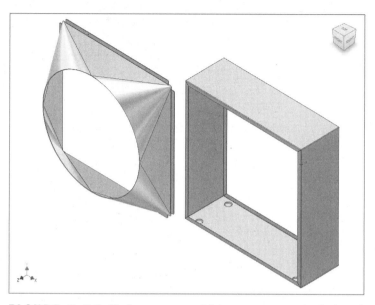

FIGURE 3.26 Moving a component into open space can make it easier to apply assembly constraints.

9. Save your assembly as Fan.iam in the Assemblies folder under C:\Data.

As you define the part's position using assembly constraints, a component's movement becomes limited. Before I get too far ahead of myself, let's discuss some of the basic concepts for building an assembly.

Creating Assembly Constraints

Assembly constraints come in a variety of flavors, but they're all based on the same principle: removing degrees of freedom. The tools that Inventor uses to create and manage assemblies are contained in the Assemble tab.

Theoretically, any part has six degrees of freedom (without that pesky gravity). A part can rotate around three axes and translate (move) in three planes. It can also move in any combination of these at the same time. However, as you can imagine, it's difficult for a complex mechanism to work unless parts are attached to one another, and those attachments limit each part's degrees of freedom.

As mentioned, by default, the first part you place is grounded. The grounded component automatically has all of its degrees of freedom removed, so be careful what component you place into an assembly first. (Should you make a mistake or change your mind, you can remove the grounded state and make another component grounded.) It's also possible to have more than one component in a grounded state, but usually one will do the trick. As other components are brought in, they're free to be positioned any way you need them. Decide which constraint is the best for creating the desired relationship between the parts; you can eventually remove all of the unnecessary degrees of freedom. Also note that you don't have to remove every degree of freedom from every part. When you place a bolt into a hole, for example, the position of the head will be difficult to predict in the real assembly, so it isn't normally necessary to define it in the assembly model.

Assembly constraints can also add intelligence to an assembly. For example, you can define constraints between two parts and use their positions to define the size of a third part that will be placed between them in the real world. If you can use assemblies to build parts, think of the possibilities for trying new ideas.

Inventor's assembly tools are available only if you've created an assembly file or if you're editing an existing assembly. Before you begin building an assembly, you need to know your options.

The Constraint Tool

You'll spend a lot of time in the Place Constraint dialog box when first creating an assembly, so let's start with it. Other tools in the Assembly Panel bar will become more useful as you define the assembly's constraints. You can find the Constraint tool in the Position panel of the Assemble tab; it has a range of options to handle the many ways you can associate geometry. Four tabs — Assembly, Motion, Transitional, and Constraint Sets — let you create a broad variety of geometric relationships. By this time, you're probably becoming good at recognizing the elements of the Inventor dialog boxes, and you understand what Inventor is looking for.

The Assembly Tab

The Assembly tab contains most of the tools you'll use on a day-to-day basis.

Before looking at the groups of options, notice the check box for displaying a preview (the eyeglasses) of the effect that applying the constraint will have. With this option checked, Inventor moves the part or parts as a preview in most cases before you apply the constraint.

Next to that is the Predict Offset and Orientation check box. This tool is useful when you have parts moved into an approximate position. When you apply a Mate or Angle constraint, the values of those constraints are automatically filled in with their current position; otherwise, Inventor would snap the parts tightly together, and you'd have to experiment with values to return them to the position they're already in.

Also notice the Solution area. As you'll see, the solution you can apply will depend on the type of constraint you're applying.

Let's look at the groups in the dialog box and go through some of the options.

Type

The Type group has four primary ways of defining an assembly constraint: Mate, Angle, Tangent, and Insert. Using these tools, you can build any rigid assembly.

Mate, the first type of constraint (the highlighted box under Solution), has two solution options. The Mate solution applies an oppositional force. It emulates elements being stuck together. A mate can also be applied between any combination of points, edges (axes), and faces. The other solution, Flush, can only be applied between faces; it's used to align faces that are parallel to one another.

An Angle constraint defines nonparallel aligned conditions. It can only be placed on edges and faces. There are three solutions for the constraint. The default solution is the Directed Angle; it applies a positive value clockwise about its axis. The Undirected Angle solution can apply a positive value about the axis in either direction. If parts unpredictably change orientation, try changing the angular constraint used on the parts to this solution. The third solution is Explicit

Reference Vector, which allows you to specify the axis directly. This gives you maximum control and predictability when defining a value. However, in most cases, it isn't necessary to use this option to get the proper, predictable result, so it isn't the default.

You can apply a Tangent constraint between a curved face and a planar face, a curved face and an edge, or two curved faces. Its two solutions behave much like those in a Mate constraint. The Inside solution tries to align the faces so that the mating face tends to be inside the curved face, and Outside holds the mating face outside the curved face.

The Insert constraint is a specialized Mate constraint. It places a Mate constraint between the axes of two curved faces and, using the Opposed solution, creates a mate condition between faces adjacent to the curved faces. Using the Aligned solution applies a flush condition between those faces. As the icon for the type shows, it's perfect for locating bolts into holes. Selections for this constraint only highlight curved edges that are planar.

Selections

The Selections group displays the input Inventor needs to create the relationship. As usual, a red arrow indicates that nothing has been selected for that group.

Offset

Offset lets you apply a value to a condition. For example, if you want to leave a space between two faces, you can enter the value for that gap. You can also build an interference condition by using a negative value. In an Angle constraint, this prompt changes to enter the angle value.

The Motion Tab

The Motion tab contains two types of constraint for creating relationships that can be activated to re-create how parts move in a mechanism: Rotation and Rotation-Translation.

A Rotation constraint can replicate gearing or rollers using the Reverse solution. You can also apply a ratio to the relationship between the two bodies to allow them to turn at different rates. The Forward solution turns the bodies in the same direction with the option of defining a ratio.

The Rotation-Translation type can emulate a rack-and-pinion joint or the movement of a slide being driven on a threaded shaft by creating a relationship between the rotation of a face and the movement of a body. The Distance value governs how far the second part moves during one revolution of the first part. To emulate a rack and pinion, you set this value to the circumference of the pinion. The Forward and Reverse solutions allow you to select the direction of the linear movement in relation to the rotation.

The Transitional Tab

The Transitional tab has only one tool. It applies a Tangency constraint that can follow a curved face such as a cam. The mating faces remain tangent as long as there is a tangency to follow.

The Constraint Set Tab

This is a specialized tool that can be very useful if you traditionally construct assemblies from a common point or in relation to datum points on various parts. By placing a User Coordinate System (UCS) in parts, you can tell those parts to align the X, Y, and Z planes of their UCS systems in one step. This is an interesting and powerful technique but beyond the scope of this book.

Let's put together your two existing components and position them properly. There are a few different ways you can assemble them accurately. For this example, we'll focus on the critical feature of your product being a fan blade and the fact that the major components are positioned around it:

1. Select the Constrain tool from the Position panel of the Assemble tab. The first thing you'll do is make the Z axis of each part line up so that you know both parts are centered on where the blade will eventually be placed.

2. Expand the Origin folders for both the housing and the duct. Using a Mate type constraint, pick the Z axis in both parts.

3. The duct snaps into place. If you have your sound on, yes, that was a cowbell.

4. Click the OK button to accept this constraint and close the dialog box.

5. Pick and drag the duct. Note that it pivots about and can still move along the Z axis. When you've moved the part, make sure the duct is place behind the housing and that the face with the two holes is toward the top, as shown in Figure 3.27.

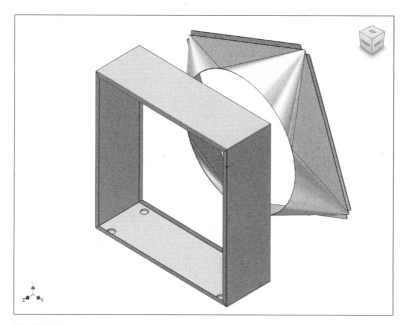

FIGURE 3.27 Moving the duct to a new position

6. Rotate your view so that it resembles Figure 3.28.

7. Start the Constrain tool again.

8. You'll use the Mate constraint again. This time, pick the flange on the housing for the first selection, as shown in Figure 3.29.

9. For the second face, hover over the face on the duct with the two holes. After a second or two, an icon appears under your cursor. By picking the arrows on either end of the icon, you can toggle the options available for the second selection. After this icon appears, you can also cycle the options by rolling a mouse wheel.

10. Pick the back of the face you hovered over for the second selection, as shown in Figure 3.30. When the correct face is highlighted, click the square in the middle of the icon.

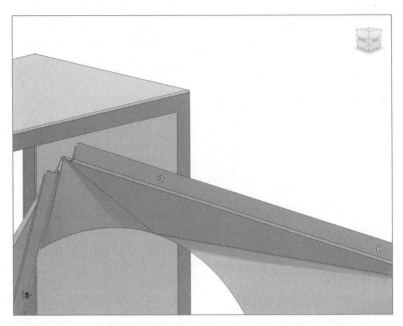

FIGURE 3.28 Having the right point of view makes placing constraints easier.

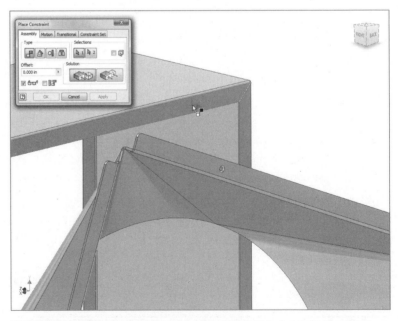

FIGURE 3.29 Having faces and edges highlight before selecting them makes it easier to see what you're picking.

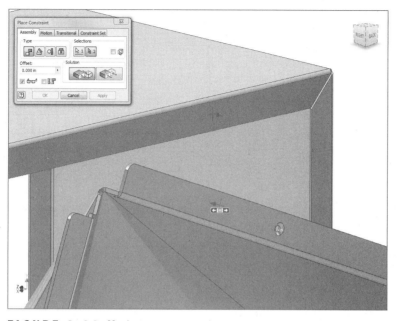

FIGURE 3.30 Moving a component into open space can make it easier to apply assembly constraints.

11. The duct moves into position — but remember, it's only a preview. Click the Apply button to create the constraint and keep the dialog available for the next constraint.

12. Rotate your view so you can see the top edge of the face on the duct (with the holes) and the top of the housing. Verify that the material of the duct mounting faces aren't intersecting with the housing. See Figure 3.31.

13. Switch the Constraint Type to Angle.

14. For the first selection, pick the top of the housing, as shown in Figure 3.31.

15. For the second selection, pick the thin top face of the duct, as shown in Figure 3.31.

16. Leave the Angle value at 0, and click OK to create the constraint.

17. The two parts should look like Figure 3.32.

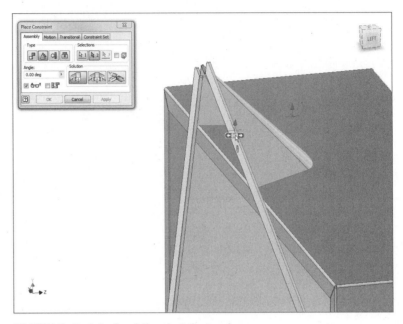

FIGURE 3.31 Carefully select the two faces.

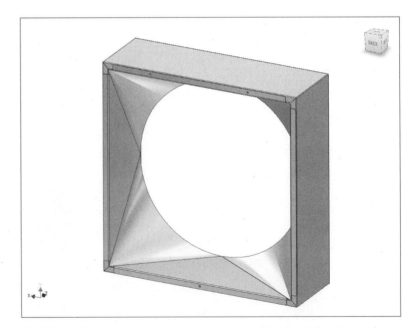

FIGURE 3.32 The two components should appear to fit together without interference.

Creating Assembly Constraints

Next, you need to create holes in the housing that line up with those you added to the duct. You could simply re-create the sketch, but for the next exercise you'll create a relationship between the two parts to define the location of the holes:

1. Close the duct and housing files if they're still open in Inventor. You should only have Fan.iam open for this exercise.

2. In the Design window, double-click the housing. This activates the part so you go from editing an assembly to editing a component. The Ribbon changes what tabs are available, and the inactive parts on the screen change in appearance, as shown in Figure 3.33.

3. Zoom into where you can see one of the holes in the duct.

4. Create a sketch on the top flange, as previewed in Figure 3.34.

5. When the Sketch tools appear, start the Project Geometry tool. Pick the bottom of the countersink hole in the duct that you zoomed into. See Figure 3.35.

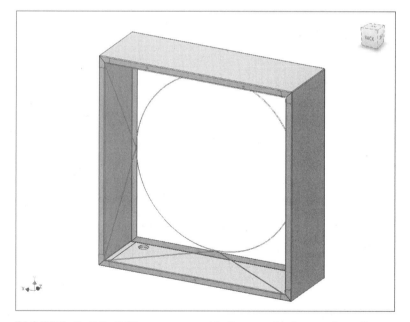

FIGURE 3.33 Editing a component in the assembly is a great practice.

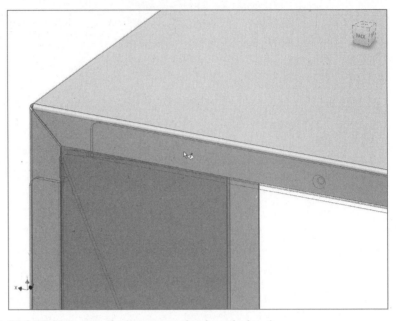

FIGURE 3.34 Creating a new sketch on the housing

FIGURE 3.35 Projecting geometry from one part to another

When you project the edge, a special icon appears next to the sketch in the Browser and next to the name of the part in the Browser to indicate that geometry in that sketch is adaptive to changes in other parts. The sketch appears simple, showing the edge of the hole and a center point; but this geometry will move if the hole changes size or location in the duct.

6. Repeat step 5 for the remaining holes in the duct.

7. Finish the sketch.

8. Start the Hole tool, and pick the center points on the three projected circles for the Placement.

9. The hole depth is again automatically set to Thickness.

10. Enter 9/64 for the Diameter value. Inventor does the math for you. This is the proper pilot-hole size for a #10 sheet metal screw. Review Figure 3.36.

11. Click OK to create the holes in the housing.

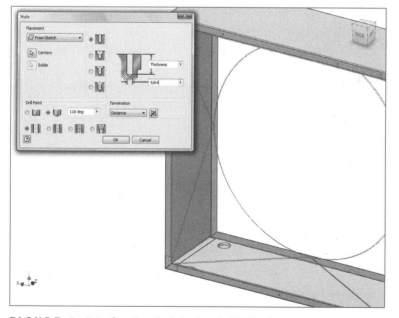

FIGURE 3.36 Creating the holes located in the duct part

12. At the end of the Model tab, pick the Return icon to go back to the assembly.

13. Save your work.

Creating components is something you'll do on a regular basis with Autodesk Inventor. But relatively few products are created without purchased components. Inventor has a few options for obtaining these components. The most commonly used is the Content Center.

Working with Standard Parts

The Content Center contains standard parts and steel shapes. If you load all the standards, there are more than 700,000. Chances are you'll only use a handful, but Inventor allows you to establish your own custom library containing only the content you'll use.

If you haven't installed the Content Center, the following exercise won't work. I can't stress strongly enough the importance of installing and understanding the Content Center. Inventor 2010 gives you two options to install the Content Center: You can use the Desktop Content for an individual user or install the Autodesk Data Management Server to share a single source of content among multiple users; it also acts as the backbone for the included data-management system called Autodesk Vault.

Not using the Content Center severely limits many of Inventor's most innovative tools. To better understand how to install and initiate the Content Center, review CC_2010_Install_guide.pdf, which is installed on your hard drive with Inventor automatically. It will guide you through the setup process.

In this exercise, you'll use the most basic technique for adding standard content to your assembly:

1. Click the down arrow under the Place icon in the Component panel.

2. Select the Place from Content Center option. Doing so launches the Place from Content Center dialog. See Figure 3.37.

3. Expand the Fasteners category. Then, expand the Countersunk category, and select Sheet Metal Screws.

   Among the tools above the category list is an icon resembling a funnel. Clicking the down arrow next to it presents a list of the standards on which the available content is based.

4. Click the down arrow next to the Filter icon, and click to the left of ANSI to filter the dialog to display only components that are members of the ANSI standard. See Figure 3.38.

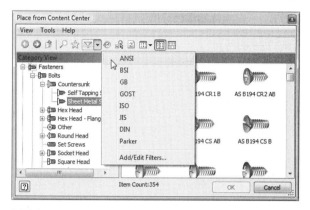

FIGURE 3.38 Filters can make it easier to locate standard parts.

5. Locate the Cross Recessed 100° Flat Countersunk Head Tapping Screw - Type B - Type I - Inch, select it in the window, and click OK.

6. A preview of the screw appears. Click an empty portion of the Design window.

7. In the dialog that appears, select the #10 Thread Description and the 0.5 Nominal Length, as shown in Figure 3.39.

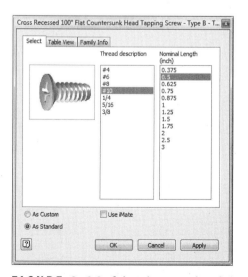

FIGURE 3.39 Select the screw thread size and length in the dialog.

8. Click OK to begin placing the component.

9. Place the screw somewhere where you can see it in the Design window.

10. Start the Constrain tool.

11. Select the Insert Type, and use the Aligned Solution for the constraint.

12. Select the top edge of the countersunk hole and the top edge of the screw, as shown in Figure 3.40. (I have turned off the preview for the screen capture. You should leave the preview on.)

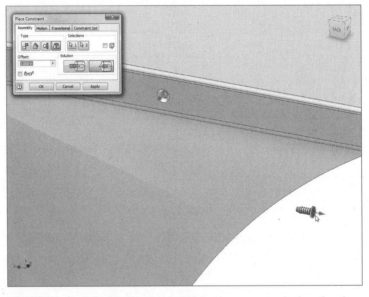

FIGURE 3.40 The Insert constraint only uses curved edges for placement.

13. Click the OK button to place the screw.

With the screw in place, you need to place the remaining two screws. You could use Place from Content Center again, but there's no need to do so because the next two screws are the same as the first.

14. In the Browser, locate the screw you just placed in the assembly. It should be at the bottom of the components list.

15. Click and drag the screw from the Browser into the Design window. Doing so creates a new instance of the screw.

16. Constrain the screw to the second hole in the duct. Repeat for the third hole.

17. Save your work.

The tools for assembling components in Inventor are defined by simple forms of geometry: a face to a face, an axis to an axis, and points to points. Occasionally, you'll use combinations of these; but if you keep the fundamental geometry in mind and place components as you want to build the physical product, you'll see that the assembly tools are easy and maybe even fun to use.

Are You Experienced?

Now you can...

- ☑ **create a sheet metal transition**
- ☑ **place components into an assembly**
- ☑ **build relationships between components in the assembly**
- ☑ **locate prebuilt standard components**
- ☑ **include those parts in the assembly**

CHAPTER 4

Working with Solid Models and Weldments

▶ Basic solid modeling

▶ Working with predefined features

▶ Creating Weldment files

▶ Creating a drawing template

▶ Creating 2D drawing views

▶ Dimensioning and detailing a drawing

Keep It Simple, Make It Work

Inventor's tools can be used to create incredibly complex parts. I hope you've seen that you can turn simple sketches into elaborate components very easily with these powerful tools. Unlike the last two chapters, this chapter will focus on the geometrically simple parts that so many machines are built from.

In this chapter, you'll build a number of parts and you'll also assemble them into groups referred to as *subassemblies* before adding them to the fan. These subassemblies should be approached just like any other assembly: with the manufacturing process in mind. If you'll be preconstructing groups of components before adding them to a main assembly, you should consider making them a subassembly. There will also be times where some machining is done in a completed assembly for increased production accuracy. In this chapter, we'll explore that as well.

Finally, we'll continue our exploration of the fact that you don't have to build every component. In this chapter, you'll use predefined metal shapes to build a frame. You'll also take the use of standard fasteners to the next level.

Making Parts

There's no need to overthink creating parts. The component you'll build in the first exercise could be made a few different ways, and none of them could be considered wrong. It's all about how you anticipate your parts changing in the future. Thinking about how your part will most likely evolve over time will guide you on how to build it to begin with:

1. Create a new file using the Standard (in).ipt template.

2. Draw a circle, using the sketch center to place the center point.

3. Use the Dimension tool to define the diameter at 2.2in., as shown in Figure 4.1.

4. Without using the Finish Sketch toolm press the E key on your keyboard. This keyboard shortcut starts the Extrude tool.

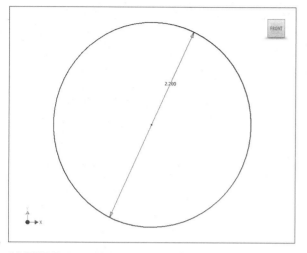

FIGURE 4.1 Creating a simple sketch

The Extrude Tool

Despite what you've done so far in this book, users most often use the Extrude tool to create initial shapes.

The Extrude tool dialog box (Figure 4.2) is typical of Inventor dialog boxes.

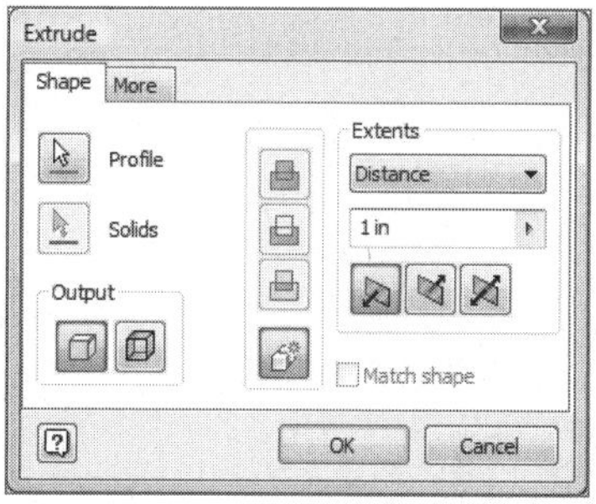

FIGURE 4.2 The Extrude dialog box

The buttons and boxes on the Shape tab ask you to select a profile or profiles, select a direction for the extruded feature to be created, and define what size the feature should be. If your sketch has only one viable profile to be used for an Extrude feature, it's automatically selected; Inventor moves on to prompt for the remaining information.

Initially, you're offered the Join tool, which creates a positive shape in the model. After your first or base feature is placed, additional options are made available in the dialog box:

Join   This option uses the sketch profile to add material to the model.

Cut   This option removes material to a depth, to a plane, or through the model, based on the sketch that was selected.

Intersect   This passes the new shape through the existing shape. Only the portions of the model that were common to both shapes remain.

New Solid   This is an option for building *multi-body* features that are regarded as separate from other features in the part. It's used for more advanced workflows.

More tab   Switching to this tab allows you to define a taper angle, which adds a draft angle to cast or plastic parts.

Continue from where you left off in the previous section:

1. Set the Distance value to .5, and use the Mid-Plane option to develop the shape equally in both directions, as shown in Figure 4.3.

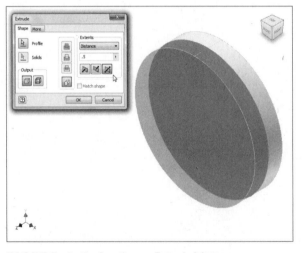

FIGURE 4.3 Creating an Extruded feature

2. Click OK to create the disk-shaped feature.

3. Set the Material for the component to Steel, and update its Mass Properties by clicking the Apply button.

4. Close the iProperties dialog, save the component into the `Parts` folder, and name it `Bearing Holder.ipt`.

That's the whole part, at least for now. A little later, you'll add a bore to the part in the context of an assembly. You're not adding the component now because the bore needs to be added after the bearing holder has been welded to the plate you're about to create; this will allow for material distortion. Welding could warp the part, and you need to have a round bore to insert a bearing cleanly.

Building the Bearing Plate

Now, let's use a technology that has been in Inventor for a few years and that quickly creates regular shapes. You can place features from the Content Center rather than drawing them:

1. Create a new file using the `Standard (in).ipt` template.

2. Click the Finish Sketch tool to get out of the new sketch.

3. Switch the Ribbon to the Manage tab, and select the Place Feature from Content Center tool in the Insert panel.

> 🖨 Feature

Doing so launches the dialog box shown in Figure 4.4, where you can select features. The features are sorted first by English or Metric units, then by geometry, and finally by whether the feature adds material or removes material from the component.

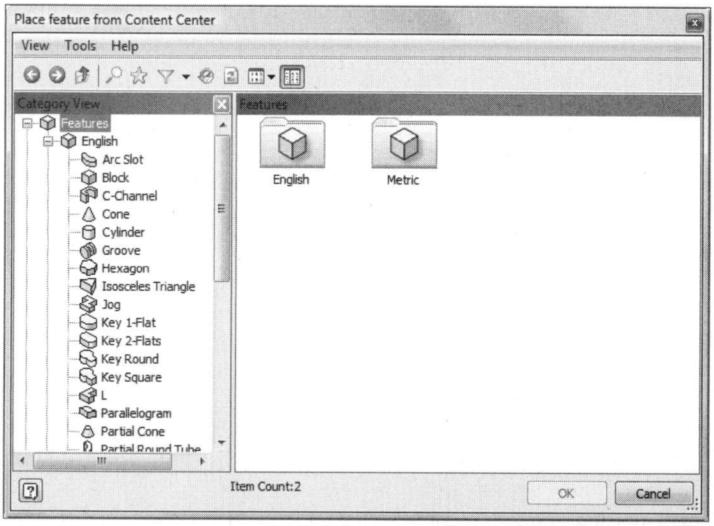

FIGURE 4.4 The Place Feature from Content Center dialog box

4. Double-click the folder containing English unit features.

5. Scroll down, and open the Rectangle folder with another double-click.

In this folder are two icons: Rectangle for adding geometry and Rectangle (Hole) for removing it.

6. Double-click the Rectangle icon. Doing so replaces the Content Center dialog with the Rectangle dialog shown in Figure 4.5.

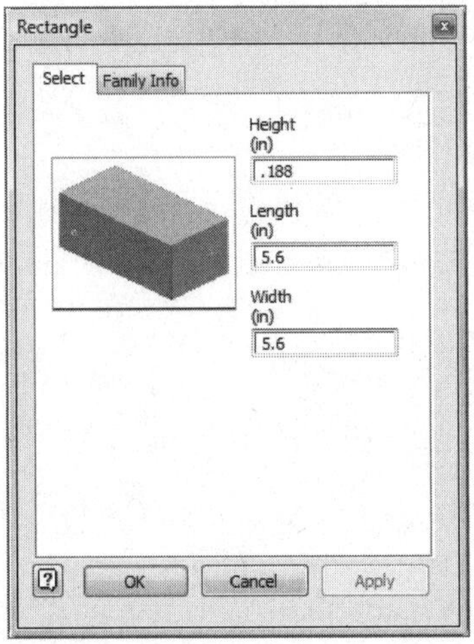

FIGURE 4.5 Sizing the Rectangle feature

7. Set Height to .188, Length to 5.6, and Width to 5.6, and click OK.

8. Because this is a first feature, you need to pick a plane to place the feature on. Expand the Origin folder, and select XY plane.

9. Press the F6 key to see the preview shown in Figure 4.6.

10. Right-click an open part of the screen, and pick Done from the context menu to create the feature.

11. Set the material for the part to be Steel. Update the Mass Properties. The plate should weigh 1.672 pounds.

12. Close the dialog.

13. Save the file as Bearing Plate.ipt in the Parts folder for your project.

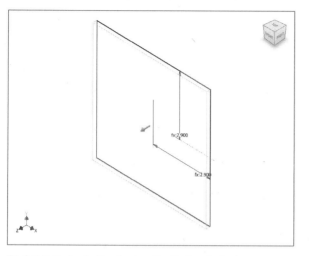

FIGURE 4.6 Previewing the Rectangle feature

The next step could be done a couple of different ways, but we'll take this opportunity to look more closely at Work features. You created a work plane in the process of defining a new sketch in the last chapter, but you can use them many ways.

Work Features

You always start a sketched feature with a sketch on a plane or planar face. Many placed features depend on placement using a plane or planar face. A part has three origin planes, but sometimes you need to create a sketch or place geometry for which no planar face is available and the origin planes aren't in the right place. In these instances, you can create a feature called a *work plane* that works as a platform.

The work plane is one of three Work features; the work axis and work point are the others. These three features are ways to build a foundation for other features of a part. In and of themselves, they don't build the part.

You can define a work plane several ways. It can be offset a distance to another plane or face; or you can create it by defining a cylindrical face and either another plane, face, axis, or edge to build a plane tangent to the cylindrical face. It can be built based on two axes (or edges) that lie in the same plane, based on an axis and a point, or by selecting three points. You can also place a work plane normal to a path in a sketch by clicking the endpoint of a line or curve and then the curve. The most important thing to keep in mind is that the work plane is associative to the geometry that you use to define it.

A work axis, like any theoretical axis, can be created by two intersecting faces or planes, by passing through two points, or by passing through a point normal to a face. Axes and planes are infinite, and another great way to build them is to make them coincident with a sketched line segment; doing so extends that piece of line beyond its normal boundaries, to add the capability of using parametric dimension to modify the plane.

You can define a work point at the intersection of an axis and a plane, but it can also be placed on top of a model point, like a corner or the midpoint of an edge, or on a point on a sketch.

How you use Work features will vary based on the type of model you make. In the exercise, the feature you placed from your library wasn't centered on the part Origin planes and axes. You'll use Work features to produce an axis at the center of your part.

The first plane will be based on the midpoint of an edge and defined to be normal or perpendicular to that edge:

1. Locate the Work Features panel on the Model tab, and select the Plane tool.

2. Move your cursor across the top edge of the part closest to you when the component is in the home view. When an icon appears at the midpoint of the edge, select it to define a point the plane will pass through.

3. Move your cursor over the same edge, and select it when it highlights to create the plane. Before you select the edge, a small preview of the plane's orientation should appear, as shown in Figure 4.7.

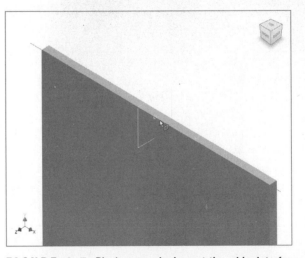

FIGURE 4.7 Placing a work plane at the midpoint of an edge

The next plane will bisect the part by locating itself between the top and bottom of the feature.

4. Start the Plane tool again.

5. This time, pick the narrow face at the top of the Rectangle feature. Doing this limits your other selection options.

6. One available option lets you pick the bottom face. Hover near the bottom; you can even select that face through the part, as shown in Figure 4.8. Pick the bottom face to create the second work plane.

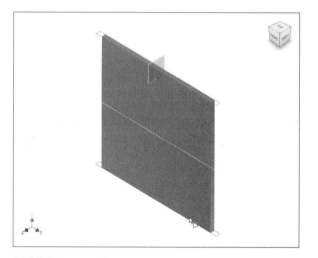

FIGURE 4.8 Previewing the bisecting work plane

The two planes should look like Figure 4.9.

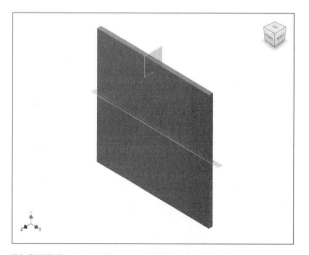

FIGURE 4.9 The two additional work planes

7. In the Work Feature panel, select the Axis tool.

8. Pick the first and second work planes. Doing so creates the work axis at the intersection of the two planes.

9. The two work planes are moved under the Work Axis 1 feature in the Browser. Turn off the visibility of the new work planes, as you did in Chapter 3, "Moving into the Assembly World." The axis remains visible, as shown in Figure 4.10.

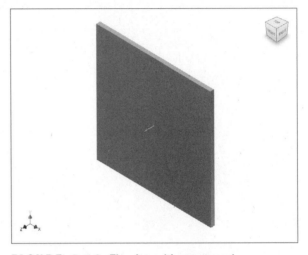

FIGURE 4.10 The plate with a center axis

10. In the Browser, click twice slowly on the words *Work Axis 1*. Done properly, this allows you to rename the feature like you rename a file in Windows Explorer.

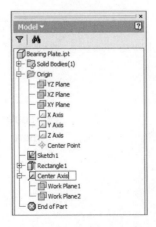

11. Rename the feature **Center Axis**.

12. Save your work.

13. Start the Hole feature.

14. Set the Placement Method to Linear.

15. Pick the large face closest to you.

16. To satisfy the references, select the top and left edge of that face, as shown in Figure 4.10. Set the dimension to the edges at 0.3.

17. Set the hole Termination to Through All and the size to be a clearance hole for a ¼″ fastener, as shown in Figure 4.11.

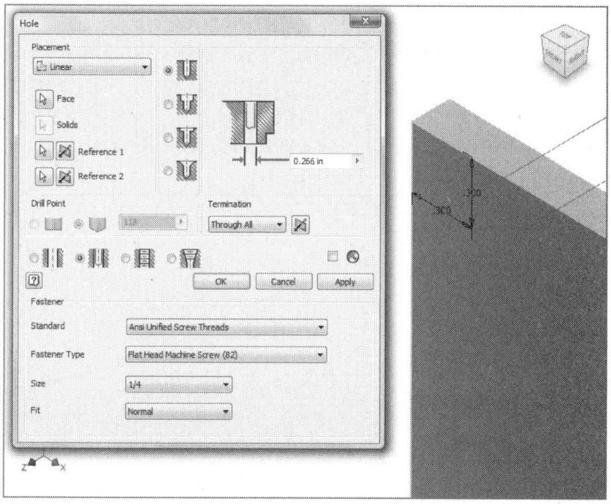

FIGURE 4.11 Locating a hole feature

18. After you've made the selections, click OK to place the hole.

19. In the Pattern panel, select the Rectangular Pattern tool.

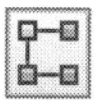

20. Select the Hole 1 feature, and then pick the edges you used to locate the hole to set the direction.

21. Make sure the number of instances is set to 2 for both directions, and set the spacing to 5. You may need to reverse one or more directions for the pattern to match Figure 4.12.

22. Click OK to create the pattern of holes.

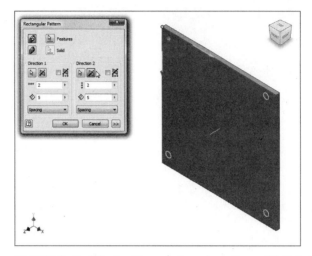

FIGURE 4.12 Creating a rectangular pattern of Hole features

Let's finish the part (temporarily) by adding chamfers to the corners next to the holes.

The Chamfer Tool

Chamfers are a common feature on machined components. This tool allows you to create chamfers on any number of edges in using three methods:

 Distance   This option creates a chamfer by displacing the selected edge down the adjacent faces based on the Distance value.

 Distance and Angle   After selecting the edge to be chamfered, you select a face to base the distance on and then enter an angle for the chamfer face in the dialog box.

 Two Distances   This option uses two distances from the selected edge to create the chamfer face.

More   Additional options are available to limit whether the Chamfer feature follows tangent edges and determine how to treat a corner where three chamfers intersect.

Continue the exercise with these steps:

1. Pick the Chamfer tool from the Modify panel.

2. Select the sharp corners of the plate, as shown in Figure 4.13, and set the value to .2.

3. Click OK to place the chamfers.

FIGURE 4.13 Select the corners of the plate to add chamfers

4. Check the weight of the part. It should now be 1.656 pounds.

5. Compare your finished part to Figure 4.14, and save your work.

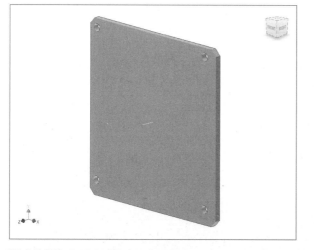

FIGURE 4.14 The bearing plate

These components were simple; but as I said, they probably represent a lot of the components you may create on a regular basis. In the next step, you'll assemble them and add features to complete them:

1. Begin a new assembly file using the Standard (in).iam template.

2. Switch the Ribbon to the View tab, and select the Tile tool from the Windows panel. Your screen should look something like Figure 4.15.

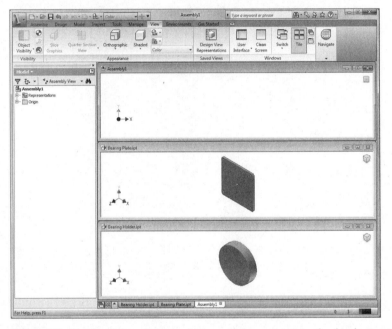

FIGURE 4.15 Using alternate views can help you manage the development of your design.

3. Click the title bar of the Bearing Plate.ipt window to make it the active file. The Browser updates to show the features that make up your latest creation.

4. In the Browser, click and drag the icon next to the words *Bearing Plate.ipt* onto the part of the screen showing the empty assembly, and release.

   Doing so adds the bearing plate to the new assembly as the grounded part.

5. Do the same for the bearing holder. You result should resemble Figure 4.16.

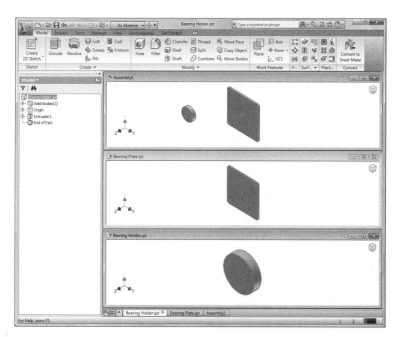

FIGURE 4.16 The components added to the new assembly

6. Maximize the assembly in the Design window.

7. Save the file to your Assemblies folder as Bearing Support.iam.

8. Start the Constrain tool from the Position panel of the Assembly tab.

9. Using a Mate constraint, select the work axis you created in the bearing plate. Then, select the cylindrical surface (see Figure 4.17) of the bearing holder to align the axes of the two parts.

10. Create a Mate constraint between the face of the bearing holder and the front face of the bearing plate, as shown in Figure 4.18

11. Change the color of the bearing holder part by selecting it in the Design window and then picking a color from the pull-down list in the Quick Access Toolbar.

N O T E   Changing the color of a component in the assembly doesn't change the color of the component in its part file.

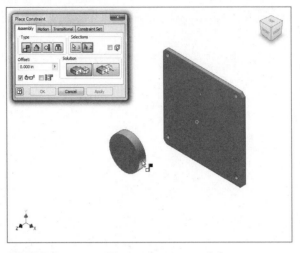

FIGURE 4.17 Aligning the centers of the parts

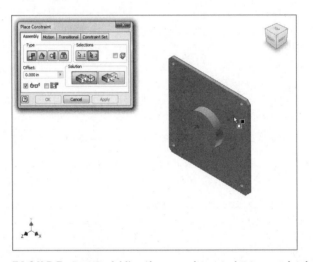

FIGURE 4.18 Adding the second constraint to completely locate the bearing holder

Now, let's make a change to the assembly. It will alter the structure of the assembly and how Inventor "looks" at it in the future. You'll change this assembly into a weldment.

Weldments

In Inventor, a *weldment* is a specialized assembly. To enable the weldment tools, you'll need to convert a saved assembly to a weldment. Doing so will open the Convert to Weldment dialog box (see Figure 4.19), where you'll set your welding standard, the bead material, and the bill of material structure that will be used.

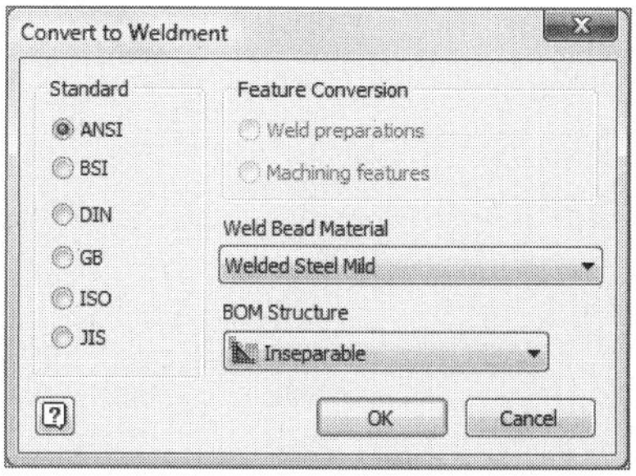

FIGURE 4.19 The Convert to Weldment dialog box

After you convert your assembly to a weldment, you can perform specialized tasks on it, such as adding beveled edges to the parts to prepare them to be welded together. What is important about this is the beveled edge (created with the Chamfer tool) generated as a feature in the weldment assembly. The individual part doesn't show this feature. This follows the traditional workflow used by most manufacturers.

Preparation features (as well as Weld and Machining features added to the assembly after it's welded) are placed in the Browser above the parts of the assembly. This keeps things organized, because these features are all part of the assembly.

A final feature of a weldment is the ability to have Inventor generate weld annotations in the 3D model, which you can reuse in the 2D drawing.

Let's convert your assembly to a weldment and finish it as a single component rather than an assembly of two separate components:

1. To make the conversion, go to the Convert panel of the Assembly tab, and select the Convert to Weldment tool.

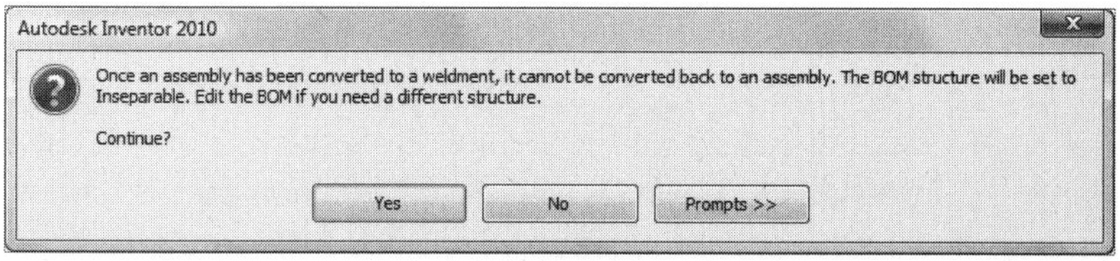

2. A message appears, warning you that if you convert your assembly to a weldment the action can't be reverted. Click Yes to continue making the conversion.

3. In the Convert to Weldment dialog, set Standard to ANSI, Weld Bead Material to Welded Steel Mild, and BOM Structure to Inseparable, as shown in Figure 4.19.

4. Click OK to complete the conversion.

5. Save the file.

A change occurs in the Browser. Along with the components, it now lists subcategories for Preparations, Welds, and Machining. These groups appear above an End of Features icon. This indicates that adding a Weld feature or a Preparation feature will only affect the weldment assembly — these changes won't propagate down to the original parts.

A new tab appears in the Ribbon and becomes active. The Weld tab contains the tools relevant to welding operations; like other tabs, it makes accessing the tools easier.

Now that you have a weldment assembly, let's weld the two parts together:

1. Click the Welds tool in the Process panel.
   Doing so activates the tools in the Weld panel.

2. Click the Fillet tool in the Weld panel to begin placing a fillet weld in the assembly.

3. You need to pick at least two faces to define the placement of the weld. For the first face, pick the cylindrical face of the bearing holder. The selection tool will continue to add faces to the first selection set until you select the icon for the second selection set.

4. Click the button for the second selection set. Pick the face of the bearing plate to which the bearing holder is mated.
   A preview of the weld appears around the base of the bearing holder.

5. Set the Bead height to .13. Set the Intermittency length to .25 and the spacing to 1.4, as shown in Figure 4.20.

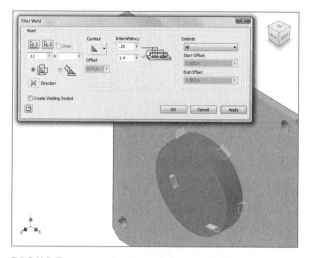

FIGURE 4.20 Applying a chain weld around the bearing holder

6. Pick the Machining icon from the Process panel. As with the welds, this activates a specific set of modeling tools.

7. Start the Hole tool from the Preparation and Machining panel.

8. Set Placement to Concentric.

9. Pick the top face of the bearing holder for the plane and the circular edge for the concentric reference.

10. Switch the type to Counterbore. Set the diameter to **1.27**, the depth to **.65**, and the drill diameter to **1**. Set Termination to Through All, as shown in Figure 4.21.

11. Pick the OK button to create the bore.

12. Pick the Chamfer tool from the Preparation and Machining panel.

13. Add a chamfer to the top inside edge of the new bore, as shown in Figure 4.22. Make the Distance value of the chamfer 1mm. Inventor does the calculation for you; but what's more important is that if you edit the chamfer later, it will remember that the original value was 1mm.

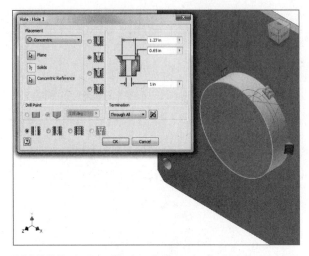

FIGURE 4.21   Placing the bore in the bearing support

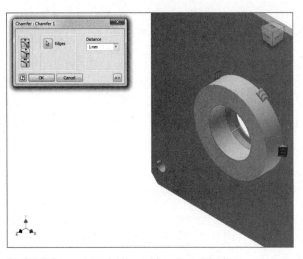

FIGURE 4.22   Adding a chamfer to the bore

14. When the settings are correct, click OK.

15. Click Return to Parent. This takes you out of the current weldment-process tools.

16. Save the file.

17. Select the bearing holder from the tabs at the bottom of the Design window to switch to that file.

Doing so reveals that none of the geometry added in the weldment machining processes has affected this part.

Now, we'll give you your first look at one of the most valuable capabilities of Inventor: creating 2D drawings.

Drawing Views

Many people exploring the idea of using a 3D design tool are probably creating 2D drawings for a living. Normally, I like to introduce users to 2D drawings as quickly as possible because it excites people when they see Inventor's potential. I'm convinced that Inventor's ease of use and the accuracy of the 2D drawings it generates are one of the best reasons to use it.

When I started out in design and engineering, the drafting board was still king. Learning AutoCAD made me see how much more easily edits could be performed; but it also made me aware of the redundancy of creating multiple lines to represent the same geometry in various orthographic projections.

When you create 2D drawing views from Inventor's 3D data, the views calculate themselves and are associative to any changes you make to the 3D model. Change the size of a hole in a part, for example, and any objects or hidden lines in the 2D drawing that represent the hole will be updated automatically.

Beginning a New Drawing from a Template

You've started all the files you've created so far by using a template. A drawing is no different. You can select any template that is appropriate for the drawing you want to create. Just because components may have been built using English units doesn't prevent you from using a Metric template.

One of the most common modifications people need early on in using Inventor is to personalize their title block so it fits the standard they're accustomed to. In this exercise, you'll create a new title block and do a basic customization to raise your awareness of where to begin. You can also import an existing AutoCAD drawing and use it as a title block for Inventor drawings.

Let's create a new drawing and set it up for your needs:

1. Click the New icon on the Quick Access Toolbar, and start a new file based on the ANSI (in).dwg template in the English tab.

   DWG? Yes, DWG. The file you just created can be read by current releases of AutoCAD without someone you send this to needing to have Autodesk Inventor.

   You can use some exciting workflows to share a DWG drawing between AutoCAD-based products and newer Autodesk technologies like Inventor. The rule of thumb, however, is that views created with Inventor are edited and dimensioned only with Inventor's tools.

2. In the Browser, expand the `Drawing Resources` folder. Note the many classes of objects that are built in.

3. Right-click ANSI - Large Title block in the `Title Blocks` folder under `Drawing Resources` in the Browser. Select Copy from the context menu or press Ctrl+C on the keyboard to copy the title block to the Windows Clipboard.

4. Right-click the `Title Blocks` folder under `Drawing Resources` and pick Paste from the context menu to create a new `Copy of ANSI - Large` title block.

5. Slowly click the name of the new title block twice, and rename it NER. Now you've created a new title block, but it's just a clone of the original. Let's give it a couple of unique features.

6. Right-click the NER title block, and select Edit from the context menu. The underpinnings of the title block appear, as shown in Figure 4.23.

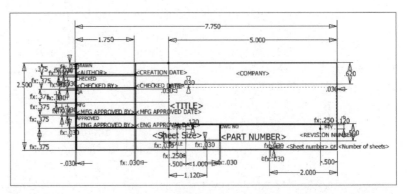

FIGURE 4.23 The power of parametric dimensioning even makes defining the title block easier.

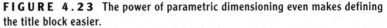

7. Change the 7.75 overall width of the title block to 8.

8. Right-click QA in the title block, and choose Edit Text.

9. In the Format Text dialog (see Figure 4.24), change QA to MASS and click OK to save the change.

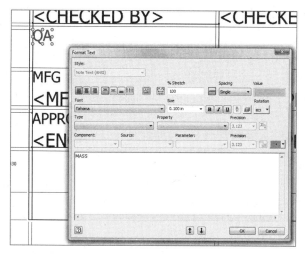

FIGURE 4.24 Editing the title block text

10. Right-click the text that reads *<ENG APPROVED BY>*, and copy it to the Windows Clipboard.

11. Paste a copy back into the title block, and click and drag it under the word *MASS*.

12. Right-click the new text, and select Edit Text as you did before.
   In this case, the text isn't really text: it's a property value. Among the iProperties of a file is a property for approval. The value you put in the iProperties automatically appears in the title block because the link is here. You need to use a different value for Mass, though.

13. In the dialog box, pick <ENG APPROVED BY>, and press the Delete key to dispose of the current value.

14. From the Type pull-down just above the text window, select Physical Properties - Model. From the Property pull-down, select Mass.

15. On the Precision pull-down, set the value to two decimal places.

16. Click the Add Text Parameter button to place the value in the dialog box. Compare your dialog to Figure 4.25, and click OK to accept the change.

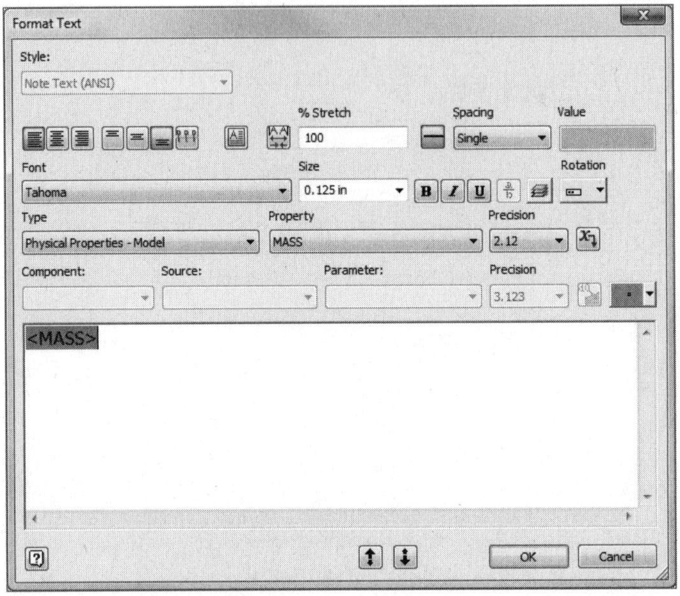

FIGURE 4.25 Adding a physical property to the title block

17. To save your work, right-click in an open part of the Design window and choose Save Title Block. You're prompted to verify that you want to save the edits.

18. Click Yes to save the changes.

The title block in your drawing is still the old title block and therefore doesn't show any changes.

19. Under Sheet:1, delete the ANSI - Large title block.

20. Under Drawing Resources, right-click the new NER title block, and select Insert to place it in the drawing.

By default, all the various linework in an Inventor drawing is black on a light background. Many people want to include more color. To show you the basics of how to do this, let's change a few things in the drawing.

21. Click the Annotate tab on the Format panel, and click the Edit Layers tool.

Doing so opens the Style and Standard Editor dialog. Basically, it's the same dialog you used to create the sheet metal rule in Chapter 2, "Building the Foundation of the Design." The dialog displays the options that are available for modifying layers in the space on the right. A small pencil icon appears next to the Hidden (ANSI) layer, showing that it's active for editing. Let's make some modifications to a couple of layers.

22. Click the black rectangle in the Hidden (ANSI) row. This launches a color-selection menu. Pick red for the layer's new color, as shown in Figure 4.26.

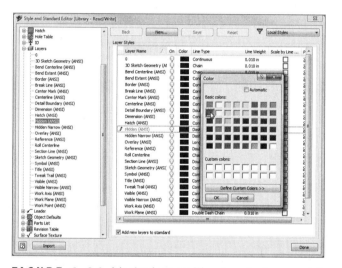

FIGURE 4.26 It's simple to modify colors, linetypes, and line widths for layers.

23. Click OK to accept the new color selection.

24. Use the same process to change the color of the Hidden Narrow (ANSI) layer to red.

25. Change the Center Mark (ANSI) and Centerline (ANSI) layers to green, the Dimension (ANSI) layer to blue, and the Hatch layer to orange. See Figure 4.27 as a reference.

26. Save the changes, and click Done to close the dialog box.

Because Inventor is based on standards and you've edited the standard by modifying the layer properties, you need to save the changes you made back to the standard. You can do this only because you're in Read/Write mode with the libraries in your project file. With multiple users, you wouldn't want this ability left open. You may also want to go back and change these settings after you're finished with this book.

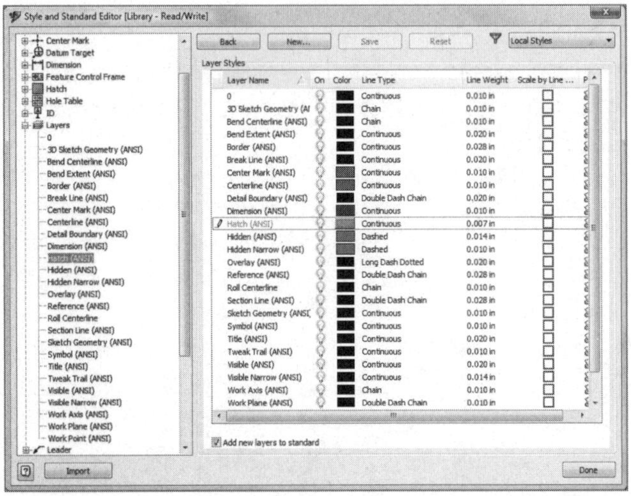

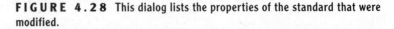

FIGURE 4.27 Make the other changes to the layer settings.

27. Click the Save button in the Styles and Standards panel of the Manage tab. Doing so opens the dialog shown in Figure 4.28.

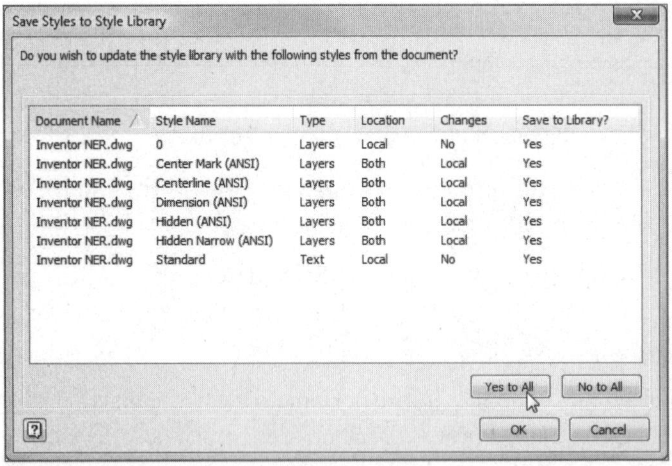

FIGURE 4.28 This dialog lists the properties of the standard that were modified.

28. You want to save all the changes to the layers to the standard, so click the Yes to All button and then the OK button to update the standard.

29. A safety message appears, warning you that you're modifying the standard. Click Yes to approve the changes.

Again, these types of changes aren't to be taken lightly. With that said, it's easy to change things back if you don't like the way they look.

Creating a New Template

Creating a new title block or modifying your border is great, but you won't want to have to do it repeatedly. You need to add this drawing as a template that can be used over and over again:

1. Click the Application menu (the big I icon) at upper left in the Inventor window. Pick the arrow to the right of Save As, and select Save as Template from the list of options.

When you select a template for a new file, the dialog contains three tabs: Default, English, and Metric. The English and Metric tabs exist because there are English and Metric folders under Templates. Adding another folder to this location adds another tab to the New File dialog. This is a great way to easily organize your template files.

2. Click the Create New Folder icon, and name the new folder **NER**. Pressing Enter activates this new folder in the dialog.

3. Give your new file the name Inventor NER.dwg, and click Save.

4. Inventor warns you that you're saving a file outside of the active project. Normally, this is a bad thing; but because you're creating a new template, click Yes to approve.

5. Close the drawing file that is open in Inventor. Say No to saving changes as it closes.

6. Create a new file using the Inventor NER.dwg template in the NER tab.

You've now come full circle. You created a new file from an existing template to create a new template from which to create a new file. I'm sure you've done that more than once before in other applications, but it's good to know that the basics are the same in Inventor.

Just as a part file needs a base feature and an assembly needs a base part, the drawing starts everything with a base view.

Creating Base Views

Detail drawings frequently require multiple views to describe the geometry properly. Because of this need, Inventor allows you to create a *base* view and project views from it.

The first view that you place on a drawing must be a base view, regardless of its orientation. You can have multiple base views on each drawing. The base view acts as a *parent view* and establishes initial scaling and other view properties for *child views*. You'll create child views later and project them from the base view.

1. To create a base view, you can select the Base tool from the Create panel on the Place Views tab or right-click a blank portion of the drawing sheet in the Design window and choose Base View. Figure 4.29 shows the context menu that appears when you right-click an empty portion of the screen.

> **NOTE**   In the coming pages, you'll find that the right-click menus contain a sizable percentage of the most common tools that Inventor users need the most. Experienced Inventor users often use this phrase: "When in doubt, right-click."

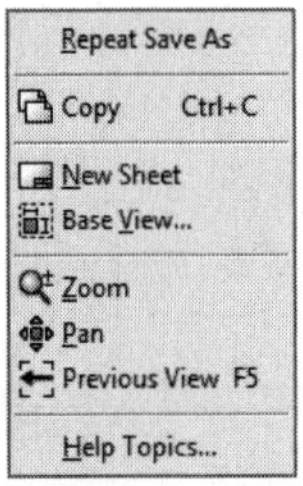

Repeat Save As

Copy   Ctrl+C

New Sheet
Base View...

Zoom
Pan
Previous View   F5

Help Topics...

FIGURE 4.29 Right-click an empty part of the screen, and choose Base View from the context menu to create a new base view.

After you initiate creating a base view, the Drawing View dialog box shown in Figure 4.30 appears. This dialog box is your toolkit for setting up different views of your drawing. In addition to its options and tool groups, notice the Component, Model State, and Display Options tabs; each offers various settings that control the display of geometry in the view:

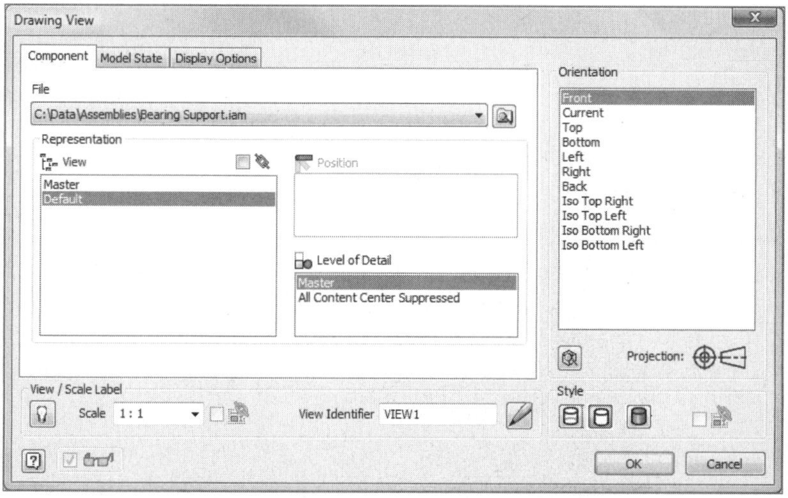

FIGURE 4.30 The Drawing View dialog box is your starting point for defining a base view.

Component   The Component tab allows you to select from a list of files that are currently open in Inventor or browse for other files on your computer or network using the icon to the right of the file list fly-out. If you're using a Vault project, you can also browse the Vault for a file.

Model State   Some files can be presented in different conditions or *states* in a drawing. This tab controls what form of the geometry is displayed in the drawing view.

Display Options   This tab controls how the geometry is represented in the drawing view. Selecting different standard views (Top, Front, Iso Top Right, and so on) from the list at right changes the drawing view preview that appears when you start the Base View command.

At upper right in this dialog box is the Orientation group. This is a listing of standard viewpoints that corresponds with the names on the ViewCube. Selecting different standard views from the list changes the drawing view preview that appears when you start the Base View command.

If none of the predefined views is suitable or you'd like to place a perspective view on a drawing, you can click the Change View Orientation icon below the list of standard orientations. This switches your view to the model with an abbreviated standard toolbar showing only view-manipulation tools. When you've found the point of view that you want to use, select the green check mark on the left to return to the Drawing View dialog box. The Base View tool will now consider the view-position changes to be your current view.

At lower left, you'll find the Scale control and display. The icon with a light bulb determines whether the view's scale and label are to be displayed. The Scale fly-out allows you to select the scale for the view. You can choose from a list of standard scale ratios or simply type in the value that you would like. As you change the scale value, the drawing-view preview also changes size, letting you more easily select a scale that you like. Parts and assemblies are always created in full scale, so this value controls their apparent size on the drawing. Dimensions applied to the view are always accurate to the model, so the use of nonstandard scales is allowable.

To the right of the Scale control and display is the View Identifier field. If you would like to give the view a specific name, such as Front, you can enter it in this field. The value you enter appears in the Browser as the name of the view; and, if you choose to make the scale and label visible, this value is also the name displayed with the view.

At lower right is the Style group. These three buttons can make things very interesting. Hidden Lines generates line objects for edges that aren't visible from the point of view selected. Hidden Lines Removed doesn't generate those lines. One of these two buttons will always be used as long as the Style group is available. In the exercises for this chapter, you'll learn to make them accessible if you choose to. The third button, Shaded, is optional for any view. It generates a shaded view of model geometry in the drawing view.

Defining the Base View

Defining the base view is always the first step, but it's also important to think about what the base view should be. Apply the same methodology you would use with any drawing, and choose the most descriptive point of view to define your base view:

1. Select the Base tool in the Create panel on the Place Views tab.

2. From the File pull-down, select Bearing Support.iam as the file you want your base view to represent.

3. Move your cursor so that you can see the preview of the view on the drawing sheet, as shown in Figure 4.31.

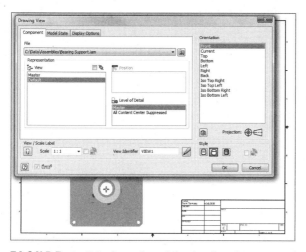

FIGURE 4.31 A preview of the drawing view ensure that you're getting the view you need.

4. Change Orientation to Bottom in the dialog, and observe the preview over the page.

5. Experiment with other standard Orientation options, and then return to using Front.

6. Click in the drawing sheet to generate the drawing view in the location of the preview.

7. When the view is placed, move your cursor near the view. The boundary of the view highlights (on my screen, it's a red, hidden-line font).

8. When the view is highlighted, click near the edge when the glyph appears on the cursor, and drag the view to a location similar to Figure 4.32.

9. Click the Save tool on the Quick Access Toolbar.

10. When the dialog opens, create a new folder named Drawings in the Data folder. See Figure 4.33.

11. Save your file with the name that it's automatically given (Bearing Support.dwg) in the Drawings folder.

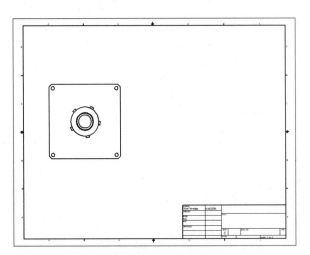

F I G U R E   4 . 3 2 Relocating drawing views is as easy as clicking and dragging the mouse.

F I G U R E   4 . 3 3 You can add folders as you're saving files.

Well, that's it. That's all it takes to create a drawing view of your assembly. Even though this is a very simple assembly, you'll find that placing views of more complex files just as easy.

Now, let's work with a tool you'll use more often than the Base tool when creating detail drawings: the Projected tool.

Creating a Projected View

A projected view can be a standard orthographic projection, or it can be an isometric view of just about any kind of parent view. Any drawing sheet can have more than one base view from which to project child views, and you can also create a projected view from another projected view.

Selecting the Projected tool in the Place Views tab doesn't launch a dialog box. Instead, the cursor changes to a special character or glyph, and on the status bar you're prompted with Select a View. This will be the parent view, to which the view that you'll now create will be associated.

This tool also has a context menu option. As with the other context menu options (and there are many), it has more of a hands-on feel. To access it, you must right-click over an existing view, or you'll only get the pop-up menu that was shown in Figure 4.29. If you right-click over the existing view, you get a much broader set of tools (see Figure 4.34), including Create View, which displays a list of different types of drawing views if you move your mouse cursor over it.

Repeat Base		
Copy	Ctrl+C	
Delete		
Open		
Bill of Materials...		
Create View	▶	
Edit View...		
Alignment	▶	
Apply Design View...		
Rotate		
Annotation Visibility	▶	
Automated Centerlines...		
Retrieve Dimensions...		
Get Model Annotations	▶	
General Dimension Type	▶	
Show Hidden Annotations		
Suppress		
Insert in Model Space		
Zoom		
Pan		
Find in Browser		
Previous View	F5	
How To...		

FIGURE 4.34 The context menu when selected from an existing drawing view

When you've selected your parent view, you'll see a line showing the direction the view will project. You should also see a preview of the item in its position. This helps you confirm that you're getting the view you want in the position on the sheet that you want. Once you select the position for a new view, the tool offers you the opportunity to place additional views. After you click to place a view, a frame appears, showing the perimeter of the new view. When you're finished placing views from this parent view, you can right-click and choose Create to generate the new drawing views.

Defining Projected Views

Projecting a new drawing view from an existing one is where many new Inventor users begin to see the real potential of using 3D to create drawing views:

1. Start the Projected tool.

2. Click the base view if it wasn't selected already.

3. Drag a view preview to the right of the base view, as shown in Figure 4.35.

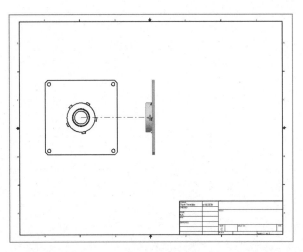

FIGURE 4.35 Previewing projected views makes spacing the views very simple.

4. Click to place the view. The tool will want to continue placing projected views.

5. Place an isometric view in the upper-right corner of the drawing sheet.

6. Right-click, and select Create to place the two new views as shown in Figure 4.36.

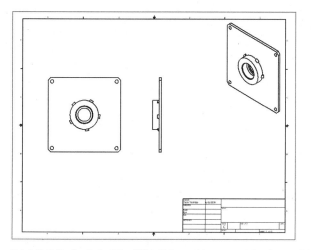

FIGURE 4.36 It's difficult to create osometric views with 2D CAD programs. Not with Inventor, though.

The isometric view you created does a good job of presenting what the assembly looks like to a layman. It doesn't need to be as large as it is, and it could be made even better to add clarity for the reviewer.

7. Double-click the isometric view to bring up the editing dialog box.

8. In the Style group in the lower-right corner, select the Shaded icon.

9. To the left, set Scale to .7, as shown in Figure 4.37.

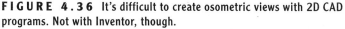

FIGURE 4.37 Modifying the isometric view to make it easier to understand

10. Click OK to make the changes to the view. You may also want to reposition the view closer to the corner.

Because the hole through the assembly was created in the weldment rather than in the individual parts, it's appropriate to have the hole shown in detail in the side view of the assembly. The base view doesn't show hidden lines, so it will be necessary to break the link between the base and the projected view.

11. Double-click the side view, and deselect the check box at lower right. This enables the tools to modify visibility options.

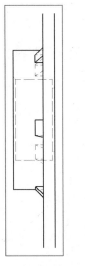

12. Select the Hidden Line option to allow the view to generate the appropriate hidden lines.

13. Click OK to make the changes shown in Figure 4.38.

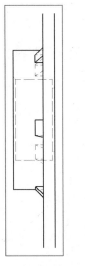

FIGURE 4.38 The hidden lines for the view are generated automatically.

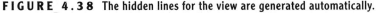

Now, let's create a projected view of a projected view.

14. Create a projected view of the right view to the right of it, under the isometric view, as shown in Figure 4.39.

As you can see in the drawing, the new view and the isometric view are interfering with each other. This is easily corrected.

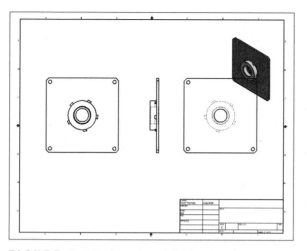

FIGURE 4.39 A preview of the drawing view ensures that you're getting the view you need.

15. Edit the base view to be scaled to .75 and the isometric view to be scaled to .5. See Figure 4.40.

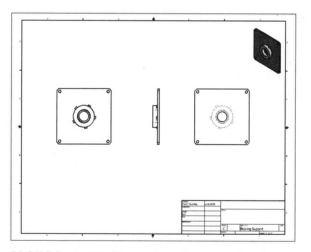

FIGURE 4.40 Nice spacing between drawing views

16. Save the drawing.

After adjusting a view location or two, it looks like you're in good shape to be able to detail your assembly. Let's make a couple more views. As with the Modeling and Assembly tools in Inventor, once you've made a couple of types of drawing views, the others seem to come naturally.

Creating Section Views

Section views are essential for many kinds of drafting and design. The Section View tool in Inventor allows you to define your section view using one or more straight segments and arcs that pass through the part. You can define the *section line* to have a relationship with geometry in the drawing view. There is no limit to the number of section views you can place on a view, and the section line doesn't have to pass entirely through the parent view to build a section view.

Defining the Section View

For this exercise, you'll create a basic section view. Section views can also be created with a section line in several segments:

1. Zoom into the base view so that you can see space beneath it in the Design window.

2. Start the Section tool in the Create panel.

3. Select the base view to see the prompt "Enter the endpoints of the section line" on the status bar.

4. Gesture over the large hole in the center of the view, and then move to the left. You see a dotted line infer the center of the hole. As you move outside of the part perimether, the inference line may show the midpoint of the side of the part. Either is acceptable. See Figure 4.41.

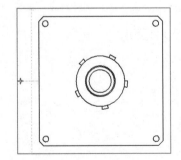

FIGURE 4.41 Inference lines help guide you when placing section lines.

5. With the inference line still showing, click to the left of the base view and drag the section line through the view. Place the second endpoint to the right of the base view.

6. The tool lets you place many segments. Right-click, and select Continue from the context menu to see a preview of the section view.

7. Place the view using the defaults in the location previewed in Figure 4.42.

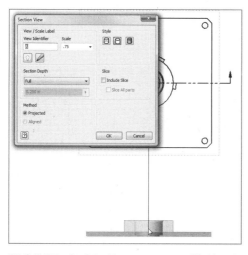

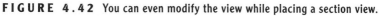

FIGURE 4.42 You can even modify the view while placing a section view.

The view placed is already hatched and ready to be used. Let's place one more view in this drawing sheet.

Detail Views

Selecting the scale for your drawing views is important, and being able to change that scale after the fact is great as well. Sometimes, though, you need a closer look at a portion of the part or assembly for clarity. You need a view with a different scale than the others. You need a *detail view*.

The Detail tool must have a parent view selected, like the section or projected view. When that parent view is selected, the Detail View dialog box (Figure 4.43) appears. This dialog box has quite a few options, but most of them are ones you've seen before, such as the Style and View Identifier options. Other options include the following:

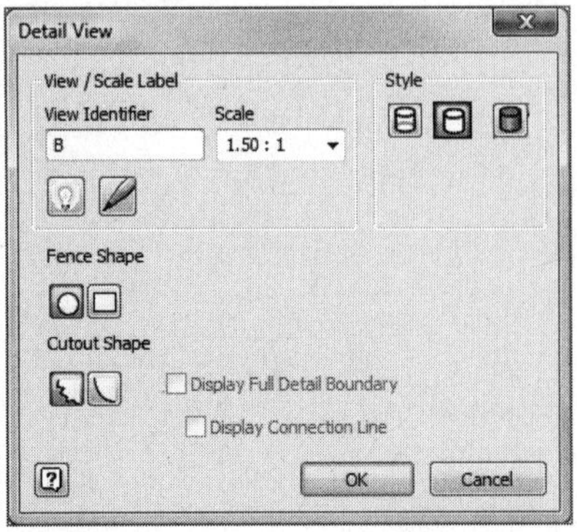

FIGURE 4.43   The Detail View dialog box

Scale   In the Scale area, you can select a standard view scale or type in a custom setting.

Fence Shape   This option defines the shape of your detail view's boundary.

Cutout Shape   This option specifies whether the detail view displays a smooth or a jagged edge. Selecting a smooth edge makes the Display Full Detail Boundary option available.

Display Full Detail Boundary   This option causes the boundary for the view to be displayed in the parent view and the detail view. Selecting this option makes the Display Connection Line Option available. If you select this option, a line is drawn between the boundaries in the parent and detail views to better illustrate the source of the detail view. This setting was added to support some standards that require this additional clarity.

Creating a Detail View

Use this exercise to create a quick detail view that will help to clarify the drawing:

1. Click the Detail tool in the Create panel.

2. Pick the section view to be the parent view.

3. Set the Scale value to 2:1. Leave the Fence Shape Circular and the Cutout Shape Jagged.

4. Drag the fence for the detail view over the section view, as shown in Figure 4.44. Your first click will be the center of the circle.

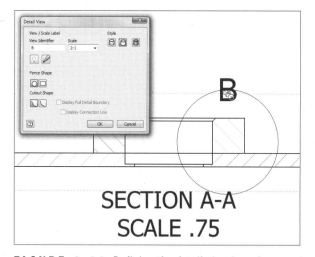

FIGURE 4.44 Defining the detail view boundary can be done in different ways.

5. As soon as you click the radius of the fence, a preview of the detail view appeaser. Place it to the right of the section view. See Figure 4.45.

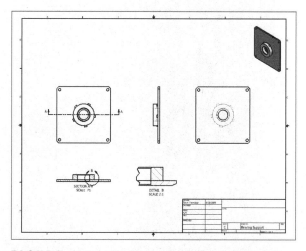

FIGURE 4.45 Placing the detail view in the drawing

In just a few minutes, you've managed to place drawing views that could take an hour or more using a traditional 2D tool. In the next exercises, you'll add dimensions and detail to these views to make this a more complete drawing.

Detailing Tools

As much as I appreciate the ease with which Inventor places drawing views, I think I like the detailing tools even more. These tools make finishing the detail drawing a snap.

More than just dimensions, detail drawings need special annotation characters to do the job completely. The detailing tools are located on the Annotate tab. They're organized in a logical fashion, as you've already seen with other tabs and panels.

You won't complete the drawing, and you'll likely create some redundant annotations. Just be patient, and keep in mind that the goal isn't to create a great drawing, but for you to learn the tools to make a great drawing of your own products.

You'll start with the basics by placing a few center marks.

The Center Mark Tool

It doesn't seem like this would logically be the first detail tool to learn, but center marks and their variations are an important detailing item in mechanical drafting. I think you'll appreciate how easy it is to place these items.

When you look at the Center Mark tool in the Symbols panel of the Annotation tab, you'll see that it has three other icons around it. The other icons are for Centerline and Centerline Bisector, which we'll also explore, and Centered Pattern, which is a powerful tool but also easily learned.

Placing a Center Mark in a View

In this exercise, you'll create center marks the slow way:

1. Zoom in on the view of the back of the assembly on the right.

2. Click the Center Mark tool in the Symbols panel.

3. Move over one of the holes in the view. As you near a hole, it highlights. When this happens, click the mouse; the center mark is placed.

4. Place center marks on the five holes in the view.

5. Press the Esc key to finish the tool, and compare your work to Figure 4.46.

6. Right-click the center mark at upper left.

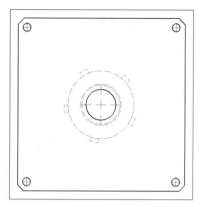

FIGURE 4.46 Place the center marks individually.

7. On the context menu, pick Edit then Align to Edge.

8. Pick the chamfer near the hole to align the center mark to it.
   It's also possible to place multiple center marks at the same time in more than one view. Let's do that next.

9. Zoom back out to the full sheet.

10. Holding your Ctrl key, click the front and side views to select both views at the same time.

11. Right-click in the Design window, and select Automated Centerlines.

In the Automated Centerlines dialog are options for the type of geometry on which you want to place centerlines in the Apply To group. In the Projection group, you can limit whether the centerlines are applied to objects in the view with the axis normal, axis parallel, or both.

12. Set Apply To for Hole features only, and set the Projection to axis normal and axis parallel.

13. Click OK to create the centerlines as shown in Figure 4.47.

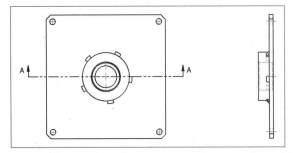

FIGURE 4.47 You can place center marks and centerlines in several views simultaneously.

Now you'll create a manually placed centerline.

Creating a Centerline Bisector

Sometimes you need to display a centerline but don't have circles or arcs to use as a basis for the Centerline tool. You'll also often want to show a centerline down the middle of parts or features such as shafts, conical parts, slots, or the side view of a hole.

In the section view, you can see the inside of the hole. The Centerline tool allows you to find the center of the hole even from the side, but the Centerline Bisector tool does this and lets you bisect nonparallel edges as well. When you select the tool, it prompts you to click a location like the other center mark tools do; but in this case, it's looking for line segments, not arcs or circles:

1. Start the Centerline Bisector tool from the Symbols panel.

2. In the section view, pick both sides of the elevated cylinder. See Figure 4.48.

3. End the Centerline Bisector tool.

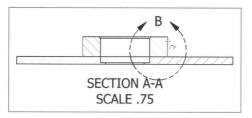

FIGURE 4.48 Select the two edges for placing the centerline.

4. In the section view, click and drag the View callout down to give the new centerline more room.

5. Click and drag the endpoints of the centerline until you can clearly see the linetype. See Figure 4.49.

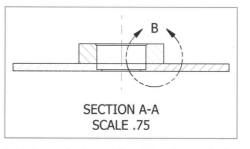

FIGURE 4.49 Pick and drag to edit the length of centerlines.

You'll have a chance to use the Centerline tool later in the chapter. For now, let's add some dimensions to the drawing.

Placing Dimensions in Inventor

Simple tools like the Center Mark tools are necessary to create drawings correctly. You'll learn other drawing tools in later chapters, but for now let's examine the ever-important dimensioning tools.

Your approach to dimensioning will vary with the national and corporate standards that you must adhere to. The dimensioning tools in Inventor follow the standards that you select for their appearance, but the basic tools are the same regardless of what that standard is. In this chapter, we'll discuss the General Dimension, Baseline Dimension, Hole/Thread Notes, Retrieve Dimension, and various dimension-editing tools.

The General Dimension Tool

Inventor has a few different tools for placing dimensions on drawing views. The one you'll work with first is the General Dimension tool. This tool lets you add dimensions to a drawing view one at a time; but as you'll see, it's a tool with multiple functions.

The single General Dimension tool can place linear, diameter, radius, aligned, and angular dimensions based solely on the types of geometry you select while placing the dimension and a few context-menu options. When you begin part modeling, you'll see this again.

To access the General Dimension command, you can click the Dimension tool in the Annotate tab; or, in most cases, you can simply press the D key on your keyboard.

The General Dimension tool is *click-sensitive*. This means that depending on the type of geometry you select, you're offered different dimension types. It's much easier to show how this works than to explain it. So, in the following exercises, let's try out some of the ways you can use the General Dimension tool.

The Inventor Help system for AutoCAD users shows five different AutoCAD dimensioning commands that are replaced by the single General Dimension command in Inventor. By the end of this chapter, I'm sure you won't miss any of those extra buttons.

Using the General Dimension Tool

You'll add a couple of dimensions to your drawing now. Keep in mind that you're not focusing on doing proper drafting:

1. Zoom in on the rear view of the assembly.

2. Start the Dimension tool, and click the top line of the drawing view.

3. Move your cursor above the view. At certain increments, the dimension preview appears dotted, as shown in Figure 4.50. This represents proper spacing based on the active standard.

4. Click to place the dimension when the dimension highlights.
   The Dimension tool is still active to allow you to continue placing dimensions. As long as it's willing, let's take advantage of it.

5. Move the cursor to the large hole in the middle of the assembly. A glyph appears, showing a circle with a diameter dimension.

6. Click to get a dimension preview.
   As you move the preview of the diameter dimension, it snaps at 15° increments. This aids in creating clean, consistent drawings.

7. Place the dimension as shown in Figure 4.51.

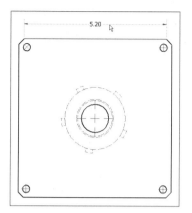

FIGURE 4.50 Dimension previews highlight when properly spaced.

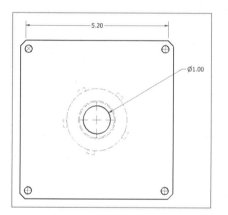

FIGURE 4.51 Adding a diameter dimension

Now for an angular dimension.

8. Pick the bottom line.

9. With the bottom line selected, pick the edge that represents the chamfer on the left. As you near the edge, a glyph appears, showing an angular dimension.

10. Place the dimension as shown in Figure 4.52.

11. Pick the hole at upper right, and then pick the hole at lower right.

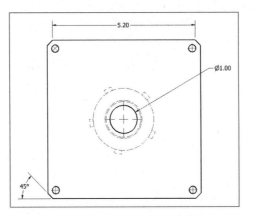

FIGURE 4.52 Selecting non-parallel lines initiates an angular dimension.

12. Place the dimension as shown in Figure 4.53.

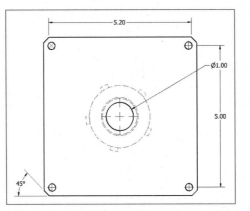

FIGURE 4.53 Dimensions can be placed between many entities.

You can place dimensions between combinations of points and edges. Note that the dimension line of the dimension you just placed has been broken to keep the diameter value clear.

13. Select the hole at upper left.

14. Pick the chamfer edge at upper left, and place the dimension as shown in Figure 4.54.

The last dimension value may have been placed on the side of the dimension that you didn't want. You can change the location of the dimension value and relocate the dimension itself.

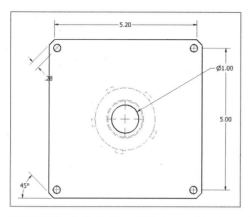

FIGURE 4.54 The ability to combine type of entities ensures flexibility.

15. Press the Esc key to end the Dimension tool.

16. Click the text of the dimension, and drag it to a new location as shown in Figure 4.55.

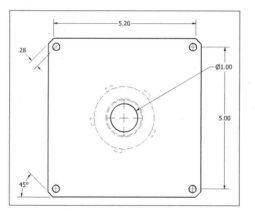

FIGURE 4.55 Modifying the location of dimension and its value is easy.

17. Zoom in on the section view.

18. Use the Dimension tool, and select the edge at the top of the hole.

19. Place the dimension as shown in Figure 4.56.
    Note that the dimension placed in the section view is a linear diameter.

20. Save the drawing.

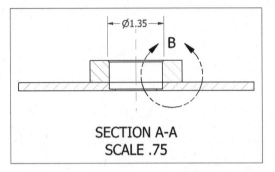

FIGURE 4.56 Add a linear diameter to the section view.

The Baseline Dimension Tool

Placing dimensions one at a time is effective, and the tools Inventor has to assist with proper spacing of dimensions are helpful, but they're no match for placing multiple dimensions simultaneously. Placing multiple dimensions that are spaced properly from a baseline is a basic need for mechanical drafting.

The Baseline Dimension tool allows you to place multiple individual dimensions at once. When you start the command, you can select the geometry you want, right-click, and select Continue. This gives you a preview of the dimensions that will be placed. It's important to note that the first geometry you select will be used as the base or *origin* of all the dimensions. After you place the initial dimensions, you can select other geometry and add a new dimension to the group in its proper position. When you've finished placing the dimensions, you must tell Inventor that you're done selecting geometry by right-clicking and selecting the Create option.

These dimensions won't preview suggested placements with dotted geometry. But if you move your cursor slowly, the tool pauses when it finds strategic placements.

The Baseline Dimension Set tool allows you to place multiple dimensions as a group so that a change to the appearance of one will affect all of them. After the group has been placed, it's possible to separate members if you want to make them unique. You can also change the origin of the group after the dimensions have been placed.

Creating a Baseline Dimension Set

As I said, creating a group of baseline dimensions or a baseline dimension set uses the same process. Let's place some dimensions and do some experimentation:

    1. Zoom in on the front view on the left side of the drawing sheet.

2. Start the Baseline Set tool from the Dimension panel.

3. Click the bottom line for the first edge of the dimension set.

4. Pick the center marks for the two holes on the left, the hole in the center, and the top for the edges to dimension.

5. Right-click, and select Continue.

6. Place the dimension set to the left, as shown in Figure 4.57.

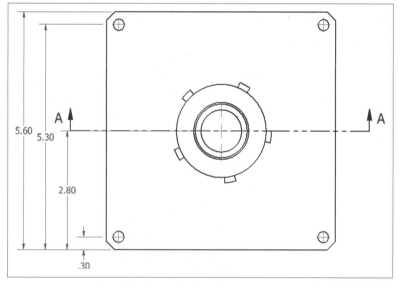

FIGURE 4.57 Adding a baseline set dimension

7. Right-click, and select Create to finish.

Hole/Thread Notes

The General Dimension tool is extremely flexible but creates relatively simple dimensions. The Hole/Thread Notes tool exchanges some flexibility for power. When you apply a hole note or a thread callout to your drawing view, the only pieces of geometry that highlight are holes or external threads. This is a good thing.

Adding Hole/Thread Notes to the Drawing

In the following exercise, you'll create a hole note and modify it:

1. Restore your view in the Design window to show the front view of the assembly.

2. Find the Hole and Thread tool in the Feature Notes panel.

3. Select the hole in the upper-right corner, and place the previewed callout as shown in Figure 4.58.

4. Press Esc to finish the command.

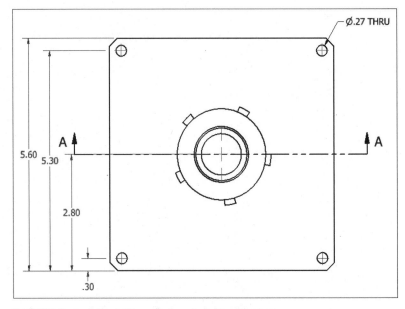

FIGURE 4.58 Adding a hole note to the drawing

The hole note has some additional functions, such as the ability to declare the type of fastener or thread for which it's a clearance hole. For your purposes, you'll ask the hole note to tell how many holes of this size are in the view.

5. Double-click the hole note displayed in the drawing.

6. When the Edit Hole Note dialog appears, place your cursor in the text window at the very beginning.

7. Click the QTY icon. Doing so inserts a note that displays the number of holes.

8. Compare your dialog to Figure 4.59, and then click OK to change the hole note.

9. Save the drawing.

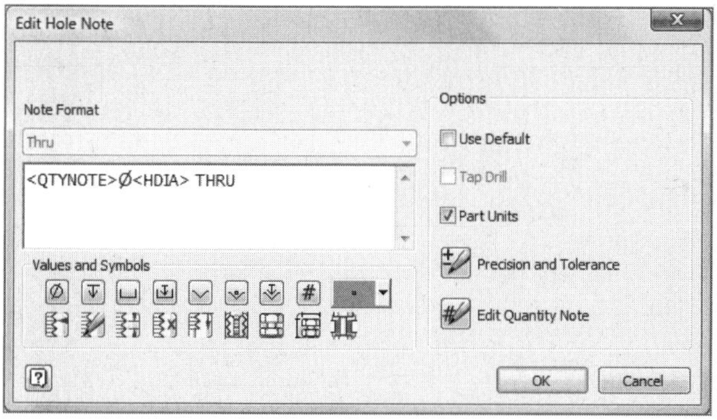

FIGURE 4.59 The Edit Hole Note dialog

Your finished drawing should look like Figure 4.60. Now, you'll modify the dimension to explore some of the options available.

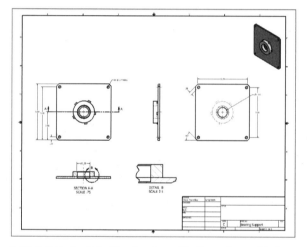

FIGURE 4.60 The drawing with dimensions added

Dimension Editing Tools

Before we move on, I want to walk through the menu in Figure 4.61 and define some of the functions. To access the dialog, right-click on an existing dimension. I'll focus on the group beginning with Copy Properties:

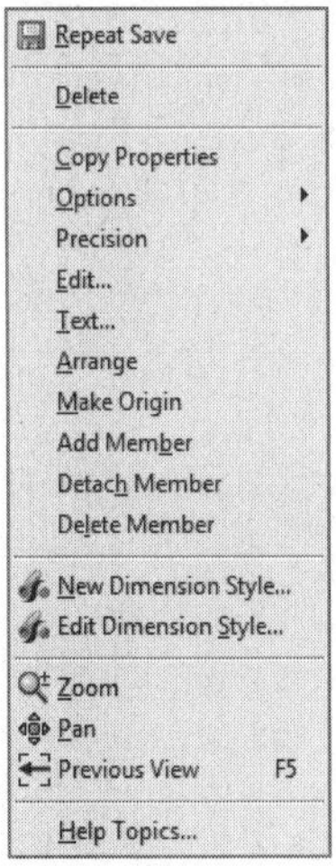

FIGURE 4.61 The Edit dimension context menu

Copy Properties   This function allows you to capture the appearance and precision information of any dimension or dimension group and transfer it directly to another dimension or dimensions in the drawing. The behavior is much like the format painter you'll find in many Windows applications.

Options   This fly-out has tools under it that are specific to the type of dimension you're editing. For example, the options for a radial dimension can force the dimension's leader to be jogged or force Arrowheads Inside. The options for a linear dimension offer the ability to disable either arrowhead or place the dimension text on a leader so it can be more easily read.

Precision   When you place a dimension, its Precision setting is based on the active dimension style. Although most of the model may have the same precision, it's often necessary to give some dimensions more or less precision than the others. This fly-out allows you to override the precision of the dimension style for one that is more suitable for the geometry or process that will be used to create it.

Edit   This offers several options. When the dialog box first opens, the value of the dimension appears as a set of characters: <<>>. These characters indicate that Inventor is obtaining the value of the dimension from the model's actual geometry. If the geometry changes, this value does as well. By checking Hide Dimension Value, you can place substitute text on the dimension, but its value won't change with the part. You can also add text before or after the value for annotation purposes. The other tabs in the dialog box allow you to add tolerance or fit information to your dimension, change the dimension's classification (reference, basic, and so on), or declare the dimension to be an *inspection dimension*. You can also access the Edit Dimension dialog box by double-clicking the dimension text.

Text   This function lets you add text around the dimension, but it also offers the ability to change the formatting of the text's appearance.

Arrange   Arrange is available only if your dimension set includes multiple dimensions. If you delete a member of the set, Arrange allows you to quickly reposition the remaining dimensions into their proper locations.

Make Origin   A baseline dimension is useful because all the dimensions reference one origin. Make Origin changes the origin for a dimension set without your having to re-create the dimension set.

Add Member   After you've created a dimension set, you can use Add Member to include new geometry in the dimension set. The new dimension automatically locates itself and rearranges other dimensions if need be.

Detach Member   When you use Detach Member, you're separating one of the dimensions in the set so it can be edited as though it were placed on its own. This is very helpful if you want to create a dimension set with many members, of which a handful need a different precision or appearance.

Delete Member   This removes the dimension from the set and deletes it from the screen. The remaining dimensions don't automatically reposition themselves, so it's common to use the Arrange tool after deleting a member.

Putting the Dimension Editing Tools to Work

Now, let's make a few changes to the dimensions to get a feel for some of the options:

1. Zoom in on the back view of the assembly.

2. Double-click the 5.20 dimension.

3. In the Edit Dimension dialog, pick the Precision and Tolerance tab, and select Reference from the Tolerance Method list. See Figure 4.62.

4. Click OK to update the dimension.

5. Double-click the 5.00 dimension.

6. Set Tolerance Method to Symmetric.

7. Set Primary Unit to 3.123 (three place decimal).

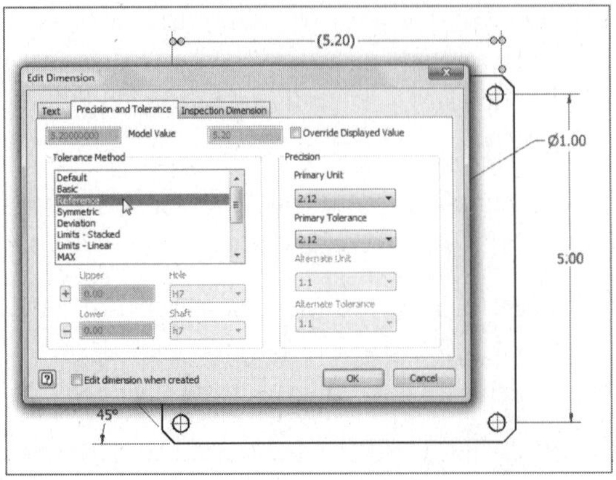

FIGURE 4.62 Picking Tolerance Method modifies the dimension.

8. Set Primary Tolerance to three places also.

9. Set the Upper tolerance value to 0.005, as shown in Figure 4.63.

10. Click OK to accept the new tolerance values.

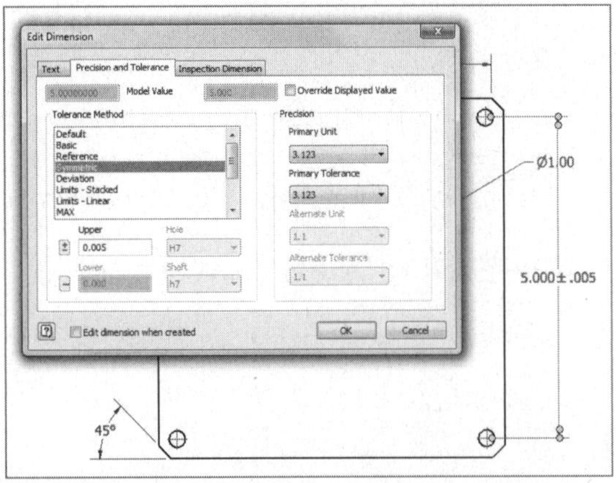

FIGURE 4.63 Changing the dimension tolerance

11. Zoom out so you can see the front view and rear view.

12. Right-click the 5.60 member of the baseline set, and select Detach Member from the context menu.

13. Right-click the 5.60 dimension, and select Move Dimension from the context menu.

14. Pick the rear view.

   The 5.60 dimension has been separated from the other dimensions, so it will no longer be affected by changes to the style. The 5.60 dimension is moved to the rear view and located with the next appropriate space.

15. Right-click the 1in. diameter, pick the Options fly-out, and deselect the Single Dimension Line option.

16. Right-click the 45° dimension, pick the Options fly-out, and select the Leader option.

17. In the Design window, pick and drag the 45° text so that it looks like Figure 4.64.

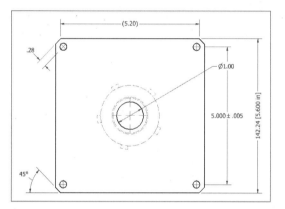

FIGURE 4.64 You can modify dimension leaders and text to make the dimensions easier to understand.

18. Make sure the Annotate tab is active.

19. Pick the 5.60 dimension.

20. In the Annotate tab, pick the lower pull-down in the Format panel.

21. From that list, pick the Default - mm [in] (ANSI) dimension style.

   The edits should appear as they do in Figure 4.64.

22. Zoom out to see your entire drawing, as shown in Figure 4.65.

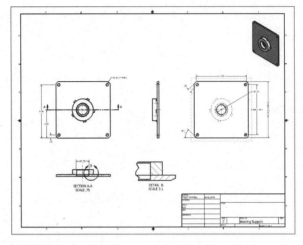

FIGURE 4.65 The completed drawing with dimensions

23. Save your work.

As you've learned in this exercise, you can access just about any modification with a double- or right-click. Now, we'll take a minute to see where the real power of Inventor drawings comes from: associativity to the 3D model.

Associativity

The principle of *associativity* simply means that any change made to the part or assembly documented in your drawing is reflected in the drawing. This is the crux of creating 2D detail drawings from 3D geometry. So far, you've been able to exploit the 3D model to quickly create a drawing. Now it's time to see the payoff: You'll change the 3D model and have the drawing update.

Drawing View Associativity

In this exercise, you'll modify the bore in the weldment and see the drawing update accordingly:

1. Right-click in any drawing view, and select Open from the context menu.

This makes the assembly active. If the assembly wasn't open already, this would open the file.

2. Edit Hole1 under the Machining fly-out in the Browser.

3. In the dialog, change the counterbore diameter to **1.57** and the counterbore depth to **.45**. See Figure 4.66.

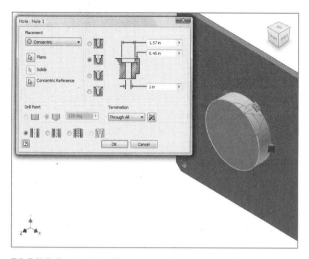

FIGURE 4.66 Updating the hole properties

4. Click OK to update the Hole feature.

5. Save your work.

6. In the Browser, right-click `Bearing Support.iam` and select Open Drawing from the context menu.

Just as opening the 3D model from the drawing activates or opens the model for editing, this option does the same for the 2D drawing.

7. Review the updated drawing. Note the change to the diameter dimension in the section view.

8. If the center mark on the large hole fails to update properly, click the red cross on the Quick Access Toolbar.

9. The first pane lists the problem. Pick Next to see a detailed description of the problem.

10. The problem highlights. Click Next to pick a solution.

11. Select the Delete Symbol option, and click Finish.

Many times, you can easily repair a problem in a drawing or model. In this case, with the overlapping section line, it's probably easier to just replace the center mark.

12. Replace the center mark, but pick the larger diameter to place the new center mark in the front view. See Figure 4.67.

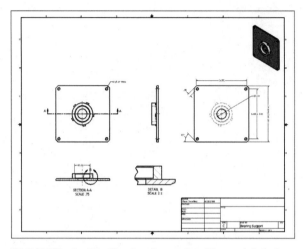

FIGURE 4.67 The drawing updated by model changes

13. Save your work.

Adding Another Sheet

To complete this quick overview of the drawing tools, I think it's important to see a little of the automation that you can access as well:

1. In the Browser, expand the Sheet Formats folder under Drawing Resources.

2. Right-click C-size, 4 View, and select New Sheet from the context menu.

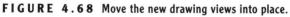

Doing so launches a dialog where you select the model you want to create a drawing of. In this case, you can select your file from the list. If you don't have the file open, you can browse for the desired file.

3. Select Bearing Plate.ipt from the pull-down menu.

4. Click OK to place four drawing views of the bearing plate in the drawing.

5. Drag the drawing views into place. See Figure 4.68.

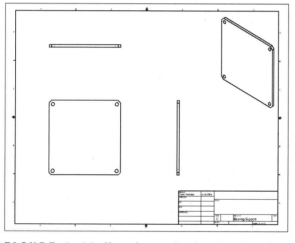

FIGURE 4.68 Move the new drawing views into place.

6. Switch back to Sheet:1 by double-clicking it in the Browser.

7. Save your work and close all files, saving any that you're prompted to.

You'll do additional drawing views in later chapters. I hope you've seen the value and the great potential that Inventor offers for creating 2D production drawings.

Are You Experienced?

Now you can...

- ☑ build basic components using traditional tools

- ☑ assemble components that will be welded together

- ☑ make modifications to components that are welded

- ☑ create a drawing template and custom title block

- ☑ create drawing views of your assembly

- ☑ add dimensions to the drawing views

- ☑ use automated tools to simultaneously create multiple views

CHAPTER 5

Working with the Frame Generator

▶ Adding standard metal shapes to an assembly

▶ Editing end treatments

▶ Using the Bolted Connection Component Generator

▶ Performing 3D grip editing

Leveraging the Assembly

As I've stated before, Inventor was built for the user to work from the assembly. In this chapter, we'll do a little more exploration of working within the assembly while you learn how to use a fantastic tool for making metal frames.

Being able to control assemblies and subassemblies is key to your success. There are times when you just can't anticipate everything or when you may want to modify the structure of the assembly strategically.

Building the Foundation of a Metal Frame

In this exercise, you'll create a part file; but doing so is really just a means to an end. Let's get started!

1. Open the Fan.iam file from the Assemblies folder.

2. On the Assemble tab, select Create from the Component panel.

   Doing so launches the Create In-Place Component dialog (Figure 5.1). You use this dialog to start a new component in the context of the assembly. It offers a place to give the part a name, select the template you would like to base it on, set the location for the new component, and even set how the component will be represented in the Bill of Materials.

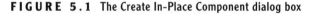

FIGURE 5.1 The Create In-Place Component dialog box

We need to review two check boxes:

Virtual Component If this is selected, Inventor creates a part that doesn't have any features. It's a placeholder for adding to the Bill of Materials an item such as paint or grease that doesn't require a model or a file to be created.

Constrain Sketch Plane to Selected Face or Plane   After you finish
filling out the dialog and select OK to create a component, Inventor
asks you to select a plane to align the new component to. With this
option selected, Inventor also creates a constraint between the
selected plane or face in the assembly and the new sketch.

3. Set the values in the dialog to create a new component named
frame envelope based on the Standard (in).ipt template in the
C:\Data\Parts folder and using the Constrain Sketch Plane to
Selected Face or Plane option.

4. Click OK to begin creating the new component in the assembly.

5. Inventor needs you to select a face or plane. Expand the assembly's
Origin folder, and select the YZ plane to base the new part on.
    This creates the new component and starts a new sketch oriented
on the plane you selected.

6. Add two rectangles to the sketch, as shown in Figure 5.2.

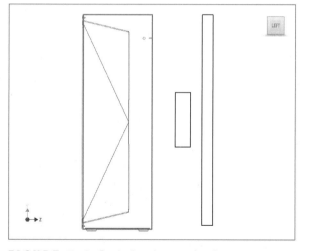

F I G U R E 5 . 2 Beginning the new sketch

7. Use the Coincident constraint to link the midpoint of the left vertical
line on the large rectangle to the midpoint of the right vertical line
on the small rectangle.

8. Dimension the width of the larger rectangle to 1in. and the width of the small rectangle to 6.5in.

9. Dimension the height of the large rectangle to 35.8in. and the height of the small rectangle to 6in., as shown in Figure 5.3.

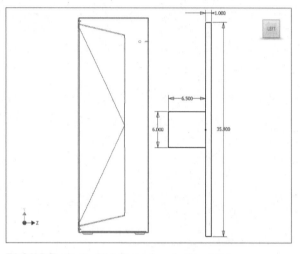

FIGURE 5.3 Add dimensions to the sketch.

10. Create a Vertical constraint between the sketch origin and the coincident midpoints of the two rectangles. Press the Esc key when you're finished.

11. Pick a portion of the sketch, and drag the rectangles from side to side. Leave the sketch outside the wireframe of the assembly.

12. Finish the sketch, and save the new component.

13. Extrude the two rectangles a distance of 6in. using the mid-plane. See Figure 5.4.

14. Use the color list on the Quick Access Toolbar to set the color of the component to Water.

15. Click the Return tool on the Ribbon to return to the assembly.

16. In the assembly, start the Constrain tool. Using a Mate constraint with a Flush solution, pick the large face on the frame envelope component and then pick the outer face of the housing, as shown in Figure 5.5. Set the Offset value to 3in.

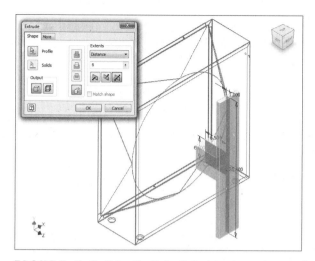

FIGURE 5.4 Using the Extrude tool to create the new shape

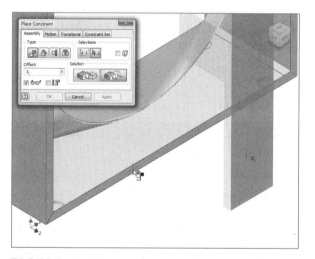

FIGURE 5.5 Applying an assembly constraint to the new component

17. Click OK to move the component.

18. Click and drag the component. It can still move vertically. You placed a constraint to one horizontal plane, and the sketch was automatically constrained when you created the component.

19. Start the Constrain tool again. Using the Flush solution with an Offset value of 0, pick the YZ plane of the frame envelope and the XZ plane of the assembly, as shown in Figure 5.6.

20. Click OK to finish constraining the component in place.

21. Save the assembly.

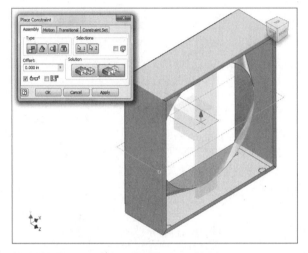

FIGURE 5.6 Beginning the new sketch

Restructuring an Assembly

Up to this point, you've built your assembly in a logical fashion. The component you just created won't be kept in this assembly; instead, it will become part of a subassembly.

So why did you bother to build it in this assembly? I had you do this to show that if you initially think you'll be using a part in the assembly, and then you discover that you want it in a subassembly, you can put it there without having to redo all your work.

You can do many things to a component in the assembly, as evidenced by the context menu you get if you right-click a component in the assembly and pick the Component fly-out. The option you want to use is Demote.

Demoting a Component in the Assembly

The act of demoting a component in an assembly requires you to add it (and other components) to a new subassembly. There is also a Promote function that lifts a part out of a subassembly into the main assembly.

Grip Snap

Move   [V]
Rotate   [G]

Pattern
Mirror
Copy
Replace   Ctrl+H
Replace All   Ctrl+Shift+H
Replace from Content Center...

Promote   Shift+Tab
Demote   Tab

Infer iMates

The extraordinary thing is that in most cases, the assembly constraints applied to the component before demoting or promoting are maintained. In this exercise, you'll put the technology to the test by demoting the components to a new assembly file that will be created in the process:

1. Right-click the frame envelope part in the Browser.

2. Click Component in the context menu, and pick Demote from the menu.

3. The same Create In-Place Component dialog is displayed as when you create a new subassembly. Set the file name to Fan Support Frame, the template to Weldment (ANSI).iam, and the location to C:\Data\Assemblies, as shown in Figure 5.7.

4. Click OK to create the component.

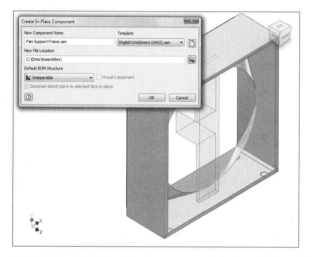

FIGURE 5.7 Creating the new assembly through demoting the part from the current assembly

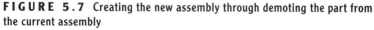

The component is replaced in the Browser by a new subassembly that is also a weldment. The constraints that were related to the frame envelope part are now related to the fan support frame assembly, as shown in Figure 5.8.

You need an assembly because you'll be building a metal frame. The frame, as you'd expect, will be made from a number of individual parts, but you won't be placing the parts in the way you've made constraints so far. You're about to use the Frame Generator.

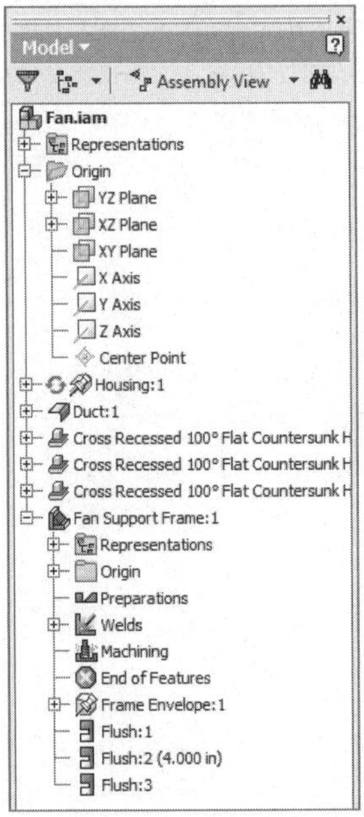

FIGURE 5.8 Constraints are maintained after the demotion.

Frame Generator

The Frame Generator is a specialized tool referred to as a design accelerator.

Design accelerators are tools that were developed under the umbrella of *functional design*. A functional-design tool automates the process of creating geometry based on standard geometric shapes; in the truly advanced tools, engineering calculations can be used to define what's needed.

The Frame Generator uses standard metal shapes from the Content Center. You can add custom shapes to the Content Center as well. Once the shapes are placed, other specialized tools allow you to edit them and build relationships between the parts that make up the frame.

You place frame members on the edges of a model, on lines or arcs in a sketch, or by selecting two points.

When you place a frame member, you're presented with the Insert dialog. This dialog box has a lot going on, as you can see in Figure 5.9:

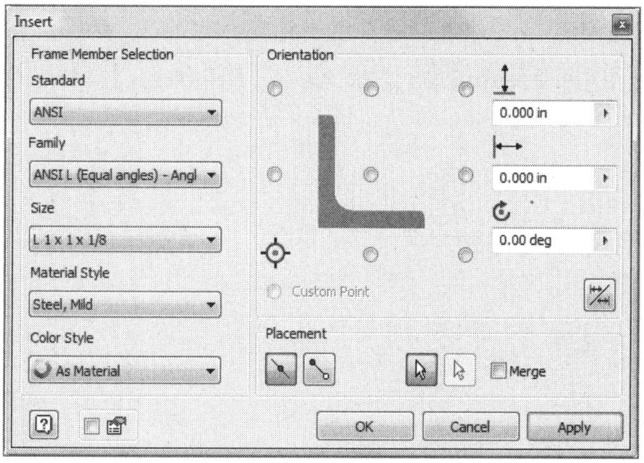

FIGURE 5.9 The Frame Generator's Insert dialog box

Frame Member Selection   In the Frame Member Selection group, you select the Standard you wish to work in and the type or Family of shapes you're looking for. After you've selected a family, you need to choose from the available sizes. You can also select a Material for the components and choose to override the color with something other than that of the material if you like.

Orientation   When you've selected the frame member information, a preview is available on the right. There are 10 points surrounding the profile, which you can use to modify the location. Selecting a point establishes how the member will be oriented when you've chosen the Placement. You can make more adjustments using the dimensional offsets to the right of the preview. The angle can also be changed.

A button beneath the angle value allows you to mirror the profile. This is a nice improvement over having to set angle values of more than 180 degrees to properly align members.

Placement   You have two options for placing members: selecting one segment, be it a line, an arc, or a model edge; or selecting two points that can be along lines or on a model.

The final option under Placement is a Merge check box. In cases where you select arcs that have other arcs or straight portions tangent to them, the Frame Generator separates the portions of the frame. The Merge option binds the tangent members together.

At lower left, next to the Help icon, is a switch that specifies whether Inventor prompts you with the naming of the files that are created.

Building a Frame

In this exercise, you'll use the frame envelope part as the basis for your frame:

1. Right-click the fan support frame, and select Open from the context menu.

2. Set your assembly to the home view.

3. Save the assembly.

4. Switch the Ribbon to the Design tab, and select Insert Frame from the Frame panel.

5. Set Standard to ANSI, and set Family to ANSI L (Equal angles) - Angle Steel.

This sets the preview in the Orientation group.

6. Set the Size value to L 1 x 1 x 1/8, and leave Material and Color Style as is.

7. In the Orientation window, set the Placement point to the corner at the base of the L shape, as shown in Figure 5.10.

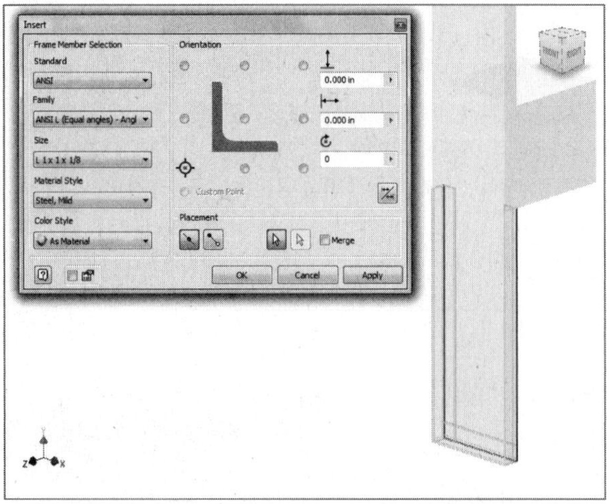

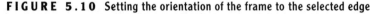

FIGURE 5.10 Setting the orientation of the frame to the selected edge

8. Pick the three edges shown in Figure 5.10. Be sure that the L shape is previewing to appear inside the frame envelope part. Picking the bottom edge first may help you get the correct preview. If you select something you don't want, remember that holding the Shift or Ctrl key and picking again deselects.

9. Deselect the file-naming option on the bottom of the dialog, and click Apply.

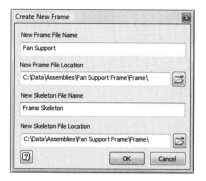

You're prompted with a dialog for the new frame subassembly. Set New Frame File Name to `Fan Support` and New Skeleton File Name to `Frame Skeleton`.

10. Click OK to approve the creation of the new files and to generate the new frame members.

11. When the Insert dialog returns, pick the eight edges shown in Figure 5.11. Again, make sure the preview shows the open portion of the angle iron going to the inside of the model.

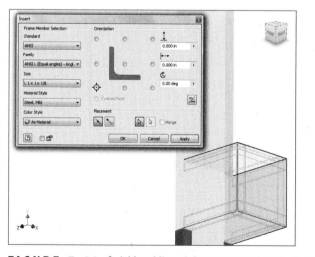

FIGURE 5.11 Quickly adding eight more members to the frame

12. Click Apply to create the new members.

13. Switch the Placement option to Insert Member between Points.

14. Pick the points at either end of the top edge, as shown in Figure 5.12. You may need to change the Orientation angle value.

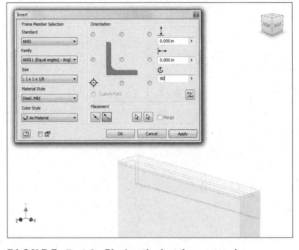

FIGURE 5.12 Placing the last frame member

15. Click OK to place the last member and close the dialog box.

16. Right-click the frame envelope component in the Browser, and turn off Visibility.

17. Compare your screen to Figure 5.13.

18. Save your work.

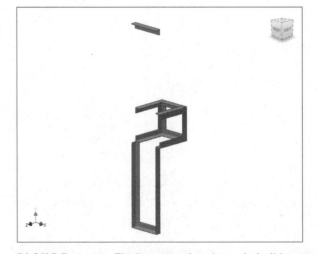

FIGURE 5.13 The frame members in need of editing to complete the model

As you can tell, this process isn't finished. In the next exercise, you'll use the very purposeful editing tools to complete the frame

Editing the Frame

The editing tools for the frame are very straightforward, but they can take some practice to get a feel for. For your frame, you don't need to use all of them, but I'm confident you'll get the feel for how they work:

1. Select the Miter tool from the Frame panel of the Design tab.

2. The Miter tool needs you to select two of the frame's members. Pick the top and the member on the left, as shown in Figure 5.14.

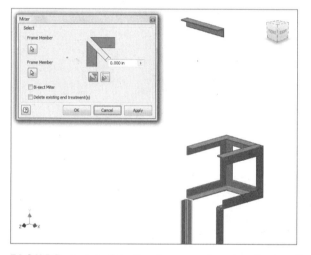

FIGURE 5.14 Selecting frame members to miter together

3. Click Apply to add the miter.

4. Add miters to the vertical member on the right and the top.

5. Miter the bottom with the two long members to complete the large frame, as shown in Figure 5.15.

    The bottom and the long sides overlap, unlike the top, which had gaps. Regardless, you can easily clean up the corners with the Miter tool.

6. Rotate the model so you can clearly see the smaller portion of the frame.

7. Miter the three members of each side. See Figure 5.16.

8. From the Frame panel, start the Trim/Extend tool. Unlike with the Miter tool, you can select as many members as you want to trim or extend to a face that you'll select.

9. Pick the two horizontal members at the back of the frame.

10. With the two members selected for trimming, pick the icon next to Face to select the trimming face.

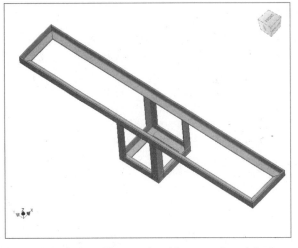

FIGURE 5.15 The completed large portion of the frame

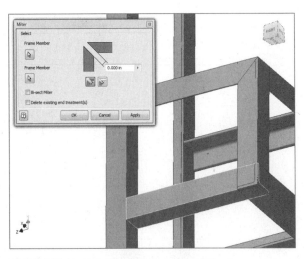

FIGURE 5.16 Mitering the sides of the frame

11. Select the narrow face on the short, vertical member that the horizontal members will butt into. See Figure 5.17.

12. Click Apply to trim the two members.

13. Repeat the process for the other end of the two members. Figure 5.18 shows small portion of the frame completed.

14. Save your work.

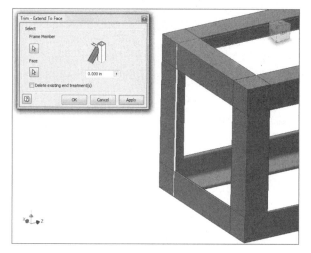

FIGURE 5.17 Trimming the two horizontal members to the vertical

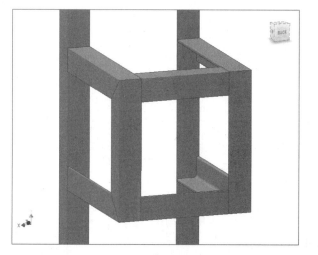

FIGURE 5.18 The updated frame after adding end treatments

You're now finished building the frame. As you notice in the dialog boxes, it's possible to include gaps for welding in the joints and when trimming members. The Frame Generator has been a huge hit with users who need to create frames of nearly any shape. If you have a need for this tool, I encourage you to explore the options further.

To finish the assembly, you'll bring in the bearing supports that you created in the last chapter.

Adding the Bearing Supports

The function of this frame is to hold the bearing supports, which in turn will hold the shaft that the fan blade will be mounted to. So, it makes sense for the bearing plate to be mounted to the frame.

1. Return the Ribbon to the Assemble tab, if it didn't switch automatically.

2. Click the Place tool. In the resulting dialog, select Bearing Support from the Assemblies folder, and click Open to insert it in the assembly.

3. Create a constraint between the axis in the bearing support and the Z axis of the assembly. See Figure 5.19.

FIGURE 5.19 Beginning to assemble the bearing support onto the frame

4. Place a Mate constraint between the back of the frame and the front of the bearing plate.

5. Add an Angular constraint with a value of 0 between the top of the bearing plate and the small part of the frame, as shown in Figure 5.20.

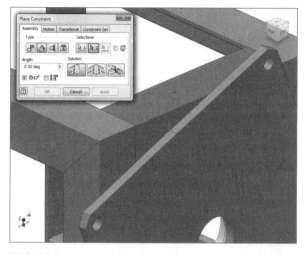

FIGURE 5.20 Aligning the bearing support and the frame

6. Locate the bearing support in the Browser. Click and drag another instance onto the screen.

7. Apply constraints to the new instance between the long vertical rails, as shown in Figure 5.21.

8. Save your work.

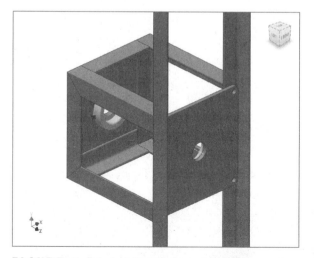

FIGURE 5.21 Locating the second bearing support assembly

Bolted Connections

You've used the Content Center to add bolts to your assembly. Now you'll see how that process can be enhanced.

In addition to selecting a bolt and its size in a dialog, it's possible to select bolts and other standard content that you use regularly and add them to a list of favorites. After an item is added to the list, you can take advantage of a technology called AutoDrop that allows you to drag and drop content into the assembly and size it after it's been brought in.

The Bolted Connection Component Generator is a design accelerator that can simply add a fastener to an assembly, add a fastener and holes to existing parts, or even use engineering calculations to help you select the right fastener for the job. The Bolted Connection Component Generator can calculate the strength of a single connection, determine how many bolts of a size are required to hold things together, what size bolts are needed, or what strength they must be.

This probably sounds complicated and difficult; but as you'll see in the following exercise, it's easy to use.

Adding a Bolted Connection

In this exercise, you'll add a bolt to your favorites and then use it to fasten the bearing supports in place:

1. In the Assemble tab, start the Place from Content Center tool. As a reminder, it's under the Place tool in the Component panel. This again launches the Place from Content Center dialog.

2. In the Category View, navigate to Fasteners ➤ Bolts ➤ Hex Head.

3. Use the Filter pull-down at the top to display only ANSI parts in the dialog.

4. Navigate to Hex Bolt - Inch in the right window.

5. Right-click the Hex Bolt - Inch icon, and select Add to Favorites, as shown in Figure 5.22.

   Doing so marks this type of fastener as a favorite. You can add entire groups of fasteners or even include the entire Content Center in your favorites if you like. Doing this doesn't modify the Content Center or the components themselves; but, as you're about to see, it makes them very easy to reach when you need them.

6. At the bottom of the list in the Category View is an icon for History. Click this icon, and a list of recent components that you've used appears in the window on the right.

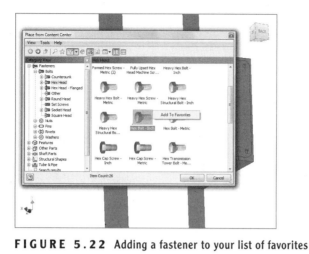

FIGURE 5.22 Adding a fastener to your list of favorites

7. Right-click the Cross Recessed Screw that you used in Chapter 3, "Moving into the Assembly World," and add it to your favorites as well.

8. Click Cancel to close the dialog box.

At the top of the Browser, next to the word Model, is an icon of a downward-pointing arrow. As with other such icons, it means that more options are available to the Browser than just displaying the structure of the active file.

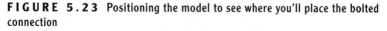

9. Open the list of Browser viewing options, and select Favorites.

10. Set your view in the Design window to resemble Figure 5.23.

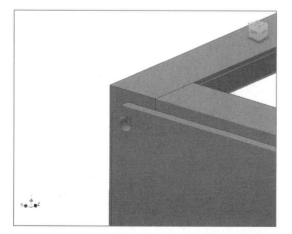

FIGURE 5.23 Positioning the model to see where you'll place the bolted connection

Placing a Bolt Using AutoDrop

Now, you'll place components from the Browser rather than using the Place from Content Center dialog:

1. Click and drag the Hex Bolt - Inch component from Favorites into the Design window, releasing your mouse button in the Design window.

   After a few moments a preview appears, showing the hex bolt and a glyph with a question mark.

2. Move your cursor over the hole in the bearing plate. The edge of the hole highlights. After a few more moments, the bolt resizes to fit the clearance hole you specified earlier. See Figure 5.24.

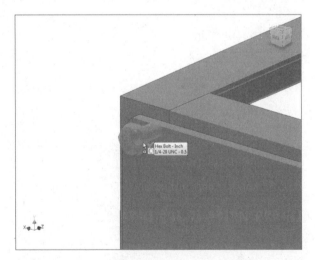

FIGURE 5.24 The bolt can detect the diameter and depth of the hole and size itself.

   This preview shows the resized fastener and gives a tooltip indicating what size it is.

3. After the preview updates, move your cursor so the edge of the hole is highlighted again. Click to begin placing the bolt into the hole.

Selecting the placement hole starts the AutoDrop dialog. It contains some interesting options, so let's quickly review them:

Follow Pattern If Inventor detects a pattern of holes, you can use the Insert Multiple option to add more than one fastener at a time.

Insert Multiple When Inventor detects more than one hole of the same size on the same plane as the selected hole, you can use this option to apply fasteners to all the holes at once.

Change Size Selecting this option brings up the selection dialog where you can choose another bolt size or length.

Bolted Connection This launches the Bolted Connection design accelerator. The icon is the same as that found on the Design and Assemble tabs.

Apply Just like any Apply button, this executes the command and keeps the dialog open so you can keep working.

Place This works like an OK button, applying the fastener and closing the tool when finished.

4. Pick the Bolted Connection button. Doing so launches the Bolted Connection Component Generator dialog, shown in Figure 5.25.

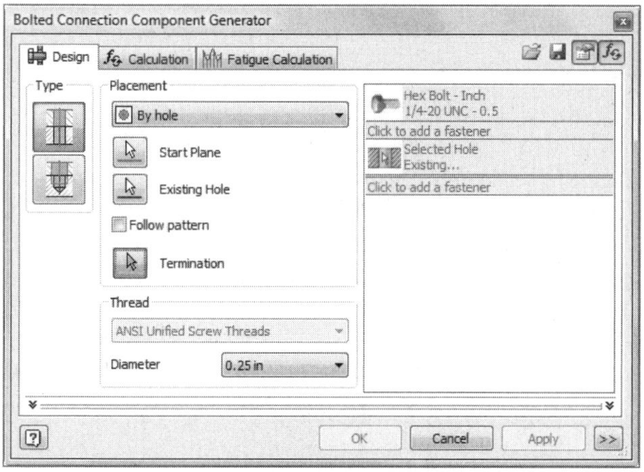

FIGURE 5.25 The Bolted Connection Component Generator dialog's Design tab

You can place two types of holes using Bolted Connection: Blind and Through. This isn't a bad thing, because just about every hole used for fastening is one of those.

The Placement options are the same as for a regular Hole feature but require input such as what face a Through hole should stop at. When the selected hole is a member of a pattern, whether circular, rectangular, or multiple holes being placed at once, you're offered a check box that lets you propagate the bolted connection across all the holes simultaneously.

The Thread group is where you select the thread type and diameter. In this situation, where you've already selected a bolt, your options are limited to the diameter. This makes sense because there's no need to be able to select an ISO thread for an ANSI bolt. The diameter displayed is selected based on the size of hole on which you placed the bolt. If you change the size here, it will also update the size of the existing hole that you chose.

The pane on the right displays the *bolt stack*. This is the combination of hole types and fasteners that will make up your bolted connection.

Expanding the dialog using the More button reveals an area where you can keep a library of standard connections. Many companies use essentially the same bolt stack in various sizes. With this library, you can select a template, choose your size, and place your connection quickly.

Now you will finish the bolted connection by adding the missing inputs.

5. The Termination button should be active. If it isn't, pick it to define the face at which your Through hole will end.

6. Hover over the section of angle steel on the frame, where the hole currently ends. The back face of that piece should highlight, as shown in Figure 5.26.

7. Click the face.

This generates a preview of the hole to be added to the piece of angle.

8. Select the Follow Pattern check box, and view the preview of all four bolted connections.

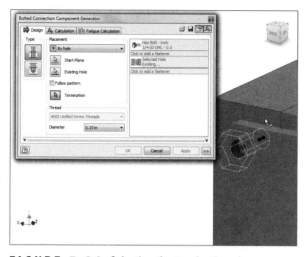

FIGURE 5.26 Selecting the termination plane

9. In the bolt stack, pick the hole that's being added, and select the ellipsis icon that appears.

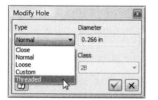

10. In the dialog, change the hole type from Normal to Threaded, and pick the icon with the check mark to make the change.

11. In the Design window, click and drag the arrow that appears at the end of the placed bolt, as shown in Figure 5.27. Set it to be ¼ UNC - 0.5.

This changes the length of the bolt — but it's important to note that Inventor only changes between standard sizes. This is a great way to not accidentally create a custom-size fastener.

12. Expand the dialog, and click the Add button.

Add...

13. You can choose a special name for the template in the Template Description dialog. In this case, keep the default and click OK to create the new template.

Doing so adds the new template to the list.

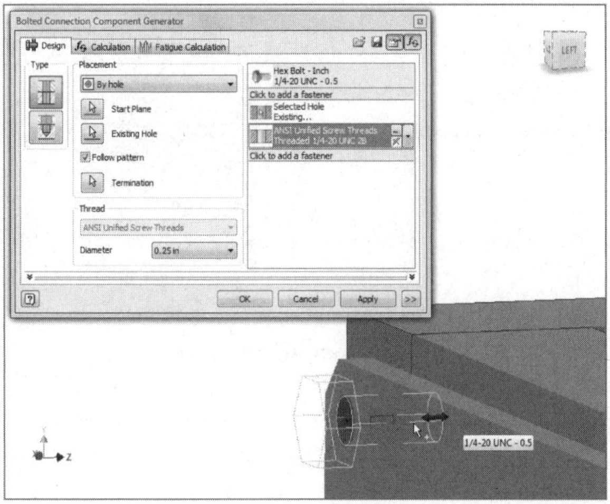

FIGURE 5.27 Dragging the length of a bolt changes the standard length.

14. Click OK to start generating the bolted connections.

15. When the File Naming dialog appears, deselect the Always Prompt for Filename check box, and click OK.

This generates the four bolts (Figure 5.28) and, in most cases, four threaded holes in the parts they go through. In this case, due to the nature of the fan support assembly — a frame with many members — the holes appear only under the part beneath the first hole of the pattern.

A simple remedy would be to project the bearing support hole locations onto the unedited parts and add the threaded holes similar to the way you added holes to the frame in Chapter 2, "Building the Foundation of the Design." For the purpose of moving forward, you'll leave the fan support assembly short a few holes. I wanted to use this as an example of an unusual condition where a design accelerator might not be able to understand all of the design intent.

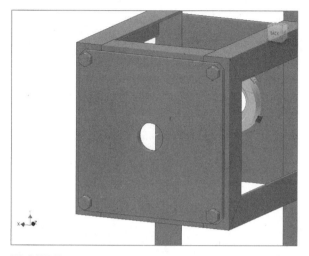

FIGURE 5.28 The bolted connections added to the assembly

Reusing a Bolted Connection Template

In this exercise, you'll perform the previous process but in an even faster way:

1. Rotate the fan support frame so you can see the other bearing support assembly.

2. Pick the Design tab in the Ribbon.

3. Start the Bolted Connection tool in the Fasten panel.
The same dialog as before appears, except it's looking for all the inputs because you haven't preselected a hole or fastener type.

4. Keep the Placement By Hole setting, and pick the front face of the bearing support for the start plane.

5. Move over the existing holes in the plate, and select the one that highlights when you pass over it. This is the parent hole to the pattern.

6. Pick the opposite face of the large vertical angle piece behind the parent hole for the termination face, as shown in Figure 5.29. Because your parent hole may be in another place, be aware that you can still select the termination face from this part.

7. Instead of building the bolt stack, highlight the template in the Library and pick the Set button.

Set

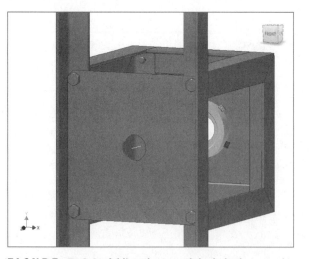

FIGURE 5.29 Select the placement of the new bolted connection.

8. Set the Follow Pattern option to On, and click OK to create the new set of bolted connections shown in Figure 5.30.

9. Save your work.

10. Select the tab for viewing the fan assembly at the bottom of the Design window.

11. Pick the Update icon in the Quick Access Toolbar to make sure the assembly is up to date and review the changes that have been made. The assembly should look like Figure 5.31.

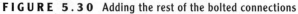

FIGURE 5.30 Adding the rest of the bolted connections

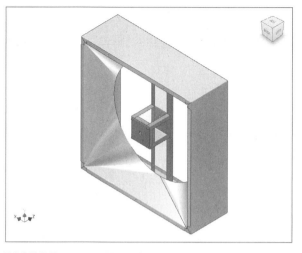

FIGURE 5.31 The updated assembly

With the assembly coming along nicely, what happens if you discover a mistake? In this case, you can use either parametric dimensions or 3D grips to edit the solid that the frame was based on.

Changing the Size of the Frame

After reviewing the updated fan support frame in the assembly, you realize that it's too long. You need to go back to the very first thing you did in this chapter and change it:

1. In the fan support frame assembly, double-click the frame envelope part to make it the active part for editing.

2. Click the face at the end of the smaller section, and select the green circle at the end to access the 3D grips. See Figure 5.32.

By selecting a face of a sketched feature and clicking the dot or *handle*, you access a special editing capability for sketched features in Inventor called *3D grips*.

As you can see in Figure 5.33, the feature switches to wireframe display; control-grip points appear along with any parametric dimensions included in the sketch.

When you hover over the grips that appear on the wireframe, they display differently based on the geometry they represent, but the capabilities are the same. Hovering over a center or a corner shows a circle with an axis running through it. You can reposition these grips. Hovering over a grip on a face center or cylindrical quadrant displays an arrow that you can use to drag the face to a different size.

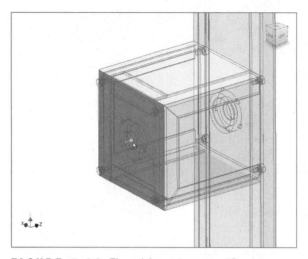

FIGURE 5.32 The quick way to access 3D grips

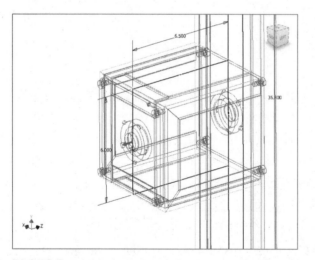

FIGURE 5.33 Activating a 3D grip makes handles accessible.

Controlling 3D Grips

While a 3D grip is being edited, you can access different options by right-clicking to display this menu (or one that is similar).

To keep the change, you also have to right-click and select Done:

Done   You must use this option to accept any change made in the 3D grips and then update the model.

Commit and Move   This additional option allows you to accept the current size or edits to the size, but then lets you reposition the feature and even move it to another face on the part, including a curved face.

Edit Extent   To modify the overall value for the feature, you use this option.

Edit Offset   This option allows you to change the value from its current setting. Entering a negative value also works to decrease a size.

Now that you have a better understanding of the 3D Grip options; you will get to use them.

3. Move your cursor near the center of the end face where you selected the 3D grip. An arrow appears, allowing you to drag the face.

4. Click and drag the face, and observe the 6.500 dimension change to a driven dimension and change value while you drag it. When you release the mouse button, the dimension reverts to a parametric dimension.

5. Right-click the same arrow, select Edit Offset, and enter any value.

6. Click OK. The model updates, and the value of the dimension that was originally 6.500 incorporates the Offset value that you added to it.

7. Double-click the dimension that was originally 6.500, and change the value to 5.5.

8. Click OK to update the 3D grip preview.

9. Right-click in an open area of the Design window, and choose Done from the context menu to save the change.

10. On the Model tab, pick the Return tool to leave the part and return to the assembly. See Figure 5.34.

11. Right-click the frame envelope component in the Browser, and select Suppress from the menu.

12. When prompted to save the changes to the frame envelope, agree and choose OK to close the dialog.

FIGURE 5.34 The frame updates per changes to the frame envelope.

13. Save the assembly.

When you save the assembly after suppressing the frame envelope, Inventor wants to create a new Level of Detail (LOD) Representation. You need to create a LOD any time you're working in the default or Master Level of Detail and suppress a component.

14. Give the new LOD the name **Envelope Suppressed**, and click Yes to create it.

15. Click OK to save the assembly.

16. Switch your Design window display to the fan assembly.

In the fan assembly, the frame envelope is still visible. This is because the fan assembly is presenting you with the Master LOD of the fan support frame assembly.

17. Right-click the fan support assembly in the Browser or in the Design window.

18. Select Representation from the context menu to open the Representation dialog.

19. From the Level of Detail Representation drop-down, select Envelope Suppressed. Click Yes to change the way the assembly is displayed in the fan assembly.

Changing the size of the fan support frame made it shorter, and now it interferes with the duct. You must edit the constraint that positions it in order to remedy the situation.

20. Locate the Flush constraint with a value of 3.00 under the fan support frame.

21. In the Browser, click the constraint. Its value appears highlighted in a text box at the bottom of the Browser.

22. Type 2 and press the Enter key to update the value.

23. Save the fan assembly, and give it a new LOD also called **Envelope Suppressed**. The completed work should look like Figure 5.35.

Because you're entering new territory by using representations, let's take some time to understand what representations can do.

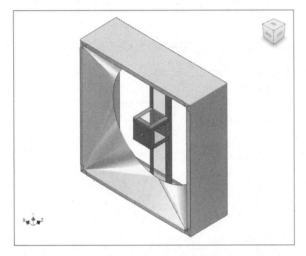

FIGURE 5.35 The fan assembly with edits to the fan support frame completed

Representations

In the preceding exercise, you were asked to suppress a component in the assembly for the sake of clarity. What if you turned off the visibility of several parts? You may have noticed that turning off the component's visibility was also an option. The result of using either is to no longer see the part — but to Inventor, these are very different things. Maybe you'd like to do more than be able to make parts visible or invisible repeatedly. Perhaps viewing parts in a different color would help clarity, but you only want to do it temporarily.

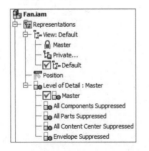

In Inventor, one of the least utilized tools in the assembly environment is the *representation*, which you can use for these purposes and more. Some regard the representation as a tool to be used for advanced purposes, but I consider it a

fundamental tool that everyone should understand. You can find the representations in the Assembly Browser, immediately under the root of the assembly. Expanding the Representations folder exposes the three types available in Inventor: View, Position, and Level of Detail.

View

View representations can be configured to change part visibility and color. You can create as many of them as you like and switch between them with a simple double-click.

Turning off the visibility of parts in a View representation (View rep.) doesn't reduce the impact the assembly has on system memory, but it can improve graphic performance.

Being able to control visibility is just the beginning. You can also set up a View rep. to control the color of parts. Views can also be locked using a context-menu option so that you can limit how many parts you see; any further parts added to the assembly don't appear in the locked View rep. Other context-menu options allow you to turn all parts on or off and override any changes to the part colors you may have made.

Position

If you work with mechanisms or assemblies that have elements that can be opened or closed, Positional representations offer you some exciting tools.

Positional representations allow you to override assembly constraints. For example, suppose you place an angular constraint on a door to keep it in its closed state. With a Positional representation, you can override the constraint value when you need to show the door open, and you can display that open state in the drawing using phantom lines to illustrate the range of motion.

You can even create a representation that turns off a constraint and lets you manipulate the assembly with a click and drag.

Level of Detail

This type of representation can change Inventor's capabilities. View representations allow you to turn off the visibility of individual parts in an assembly, but with a LOD representation, you can suppress a part or parts from system memory without interfering with the assembly. This means that when you work with LOD representations, you can manipulate extraordinarily large assemblies without having to use a supercomputer.

You can even replace entire assemblies by fusing the assembly into a single part to simplify things further; and you can replace an entire assembly with a single part that will allow the user to still see where the assembly is but task memory with only one part instead of perhaps thousands. All this happens without compromising the assembly's understanding of what components are used to make it.

To make it even easier, you can copy an existing View representation to create a new LOD representation by right-clicking and using a context menu option to do so.

Creating a View Representation

This is a simple tool to use, but taking a little time to walk through the process will be well worth the effort:

1. Set the view of the fan assembly to look like Figure 5.35.

2. Right-click the icon for View:Default in the Browser, and select New from the context menu.

    This creates a new representation named View1.

3. Slowly double-click the name of View1, and rename it **Fan Drive**.

4. In the Browser or in the Design window, select the fan support frame, right-click, and select Isolate from the context menu.

    Doing so turns off the visibility of all other components in the assembly. It doesn't affect the number of components listed on the status bar as being used or displayed by Inventor. As I mentioned in the introduction to representations, turning off the visibility of a part only helps you see things more clearly and offers some graphic performance benefits.

5. On the status bar, note the number of parts that are displayed and in memory.

6. Under the assembly's `Level of Detail` folder, switch the Active LOD to Envelope Suppressed and note the change on the status bar.

7. Right-click the Fan Drive, and select Copy to Level of Detail from the context menu.

8. Save the assembly.

9. Double-click the Fan Drive LOD.

    This removes the housing, duct, and fasteners from system memory.

    So far, you've modified the representations of the overall fan assembly. Let's modify the way the fan support frame is shown in the assembly.

10. Right-click the fan support frame assembly in the Design window or the Browser.

11. Select Representation from the context menu, and choose a LOD of Envelope Suppressed.

    You've now pared down your assembly considerably.

12. Save the assembly to keep the changes to the Fan Detail LOD.

13. Right-click the Fan Drive View representation, and delete it.

14. Switch back and forth between the Fan Drive and Master LODs, noting the change in the number of active parts.

15. Activate the Envelope Suppressed LOD, and save the assembly.

Before we go further with the concept of representations we're going to take a detour and look at a tool that makes manipulating the assembly much easier: selection filters.

Selection Filters

I mentioned selection filters in passing in Chapter 1, "Finding Your Way in the Inventor Interface," as an item that was worthy of exploration. This is a great opportunity to look into these tools, at least to get the basics.

A lot of options are associated with the filters, and we'll focus only on the first five options. These options are the ones most commonly used to access parts — or even features of parts that are several layers of hierarchy beneath the assembly you may be working on.

A filter affects what highlights as you move your cursor over an assembly, a part, or a drawing. The filters that are available to you may change depending on the file you're in. Each filter has a specific type of object it highlights. Let's give some definition to the top five filters:

Select Component Priority   I have used the terms *part* and *component* somewhat interchangeably. When discussing individual parts, they can be regarded as components. In an assembly, the distinction becomes a little clearer. In your fan assembly, the duct, frame, bolted connections, and fan support frame are components. The pieces of steel that make up the frame are parts. Passing over the assembly, these components will highlight. The frame is made up of many parts but highlights as a whole because this is the default selection filter.

Select Part Priority   As I just stated, there is a difference between a part and a component. If you select this mode, the individual pieces of the fan support frame will highlight, or a single screw of the bolted connections will highlight. This is a fantastic tool for accessing a part that is buried in a subassembly of a subassembly in an assembly.

Select Feature Priority   This filter goes even deeper. It lets you select the Hole feature on a part that is at any level in the assembly. It's also the default mode when working in a Part file.

Select Faces and Edges   As with all the filters, the name is the description. This option can help you locate a specific face to build a work plane or sketch on.

Select Sketch Features   This is the default mode in the drawing file. When you share a sketch across features, you may accidentally leave it visible. If you do that some time, try switching this filter on, selecting the sketch, and turning its visibility off from the assembly. You'll really appreciate it if you've already dug many layers deep to try to figure out where the visible sketch is hidden in the Browser.

After you select a filter and pick the part, feature, or face you want, you can do anything you need to. Remember, Inventor was built from the assembly out, so this type of tool is second nature to Inventor — the trick is remembering to leverage it.

Other selection filters allow you to select multiple components by size or all the instances of a particular component. This is a great way to select parts for suppression or isolation to build representations.

Before you practice using your filters, we should discuss one last item: highlighting.

Enhanced Highlighting

Passing over components in the assembly, you see the edges of the components highlight. This indicates which one you'll interact with if you pick your right or left mouse button.

There is another mode for highlighting, called *enhanced highlighting*. Rather than just the edges of the component highlighting, the entire part highlights. To make this the standard mode of operation, you need to engage it in the Application Options.

Let's switch this on.

Turning On Enhanced Highlighting

Remember, the settings in the Application Options affect Inventor as a whole. Using this option is a matter of taste; but if you like it, you'll probably want to use it all of the time. So, set it and forget it:

1. Select Application ➤ Options to bring up the Application Options.

2. On the General tab, pick the Enable Enhanced Highlighting check box.

3. Click OK to save the changes. If you like, you can always export the settings to a new profile.

4. In the Design window, move your cursor over some of the components to see the effect of the new setting.

Working with Colors

With your new knowledge of selection filters and enhanced highlighting, let's do another exercise to create a View representation that may not look as realistic but may make it easier to see what parts form the assembly:

1. Right-click the Master View representation, and select Copy from the context menu.

2. Rename the new View representation **Circus**.

3. Make Circus the active View representation.
   Right-click context menus are an enormously valuable resource, and of course they're not wasted on the selection filters. In this case, because primary tools are available through the right-click menus, selection filters are accessed by adding a keystroke.

4. Hold the Shift key, and right-click in an empty part of the Design window.

5. Set Select Part Priority as the selection mode. See Figure 5.36 for the full context menu.
   Now, as you pass over the assembly, the individual elements highlight.

6. Pick a component on the screen. When it's selected, choose a new color for it from the pull-down menu on the Quick Access Toolbar.

7. Repeat the process for a number of parts in the assembly. See Figure 5.37 as an example.

Repeat ApplicationOptions

Select Component Priority
Select Part Priority
Select Features
Select Face and Edges
Select Sketch Features

Select Visible Only
Select Prehighlight

Invert Selection
Previous Selection

Select All Occurences
Select Constrained To
Select Component Size...
Select Component Offset...
Select Sphere Offset...
Select by Plane...
Select External Components
Select Internal Components
Select All in Camera
Replace from Content Center...
Place from Content Center...

FIGURE 5.36 The full selection priority context menu

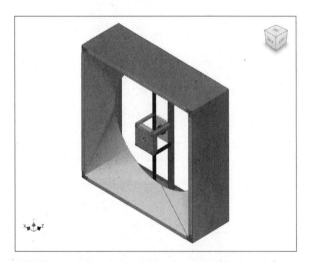

FIGURE 5.37 An example of using contrast to more easily see individual parts

8. Save the assembly.

9. Switch the LOD to Fan Drive.

You can use View and LOD representations in tandem. By using the LOD to limit the number of parts and the View representation to accentuate the different parts that remain, you make visualizing the true structure of the product much easier.

10. Switch the View and LOD representations to Master to restore the realistic coloring of the parts.

11. Save your work.

Going forward in the book, you can choose to use different colors for your components. You'll use the LOD representation in the next chapter for no other reason than to make it easier to see what is going on in your assembly — which is precisely the reason you'll probably use them in your production work.

Are You Experienced?

Now you can...

☑ **create a metal frame**

☑ **establish a list of commonly used standard components**

☑ **use the Bolted Connection Component Generator to place fasteners**

☑ **use 3D grips to edit a solid model**

☑ **create a Level of Detail representation to reduce the system memory load**

☑ **use selection filters to more easily work in an assembly**

CHAPTER 6

Working with Purchased and Multipurpose Parts

- ▶ Leveraging content created by other Inventor users
- ▶ Cast part workflows
- ▶ Accessing components made by vendors
- ▶ Modifying existing components
- ▶ Defining named parameters

Reusing Your Own Parts

So far, you've had a couple of opportunities to interact with the Content Center. Of course, we're just scratching the surface of all its potential. But the Content Center doesn't contain components that you've created yourself and want to reuse.

It's possible to add components that you've created to the Content Center and make it possible for everyone to access them. I think that topic goes beyond the scope of this book, but I did want to show you an option for automating constraints for commonly used components.

iMates

Every assembly constraint has two halves. A face or an edge on one part is related to a face or edge on another. To completely constrain a part in the assembly, you need to repeat the process of applying these constraints several times on a part.

The iMate concept allows you to construct half of the assembly constraints for a component ahead of time and store them in the components. To really exploit the function, you can apply the incomplete constraints to several interchangeable parts; doing so lets you swap them for one another in an assembly without having to reapply constraints.

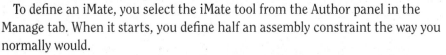

To define an iMate, you select the iMate tool from the Author panel in the Manage tab. When it starts, you define half an assembly constraint the way you normally would.

If you have a component constrained in an assembly and you would like to incorporate its existing constraints into iMates, you can select the constraints in the Browser and select Infer iMates from the right-click context menu. You won't do that in this chapter, but it's good to be aware of the option.

Let's use the manual method to develop an iMate set.

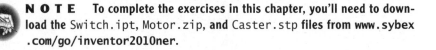

N O T E   To complete the exercises in this chapter, you'll need to download the `Switch.ipt`, `Motor.zip`, and `Caster.stp` files from www.sybex .com/go/inventor2010ner.

Creating an iMate

In this exercise, you'll review an existing iMate set and build a companion set in the fan assembly:

1. Place the `Switch.ipt` file in the `C:\Data\Parts` folder.

2. Open the switch part in Inventor. See Figure 6.1.

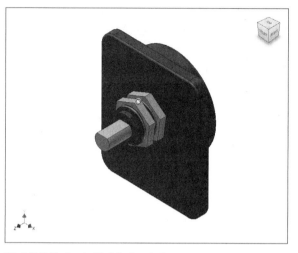

FIGURE 6.1 Finished switch containing iMates

3. In the Browser, locate the iMates folder and expand it.

4. The folder contains a composite iMate named Switch. Expand it to reveal the two constraints that define the position of the part.

A *composite* iMate is a way to combine single iMates within a component. You may have more than one group of iMates, and linking them together in a composite makes it easier to manage them.

5. Open the fan assembly or make it the active file in the Design window.

6. Double-click the housing in the Design Window to edit it in the assembly.

7. Switch the Ribbon to the Manage tab.

8. Start the iMate tool from the Author panel.

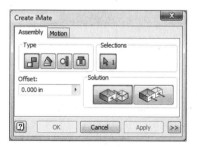

Doing so opens the Create iMate dialog. It's similar to the Place Constraint dialog, except that it's looking for only one selection.

9. In the Create iMate dialog, set Type to Insert and pick the outer edge of the hole in the housing, as shown in Figure 6.2.

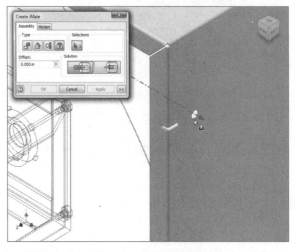

FIGURE 6.2 Creating an Insert iMate

10. Click Apply to create the iMate and keep the dialog open.

11. Switch the constraint type to Angle, and pick the flange on the edge of the housing, as shown in Figure 6.3.

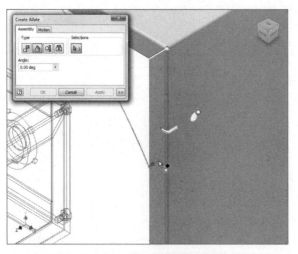

FIGURE 6.3 Adding the Angle iMate constraint

12. Click OK to create the iMate and close the dialog.

You can rename the iMates in the Browser. When you have more than one iMate, it can be very useful to sort out what is what. It's critical to know that in order for iMates to work, all the names of the iMates between the two components must be identical. In the case of composite iMates, not only must they have the same name, but the iMates within them must have the same names; and there must be the same number of iMates in both parts.

13. Expand the folded model in the Browser.

14. Expand the `iMates` folder to see the two iMates you created.

15. In the Browser, hold the Ctrl key, and pick both of the iMates you created.

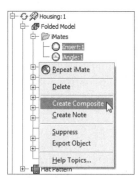

16. Right-click, and select Create Composite from the context menu.

17. This creates a composite iMate named *iComposite:1* under the `iMates` folder. Rename this item *Switch*.

18. Save the part, and use the Return icon to go back to the assembly.

Now you've prepared the assembly to take advantage of the work someone else has done in the switch part. Let's see what the results are by placing the switch into your assembly.

19. Start the Place tool, and select the `Switch.ipt` file in the `Parts` folder.

20. At the bottom of the Place Component dialog, select the Automatically Generate iMates on Place option, and click Open to place the switch into the assembly.

The switch automatically locates itself in the assembly.

21. Restore the assembly's home view, and save your work.

When you have components that are interchangeable in an assembly and that are frequently substituted for one another, explore the capabilities of iMates. In this case, if you had another switch with the same iMates, you could simply replace this on with it and never have to manually apply assembly constraints.

Next, you'll build a part that will be used by other parts. This is the same philosophy of reuse that we explored by working with iMates.

Creating a Cast Part

To create the cast part, you'll use traditional solid-modeling tools. We'll include some new tools that you haven't had an opportunity to work with yet, to add another level to your expertise.

Defining the Basic Shape

In this exercise you will build a part using traditional solid modeling techniques.

1. Create a new part from the Standard (in).ipt template.

2. Use the Rectangle tool, and use the sketch centerpoint as the upper-left corner of the rectangle shown in Figure 6.4.

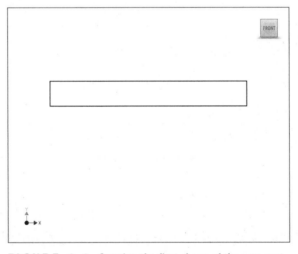

FIGURE 6.4 Creating the first shape of the new part

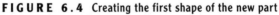

3. Start another rectangle, and draw it vertically from the endpoint of the last one. See Figure 6.5.

4. Start the Line tool, and pick the bottom-left corner of the first rectangle to begin a vertical line (Figure 6.6) that goes down roughly .3 inches.

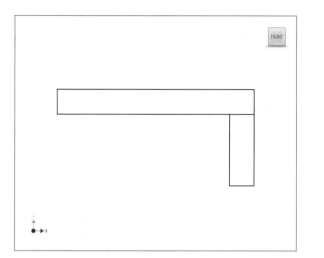

FIGURE 6.5 Start the new rectangle based on the corner of the first.

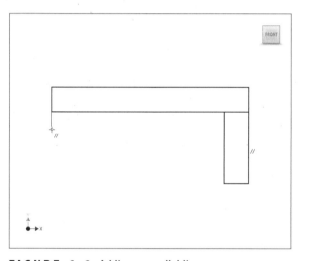

FIGURE 6.6 Adding a parallel line

In Inventor, you can create an arc tangent to a line by moving your cursor over the endpoint of a line segment and then clicking and dragging your mouse off the end of the line. You can use the same technique to create an arc that ends *normal* to the end of a line segment.

5. With the Line tool still active, hover over the last point you selected.

6. When the gray dot appears, click and drag your mouse to the right of the endpoint. This should generate an arc like that shown in Figure 6.7.

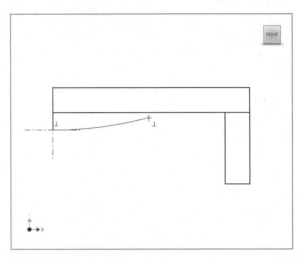

FIGURE 6.7 A click-and-drag operation can create an arc while in the Line tool.

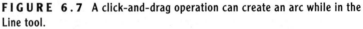

7. Drag the new arc to the intersection of the two rectangles, as shown in Figure 6.8, and release the mouse button.

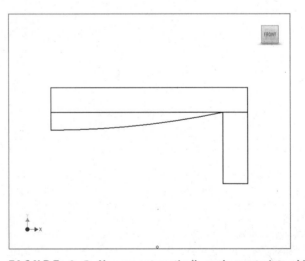

FIGURE 6.8 You can automatically apply constraints while dragging.

8. Repeat the process for the vertical leg by creating a horizontal line and an arc that goes to the same point as the last one, as shown in Figure 6.9.

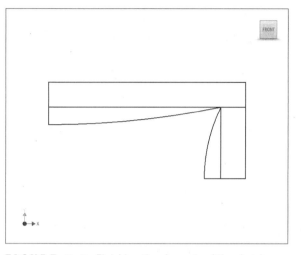

FIGURE 6.9 Finishing the elements of the sketch

9. Save the file to the Parts folder as **Cast Handle.ipt**.

10. Reactivate Sketch1, and add an Equal constraint to the short sides of the two rectangles.

11. Restart the Equal constraint, and create a relationship between the short line segments that the arcs extend from.

12. Dimension the sketch as shown in Figure 6.10.

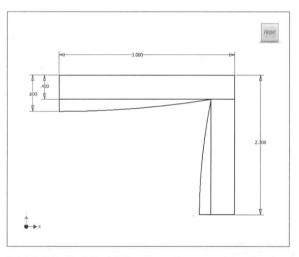

FIGURE 6.10 Adding dimensions completes the sketch.

13. Finish the sketch, and save the Part file.

14. Extrude all the profiles a distance of .3in, as shown in Figure 6.11.

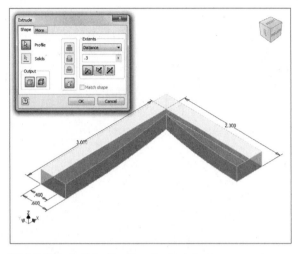

FIGURE 6.11 Creating the base feature

15. Save the part with the new feature.

Next, you need to add a draft angle to most of the part's faces. You can add draft when you're creating the extrusion, but in this case it would be improper to add a draft angle to one of the faces. This is where the Draft tool comes in.

Adding Draft

Plastic and cast parts require a draft angle to be applied. You can apply this with the Taper value in Extrude and a couple of other commands, but sometimes it's best to do so after you've placed the primary features.

The tool is very simple and provides only two ways to define the feature. These two features allow for all the flexibility you'll usually need:

Fixed Edge   If you need to apply a draft as it runs along an edge, you use the Fixed Edge option. This edge doesn't have to be a simple, straight edge. It can be a curve or a complex combination of geometry. You can also select a face for your plane, but the behavior is different than the Fixed Plane method. After you've selected your edges, you select the faces to draft and then set the direction of pull that will control whether the applied draft angle faces in or out. Finally, you set the Draft Angle required in the text box at right.

Fixed Plane   This option pivots the selected face about a plane. The farther the selected face is from the plane, the more dramatic the effect is. The other options required are the same as for the Fixed Edge method, but the results can be very different.

Adding Draft to the part

Now you'll add draft to the free faces on the part:

1. Start the Draft tool from the Modify panel on the Model tab.

2. Select the XY plane of the part for the Pull Direction. The Direction indicator should be pointing in the Z direction.

3. Select the faces shown in Figure 6.12. The preview should show the faces tipping into the part.

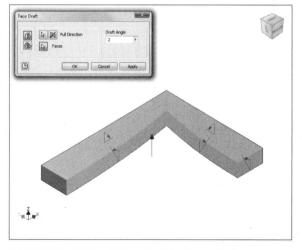

FIGURE 6.12 Adding draft to the part's faces

4. Set the Draft Angle to 2 degrees.

5. Click OK to modify the part.

6. Save the changes.

Next, you need to round off the sharp edges of your part.

The Fillet Tool

The Fillet tool may be the most used feature in typical part modeling, because there are so many reasons for rounding an edge on a part. The Fillet dialog box provides a large number of options for creating fillets.

On the left are the primary fillet construction types.

Edge Fillet

To use this type of fillet, you select an edge or several edges and define a radius you would like applied to the edge. The dialog box also offers one or more tabs of options, depending on the type of fillet you've selected. For an edge fillet, you see three tabs:

Constant Tab You can select multiple edges; and by clicking Click to Add, you can also place fillets with differing radii in one feature by changing the value of the radius. An additional option lets you define whether the fillet is tangent to adjacent faces or continues the curvature; for the latter option, click the down arrow, and select Smooth (G2). You also have several options for how to select edges, and you can mix and match them. For example, the Edge option has you select each edge to be rounded individually, whereas the Loop option has you try to select multiple edges based on a face or the edges of a surface. By mixing them, you can set a fillet radius, select multiple edges using the Loop option, and select additional edges by changing Select Mode to Edge. A display shows how many edges are selected as you go. Choosing the Feature option selects all the edges of a specific feature. If you've created an extrusion with a large number of edges, you can select them all by switching to Feature mode.

With cast or plastic parts, you may not want any sharp edges. The All Fillets and All Rounds options do as they say and select every sharp edge that is external for all fillets and every sharp edge that is internal for all rounds.

Variable Tab   This tab allows you to place a fillet or round that changes size as it moves along the edge. You can reference points along the edge to define a different radius between the beginning and end. You can do this after you've selected the edge on which you want to place the feature by moving your cursor to the end and clicking where you want to add another radius.

Setbacks Tab   The options on this tab add additional control to the shape of a corner where several fillets meet. This lets you soften the corner to a larger radius than is used on the edges.

Face Fillet

This method has only one group of options. You can override whether the fillet includes faces that are tangent to the ones you selected to build the fillet between.

Optimize for Single Selection allows you to select your two faces quickly. If this option is deselected, you can build a collection of faces for Face Set 1 and another individual face or collection of faces for Face Set 2 to build a complex fillet feature. This type of fillet also needs a radius specified, but you can only place a fillet with one radius.

Full Round

This fillet type calculates the only radius it can use based on the geometry you select. You have the Optimize for Single Selection option as well as the Include Tangent Faces option.

These additional options appear in the Fillet dialog box:

Solid   This option enables you to pick the body or bodies to apply the fillets to.

The icon with the eyeglasses next to the check box allows you to disable a preview of the Fillet feature if the performance of your system is suffering.

You can find four other options by clicking the More button and expanding the dialog box. These options affect how the fillet or round is generated:

Roll Along Sharp Edges   When this option is selected, Inventor varies the fillet radius in order to maintain a sharp edge corner where it intersects. If this option is off (the default), Inventor maintains the radius by pulling the face it meets up into the radius. It's as if a fillet was put around an object and then part of the fillet was milled off.

Rolling Ball Where Possible   This option controls how corners are resolved where multiple edges meet at a corner. With Rolling Ball Where Possible selected, the corner shows a spherical radius that is the same as the edge radius. With the option off, Inventor enlarges the corner and extends the radius back down the edge to create a smoother appearance.

Automatic Edge Chain   Automatic Edge Chain is on by default. When it's disabled, selecting an edge won't automatically select edges that are tangent to it.

Preserve All Features   Preserve All Features takes features that are affected by the fillet into consideration for the calculation. You would use this option primarily when placing a fillet has the effect of removing another feature. For example, if you cut a notch into a face near an edge and then place a fillet that passes over the notch, the notch may disappear even though the notch is deep enough that you expected it to remain. With this option turned on, the Fillet tool recognizes that there is a cut that shouldn't be removed and calculates its rounded face with the notch built into it.

Even with all the options and flexibility, placing fillets and rounds on a part can be challenging to do exactly right. The order in which you place fillets, along with the numbers and combinations of edges you select, affect how the fillets appear on the model. This takes time to master, and you have to look at the model to make sure you're getting the result you want. The good news is that if it doesn't come out right the first time, it's easy to try it another way.

Let's do a sampling of the different fillet types on the part.

Adding Fillets to the Edges

For the same reasons you needed to add draft, you need to soften the external edges of the part:

1. Start the Fillet tool from the Modify panel.

2. Using an edge fillet, click the inside edge of the part as shown in Figure 6.13.

3. Set Radius to .2in, and click Apply to create the fillet.

4. Change Radius to .1, and pick the five edges shown in Figure 6.14. You may need to click the Pencil icon to be able to select edges. Don't click OK or Apply after picking the edges.

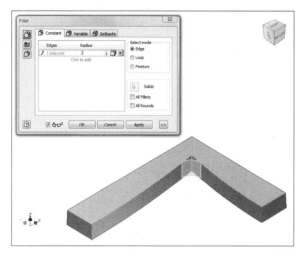

FIGURE 6.13 Edge selected for fillet

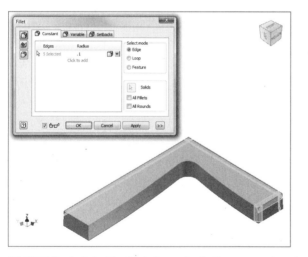

FIGURE 6.14 The first stage of selecting many edges for a single Fillet feature

5. Switch the Fillet dialog to the Variable tab.

6. Pick the edge selected in Figure 6.15.

7. Set Start Radius to .1 and the End Radius to .25.

8. Pick the tangent point where the curve meets the first fillet you added for an additional radius. This point is highlighted in Figure 6.15.

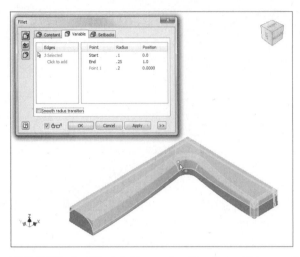

FIGURE 6.15 Selecting and setting the radii for a variable-radius fillet

9. Set the Radius value to .2.

10. Return to the Constant tab, and pick where it says Click to Add.

11. Set a new Radius of .3in, and pick the outer vertical edge shown in Figure 6.16.

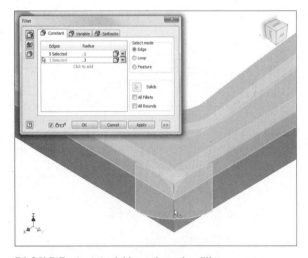

FIGURE 6.16 Add another edge fillet.

12. Pick the Setbacks tab in the dialog.

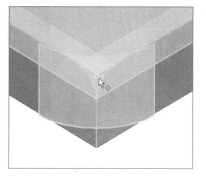

13. Select the top outer corner for the vertex to define setbacks.

14. Define the distance of the setbacks as .4in along the long edges and .25in for the vertical edge. Refer to Figure 6.17 to compare your results.

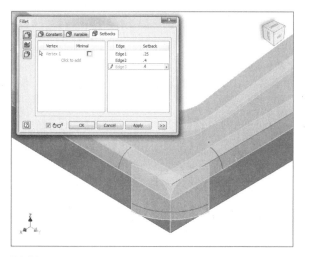

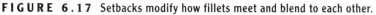

FIGURE 6.17 Setbacks modify how fillets meet and blend to each other.

15. Click OK to place all the fillets at once. See Figure 6.18.

16. Save your work.

To this point, you've defined one fourth of your part. Now you can finish creating the cast handle using the Mirror tool.

FIGURE 6.18 The finished filleting

Mirroring the Incomplete Part

In this exercise, you'll complete the cast handle by replicating the geometry you've already created:

1. Start the Mirror tool from the Pattern panel.

2. Set the Mirror a Solid option, and pick the flat face at the end of the part as shown in Figure 6.19.

3. Click OK to create the Mirror feature.

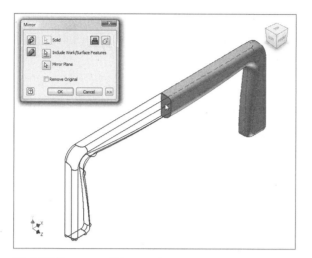

FIGURE 6.19 Mirroring the entire body to form half the part

4. Press the Enter key to start the Mirror tool again.

5. Using the Mirror a Solid option again, click the flat face shown in Figure 6.20.

6. Click OK to finish creating the entire solid body.
    Now, let's add a finishing touch to the completed handle.

7. On the Quick Access Toolbar, set Part Color to Aluminum (Cast). See Figure 6.21 to compare your finished part.

8. Save your work, and close the file.

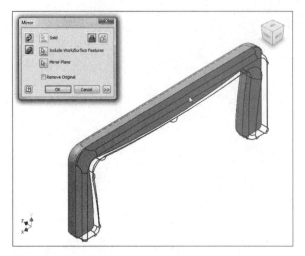

FIGURE 6.20 Using the Mirror tool again to complete the body of the part

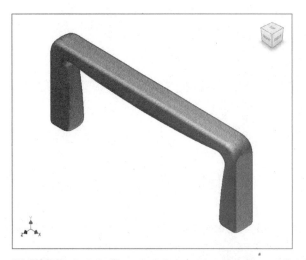

FIGURE 6.21 The completed cast handle with cast finish applied

Often, companies choose to make a part a casting because they need the same basic geometry for several parts but each part may have critical surfaces or features that differ from one another. With that in mind, let's create a new part using your cast part as its foundation. To do this, you must use a derived part.

Derived Parts

Inventor's Derived Parts technology is primarily a tool for part modeling, but it can be used in many ways, including complex assembly designs.

The most common use for derived parts are to create one part model based on another and keep the resulting model associated with the original. Another use is to be able to fuse the parts of an assembly into a single part file. A third, very powerful option is to extract dimension values and parameter values from one part for reuse in another part. This is a great way to build enduring relationships between parts without using adaptive modeling. This method even allows you to draw model values from several parts into one so that the part responds to changes from multiple sources.

At some companies, the use of derived parts can completely change the way they're doing their job. I think it's important to at least dabble in this great technology.

Creating a Machined Handle

In this exercise, we'll review a basic workflow for converting a cast part to a machined part without modifying the original casting so that other machined versions can be made from it:

1. Create a new part from the **Standard (in).ipt** template.
   As usual, this opens a new Part file in the Design window with an active sketch. For this purpose, you don't need a sketch at this time.

2. Select the Finish Sketch tool to exit the active sketch.

3. Set your Ribbon to the Manage tab, and pick Derive Tools from the Insert panel.
   Doing so brings up the Open dialog. This lets you select the file from which you want to extract data or geometry.

4. Select Cast Handle.ipt from the Parts folder, and click Open.
   This opens the Derived Part dialog, similar to Figure 6.22. In this dialog, you can choose from many types of information available in the source part. In this case, the solid geometry is available as well as any parametric dimension that has been created.

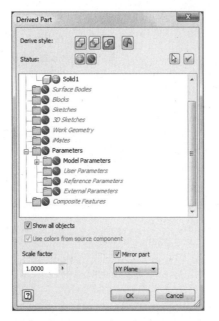

FIGURE 6.22 The Derived Part dialog makes it possible to select what type of data you want to reuse.

In addition to selecting the data you want to link to in the source file, you can also select how any geometry will be used. Four Derive Style settings determine how imported data is used in the assembly:

Single Solid Body Merging Out Seams between Planar Faces   A name like that doesn't leave much need for definition. If you link to an assembly with three parts that are end to end, the parts are merged into a single solid using this method.

Solid Body Keep Seams between Planar Faces   Also used for working with links to assemblies, this option maintains separated faces similar to multibody solids, but in reverse.

Maintain Each solid as a Solid Body   This option brings an assembly to a multibody solid state in the single part.

Body as Work Surface   If you need to build a part that conforms to the contours of another part or assembly, you can use that component's surfaces to build up against or to cut your current part.

Other options exist for selecting the components in the context of the source file and for picking what is and isn't included in the derived body. You can also modify the scale of the source data in the new part and create a mirror of the source data based about a selected plane.

Now let's begin the process of making a new part from the cast part.

5. Click OK to accept the default in this case.

In the Design window, you see the exact data that you just created. It doesn't have parametric intelligence that is maintained in the source file. Think of it as a kind of template from which to start your new work.

6. Turn on the visibility of the XZ plane in the Origin folder.

7. In the Work Features panel on the Model tab, start the Plane tool.

8. Select the XZ plane, and drag a new work plane –1.85 inches below, as shown in Figure 6.23.

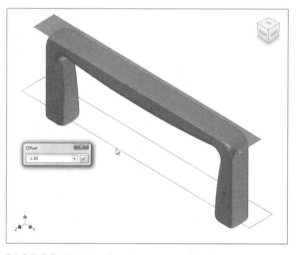

FIGURE 6.23 Creating a new work plane

9. Click the check mark to create the new work plane.

10. Save the file as **Machined Handle.ipt** in the Parts folder.

The Split Tool

Many tools in Inventor work differently depending on the options you choose, but the Split tool can work like two different tools depending on the options you select. It can either remove a portion of the target part or simply split its geometry.

Either way, you can use a sketch, surface, or plane to split a part or faces of a part by first selecting the tool you want to cut with and then choosing what elements of the part it will pass through to divide.

Method

Choosing the split method is the big difference in how the tool behaves:

 Split Face   This option doesn't remove any geometry from the part, but it breaks faces based on the geometry of the tool.

 Trim Solid   This option removes a portion of the target part. With this option, you can also set the direction to choose which portion will be removed.

Split Solid   A different tool in some ways, the Split Solid option divides the split body into separate bodies. You can modify these bodies independently even though they're part of a single solid. This is a gateway to using a single solid to define an assembly. It's referred to commonly as a *multibody workflow*.

Faces

You can also select whether all or only specific faces are affected by the tool while using the Split Face method:

All   Any face that the tool passes through is divided along the tool's geometry.

Select   This allows you to select the faces to split. If a face (such as a cylinder) can be passed through more than once, the face is split more than once.

Remove

This option appears when you're using the Trim Solid method. Selecting the direction arrow determines which side of the solid model is removed by the operation.

Let's use the Split tool to machine the mounting surface of your handle so that it rests flat against the fan housing.

Using Split on Your Derived Part

You've already defined your cutting surface by creating the work plane. The rest should be easy:

1. Start the Split tool in the Modify panel.

2. Switch the method to Trim Solid.

3. Select the recently created work plane as the Split tool and make sure the arrow is pointing toward the open portion of the part as shown in Figure 6.24.

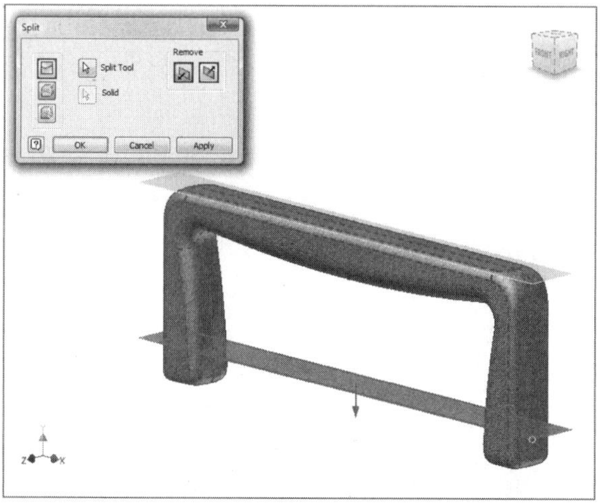

![Screenshot showing the Split dialog and a handle model with a work plane used as the Split tool]

FIGURE 6.24 Using a work plane as the Split tool

4. Click OK to trim off the bottom of the part.

5. Turn off the visibility of the XZ plane and the work plane you created. See Figure 6.25 for the result.

Now, let's place some mounting holes in the part.

6. Create a new sketch on the work plane you created by starting the Create 2D Sketch tool and selecting Work Plane 1 in the Browser.

7. Use the View Face tool (PgUp key) to get a view of the machined faces.

8. Use the Point tool to create a sketch point in the middle of each of the two faces. See Figure 6.26.

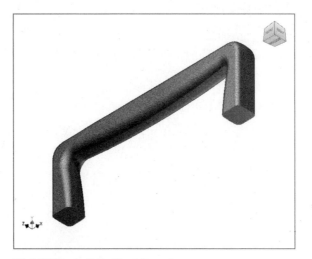

FIGURE 6.25 The trimmed part

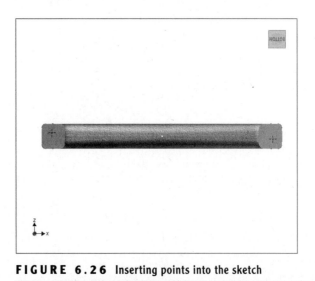

FIGURE 6.26 Inserting points into the sketch

9. Use the Horizontal constraint to align the two points with the sketch centerpoint.

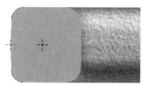

10. Start the Project Geometry tool to project the point where the two drafted faces meet on the sides of the handle.

11. Place a dimension of .3 inches between the two points, as shown in Figure 6.27.

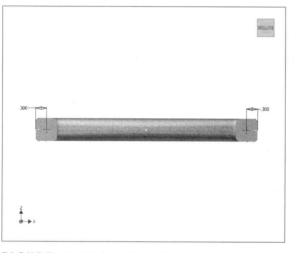

FIGURE 6.27 Locating the hole centers

12. Finish the sketch.

13. Start the Hole tool, and place two holes on the sketched points. Hold the Ctrl key, and deselect the projected points for placing the holes.

14. Set the parameters of the holes according to the dialog shown in Figure 6.28.

15. Click OK to place the holes.

16. Save your work, and compare it to Figure 6.29.

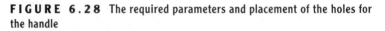

FIGURE 6.28 The required parameters and placement of the holes for the handle

FIGURE 6.29 The finished handle

Now you'll see what happens to your finished part if the casting changes.

Modifying the Derived Component Source

Let's make a change that is a lot more extreme than you would usually see done to a cast part from which machined variations are made:

1. In the Browser of the machined handle part, right-click the Cast Handle.ipt link and select Open Base Component from the context menu.

2. When the cast handle part is open, edit Sketch1 under Extrusion 1.

3. Change the 3.000 dimension to 4.000 and the 2.300 to 2.000, as in Figure 6.30.

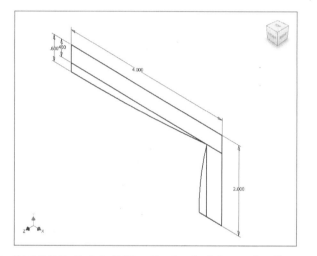

FIGURE 6.30 Editing the sketch of the cast handle

4. Finish editing the sketch.

5. Save the changes, and close the file.

6. When you return to the machined handle part, nothing has changed. Pick the Update tool in the Quick Access Toolbar to bring the part up to date.

    The updated part looks like Figure 6.31.

7. Save the changes to the machined handle, and close the file.

As I said, this was an extreme change to the cast part. But by thinking through the likely changes when defining your machining, you ensure that the updates are successful.

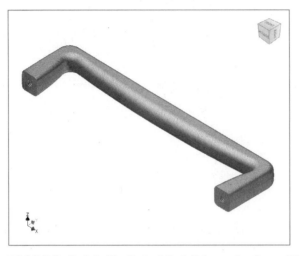

FIGURE 6.31 The Derived Part dialog makes it possible to select what type of data you want to reuse.

In this case, using the XZ plane as a datum for making the cut not only makes sense but is a good stable foundation that won't be affected by a change to the casting. Using the draft-convergence points for locating the holes also makes sense because the model is mirrored about the planes; it's highly unlikely that those points will be broken, because the drafted faces will be kept in a cast part.

So far, we've looked at scenarios that make it easier to reuse data that is created in house. Now more than ever, a portion of designs are often sourced from outside companies.

Supplier Content Center

Many experienced CAD users are accustomed to working with IGES or STEP data. Inventor offers other options as well, including the ability to import data from (and export data to) several other CAD systems (see Appendix B) without having to use the neutral file formats. Along with a lot of flexibility regarding import/export formats, Inventor comes with links for access to online content from dozens of vendors in the Supplier Content Center.

Selecting the Supplier Content icon from the Web panel on the Manage tab connects you to online resources for locating purchased components or components created by members of the Autodesk Manufacturing Community (Figure 6.32). There are also links to sites where vendors have posted tens of thousands of components for their customers.

FIGURE 6.32 Autodesk Manufacturing Community Content page

These sites have search capabilities that allow you to find components based on specifications so you don't have to know the name or part number of the component you need to find it. I highly recommend creating a membership in the Manufacturing Community as well as the part sourcing sites to explore what is available. You may save yourself some time modeling purchased components or discover another component from an unfamiliar manufacturer that will suit your needs.

For the sake of simplicity, I have downloaded two components for your assembly from the Supplier Content Center. One is in Inventor format; I've converted the other to a STEP neutral file so you can experiment with that process as well.

Using Supplier Content

First, you need to locate the components in a place where Inventor can easily find them:

1. Create a new folder named C:\Data\Supplier Content.

2. Place the Caster.stp file you downloaded earlier in the Supplier Content folder.

3. Expand the previously downloaded Motor.zip in the Supplier Content folder, creating a subfolder named Motor that contains the model files.

Now you have the files in place. It's important to remember the structure of your project file, and creating a new folder in that structure allows you to keep things sorted but easily accessible to Inventor.

Let's use the new data to enhance your assembly:

1. Open or activate the fan assembly.

2. Set your view in the Design window by selecting the corner of the ViewCube that makes Bottom, Right, and Front visible.

3. Start the Place tool.

4. Change the Files of Type value to STEP files (*.stp, *.ste, *.step).

5. Change the Look In folder to Supplier Content.

6. Pick **Caster.stp**, and click OK or double-click the file to begin placing it.

7. Place one instance of the component into the assembly. See Figure 6.33.

8. In the Position panel, pick the Rotate tool or press the G key on the keyboard.
   Doing so starts a tool that lets you rotate a component in the assembly regardless of its existing constraints.

9. Pick the caster. A Reticle appears, just as it does with the Orbit tool; but this affects only the selected part.

10. Click and drag until the caster is in roughly the same position shown in Figure 6.34.

11. Right-click, and select Done to stop rotating the part.

12. Start the Constrain tool, and place a Mate constraint between the side of the housing and the top of the caster as shown in Figure 6.35. Use the Apply button to place it, because you'll need more constraints.

Rotate

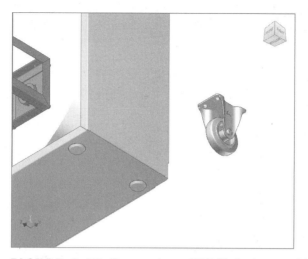

FIGURE 6.33 You can place a STEP file in the assembly without converting it first.

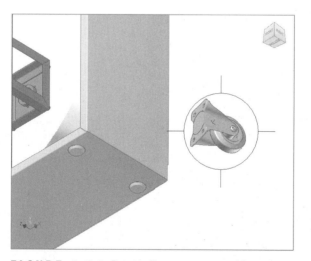

FIGURE 6.34 Rotate allows you to reposition a part even if it has constraints.

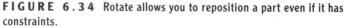

13. Place another Mate constraint with a Flush solution between the side of the caster and the side of the housing with a .5in. offset (Figure 6.36). Click Apply.

Picking the caster first avoids having to make the value negative to position it as it's shown in Figure 6.37.

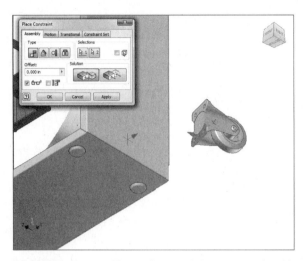

FIGURE 6.35 Mating the top of the caster to the side of the housing

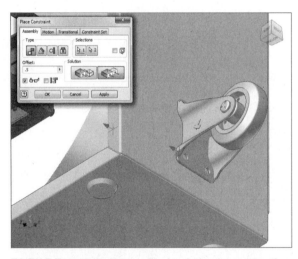

FIGURE 6.36 Using a Flush solution to position the caster from the side

14. Place the caster flush and .5in. from the bottom of the housing, as shown in Figure 6.37.

15. Click OK to place the constraint and close the dialog. The final result should look like Figure 6.38.

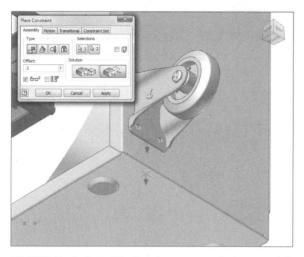

FIGURE 6.37 Aligning the caster to the bottom of the assembly

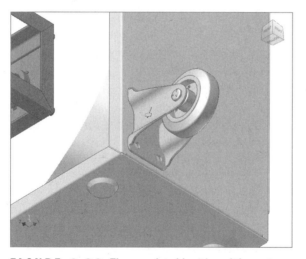

FIGURE 6.38 The completed location of the caster

16. Place another instance of the caster, and constrain it to the assembly on the other side of the assembly per Figure 6.39, using the same distances.

17. Save your work.

FIGURE 6.39 Add a second caster to the assembly.

Now, you'll place the motor into the assembly. The files provided by the manufacturer include an assembly and two part files: one is the model, and the other includes additional location geometry. You only need the model, so you'll use its part file rather than the assembly.

In Chapter 3, "Moving into the Assembly World," we discussed how a component placed into the assembly (that isn't the base component) has six Degrees of Freedom (DOF). Inventor has a mechanism that lets you visualize how you're removing the Degrees of Freedom as you place constraints. The next exercise includes the use of this tool for visualization:

1. Set the view of the assembly so that the ViewCube displays the Top, Front, and Left of the assembly.

2. Place the 34LY1371_frame_10_96_N.ipt file from the C:\Data\ Supplier Content\Motor folder. You'll need to change File of Type to Inventor Component Files to see the part file.

3. Switch the Ribbon to the View tab. In the Visibility panel, pick the toggle that turns on the display of DOF (keyboard shortcut Ctrl+Shift+E).

4. Because the motor has full freedom, it initially displays the full icon, as shown in Figure 6.40.

5. Constrain the back of the motor to the inside of the housing as shown in Figure 6.41, with a .5in. offset.

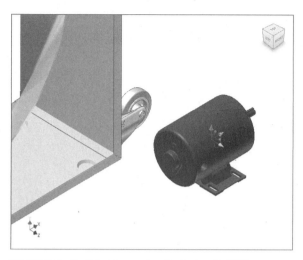

FIGURE 6.40 The motor displaying its DOF

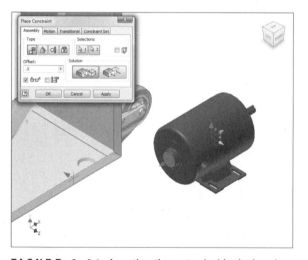

FIGURE 6.41 Locating the motor inside the housing

6. Click OK to place the constraint.

7. Use Rotate to position the motor so you can see the bottom of the mounting plate. Note how the DOF icon is now showing one rotational DOF and two translational degrees.

8. Add a Mate constraint with no offset to bind the bottom of the motor's mounting plate to the inside, bottom of the housing. See Figure 6.42.

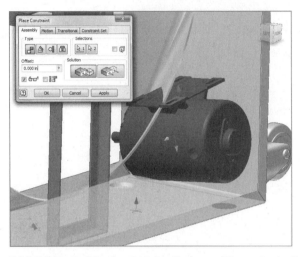

FIGURE 6.42   Constraining the base of the motor to the housing

9. Click OK to add the constraint.

10. Only one remaining DOF exists. Click and drag the motor to see that you can still move in the unconstrained DOF. See Figure 6.43.

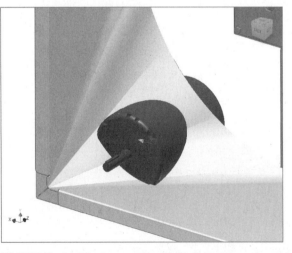

FIGURE 6.43   A remaining DOF lets you move the motor.

11. Toggle off the DOF display by selection the icon again.

12. Save your work.

As you've probably noticed and can see in Figure 6.42, you have a bit of an interference issue between the motor and the duct. In the next chapter you'll calculate the proper location of the motor; then, you can modify the duct to accommodate it. For now, though, I want to simplify the motor to make it easier to reuse its geometry.

Advanced tools in Inventor let you take entire assemblies and replace them with a single part or find just the exterior features and create a shrinkwrap model that removes the interior detail for enhanced performance. In this case, the changes you need are very simple and best done on the model itself.

Modifying Supplier Content

In the following steps, you'll simplify the motor without limiting its value or compromising its accuracy:

1. In the Browser or the Design window, right-click the newly placed motor, and choose Open to bring it up in its own window.

2. Pass your cursor over the features in the Browser to get a sense of how the part was built.

3. Pick Extrusion 1 in the Browser. This highlights what appears to be a shaft key.

4. Hold the Shift key, and select Extrusion 6. This highlights all the features between Extrusion 1 and Extrusion 6, as shown in Figure 6.44.

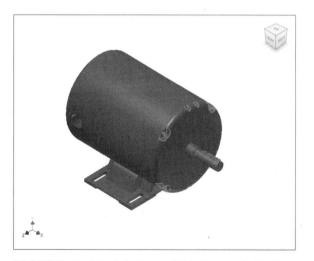

FIGURE 6.44 Selecting multiple features in the Browser

5. Right-click in the Browser, and select Suppress Features from the context menu. See the result in Figure 6.45.

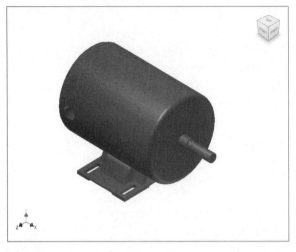

FIGURE 6.45 The motor with suppressed features

6. Save the motor, and close it.

7. When Inventor returns to the fan assembly, save it.

Now, you need to add your machined handle to the assembly. But you first need to figure out where to place it.

Assembly Sketches

In Chapter 3, you worked in the weldment environment, where you were able to add a machining feature to the assembly that existed only in the assembly. It's also possible to add features to assemblies that aren't weldments. You can add sketches to the assembly that are only used as sketches and not converted to features.

In order to properly locate your handle, you need to figure out where the handle needs to be positioned so that it's useful for moving the fan. You could do this on the physical prototype, but the goal of using these 3D models is to develop a digital prototype that lets you validate the design and know it's correct the first time you build it in the physical world.

In a 2D CAD system, you'd assume that the best way to do this would be to create a layout sketch—and you'd be correct. The question is whether most people would think to use the same approach in a 3D model. Well, that is exactly what you'll be doing. You'll create a 2D sketch in your assembly that is based on the geometry of your 3D parts, so that if they change, the sketch will adjust and give you the proper information.

Creating the 2D Layout

In this exercise, you'll project edges and points from the parts you've placed in the assembly:

1. Make the fan assembly the active file.

2. Restore the Front view from the ViewCube.

3. Press the S key to start a new sketch, or switch to the Model tab and pick Create 2D Sketch from the Sketch panel.

4. Place the new sketch on the bottom face at the front of the housing. See Figure 6.46.

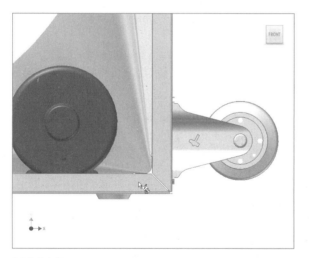

FIGURE 6.46 Locating the new sketch in the assembly

The interface is updated to offer you the sketching tools, and the Browser updates to show that you're in Sketch1 of the assembly.

5. Start the Project Geometry tool, and pick the outer diameter of the caster to project it into the sketch.

6. Project the point at lower-right on the housing, as highlighted in Figure 6.47.

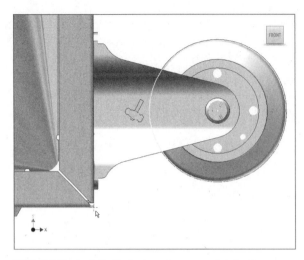

FIGURE 6.47 Project a reference point for the corner of the housing.

7. Start the Line tool. Move near the bottom of the projected circle from the caster. When the glyph appears, showing a relationship to the edge, pick and drag to the left.

Doing so creates a new line that is automatically tangent to the circle. This line will be used to represent the floor if and when the fan is rolled on the caster.

8. Drag the end of the tangent line below the housing, as shown in Figure 6.48.

9. End the Line tool.

10. Right-click the new line, and select Properties from the menu.

This launches a dialog that lets you alter the way a sketch element is displayed in the sketch. It doesn't alter whether the line is a normal, construction, or center line.

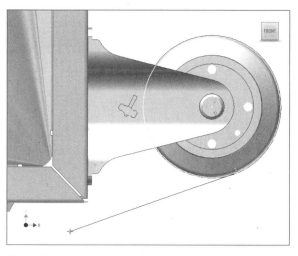

FIGURE 6.48 You can drag a line segment tangent to an arc or circle.

11. Set Line Color to Red and Line Weight to .055in.

12. Click OK to make the changes to the line.

13. Start the Dimension tool, and place a dimension between the projected point and the newly created line. Set the value to 0.8in., as shown in Figure 6.49.

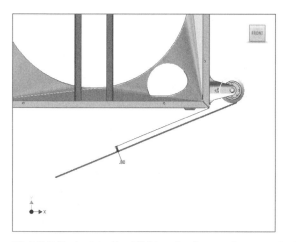

FIGURE 6.49 Establishing the distance between the housing and the floor

This dimension allows you to modify the angle of the line by setting a clearance between the point and the line representing the floor.

14. Zoom out so you can see the left side of the housing.

15. Drag the endpoint of the tangent line to make it about half as long as the assembly is wide. Press Esc to end the Dimension command if needed.

16. Draw a perpendicular line starting on the end of the first line, as shown in Figure 6.50.

17. Dimension the line's length to a value of Standing_Height=30, as shown in Figure 6.50.

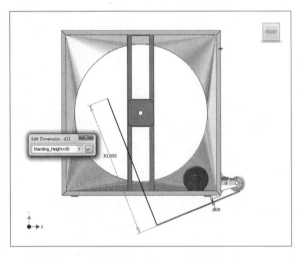

FIGURE 6.50 Adding the perpendicular line

This new line sets the target height for the handle from the floor when the person moving it is standing. It also creates a named parameter that will make it easier to locate and modify in the Parameters table.

18. Create a Coincidence constraint between the endpoint of the 30in. line and the left, vertical edge of the housing. See Figure 6.51. Be sure not to pick the midpoint of the edge.

19. Add a dimension between the endpoint of the 30in. line and the point you projected early on. Click to place the dimension.

When you attempt to place the dimension, you receive a warning that the dimension will "over-constrain" the sketch. You're offered a chance to place the dimension as a driven dimension. You want this dimension to be driven because it's going to provide you with the distance you're looking for.

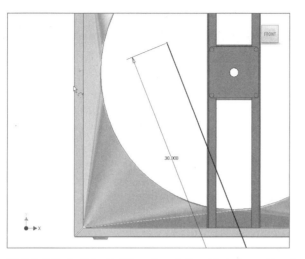

FIGURE 6.51 Building the relationship between the standing height and the side of the housing

20. Click Accept to place the dimension. See Figure 6.52.

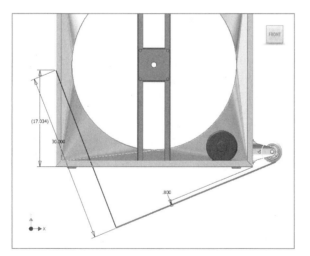

FIGURE 6.52 Adding a driven dimension to monitor the distance from the bottom of the housing

21. Make note of the new dimension's value. Click the Manage tab, and select the Parameters tool.

   The Parameters dialog appears (Figure 6.53), showing a list of all the parameters being used by the assembly. The values of assembly

f_x
Parameters

constraints and the parametric dimensions appear in the Model Parameters rows. The dimension you want to work with is listed under Reference Parameters.

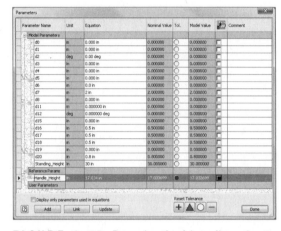

FIGURE 6.53 Renaming the driven dimension to a recognizable parameter

In this dialog, you can rename any parameter or change its value. You can also link the file to a spreadsheet or another model to extract parametric values from. In the Tolerance column, you can tell a parameter to be generated to its Maximum, Minimum, Mean, or Nominal tolerance value if you've included a tolerance in the parametric value.

22. Change the name of the dimension under Reference Parameters to **Handle_Height**.

23. Click Done to complete the change.

24. Click the 17.034 dimension to highlight it.

25. Right-click, and select Dimension properties from the context menu.
   Doing so opens the Dimension Properties dialog, where you can also give the dimension a new name, change its evaluated size, and set its tolerance method. The Document Settings tab (Figure 6.54) offers you tools to change the display of the dimension and the precision that is displayed. Regardless of the precision that is displayed, Inventor still calculates the accuracy to a very high degree.

26. Set the Modeling Dimension Display value to Show Expression.

27. Set the Linear Dim. Display Precision to the second decimal, as shown in Figure 6.54.

28. Click OK to apply the changes. Compare your screen to Figure 6.55.

29. Double-click the 0.8in dimension, and change the value to **1.5** to see what happens to Handle_Height if you increase your floor clearance.

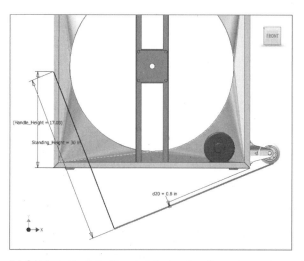

FIGURE 6.54 Modifying the display of the sketch dimensions

FIGURE 6.55 The sketch showing dimension names and values

30. Click the check mark to see the change, as shown in Figure 6.56.

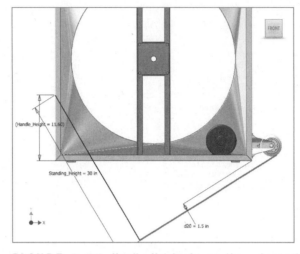

FIGURE 6.56 Handle_Height changes if you change the floor clearance.

31. Restore the clearance to .08in., and click the check mark to update.

32. Click the Finish Sketch tool to leave the sketching environment.

33. Save the file.

The entire purpose of creating the sketch was to model the height at which your handle needs to be mounted from the bottom of the housing so that when you pick it up, the handle is at the height you want. You can use your digital model to evaluate the options. Giving the housing a 1.5in. clearance from the floor when moved places the handle at an uncomfortably low position for picking it up.

Now that you've made your evaluation, you can reuse the information in the context of your assembly.

Using the Named Parameter

Let's use the Handle_Height parameter from your sketch to set the height of the machined handle in the assembly:

1. In the fan assembly, locate Sketch1 below the `Origin` folder in the Browser, and turn off its visibility.

2. Use the Place tool to add one instance of the machined handle to the assembly.

3. Create a Mate constraint between the XY plane of the assembly and the YZ plane of the machined handle, as shown in Figure 6.57.

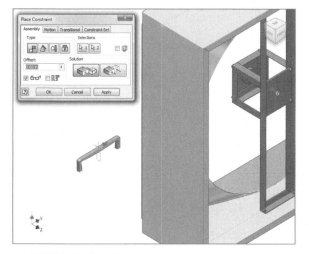

FIGURE 6.57 Constraining the handle to be centered on the side of the fan

4. Click OK to place the constraint.

Your handle may be moved into the middle of the assembly. If so, click and drag it into a position that is easy for you to see.

5. Add a Mate constraint between the machined face of the handle and the left side of the housing. See Figure 6.58.

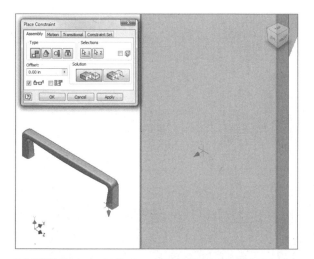

FIGURE 6.58 Mating the machined face to the housing

6. Click Apply to place the constraint.

7. Create another Mate constraint by first selecting XY plane of the handle where the parting line of the casting and then the bottom of the housing.

8. In the Offset box in the dialog, click the arrow pointing to the right. Doing so opens a context menu.

9. From the menu, pick List Parameters.
This opens another dialog with a list of named parameters.

10. Double-click Handle_Height to set it as the value for the constraint offset.

11. Be sure Handle_Height is the only value in the dialog, and then place a hyphen before Handle_Height to make the value negative. See Figure 6.59.

12. Click OK to place the constraint.

13. Save the assembly.
As it seems is always the case, just when you think you have it all figured out, someone makes a change. In this case, it's been determined that the height of the handle while moving the fan should be 32 inches.

14. Set the Ribbon to the Manage tab and open the Parameters dialog.

15. Change the value of the Standing_Height parameter to 32 in., and click Done to close the dialog.
Normally, the Update icon on the Quick Access Toolbar updates an assembly constraint. But when you make a change to a constraint value based on a calculation based on a dimension, it's a good idea to use something with a little more strength to execute the update.

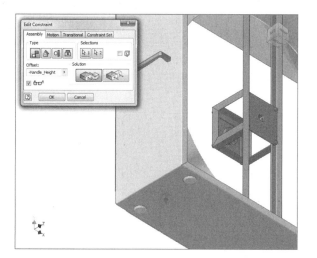

FIGURE 6.59 Setting the height of the handle based on the Handle_Height parameter

16. In the Update panel of the Manage tab, click the Rebuild All tool.

After a few seconds, the machined handle should move up, and the value for the dimension that located it should update to 19.19 inches. With Inventor doing the geometry calculations for you, it's easy to be confident about the correct result.

17. Save your work, and compare it with Figure 6.60.

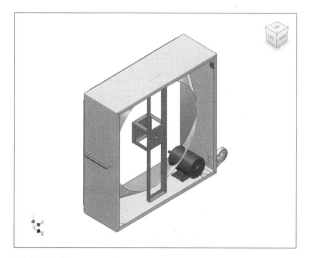

FIGURE 6.60 The updated handle location

This example is a very simple one for Inventor. It's also possible to use multiple sketches and build entire assemblies using 2D elements inside Inventor.

We could continue and have you add the bolted connections to attach the handle and the caster, but instead we'll move on to other new topics.

Are You Experienced?

Now you can...

- ☑ **create and access iMates to automate assembly**

- ☑ **use derived parts to create a part based on another part**

- ☑ **work with components sourced from others**

- ☑ **recognize available Degrees of Freedom**

- ☑ **use parametric 2D sketches to do calculations for you**

CHAPTER 7

Functional Design Using Design Accelerators

▶ Selecting bearings based on needs

▶ Designing shafts

▶ Creating V-belts

▶ Editing components created by design accelerators

▶ Modifying sheet metal parts

Design Accelerators

The design accelerators exist for one reason: design. As powerful as Inventor is, most of what you've been doing to this point is modeling, and any 3D system should be able to model parts. Design is a different issue. Design means using engineering calculations to determine the correct component for the job rather than hoping you have it right.

The geometry of a part is the solution, not the question; so although tools like finite element analysis are still the best solution for creating custom parts, using time-tested data to find which standard components meet your requirements is the more intelligent approach when working with common parts of a typical machine design.

You've already tried an example of this approach, when you worked with the bolted connection design accelerator in Chapter 3, "Moving into the Assembly World." Bolted Connection is a great tool that follows the design approach I've just described, and I highly encourage you to explore it in full. There are many more design accelerators than I have room to cover in this chapter, so I'll focus on demonstrating a few that are particularly useful in assembly design: the Bearing Generator, the Shaft Component Generator, and the V-Belts Component Generator. To learn more about the design accelerators, see *Mastering Autodesk Inventor 2010*, by Curtis Waguespack (Wiley, 2009).

Like other Inventor tools, the design accelerator dialog boxes generally all work in the same way: the Design tab handles modeling considerations such as size and shape, and the Calculation tab focuses on engineering or product design considerations.

The Bearing Generator

🔲 Bearing

The first design accelerator you'll use is the Bearing Generator. You should open the dialog to follow along. It's located on the Design tab in the Power Transmission panel.

Like most design accelerators, it can be used two ways: to place geometry based on the size you want or to calculate what geometry is needed to fulfill the engineering requirements. Again, the first use is the approach we've taken so far with the Bolted Connection Component Generator; the second is a capability we'll begin to explore here. In practice, you'll often combine the techniques.

This tool is unique in that the dialog box can present a list of suitable bearings based on a query. You can use the two tabs back and forth to help limit the list based on the standards you search and the engineering requirements placed on the design.

The Design Tab

This tab has some straightforward inputs, but don't let the simplicity fool you — you can quickly locate a huge amount of data using this tab.

The pull-down list at the top launches a dialog box similar to the one used for placing components from the Content Center. The dialog box includes two pull-down lists that allow you to filter based on the standard or the category of bearing. After you set the filters, the bearing standards are displayed as icons. The dimensional range at upper right limits the selection of bearings based on space considerations.

The selection arrows at left let you select geometry directly in the assembly for the diameter and starting plane used to placing a bearing.

After you've selected your search criteria, you can update the rules to have Inventor search the Content Center for the matching items. The list appears in the Select Bearing area in the lower half of the window.

The Calculation Tab

The Calculation tab is intended to be used quite differently than the Design tab. You input your requirements, and Inventor calculates which standard bearings meet your needs.

Discussing every option here would lead us into engineering topics that are beyond the scope of this book. The bottom line is that if you want to be absolutely certain that the bearing you select will do the job, this is where to find out. There are a couple of key elements that every user should be aware of.

Type of Strength Calculation

The first pull-down option is located at upper left in the dialog box and controls which method is used to evaluate the bearings:

Check Calculation   When you select a bearing from the list at the bottom of the tab, its properties are displayed based on the loads specified in the Loads group.

Bearing Design   By also calculating the effect the loads will have on the life of the bearing, this option filters the list further and makes it easier for you to select the proper bearing.

Loads

It's critical that you enter the appropriate Radial and Axial loads as well as the number of shaft rotations per minute that will occur, in order to validate the bearings for selection.

Bearing Life Calculation

This pull-down list selects which ANSI or other standard method will be used to calculate the life of the bearing. Be sure to use the appropriate methodology to ensure the results you need.

Messages

At the very bottom and on the right side of most design accelerator dialog boxes are double arrows that expand the dialog box to show messages relating to the calculation. If the bottom or right edge of a design accelerator dialog box turns red after a calculation, expand this area to see the error message.

Let's use the Bearing Generator to verify that the bearing that I have in mind for your fan is acceptable.

Using the Bearing Generator

You'll test your selection, keeping in mind that you can generate a list of bearings purely by selecting a class and loading the performance conditions:

1. Activate or open the fan assembly.

2. In the Browser, expand Fan Support Frame and pick Bearing Support:2.

3. Right-click, and select Isolate in the context menu.

4. Zoom in on the bearing support assembly.

5. Switch the Ribbon to the Design tab.

6. Pick the Bearing tool from the Power Transmission panel.

7. Set the Bearing type to Angular Contact Ball Bearing.

8. Set the outer diameter range with a From value of 1.4 and a To value of 1.6.

9. Set the inner diameter with a From value of .5 and a To value of .65. See Figure 7.1.

10. Click the Update icon to refresh the list of bearings.

11. Switch the dialog to the Calculation tab. See Figure 7.2.

12. Change Type of Strength Calculation to Bearing Design.

13. Set the Radial Load value to 100 lbforce and the Axial Load value to 20 lbforce.

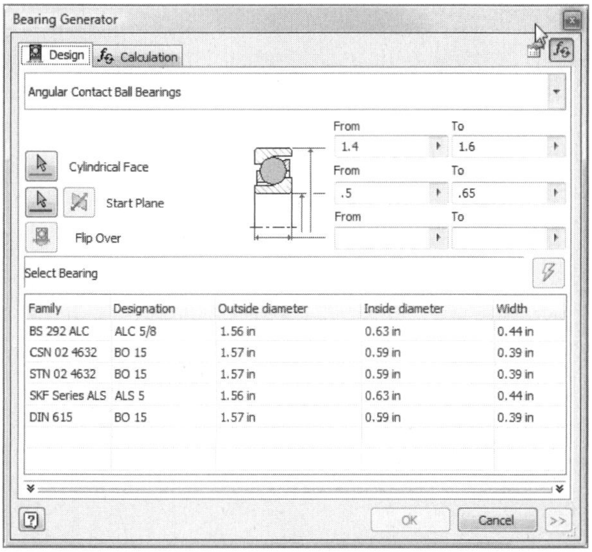

FIGURE 7.1 The Bearing Generator dialog box's Design tab

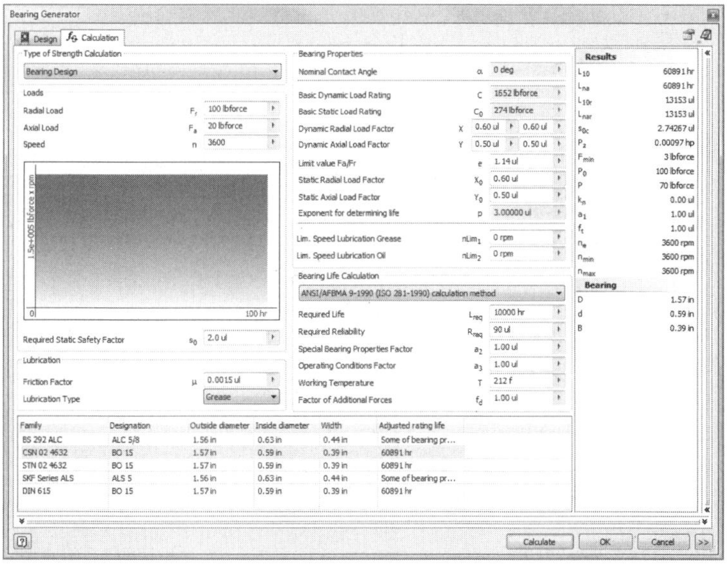

FIGURE 7.2 The Calculation tab of the Bearing Generator dialog box. On the right are the results calculated from the input.

14. Set the Speed value to 3600.

15. At the bottom of the dialog, select SKF Series ALS from the list of families.

16. Click the Calculate button.

A dialog appears, warning you that the calculation may take considerable time.

17. Click Yes to start the calculation.

A rule of thumb for design accelerator dialogs is that no red is good. This calculation should be fine.

18. Switch back to the Design tab.

19. Pick the SKF Series ALS bearing from the list in the lower section of the dialog, and click OK to generate the physical model of the bearing.

20. Place one model of the bearing in your assembly, and click the Esc key to end the command. See Figure 7.3.

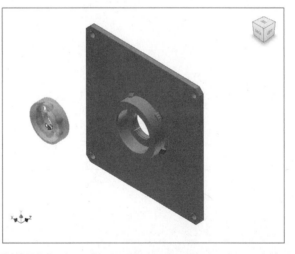

FIGURE 7.3 Placing the bearing that has been evaluated

21. Use an Insert constraint to place the bearing into the bearing support assembly. See Figure 7.4.

22. After the bearing is constrained, right-click an open area in the Design window and select Undo Isolate from the context menu to turn the other components' visibility back on.

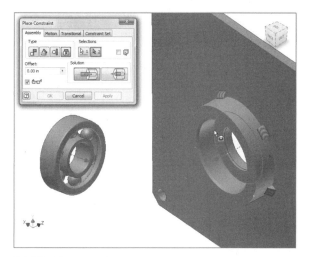

FIGURE 7.4 Constraining the bearing into place

23. Locate the bearing that was just placed at the bottom of the Browser.

24. Click and drag another instance into the Design window.

25. Use another Insert constraint to place the bearing into the other bearing holder, as shown in Figure 7.5.

26. Save your work.

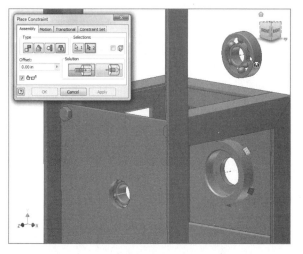

FIGURE 7.5 Locating the second bearing

Now you've placed a bearing, and you know that it's capable of doing the job. Using the standards that govern the production of the bearings to help guide your selection ahead of time rather than doing hours of testing can be a huge cost savings. This too is an example of using a digital prototype.

Let's build the shaft that the fan blade will be mounted to. But rather than using Extrude or Revolve, you'll use another design accelerator that is purpose-built.

The Shaft Component Generator

This tool builds round things. It's especially adept at round things that spin, so it offers some great features for rotating shafts.

Like all design accelerators, the Shaft Component Generator can be used simply as a quick way to draw a shaft; but it has extraordinary tools to validate a shaft based on what you need for performance.

In the upper-right corner are icons that allow you to save the shaft configuration to a template file for future use. You can also generate a report of the results for review. See Figure 7.6 for a partial preview.

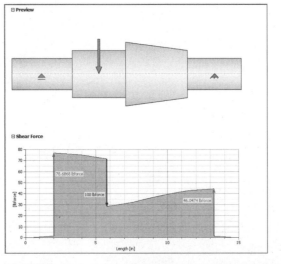

FIGURE 7.6 One portion of the extensive calculation report

The Shaft Component Generator dialog box's Design tab, shown in Figure 7.7, uses a list of shaft elements and special treatments to develop the geometry of the shaft. Let's go over a few of the special items in the dialog box.

FIGURE 7.7 Shaft Component Generator's Design tab

The Design Tab

As with the other design accelerators, you use the Design tab when you want to start by defining the initial geometry rather than by calculating the geometry from the engineering requirements:

Placement   This group of tools allows you to select the geometry the shaft is centered on, where it starts, and the direction in which it's developed. The Mate check box will even place a constraint between the new shaft and its location as you define it.

Sections   This fly-out menu controls which geometry is being placed in the shaft at any given time:

> **Sections**   In this mode, geometry that you add constitutes the exterior of the shaft.

> **Bore on the Left/Right**   The other two modes remove geometry from the interior of the shaft, starting on either the left or the right end.
>
> The buttons to the right of the pull-down list add segments to the shaft or control the display of its elements.

The Calculation Tab

The Calculation tab for the Shaft Component Generator features a graphical display of the shaft geometry that you can use to position the shaft's loads and supports:

Material   You can specify a material for use by selecting it from the pull-down list or entering the physical values directly, or you can simply accept the material that is set for the part in its iProperties.

Loads & Supports   You can add as many loads or supports as the shaft will encounter in real use to validate the design. Some loads, such as torque, must have a countering load to be properly defined.

The Graphs Tab

In the Graphs tab, you can select which calculation-result graph you want to display. With the Shaft Component Generator, graphs you can display include Shear Force, Bending Moment, Bending Stress, and several other critical measurements. The graph appears under the profile of the shaft to provide visual feedback about the shaft's behavior. You can also move the load and support positions for a better understanding of how they affect the result.

Creating a Shaft

In this exercise, you'll use the Shaft Component Generator in a very conventional way. You'll define the shaft in the Generator and constrain it into place:

1. Activate or open the fan assembly.

2. Change the Level of Detail (LOD) representation to Fan Drive.

3. Suppress the handle, switch, and caster that were added to the assembly after the unlocked LOD was created.

4. On the Design tab, select the Shaft tool from the Power Transmission panel.

5. When the dialog for the Shaft Component Generator appears, click the Delete icon on the bottom three sections.

6. Click Yes to approve of deleting the segments.

Each shaft section has four icons that control the beginning condition, the section shape, the end condition, and any special geometry on the section. After the icons is a listing of the section's size and general shape. Each icon has a pull-down you can use to select the shape. Clicking one of the icons lets you change the values associated with that shape.

The remaining shaft section (Figure 7.8) begins with a chamfer and a cylinder and ends with a fillet. The size is presently 2 inches in diameter by 4 inches in length.

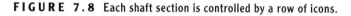

FIGURE 7.8 Each shaft section is controlled by a row of icons.

7. Click the chamfer on the left end of the shaft section. This brings up the Chamfer dialog.

8. Change the Distance value to .05. Pick the check mark to close the dialog.

9. Click the cylinder, and set the Diameter value to **.625** inches and the Length value to 3 inches in the dialog. Click OK to close the dialog.

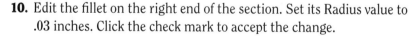

10. Edit the fillet on the right end of the section. Set its Radius value to .03 inches. Click the check mark to accept the change.

11. In the dialog, pick the Cylinder icon next to the sections pull-down. Doing so adds a new cylindrical section to the shaft. The fillet that you just edited disappears because the new section is the same diameter as the first.

12. Click the cylinder portion. Set Diameter to .93 inches and Length to 4.74. Click OK to finish the edit.

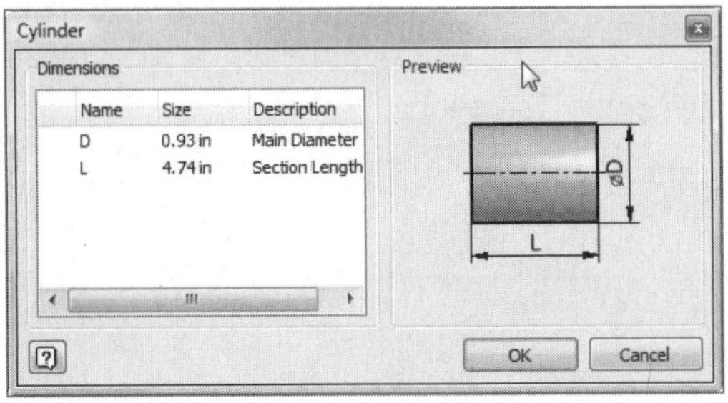

Now, you want to create another shaft section with some of the same attributes as the first section.

13. Highlight the first shaft section.

14. Click the Cylinder icon again; doing so creates a new section of the same size as the first.

15. Click and drag this new section (the second one) to the bottom of the list.

16. Edit the new section with a .03 inch fillet on the left, a .05 chamfer on the right, and a length of 2.25 inches, as shown in Figure 7.9.

FIGURE 7.9 Setting the values for the shaft

17. Click OK to generate the shaft.

18. Pick a place on the screen to insert the shaft. See Figure 7.10.

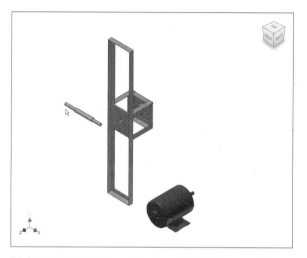

FIGURE 7.10 Inserting the shaft in the assembly

19. Add an Insert constraint to place the shaft in the assembly. Constrain the end with the 2.25in. end to the bearing on the smaller end. See Figure 7.11.

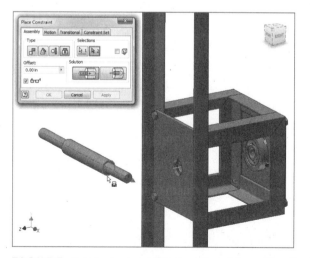

FIGURE 7.11 Apply an Insert constraint to position the shaft in the assembly.

20. Click OK to place the constraint. Compare your result to Figure 7.12 to make sure the shaft is pointing in the correct direction.

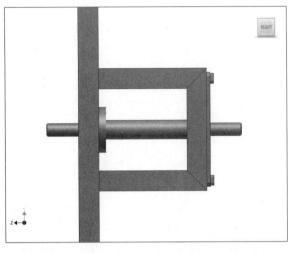

FIGURE 7.12 Make sure the shaft is pointing the correct direction.

21. Set your Design View representation to Default, and save your work.

You've used the Shaft Component Generator to place geometry that you knew to be correct. You can also use the calculation tools to verify the function of the shaft. Let's continue, and generate the belt that will link your motor and your shaft.

The V-Belts Component Generator

Machines use several types of belts. That's why more than one design accelerator deals with this type of power transmission. Along with the V-Belts Component Generator are a Synchronous Belts Generator and a Chain Generator.

As you would expect from the name, the V-Belts Component Generator focuses on V-belts from many different standards. The dialog for the V-Belts Component Generator is essentially similar to the others. It's built so that someone needing to do belt design can find their way through easily.

The Design Tab

There are two option groups on the Design tab to do the initial specification:

Belt   At the top of the Design tab is the Belt selection. You can choose from Classical or Narrow belt designs by picking the belt image.

Below that, you set the placement. Setting the Belt Mid Plane is the first step; then, you can adjust the location by setting a Mid Plane Offset value. When there is a high degree of stress on the system, you may need to add additional belts instead of or as well as switching to a higher-strength belt design.

You can use the Datum Length pull-down to pre-select one of the available sizes of the class of belt. As you'll see in the exercise, the design accelerator lets you know when you have a purchasable size.

Pulleys   The key to this group is the Click to Add Pulley line below the initial list of pulleys. Clicking that line and adding more and different types of pulleys lets you create extremely complex pulley sets.

Similar to the Shaft Component Generator, options are set into columns of icons. The first icon specifies whether Inventor generates a pulley, uses an existing one, or models the belt size on a virtual pulley. The second establishes how the pulley is positioned or constrained in its movement options.

More   Using the More icon to expand the dialog exposes a toggle for displaying the coordinate system for the belt set, and whether the belt length can switch between available sizes or only use the one that you selected. There is also a display option. You can choose to display the belt only as a centerline, as a solid, or as a synchronous belt to show full tooth detail.

The Calculation Tab

Although it's considerably less spooky than the Calculation tab in the Bearing Generator, this tab it's no less powerful. You'll probably need to work in two areas:

Type of Calculation   Do you want to calculate the number of the belts you selected or do a strength check? Those are the options.

Load   From the drop-down menu, pick what you know about your machine, and let the computer calculate the missing information.

Now, let's generate a belt and make sure it will handle the stress by performing calculations in the digital prototype rather than finding out on a physical one.

Adding a V-Belt

Remember that your motor still has a Degree of Freedom (DOF). That is because you didn't know how or what belt you would be driving with it. Let's figure that out now:

1. Rotate the view of the fan assembly to resemble Figure 7.13.

2. Pick the V-Belts tool from the Power Transmission pane to open the V-Belts Component Generator dialog.

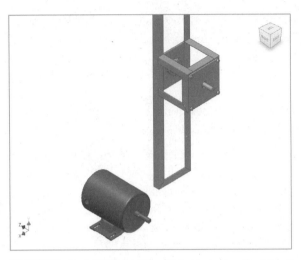

FIGURE 7.13 Having the right view makes it easier to place the V-belt.

3. The dialog is looking for a Belt Mid Plane. Pick the end of the shaft that you created. See Figure 7.14.

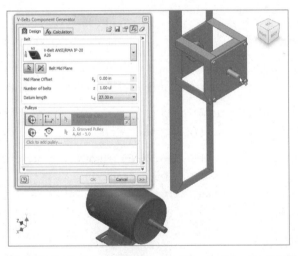

FIGURE 7.14 Select the end of the shaft for the Belt Mid Plane.

When you select the mid plane, a preview of the current belt configuration appears.

4. In the dialog, set the Mid Plane Offset value to –.5. The preview updates by moving closer to the frame.

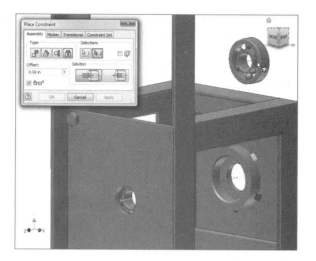

5. For Pulley1, set the Position option to Direction Driven Sliding Position.

6. Pick the selection icon for Pulley1.

7. Locate the 34LY1371_frame-10.96-N part in the Browser, and expand the Origin folder.

8. Pick the XZ plane of the motor, to align Pulley1 to it. The result is shown in Figure 7.15.

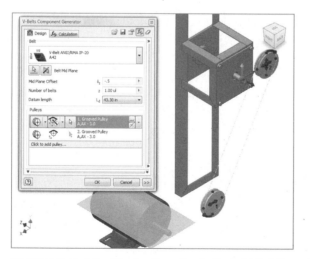

FIGURE 7.15 Aligning the pulley to the height of the motor shaft

Now Pulley1 can move from side to side at the height of the shaft of the motor. This way, you can find an available belt length by simply dragging the preview after you've locked down the position of Pulley2.

9. Set the Position control for Pulley2 to Fixed Position by Selected Geometry.

10. Pick the selection icon for Pulley2, and pick the shaft you created.

Doing so updates the preview of the belt (Figure 7.16), but the belt still hasn't been placed. Before you can finish placing, it you need to set the ratio for the pulleys.

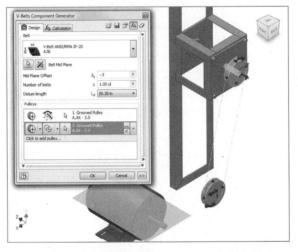

FIGURE 7.16 Both pulleys are constrained in their movement, with Pulley1 maintaining a single DOF.

11. Select the Ellipsis icon in the Pulley2 row to bring up the Groove Pulley Properties dialog.

12. Set the Diameter value for Pulley2 to 9. Click OK to update the V-belt.

13. Drag Pulley1 to be near the shaft of the motor, as shown in Figure 7.17.

14. Click OK to generate the V-belt.

15. Save the assembly.

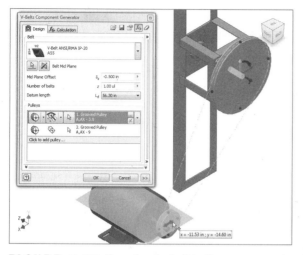
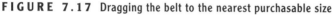

FIGURE 7.17 Dragging the belt to the nearest purchasable size

If you want to edit components created by a design accelerator, you can't double-click or use the right-click ➤ Edit operation that you normally use. These techniques allow you to edit the models of the design accelerator components but not access the methodology or intelligence.

To edit a design accelerator's intelligence, you select the geometry from the Browser or Design window and select Edit Using Design Accelerator from the context menu. This brings up the design accelerator dialog used to define the component; now you can use the dialog for editing.

Editing the V-Belt

In this case, you don't want to modify the V-belt — you want to validate it to see if you need to modify it:

1. Right-click the V-belt, and select Edit Using Design Accelerator from the context menu.

2. Switch to the Calculation tab.

3. In the Power field, set the value to .33.

4. Put **1200 rpm** in the Speed field.

5. Click the Calculate button at the bottom to test the strength of the belt. The belt should pass with no issues.

6. Click OK to close the dialog.

If the belt's elements aren't properly located, you can't run the calculation. This is a great tool that can help you design with confidence.

Now, let's move on to learn the full effects of adding the belt to your assembly.

Locating the Motor

Now that you've set a length for the belt, let's locate the motor to it:

1. Start the Constrain tool.

2. Place a mate between the axis of Pulley1 and the shaft of the motor. See Figure 7.18.

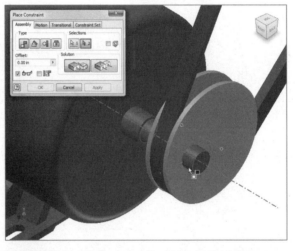

FIGURE 7.18 Locating the motor to the pulley

3. Click OK to create the constraint.

4. Restore the Envelope Suppressed LOD.

5. Save your work, which should now look like Figure 7.19.

Now that you've added the critical elements to the function of your assembly, you can go back and make some changes for clearance as well as reduce the strain on some of the power train.

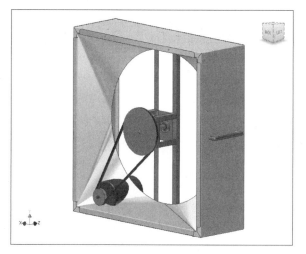

FIGURE 7.19 Bearings, shaft, and belts added to the assembly

Modifying Pulley2

Let's start out by reducing the mass of Pulley2. When the V-Belts tool places the pulleys, the assumption is that you'll want to modify them in the way that you traditionally build these components; so, Inventor creates blanks. With that, let's lighten the load:

1. Set your selection filter to Select Part Priority.

2. Pick Pulley2, right-click, and select Open to bring up Pulley2 in a new window.

3. Use the ViewCube to orient the part so that you're looking at the front view and the word *Front* is legible.

4. Start a new sketch of the face closest to you.

5. Draw two circles concentric to the sketch center.

6. Set their diameters to 7.8 and 1.3, as shown in Figure 7.20.

7. Start the Extrude tool.

8. Set the function to cut and select the ring between the two sketched circles. Set Extents to All, and make sure the cut is going through the part as shown in Figure 7.21.

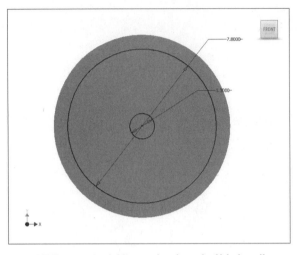

FIGURE 7.20 Adding a sketch to the V-belt pulley

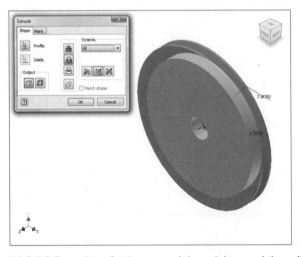

FIGURE 7.21 Cutting most of the weight out of the pulley

9. Click OK to make the cut.

Doing so creates a gap in the pulley. This is sometimes referred to as a *disjointed feature*. Although this used to prove troublesome to other CAD systems, Inventor has always used conditions like this to offer creative ways for you to define geometry.

You need a plane that bisects the thickness of the pulley. On this plane, you'll create the shape of a spoke to reinforce the pulley. Let's create a work plane to do the job.

10. Start the Plane tool.

11. Select the far face on the hub of the pulley, and then select the near face on the hub. See Figure 7.22.

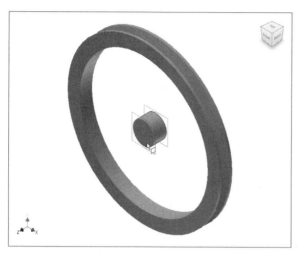

FIGURE 7.22 Creating a work plane that bisects the pulley

12. Create a new sketch on the work plane.

13. Restore the front view.

14. Right-click the work plane in the Browser, and turn off its visibility.

15. Right-click and select Slice Graphics from the context menu, or press the F7 key. Doing so makes the geometry between your point of view and the sketch plane disappear, as shown in Figure 7.23.

16. Draw a circle centered on the sketch centerpoint using the Construction override, and make its diameter 8.2.

17. Press the Esc key to end the Dimension tool.

18. Draw a vertical construction line from the sketch centerpoint to the circle.

19. Restart the Line tool, and create a tangent arc starting from the sketch centerpoint to the circle, as shown in Figure 7.24.

20. Start the Dimension tool, and add an 8-inch radius to the arc. Use Esc to end the dimension tool.

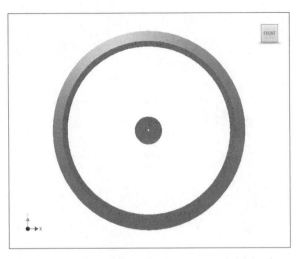

FIGURE 7.23 Having the right view makes it easier to place the V-belt.

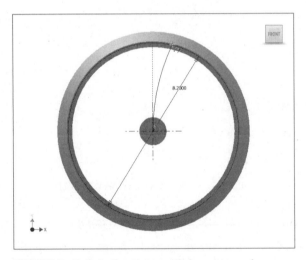

FIGURE 7.24 Creating a path for a new spoke

21. Finish the sketch.

22. Save your work.

Now that you have the path for a spoke defined, you need to add the shape:

1. Create a new sketch on the XZ plane.

2. Rotate the view of the part so that it's similar to Figure 7.25.

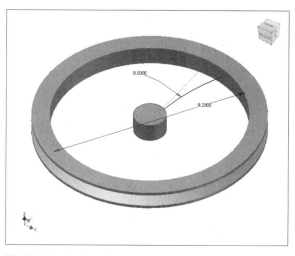

FIGURE 7.25 Preparing to build the spoke

3. Use the Slice Graphics tool to cut away the material down to the sketch.

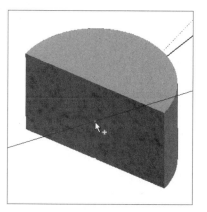

4. Project the endpoint of the arc into the current sketch.

5. From the Draw panel of the Sketch tab, select the Ellipse tool.
To draw an ellipse, you pick a centerpoint and then select two axis endpoints.

⊕ Ellipse

6. Pick the projected point as the center of the ellipse.

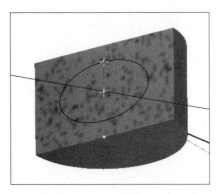

7. Drag the first Axis Horizontal (in the X direction) and the second Axis will be perpendicular to it by default.

   Dimensioning an ellipse is a little different than arcs or circles as well. The dimensions are applied to half the overall size in each direction. You also apply the dimension by picking the perimeter of the ellipse and then dragging the dimension out.

8. Add a .3-inch dimension to the X direction and a .18-inch dimension to the Y direction, as shown in Figure 7.26.

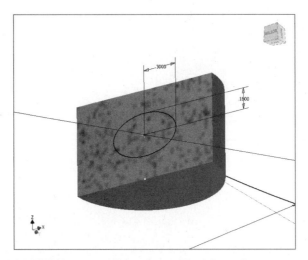

FIGURE 7.26 Sizing the profile of the spoke

9. Click Finish Sketch to exit the sketch and end the Dimension tool.

10. Save your work.

It's time to create the spoke. For that, you'll use the Sweep tool.

The Sweep Tool

An extrusion builds a body based on projecting a profile so that it's normal to its sketch plane. Sometimes you need that sketch to follow a path but you don't need it to change shape, so a loft isn't appropriate. This is what the Sweep tool is for.

Because the concept is similar to extrusion, the Sweep dialog box has a lot of the same elements as Extrude. Other features are genuinely unique and demonstrate some truly spectacular capabilities.

Type

The basic idea for having a profile follow a path is powerful. But you can select additional ways to define the feature from the Type pull-down list:

Path　The simplest and most common type, this option only needs a profile and a path to follow. The path doesn't need to intersect the profile.

Path & Guide Rail　Along with the profile and a path to follow, this option requires you to select a second rail that modifies the transition of the profile along the selected path.

Path & Guide Surface　Rather than using a basic sketch to modify the profile transition, this option takes into account the normal of a surface to control the profile. If you need to create a shape that transitions across a complex surface yet maintains its position, this is your tool. Think about running a machine-tool bit across a surface and keeping the bit normal to the face; this lets you emulate that.

Orientation

For the Path option, you have the ability to define how the profile follows the path without using a guide rail or surface:

Path   This option keeps the profile normal to the path as it transitions.

Parallel   While the profile moves along the path, this setting keeps the profile parallel with its sketch plane.

Now, you'll build your spoke by doing a very simple sweep.

Constructing the Spoke

You've already built the profile and path needed for a Sweep feature. All you need to do is execute the tool:

1. In the Create panel of the Model tab, pick the Sweep tool.

2. Because there is only one enclosed profile and one viable path, the tool immediately gives you a preview of the new feature. See Figure 7.27.

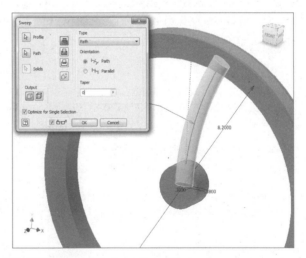

FIGURE 7.27 A preview of the spoke

3. Click Parallel Orientation to see the effect that using that technique would have on the shape of the feature.

4. After reviewing the change, reselect Path for the Orientation.

5. Click OK to create the feature.

Rotate your model, and inspect how the spoke is formed into the rest of the model. Looking closely at the belt groove, it appears that the feature is penetrating into the groove (Figure 7.28). This isn't good. You need to modify the Sweep feature to prevent this.

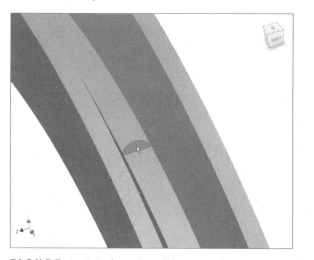

FIGURE 7.28 A portion of the sweep feature penetrates the belt groove

6. Under the Sweep1 feature in the Browser, double-click Sketch3 to edit it.

7. In the sketch, edit the 8.200 dimension and make its new value **8.000**.

8. Pick Finish Sketch to update the model.

9. Save your work.

This should remedy the problem, as shown in Figure 7.29. Let's keep modifying the pulley.

You want to round the inside of the rim of the pulley. You can still add a fillet to the edges now, and Inventor's model healing will understand what you want; but just to be sure, you'd like to go back in time to make the modification.

You don't want to delete or undo the work you've done on the spoke; instead, you'll tell Inventor that you haven't done that work yet.

In the Browser is an icon I'm sure you've noticed: the End of Part marker. Wherever this marker sits, Inventor considers the end of the features. If you move the End of Part marker, you can truncate the list of features Inventor will generate.

FIGURE 7.29 The updated spoke doesn't interfere with the belt.

You want to temporarily forget that you've built the Sweep1 feature, and you can use this tool to make that happen:

1. In the Browser, click and drag the End of Part marker above the Groove feature, and release the mouse button.

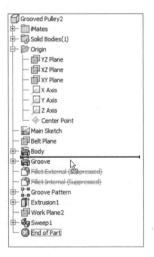

This causes Inventor to recalculate the model and stop at the marker. The results are pretty dramatic, as you can see in Figure 7.30

2. Move the End of Part marker to just below Extrusion1, and release.

3. Start the Fillet tool, and add a .3-inch fillet to the two inside edges of the rim, as shown in Figure 7.31.

4. Click OK to create the fillets.

5. Move the End of Part marker back to the bottom of the feature tree in the Browser.

One spoke is good, but you really need to have several spokes distributed around the hub.

Earlier in the book, you used a rectangular pattern. A circular pattern follows the same workflow and shares many of the same options.

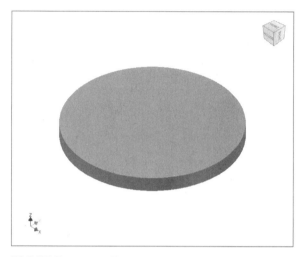

FIGURE 7.30 Moving the End of Part marker can roll back time.

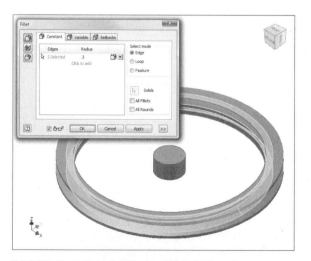

FIGURE 7.31 Adding the fillets before the sweep

6. Start the Circular Pattern tool on the Pattern panel.

7. Select Sweep for the Feature, and set the Rotation Axis using one of the cylindrical surfaces.

8. Set the Placement value to 5, and click OK to create the pattern shown in Figure 7.32.

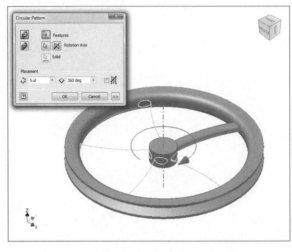

FIGURE 7.32 Creating the pattern of spokes

The foundation of the pulley is complete. You need to add just a couple more features.

An amazing new tool added to Inventor 2010 is the rule fillet. Unlike the feature fillet you've used, it's based on relationships between features rather than just on edges or faces.

The Rule Fillet

This feature can build relationships that can be temporarily broken and renew themselves when conditions are restored. A single rule fillet can tell a feature that it's blended to one feature with a .05 radius, another feature with a .1 radius, the rest of the part with a .2 radius, and any free edges with a .03 radius. You can do all this without picking a single edge.

Adding a Rule Fillet

Let's use this tool in a simple example:

1. Start the Rule Fillet tool from the Plastic Features panel of the Model tab.

2. Because a rule fillet is feature based, you must select a feature to affect. Pick the Sweep feature and the circular pattern.

   Doing so creates a fillet preview (Figure 7.33) on both ends of the Sweep feature. The rule that is being applied is the selected feature Against Part. So, anywhere this feature meets the rest of the part, it's applying the Radius value.

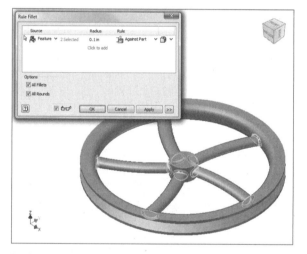

FIGURE 7.33 A preview of the rule fillet

3. Leave the Radius value at .1, and click OK to create the fillet.

4. Let's find a new color for the pulley — something to make it stand out a bit. Pick something different from pull-down on the Quick Access toolbar.

5. Switch to the Fan.iam window to see that your changes to the model have already updated the assembly.

6. Switch back to the pulley model.

Let's add one more feature to the pulley. In a sketch, you can add lines, arcs, circles, and so on, but you can also add text. This text can be used for several things, from simple nomenclature to a profile for engraving or embossing.

To create text on an arc, you can use a specialized version of the Text tool called Geometry Text.

Applying Geometry Text

Adding a text box to an Inventor sketch is a very simple process. Geometry text is more involved, but it can create a great result:

1. Restore the Front view of your pulley.

2. Create a new sketch on the flat face of the pulley rim.

3. Draw an 8.75-inch diameter circle centered on the sketch. See Figure 7.34. Be sure to exit the Dimension tool after sizing the circle.

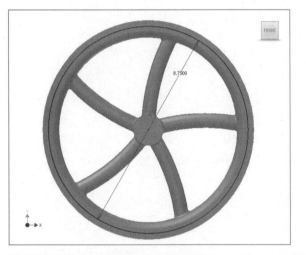

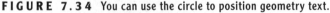

FIGURE 7.34 You can use the circle to position geometry text.

4. Under the Text tool in the Draw panel is a fly-out option for the Geometry Text tool. Start the Geometry Text tool.

5. Pick the circle to establish that you want the text aligned to it. the Geometry-Text dialog box opens.

   The dialog itself has a number of options. I tend to do a good deal of experimentation to get the precise look I want. One of the keys is the Update button, which refreshes the display of the text in the Design window and gives you the feedback you need to get the text just right.

6. In the text box near the bottom, enter the word **ROTATION** in capital letters.

7. Set Position to Center Justification, Start Angle to **90**, and the Offset Distance to –.06 (half the text size).

8. Click the Update button to refresh the text preview, which should look like Figure 7.35.

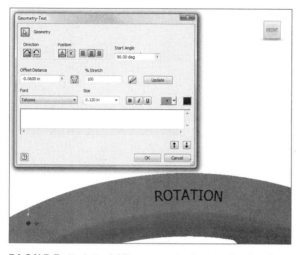

FIGURE 7.35 Adding geometry text to the sketch

9. Pick OK to add the geometry text to the sketch.

10. Change the circle to be construction geometry.

11. Freehand a sketch of a triangle with its point going to the left to create an indicator arrow, as shown in Figure 7.36.

    I want you to deliberately leave the sketch of your triangle underconstrained to prove that you can do so and still get results. The only requirement is that the endpoints of the sketch elements must be coincident to form a closed profile.

12. Start the Extrude tool by pressing the E key. This will exit the sketch and move right to the tool.

13. Set the type to Cut and the Distance value to .01. Pick your pointer and the text, and click OK to cut those shapes into your pulley.

14. In the Browser, pick the new Extrusion feature.

15. While the feature is highlighted, use the pull-down menu in the Quick Access Toolbar to set the color of the feature to Black by extending the list and picking the color. See Figure 7.36.

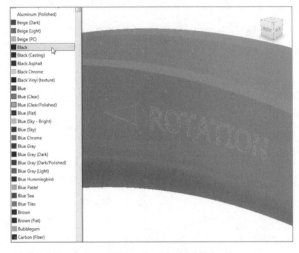

FIGURE 7.36 With a feature highlighted, you can override its color.

16. Save your work, and close the pulley.

17. With Part Selection Priority still active, pick the pulley. Use the Rotate tool to turn the pulley over so the word *ROTATION* is at the top.

18. Update the assembly, and the pulley will be re-constrained.

19. Make sure the pulley is up to date in the assembly, and save that file as well.

When editing the pulley, you may have noticed that the hub doesn't have a hole in it. As I mentioned before, the V-Belts Component Generator produces the pulleys as blanks. You've modified your large pulley with some additional features, but you'll use another design accelerator to prepare it for the shaft.

Parallel Key Connection Generator

This tool has a lot of similarities to the others, but it's more interactive when you're selecting what key will be used when you select the geometry to place it on. This is reasonable because keys are commonly sized based on the shafts that they're placed in.

The Design Tab

There are four groups of tools on the Parallel Key Connection Generator's Design tab:

Key   You can select the class of key you'd like to use. You can also preselect the size of the key or select it later. You can set the angle at which the key will be placed in the model about the axis of the shaft as well as the number of keys to be placed.

Shaft Groove   This group allows you to select from three different types of shaft grooves. Once selected, you can specify the location of the groove.

Hub Groove   The selection icons in this group establish where the groove is placed in the hub.

Select Objects to Generate   These three toggles establish what elements of the key connection are generated by the result.

The Calculation Tab

The tools in this tab let you specify the load to be applied as well as override the material of the components involved in the key connection.

As with the V-Belts Component Generator, it's possible to select which inputs you can provide and have the tool calculate the other information to do a complete test.

Creating a Key Connection

In the following exercise, I've turned off Enhanced Highlighting mode in the Application Options. The preview of the key and keyway can be obscured when entire parts or faces highlight.

You can do a lot of work on the key connection in the Design window. You'll do several steps in this exercise where you grab 3D grips to position the key and keyway.

Let's create your key.

Creating a Parallel Key Connection

1. Restore the Fan Drive LOD representation.

2. Set your view in your Design window so that you're close to the hub of Pulley2 and viewing it somewhat from the side, as shown in Figure 7.37.

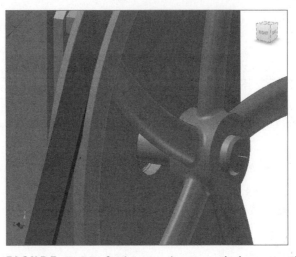

FIGURE 7.37 Setting up a view to see the key connection

 Key

3. Start the Key tool from the Power Transmission panel.

This brings up the Parallel Key Connection Generator dialog. Several steps in this exercise require you to look at your screen with a critical eye to make sure you're going in the right direction. This is one of those tools where it's almost easier to experiment to get used to it.

4. Leave the Key type at Rectangular or Square Parallel Keys.

5. In the Shaft Groove group set the groove type to Groove with One Rounded End.

6. The selection icon for Reference 1 in the Shaft Groove group should be active. Pick the surface of the shaft that you created where it runs through the pulley.

7. Selecting the surface of the shaft makes the Reference 2 selection active. Pick the end of the shaft as shown in Figure 7.38.

By picking the second reference for the shaft groove, you give Inventor enough information to calculate the size of the appropriate key and groove for the shaft. A preview of the key and a short groove appear.

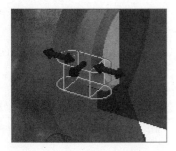

The key has three grip arrows like those you saw when working with 3D grips earlier. The double-headed grip near the end of the shaft moves the key, the double-headed grip to the inside changes the length of the key, and the single arrow on the side of the key alters the position around the shaft where the key is located.

FIGURE 7.38 Selecting the shaft to determine the size of the key

To properly size the shaft groove, Inventor needs to know the length of the hub and its groove.

8. To define Reference 1 of the hub groove, select the face highlighted in Figure 7.39. This defines the face where the groove will begin.

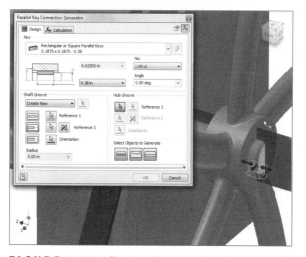

FIGURE 7.39 Showing Inventor where to begin cutting the hub groove

9. For Reference 2 (Centering), pick the outer edge of the hub as shown in Figure 7.40.

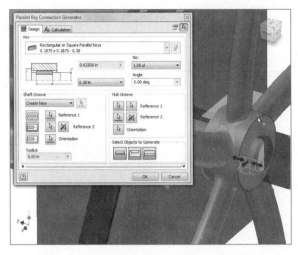

FIGURE 7.40 Locating the center of the hub

Now that the key size has been selected, you can set the length and position of the key.

10. Click and drag the angle grip to reposition the key 180 degrees from where it initially previewed. See Figure 7.41.

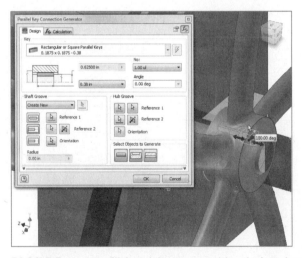

FIGURE 7.41 Click and drag to reposition the key about the circumference of the shaft.

11. Click and drag the length of the key to be .75. You'll need to click again to accept the length. See Figure 7.42.

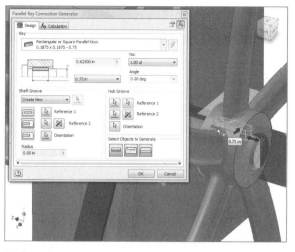

FIGURE 7.42 Drag the length. Note that it steps only in standard lengths.

12. Compare your preview with Figure 7.42 and click OK to make the modifications to the shaft and pulley and generate the key.

13. The finished geometry should look like Figure 7.43.

FIGURE 7.43 The completed key and grooves

14. Double-click the pulley to activate it in the context of the assembly. You should see a groove and the diameter of the shaft cut from the pulley.

15. Pick the Return icon on the Ribbon to return to the assembly.

16. Set the view to the home view, and restore the Envelope Suppressed LOD.

17. Save your work.

Take away the ability to use the Calculation tab and verify the function of these components before creating the geometry, and you'd still have a powerful tool. The calculation tools are available, though, and not using them would be a shame — especially if you do any sort of machine design.

The last thing you need to do for this chapter is correct the issue with the motor and the duct casually overlooking one of the laws of physics. You won't just make room through the duct for the motor, you'll use the motor to help define how it will go through the duct.

It's preferable not to have to make a cut in the duct to accommodate the pulley, but you need to make sure there is room to get the belt onto the pulley. You'll do a quick measurement similar to what you did early in the book, but in this case you want to find the minimum distance between the two bodies.

You also need to be able to clearly see the components you're working on:

1. Create a new design view, name it **Duct Clearance**, and make it the active View representation.

2. With the Part Selection Priority still on, hold the Ctrl key and pick the motor, the duct, and the small pulley.

3. Right-click in an empty portion of the Design window, and pick Isolate from the context menu. Your screen should look like Figure 7.44.

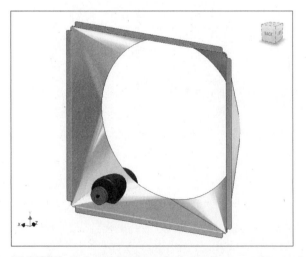

FIGURE 7.44 Isolating only the parts you need to work with

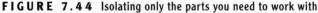

4. Start the Distance measurement tool from the Measure panel on the Inspect tab.

Selection filters are available for working in the assembly, and the Measure Distance tool has filters too. The default is geared toward selecting edges and faces. This is completely logical because that is the most common query people use. There is a filter for Component Priority that, like its assembly counterpart, looks at the bigger picture of selecting an entire subassembly as a single item. Because the pulley is a member of the V-belt component, you need to use the Part Priority, which looks through the assembly structure and allows you to pick parts directly.

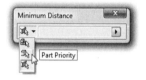

5. From the Filters pull-down in the Distance Measurement dialog, select Part Priority.

6. Pick the pulley and then the duct. The Minimum Distance and In Depth values appear in the dialog, along with a display of where that distance is. See Figure 7.45.

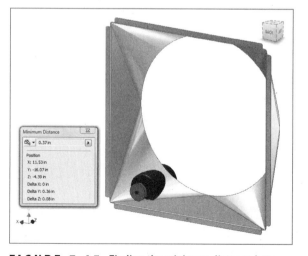

FIGURE 7.45 Finding the minimum distance between parts

7. Press the Esc key to end the Measure tool.

The belt you selected is 5/16 (.3125) of an inch thick, and your minimum distance is .37 inches, so you can fit a belt onto the pulley. On to the next problem: what kind of hole do you need in the duct?

To solve this problem, you'll use tools that aren't commonly used with sheet metal but that are perfect for your needs.

The Copy Object Tool

You've built relationships between components in the assembly, but sometimes the relationship needs to be much deeper. Linking parameters from another part can be useful, and using a derived component to link to another part can work too. But what if you need only one surface or a part of a body?

The primary function of the Copy Object tool is to link the geometry of one component to another. When it's done, the geometry that is copied into the second part remains associated with the original.

The Copy Object dialog has only two sets of criteria: choosing how and what geometry needs to be copied, and what to make from the copied geometry.

Copying Geometry from One Part to Another

Let's use the tool and see its options in action:

1. Double-click the duct to edit the part in the Design window of the assembly.

2. Switch the Ribbon to the Model tab.

3. Select the Copy Object tool from the Modify panel.

Copy Object

4. For the Select option, choose Face.

5. Under the Create New options, select the Composite option.

6. In the Design window, pick the three surfaces on the motor shown in Figure 7.46.

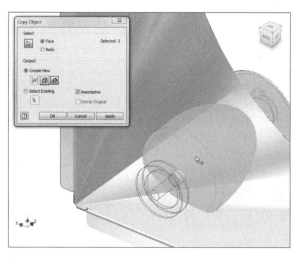

FIGURE 7.46 Choosing the surfaces to link into the duct

7. Click OK to create the new surfaces in the duct part.

This step has created the surface geometry you need to make clearance for in your duct part. Now you need to define what that clearance is.

The Thicken/Offset Tool

If you need to build a feature that has a basic shape or a complex contour, and you want to have a consistent thickness but don't want to use the Shell tool to remove all but one side, you can use Thicken/Offset.

It's two features in one. Thicken develops a solid body from an existing face or surface. Offset takes an existing face or surface and creates another surface with a space between it and the original.

The dialog box for the tool has one unique feature that you haven't encountered yet: you can select either a face (or several faces) or a quilt. A *quilt* is a number of surfaces that are tangent to one another and that form a continuous surface.

Defining the Clearance Envelope

For your design, you'll create an offset surface that defines the clearance for the hole in the sheet metal:

1. Start the Thicken/Offset tool found in the Surface panel of the Model tab.

2. Set the Output option to Surface, and set Distance to .35.

3. Select the surfaces you copied into the duct, as shown in Figure 7.47.

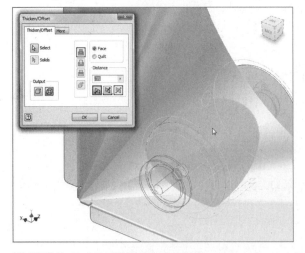

FIGURE 7.47 Offsetting surface to create a clearance model

4. Click OK to create the new surfaces.

5. Expand the folded model in the Browser.

6. Locate the Composite1 feature, which you created with the Copy Objects tool, and turn off its visibility.

The next step is to translate the shape of your clearance onto the model. You can use a couple of different tools to do this, but the one that keeps you closest to a typical sheet-metal workflow maps the perimeter of where the surfaces meet as a 3D sketch and then uses that to define your cut-out.

You'll begin by creating a 3D sketch.

Creating a 3D Sketch

3D sketches have hundreds of uses, and without the tool you wouldn't be able to calculate the intersection easily:

1. In either the Sheet Metal or Modeling tab, expand the Create 2D Sketch tool and pick the Create 3D Sketch tool.

The 3D Sketch tab appears and becomes active just as the Sketch tab does for a 2D sketch. Some of the tools will seem familiar, but a number of tools extract geometry from existing sources to form the 3D sketch. One of those tools is the Intersection Curve. This tool creates an edge at the intersection of surfaces, which is exactly what you need.

2. Select the Intersection Curve tool from the 3D Sketch tab's Draw panel.

The 3D Intersection Curve dialog appears. It's very simple and only needs you to select two sets of geometry. You may need to reselect one of the icons to add additional surfaces to one set or the other, but careful selection of the first surface is the most important.

3. Move over the offset surface, and make sure the entire surface highlights (Figure 7.48) before selecting it.

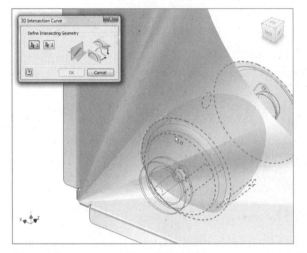

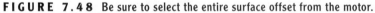

FIGURE 7.48 Be sure to select the entire surface offset from the motor.

4. For the second set, you can pick the surface of the bend and the flat surface at the base of the duct, as shown in Figure 7.49.

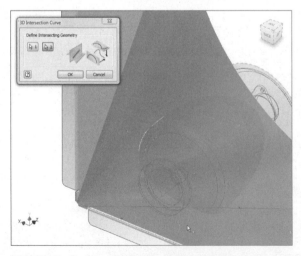

FIGURE 7.49 Pick both surfaces that intersect the motor clearance.

5. Click OK to create the 3D sketch curvature shown in Figure 7.50.

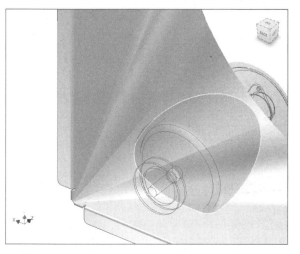

FIGURE 7.50 The projected 3D curve

6. Pick the Finish Sketch tool to exit the 3D sketch.

The next step is to apply that curve to the faces of the sheet metal itself. By splitting the faces, you can unfold the metal and see how the curvature would look in a flat pattern.

Splitting the Folded Faces

For this exercise, you'll use the Split tool and cut the surfaces of the sheet metal:

1. In the Model tab, select the Split tool from the Modify panel.

2. Set the Faces option to All.

3. For the Split Tool, select the 3D sketch.

4. Select the body of the duct for the faces. Click OK.

5. Turn off the visibility of the OffsetSrf1 feature.

6. Move your mouse over the area that should have been split. There should be two new faces: one on the bend and one on the flat portion of the lofted flange. Hold the Ctrl key, and select the two new faces.

7. Right-click, and select Properties from the context menu.

8. Pick a new color for the faces. Compare to Figure 7.51.

9. Save your work.

FIGURE 7.51 The colored faces provide a preview of what needs to be removed.

When you made the housing, you created a sketch and used that sketch to make a cut across the bend. This is a significantly more complex problem, so you have to use a different technique to find the shape of what needed to be cut. Using tools like this is much more cost effective than doing several physical prototypes, and it's ultimately more accurate. If you were to discover that the belt you selected was in limited supply, and you had to switch to another version, you could relocate the motor and recalculate all this in a minute or two.

Next, you need to make the cut in the metal. To do this, you'll flatten the bend and make a cut.

The Unfold and Refold Tools

Inventor has the ability to preview the flat pattern in a sketch (as you did in Chapter 2, "Building the Foundation of the Design") to establish how that feature will appear in the flat pattern. Sometimes you need to be able to see a portion of the part in an unfolded state to add geometry.

A great example is adding a stiffening feature across a bend. You unfold the bend, add the stiffener to the flattened portion, and refold the model, including bending the stiffener.

Unfold

Stationary Reference (A)

Unfold Geometry (B)

Bends

Add All Bends

Copy Sketches (C)

Sketches

☑ Parent is Visible

OK   Cancel   Apply

Unfold and Refold are arguably the same tool, but they need to be calculated independently because you may need to create more than one unfold and refold or a different set of unfold features at once. Even the dialog boxes for the two are the same except the name at the top.

The dialog requires a stationary reference to get started. This can be a flat face or an edge. Most often it'll be a flat face, unless you have a bent part without a flat portion. I select the stationary reference as though it were the portion of the part I would hold on the table while flattening the bend(s) that I wanted to flatten.

You can unfold as many bends as you like; there's even an Add All Bends option to speed things up. As you select bends to be unfolded, give Inventor a moment; it will calculate a preview of how the part will look.

If there are 2D sketches on a face or hanging over a bend from a face, you can include them in the Unfold feature as well.

You'll use the Unfold tool to see what your cut needs to be. Then, you'll refold your part after you make the cut.

Making the Cut

When you unfold a part, you're in essence re-creating the flat pattern. On a complex part like this, I sometimes clear the flat pattern before using Unfold:

1. In the Browser, locate and delete the flat pattern for the duct.

2. Start the Unfold tool, which is in the Modify panel of the Sheet Metal tab.

3. The dialog needs a stationary reference. Pick the flat, vertical face to the left of the bend that you split. See Figure 7.52.

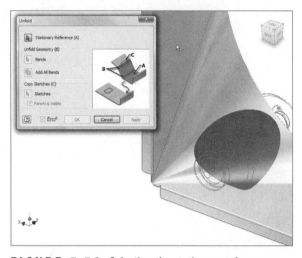

FIGURE 7.52 Selecting the stationary reference

4. When you select the stationary reference, all the bends on the part highlight. Pick only the large bend that was split.

5. After a moment, a preview appears (Figure 7.53) to show the result of unfolding the large bend. Click OK to create the Unfold feature.

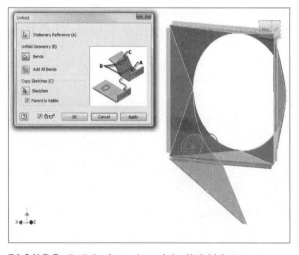

FIGURE 7.53 A preview of the Unfold feature

6. Create a new 2D sketch on the unfolded face.

7. Use the Project Geometry tool, and select the edges of the shape to be cut out. See Figure 7.54.

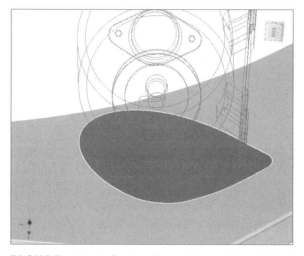

FIGURE 7.54 Creating the perimeter of the cut that is needed

8. Finish the sketch.

9. Start the Cut tool. The profile should be selected immediately and offer a preview.

10. Click OK to create the cut as shown in Figure 7.55.

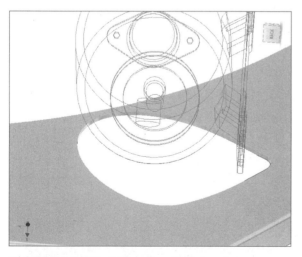

FIGURE 7.55 Cutting the unfolded part

11. Select the Refold tool (directly below Unfold).

12. Pick the same stationary reference face. Doing so highlights any unfolded bends.

13. Select the bend that you selected before. This creates a preview of the refolded part. See Figure 7.56.

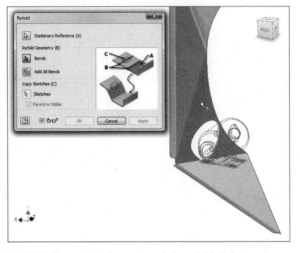

FIGURE 7.56 A preview of the refolded duct

14. Click OK to complete the edit.

15. Select the Create Flat Pattern tool.
    This opens the duct part in a separate window to display the flat pattern with the new cut included.

16. Click the Go to Folded Part icon on the end of the Ribbon. You many need to Zoom All to see the part.

17. Save your work, and close the duct part. Figure 7.57 shows the perfectly formed clearance hole.

18. Restore the Default Design View representation, and save the assembly.

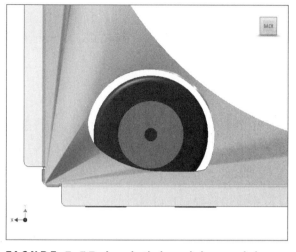

FIGURE 7.57 A perfectly formed clearance hole

This was a big chapter. The tools and techniques we covered show some of the automation and intelligence that are built into Inventor. Systems have been around for years that could create most of the geometry you've worked with, but Inventor's knowledge base makes it much more productive for this type of work.

Your product is really taking shape, and in the next chapter you'll finish building it. Let's take another look at what you've done; see Figure 7.58.

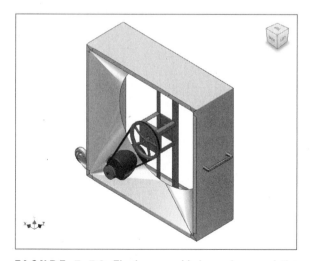

FIGURE 7.58 The fan assembly is nearing completion.

Are You Experienced?

Now you can...

☑ **define and generate bearing based on their performance**

☑ **create a shaft using automated tools**

☑ **easily find a V-belt that can be purchased**

☑ **create a Sweep feature**

☑ **use solid-modeling tools to complete a complex edit to a sheet metal part**

CHAPTER 8

Creating Contoured and Plastic Parts

▶ Using surfaces to define a solid

▶ Adding text as a model feature

▶ Lofting between shapes

▶ Advanced filleting

▶ Creating hollow parts

▶ Adding specialized plastic features

Working with Plastic Parts

So far, everything you've done has focused on machined, cast, or sheet metal parts. Every type of material or process affects the way that you define a component, but people who create plastic parts work with a different approach and even have a language all their own. I won't attempt to describe how it's all done, but I do want to walk you through some of Inventor's specialized features that help the experts in this field work more efficiently.

A workflow called *multibody modeling* can be used in a number of situations. I've mentioned it before, but now we'll take the time to explore it.

The Multibody Part

Many consumer products appear to be single monolithic components even when they're made up of several parts. Although these components are an assembly, it can be very frustrating to have to edit the individual components. This is the case particularly if the change is to the overall contour and must be repeated for each part.

The concept of a multibody part allows a Part file to simulate an assembly for the development process. After the elements are developed, you can use the single file as a source for an assembly that remains associative to the single part much as drawing views are based on the parts or assemblies they represent.

The Browser has a Solid Bodies folder that contains information about the body (or bodies) that make up the part. As a single solid is broken into multiple bodies, this folder acts as a resource for isolating which body you want to work with or give a special appearance to. It's also dynamic. Because you're really working with a single part, if you edit a feature that existed before a part was divided, you'll see that the folder presents only the single body while you're editing that feature. The process is easy to follow but extremely powerful.

Building the Basic Part

In this exercise you will build a simple part that you will eventually transform into an assembly of complex parts using automated tools.

1. Open or activate the Fan.iam file.

2. Set Level of Detail to Fan Drive.

3. Use the Create tool in the Component panel of the Assemble tab to add a new component to the assembly.

Create In-Place Component

New Component Name

Bearing Cover

Template

English\Standard (in).ipt

New File Location

C:\Data\Parts

Default BOM Structure

Normal   ☐ Virtual Component

☑ Constrain sketch plane to selected face or plane

OK   Cancel

4. Using the Standard (in).ipt template, create a new component named **Bearing Cover** in the Parts folder.

5. Place the new sketch on the vertical face of the fan support frame, as shown in Figure 8.1.

FIGURE 8.1 Align the new part with the fan support frame.

6. Project the points where the horizontal frames meet the new sketch face, as shown in Figure 8.2.

7. Draw a rectangle using the two projected points.

8. Project the origin centerpoint of the assembly into the sketch.

9. Create a circle, using the sketch centerpoint to locate it in the sketch.

10. Set the diameter of the circle to 9.25 inches. See Figure 8.3.

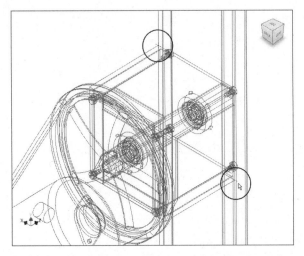

FIGURE 8.2 Project the corners of the frame members.

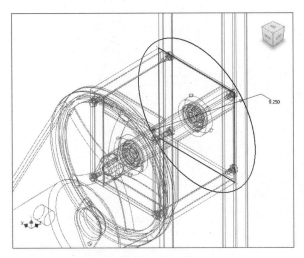

FIGURE 8.3 Add the circle to the sketch.

11. Extrude the outer area of the sketch to a distance of 5.5 inches. See Figure 8.4.

12. Click OK to create the feature.

13. Add a .3-inch fillet to the ends of the extrusion, per Figure 8.5. Click OK to apply the fillets.

14. Change the color of the part to Plastic (texture).

15. Save your work.

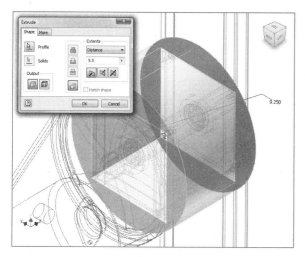

FIGURE 8.4 Extruding the sketch

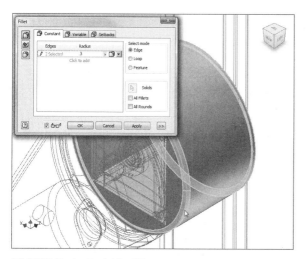

FIGURE 8.5 Add a fillet to the ends of the feature.

The Shell Tool

When you need a part to be hollow and (usually) have a consistent remaining
wall thickness, you can use the Shell command to remove a large portion of the
body rather than modeling the walls of a model individually. To do this, you select
a face or faces to be removed. The faces that you don't select are thickened and
remain a solid.

The Shell dialog box has relatively few options, but a few of them are worthy of more explanation.

The Shell Tab

In most cases, the Shell tab gives you all the tools you need to create a Shell feature.

Shell Types

 Inside Shell   This removes material from the interior of the part, leaving the body that you created intact.

 Outside Shell   This option adds material beginning at the surface of the body that you created. In essence, you create a model of the void and add material to it.

 Both   This option uses the surface of your model as the mid-surface, adding thickness in both directions simultaneously.

Automatic Face Chain

The Automatic Face Chain option is checked by default. Deselecting it enables you to select faces for removal without automatically selecting tangent faces as well.

Solids

You may want to shell more than one body. By selecting the participating bodies, you can use a single Shell feature to affect the multiple bodies.

Unique Face Thickness

 The Shell dialog box has a More button at the bottom to expand the dialog box. Doing so exposes the additional option of adding a Unique Face Thickness setting.

By default, selecting a face for removal applies the thickness to all of the remaining faces. If you want a different thickness applied to a specific face, you can use the Click to Add function and add the special face and a unique thickness for it to the list. You can add multiple faces and, in theory, hollow out a part and give each remaining face a different thickness.

The More Tab

Sometimes you may have difficulty getting a shell to calculate. The More tab offers several workflows that should help you get the part to shell.

Allow Approximation

This option is on by default. Optimized shelling creates the shell quickly; but in order to do so, it allows infinitesimally small variations in the thickness. In all but a handful of cases, this shell is more accurate than most people need. If you require extreme accuracy, you can deselect this option:

Mean   This approximation allows the thickness to vary and be either slightly thinner or thicker than the Thickness value.

Never Too Thin   If the shell thickness is critical, this option allows the variation to be thicker — but never thinner — than the specification.

Never Too Thick   With this option, the shell can be thinner than the callout but not thicker.

Specify Tolerance   To allow deviation but limit it to a tolerance, you can specify a value along with the solution. Doing so can add time to creating the shell; but in cases where you must be sure, this is the way.

When I approach a multibody part, I create as many features as possible that will be common to all (or many) of the parts before dividing the part.

Shelling the Part

The last common feature of the parts is they all have the same wall thickness:

1. Start the Shell tool from the Modify panel.

2. Select the four internal faces (Figure 8.6), and set the Thickness value to 0.1 inches.

3. Click OK to calculate the Shell feature.

4. Save the part.

Now. it's time to separate your part into two.

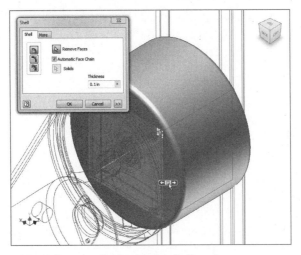

FIGURE 8.6 Apply a shell to hollow the part.

Splitting the Part

In Chapters 6 ("Working with Purchased and Multipurpose Parts") and 7 ("Functional Design Using Design Accelerators"), you used the Split tool to divide faces and trim off a portion of a part. Now you'll use it to divide a part into two parts:

1. Start the Plane tool in the Work Features panel.

2. Right-click, and select Create Axis from the context menu.
   This allows you to generate an inline work feature that is used to define the feature you're focused on creating.

3. Move over the cylindrical body of the bearing cover. When it highlights, select the cylindrical face to place an axis.
   Inventor prompts you for a face to align the work plane to.

4. Select the XZ plane of the cover, and set the angle to 0 degrees. See Figure 8.7.

5. Start the Split tool in the Modify panel of the Model tab.

6. Select the Split Solid option.

7. Use the new work plane as the Split tool, as shown in Figure 8.8.

8. Click OK to create the two separate bodies.

9. Hide the visibility of the work plane.
   Two new solids are created in the `Solid Bodies` folder.

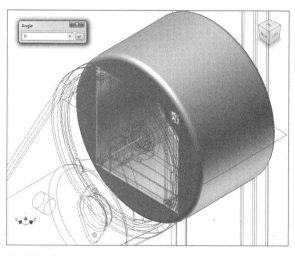

FIGURE 8.7 Adding an angular constraint.

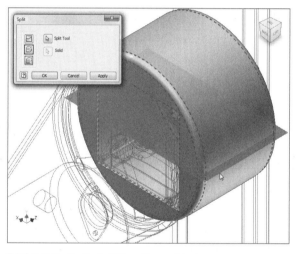

FIGURE 8.8 Splitting the part in two

10. Rename the two bodies **Top** and **Bottom**, per their position.
For clarity, you'll do the rest of the exercise by editing the part model.

11. Save the file.

12. Pick the Return button on the Ribbon to return to the assembly.

13. In the Design window or the Browser, right-click the bearing cover, and select Open from the context menu. This opens the part in its own window.

14. Right-click the Bottom solid in the Browser, and select Hide Others from the context menu. See Figure 8.9.

15. Create a new sketch on the work plane you created to split the solid.

16. Using construction lines, project the edge of the cylindrical face and the edge highlighted in Figure 8.10.

17. Turn off the visibility of the work plane.

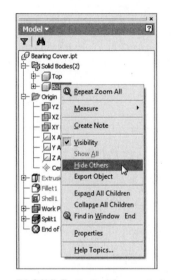

FIGURE 8.9 It's easy to isolate which body you want to work on.

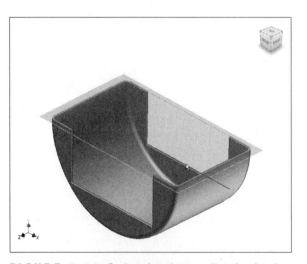

FIGURE 8.10 Project the edges to align the sketch to.

18. Place a rectangle in the sketch, and use the Horizontal and Vertical constraints to center the rectangle based on the projected edges.

19. Dimension the rectangle as shown in Figure 8.11.

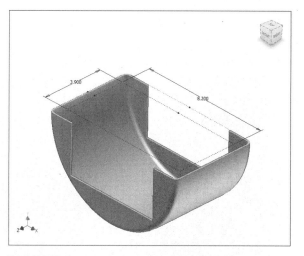

FIGURE 8.11 Set the size of the rectangle in the sketch.

20. Finish the sketch, and save the file.

You'll use this sketch to add some new features to the part. These new features are unique to plastic parts and, as you'll soon see, very impressive.

Plastic Part Features

In the Model tab are a number of powerful tools grouped together based on their general purpose. The Plastic Part panel contains six very highly specialized tools. You'll use only a couple of these tools here; but if you work with plastic parts, you'll want to devote some significant time to exploring these powerful features.

Grill

In electronics, it's important to allow airflow through the housing. The Grill tool has an incredible number of options, yet it remains easy to use. You construct a grill feature by using a boundary to locate it and adding islands, ribs, and spars, all of which can have draft added to them at once.

Snap Fit

A Snap Fit has two halves. One is the tab and the other, the catch. They are located by placing points in a sketche or by using points that occur in the model. Once the points for locating the snap are selected, a wizard will walk you through sizing and positioning the feature.

Boss

If your components will be fastened together using screws, then Boss is the tool you want. It too is a multifunction tool, creating the boss into which the screw is recessed and the one the screw fastens to on the opposite part.

Rule Fillet

The regular Fillet tool that you've been using is very flexible, but it's based on edges, faces, and other selected elements. The Rule Fillet tool can tell one feature that if it comes in contact with another feature, it automatically constructs a fillet of a specified radius. A number of different rules can be applied, all of which are fantastic.

Rest

It can be difficult to mount things to highly contoured parts. A *rest* is a feature that builds a place to attach to. Based on a sketch, it adds or removes material in order to create a flat face from the sketch.

Lip

Lips are among the most common features on plastic parts. These overlapping features locate parts to one another and are critical for creating the effect of a seamless body.

You've already been exposed to the rule fillet, and you'll use other plastic-part tools as we go through the next several exercises.

Placing the Bosses

Let's begin by placing Boss features on the Bottom solid; then you'll place them on the Top solid:

1. Start the Boss tool from the Plastic Features panel.

2. Select the four corners of the sketched rectangle for placement.

3. Set type to Head.

4. On the Shape tab, set the Fillet value to .03.

5. Set the values on the Head tab as shown in Figure 8.12.

6. Click OK to place the Boss feature. Figure 8.13 shows the result. Now, you'll add the threaded side of the boss to the top part.

7. In the Browser, right-click the Top solid, and select Hide Others to focus on the top part.

8. Share the sketch under the Boss1 feature.

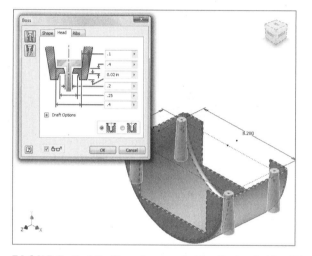

FIGURE 8.12 The values needed for the head side of the Boss feature

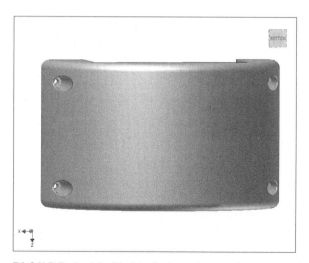

FIGURE 8.13 Placing the boss changes the geometry inside and outside the part.

9. Start the Boss tool again, and set the type to Thread.

10. Select the same four corners of the rectangle for placement.

11. Set the Fillet value on the Shape tab to .03.

12. On the Thread tab, set the Hole type to Depth, and set the values to match those in Figure 8.14.

13. Click OK to add the bosses shown in Figure 8.15.

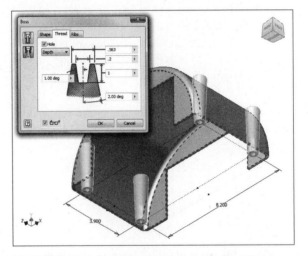

FIGURE 8.14 Adding the thread-side Boss features

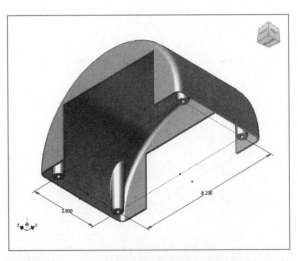

FIGURE 8.15 The opposite bosses added to the solid

14. Turn off the visibility of the sketch you used to place the bosses.

15. Save your work.

Next, you'll add a feature to hold the edges of the bodies in place.

Adding a Lip to the Solids

The Lip tool creates an interlocking feature to keep the side of the parts aligned:

1. Start the Lip tool from the Plastic Features panel.

2. Set the Lip type to Lip.

3. Set Path Edges to the outer edge of the part, and pick the flat highlighted face as the guide face. See Figure 8.16.

4. Set the values on the Lip tab as shown in Figure 8.16.

FIGURE 8.16 Adding a lip to half of the Top solid

5. Click OK to add the lip.

6. Repeat the Lip feature for the B solid, as shown in Figure 8.17.

7. Click OK to place the lip.

8. Use Hide Others to make the Bottom solid visible.

9. Start the Lip tool again.

10. Switch the Lip tool to place a groove.
The size values should carry over from placing the lip.

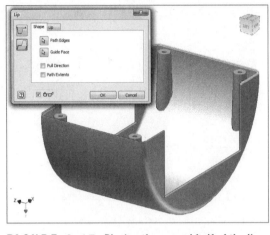

FIGURE 8.17 Placing the second half of the lip

11. Select the outer edge on the bottom and one of the faces, as shown in Figure 8.18, to define the placement of the Lip (Groove) feature.

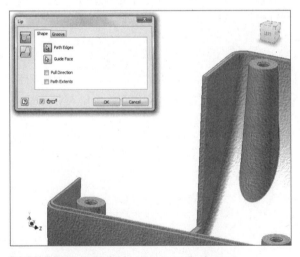

FIGURE 8.18 Add a groove to the bottom.

12. Click OK to create the groove.

13. Repeat placing the groove on the other side. See Figure 8.19.

14. Right-click one of the solids in the Browser, and pick the Show All option. See Figure 8.20 for the final result.

15. Save your work.

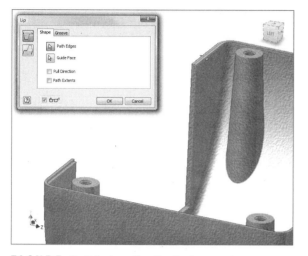

FIGURE 8.19 Inserting the final groove

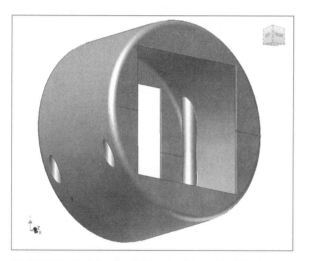

FIGURE 8.20 The finished solid model of the bearing cover

As far as the solid model goes, you're finished with your work. But it could be just the beginning for these interrelated parts.

Making Components

Using the multibody workflow in the part is a great way to develop the basic concept with assurance that your features are consistent — but it's only part of the value of the methodology. It's also only part of the bigger picture from a workflow perspective. You'll still want to manage this type of design as an assembly in order to completely document the individual bodies as full-fledged components.

Inventor has a tool that converts the bodies in the part to separate part files and ties them back to an assembly file. As mentioned before, this assembly and its components remain associative to the source part file.

The Make Components tool is a wizard-style tool that walks you through the conversion process. Let's use it now to create a new assembly.

Creating an Assembly from the Part

In this exercise, you'll create an assembly that is linked to your part and remains associative:

1. Switch to the Manage tab, and select Make Components from the Layout panel.

   In order to use the Make Components tool, you need to select which bodies will be copied to components.

2. Pick the two solids. They appear in the dialog as you do.

3. Set Target Assembly Location to the C:\Data\Assemblies folder. See Figure 8.21.

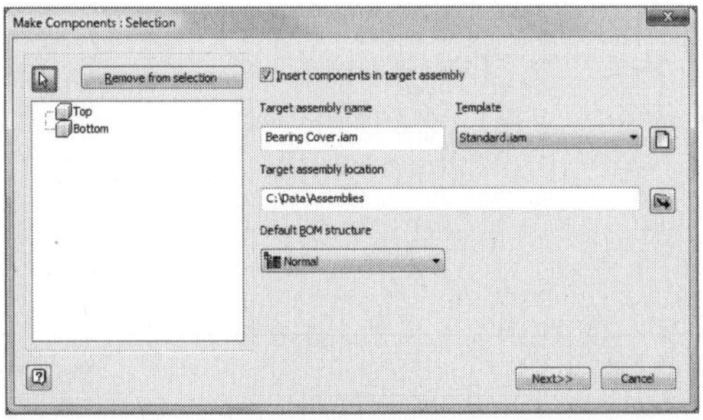

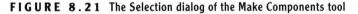

FIGURE 8.21 The Selection dialog of the Make Components tool

The name of the assembly is populated based on the name of the part model. You can select a different template to base the part models on. This offers a great opportunity to build a new file from a different standard than the one you started with. You can also alter the Bill of Materials structure if some components are purchased or are considered inseparable if an assembly comes as a single purchase kit.

4. Click the Next button to set the options for the Part files.

On this tab (Figure 8.22), you can modify the template for each component. You can also change the scale or path, or even mirror the parts as they're created.

FIGURE 8.22 The Bodies dialog for the Make Components tool

5. Click OK to create the new part and assembly files.

6. When the new file opens, it may appear blank. Use the Home View tool to bring the model into view.

7. Use the Save tool to create the new assembly and part files. Click OK to update and create the files.

Even though you started by creating a part file in the assembly, you really need to have the bearing cover assembly in the fan assembly. To do this, you need to replace the single part component with an assembly component.

The Replace Tool

By now, I'm sure you've become aware that the right-click context menus are a gold mine. You can find the Replace tool and the Replace All tool in the context menu after you select a component. You can also find them in the Component panel of the Assemble tab.

These tools can take a component or all instances of a component and replace them. In cases where the geometry is similar enough, you don't even need to reapply assembly constraints.

Replacing a Component in the Assembly

In this case, you have only one instance, so that makes tool selection easier:

1. Pick the Replace tool on the Component panel.

2. Pick the bearing cover part. This opens the dialog shown in Figure 8.23.

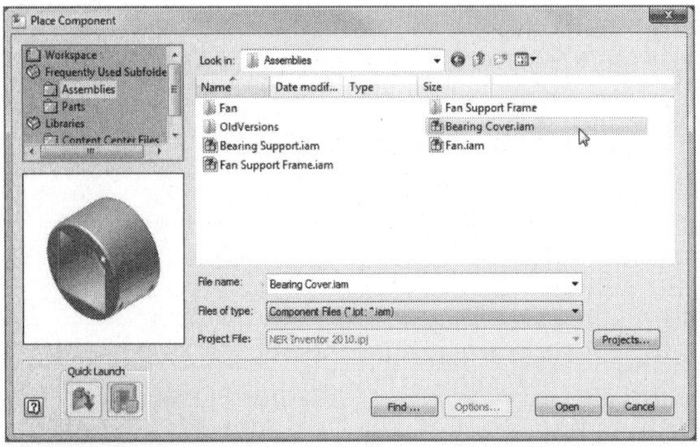

FIGURE 8.23 Selecting the replacement component

3. Navigate to the Assemblies folder, and select Bearing Cover.iam.

4. Click OK to replace the part with the assembly.

You're shown a dialog explaining that some constraints may be lost. Click OK to accept this.

When the bearing cover assembly is placed in the fan assembly, it isn't constrained. A change this dramatic is too much for automatic constraint updates, but the geometry is placed correctly in the file. You can add constraints to locate it as it was, but in this case you'll just make it stay put.

5. Right-click the bearing cover assembly in the Design window, and select Grounded from the context menu.

6. Restore the Envelope Suppressed Level of Detail (LOD), and save your work.

7. If it's available, click the Update icon in the Quick Access Toolbar to refresh any assembly constraints that need restoration. See Figure 8.24 for an update on the assembly's appearance.

I've been experimenting with different uses for multibody solids, and I've been shocked at how many types of assemblies I've built over the years that could've benefited from them. On that note, let's move on to the next plastic part: the fan blade!

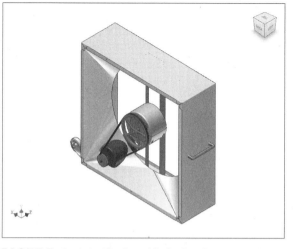

FIGURE 8.24 The fan with the Bearing cover added

What makes a fan a fan is the blade, and being able to create a complex contour is essential. To make this contour, you want to transition from one shape to another. When you did this in sheet metal, it was referred to as a *lofted flange*. In solid modeling, it's referred to as a *lofted feature*. You create these by using the Loft tool.

The Loft Tool

When it comes to creating the complex surfaces that are sought for many modern designs, extrusions and revolved features can fall short. Lofted features create solids and surfaces by calculating the shapes that transition between sketches.

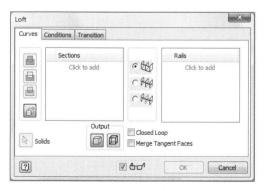

The Loft tool's dialog box has quite a few options. The basic functions such as Join, Cut, Intersect, and New Solid are the same as those for other sketched features. The tool itself uses several techniques to construct how the loft is created. These techniques are reflected in the grouping of options on three tabs: Curves, Conditions, and Transition.

The Curves Tab

This tab is where you define the curves and profiles that are used to construct the loft. You also select the method to use for the definition of the feature:

Sections   As noted, a loft is built based on sections, which can be sketches or model edges. As you select the sections you want to build with, the selections appear as a list in the Sections area of the tab.

Loft Types   Between the Sections and Rails lists are three options for the type of loft solution that will be applied:

> **Rails**   To use this solution, you must have at least two sections and a third curve that you select as a rail. This rail must come in contact with geometry in each of the sections.

> **Center Line**   This works just like the Rails definition, but the centerline doesn't have to contact the sections.

> **Area Loft**   This is a useful option if you're building manifolds or need to control flow. It works like the Center Line option but allows you to calculate the area of the shape as it transitions down the centerline.

Rails/Center Line/Placed Sections   This list changes names based on the construction technique, but it displays the options used to guide your sections to form the lofted shape.

Closed Loop   Selecting this option causes the end section to transition back into the beginning section.

Merge Tangent Faces   As Inventor develops a loft, it generates separate surfaces for each segment in a section sketch. If you select this option, it merges those separate surfaces together if they're tangent to one another.

The Conditions Tab

Each section selected (sketched or part edge) is listed on this tab with a transition condition applied. Several types of transitions can either be applied by the program automatically or selected from the pull-down list. Not all conditions are available for all sections:

Free Condition   This is typical of using open sketches and offers no additional control or capability. It just takes the shape the way it is.

Direction   Using this condition, you can control the angle at which the loft transitions from the sketch plane. This is available only for a sketched section.

Tangent   This option allows you to guide the lofted surface based on an existing surface or face that is adjacent to the selected section sketch or selected face edges.

Smooth   The Smooth option is similar to Tangent but is enhanced by focusing on the overall curvature of the original and resulting faces to maintain continuous curvature.

Sharp Point   This option allows you to loft from a loop (open or closed) to a single point.

Tangent (to Point)   When transitioning from a loop to a point, you can add curvature to the surface by bringing the surface tangent to the sketch plane of the point.

Tangent to Plane   This option is similar to Tangent but also offers the ability to specify what plane the surface is tangent to as it approaches the point.

As you use some of these options, you may be presented with prompts for additional modification:

Angle   When using the Direction condition, you can specify the angle that the shape begins to transition along as it moves to the next curve.

Weight   Use this value to control how quickly the shape of one section begins to transition to the shape of another. This value is referred to as *unitless*, meaning it's an arbitrary value that you can change until the effect is appropriate.

The Transition Tab

Inventor automatically maps how a surface will transition between edges on the various sections. You can override these selections on this tab and specify how a surface is defined by selecting beginning and ending points for the surfaces of the loft. With care, you can even introduce twist into the shape.

A lot of the options are selected for you automatically, and very often the automatic result will give you the look and shape that you need.

Constructing the Fan Blade Shape

The loft is a sketched feature, so as usual that's where you'll begin. In this case, rather than using origin planes or work planes that you create, I want to show you a construction technique that I frequently use to figure out shapes. I have used this for extremely complex shapes, but what you'll be doing would be even more challenging without it:

1. Create a new part based on the Standard (in).ipt template.

2. Using a Construction linetype draw a circle with roughly a 4.5-inch radius based on the sketch centerpoint.

3. Draw a rectangle with normal lines above the circle, as shown in Figure 8.25.

4. Use a Vertical constraint to center the middle of the rectangle.

5. Add a Coincidence constraint between one of the bottom corners of the rectangle and the top of the circle.

6. Add dimensions as shown in Figure 8.26.

7. Finish the sketch, and start the Extrude tool.

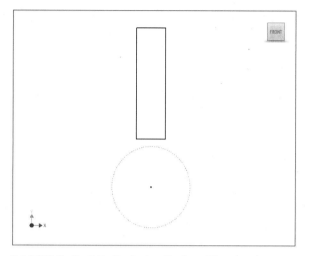

FIGURE 8.25 Beginning the fan with a sketch

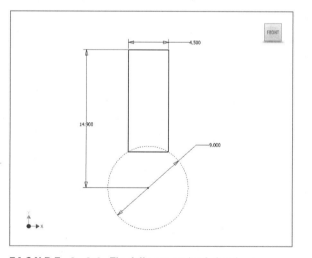

FIGURE 8.26 The fully constrained sketch

8. Change the Output type to Surface and set the Distance value to 1.5. See Figure 8.27.

9. Click OK to create the surface.

Rather than creating a series of work planes, you'll use these surfaces to construct the sketches that define the Loft feature.

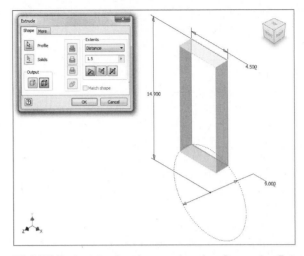

FIGURE 8.27 Creating a series of surfaces using Extrude

10. Save the new file as Fan Blade in the Parts folder.

    For the next step, I'll refer to the surface faces based on the face of the ViewCube that lets me look directly at them. I'll do my best to keep the images clear; but if I refer to the top face, use the ViewCube as a safety check.

    You'll also place sketches on the faces based on the home view rather that rotating the part to get views external to the surface.

11. Create a sketch on the bottom surface.

12. Using a Construction linetype, project the edges that intersect with the left and right surfaces into the sketch.

13. Using a Construction linetype, draw a line from the right edge outward and perpendicular to the projected line.

14. Dimension the line's position as shown in Figure 8.28.

15. Switching to the Normal linetype, draw a tangent arc using the Line tool from the dimensioned line to the opposite projected line. Dimension it as shown in Figure 8.29.

16. Finish the sketch.

17. Start a new sketch on the top surface, and replicate the last steps with the different dimension values shown in Figure 8.30.

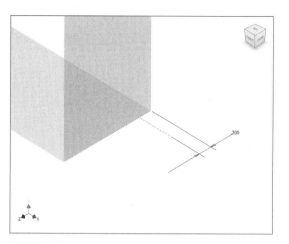

FIGURE 8.28 Setting up the sketch's construction geometry

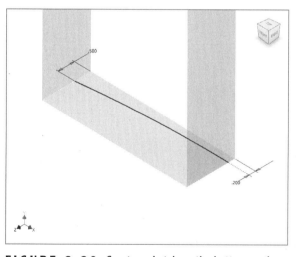

FIGURE 8.29 Create a sketch on the bottom surface.

18. Finish the sketch on the top and create a new one on the right surface.

19. In the new sketch, project the endpoints of the arcs that contact the right surface.

20. Draw a line between the two projected points. See Figure 8.31. Finish the sketch.

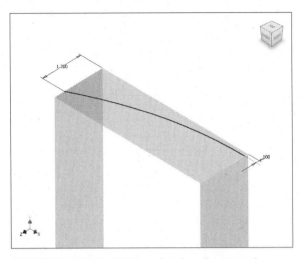

FIGURE 8.30 Adding a sketch to the top surface

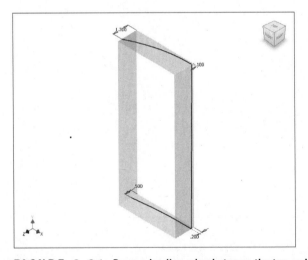

FIGURE 8.31 Draw a leading edge between the two points.

21. Create a new sketch on the left surface.

22. Project the points of the arcs that come in contact with the left surface.

23. Create a short, vertical construction line to establish tangency from the projected point at the top surface.

24. Draw a tangent arc between the points, as shown in Figure 8.32.

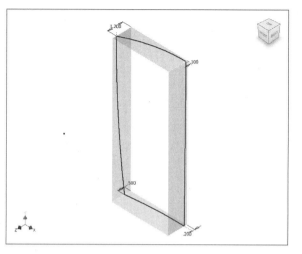

FIGURE 8.32 Sketching the trailing edge between the arcs

25. Finish the sketch, and save the file.

   What you've done is construct the profiles and the rails of the loft you're about to create.

Creating the Blade

In this case, you've used open sketches, so you can only create a surface between the profiles. After you've done that, you can use the Thicken tool to create the solid blade:

1. Start the Loft tool from the Create pane on the Model tab.

2. When the Loft dialog appears, pick the sketches on the top and bottom surfaces for the profiles.

3. Click the Click to Add option in the Rails section, and then pick the sketches on the left and right surfaces. The preview should appear like Figure 8.33.

4. Click OK to create the lofted surface.

5. Turn off the visibility of the extrusion you based the sketches on.

6. Start the Thicken/Offset tool, and select the lofted surface.

7. Set Thickness to .1 inches, and set the direction so that the new body is toward the front. See Figure 8.34.
   Click OK to create the blade.

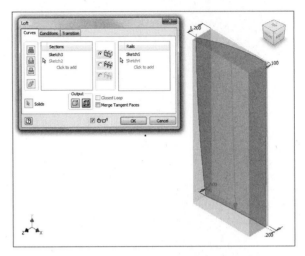

FIGURE 8.33 Creating the lofted surface

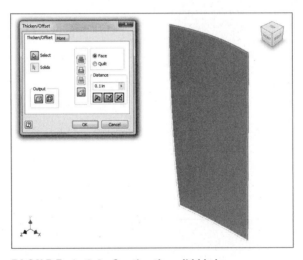

FIGURE 8.34 Creating the solid blade

8. Turn off the visibility of the lofted surface.

9. Change the model's Color to Plastic (White).

10. Save the file.

11. Start the Fillet tool, and add a 0.5-inch radius fillet to the small edges at the upper-left and upper-right corners, as shown in Figure 8.35.

12. Start the Fillet tool again, and set it to Full Round Fillet.

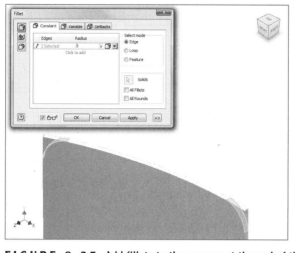

FIGURE 8.35 Add fillets to the corners at the end of the blade.

13. For the three faces, select the front face, the edge, and the rear face. The preview should look like Figure 8.36.

14. Save the file.

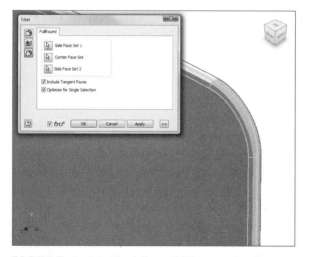

FIGURE 8.36 The full round fillet smooths all the moving edges of the fan at once.

Now that you've created your blade, you need to create the hub. The hub will spin or revolve around the axis of the shaft. To build it, you'll use a tool that is suitably named.

The Revolve Tool

The second most frequently used tool for creating the base feature in a model is Revolve. Whereas the Extrude feature builds a sketch in one direction, Revolve wraps a sketch around an axis. The axis doesn't have to be part of the sketch or geometry that is part of the profile. This allows for the use of origin axes, and it also lets you use an axis separate from the profile to create a hollow part.

To revolve a sketch, you need two fundamental items: the *profile*, or shape, and the *axis* to revolve around. As with Extrude, you'll initially only be able to use Join for the base feature. Cut and Intersect options are available once you have a base feature.

The Extents group allows you to select termination options for the feature. The Revolve tool's window (see Figure 8.37) includes the following options:

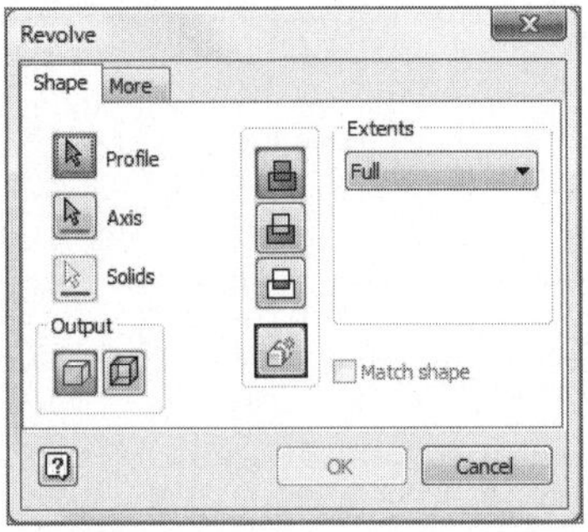

FIGURE 8.37 The Revolve dialog box

Extents

Five options define how far the profile is revolved around the axis:

Angle   Develops the shape through the specified angle. You can change the direction from one side of the sketch to the other or make an equal division with the sketch in the center.

To Next   Revolves the profile until it intersects with the first body it meets in the direction selected. This option isn't available for creating the base feature.

To   Similar to To Next, but available as a base feature. You can select a terminating plane or surface that has been created or imported.

From To   Revolves the shape between two selected planes or surfaces.

Full   Revolves the sketch 360 degrees about the axis.

Building the Hub

In reality, you're going to build only a portion of the fan blade. Then, you'll pattern that portion to make the complete blade. This saves time, but it's also better practice because it allows for simplicity and consistency.

Let's also start testing your retention a little by giving you fewer instructions for how to do things. It's OK to go back and look things up. I think it's important for you to fill in the gaps, though, to really learn these tools:

1. Create a new sketch on the origin YZ plane.

2. Using techniques you've already used in previous exercises, create the sketch and dimensions shown in Figure 8.38. Start the vertical centerline at the sketch centerpoint.

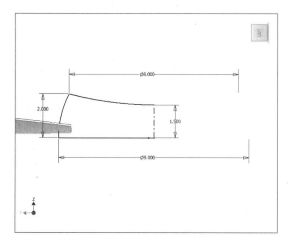

FIGURE 8.38 Set the vertical line to be a centerline, to get the linear diameter dimensions.

3. Return to the home view.

4. Start the Revolve tool.

5. Set Extents to Angle.

6. Set Angle to 90 and the solution to be from the Middle. Compare your preview to Figure 8.39.

7. Click OK to create the new feature.

8. Add a 0.3-inch fillet to the top of the hub, as shown in Figure 8.40. Click OK to place the fillet.

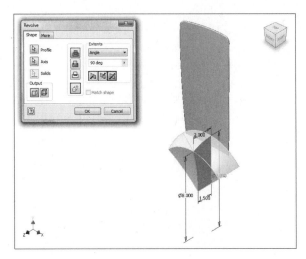

FIGURE 8.39 The preview of the revolve

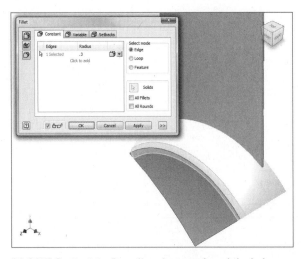

FIGURE 8.40 Rounding the top edge of the hub

9. Use the Shell tool with a Thickness value of 0.15 inches to remove the flat faces at the back, lower left, and lower right of the hub.

Click OK to place the feature, which should look like Figure 8.41.

10. Position your view of the model so you can see the intersection of the blade and the hub.

11. Start the Fillet tool again.

12. Set the Fillet type to Face Fillet.

13. Pick the large curved face of the hub and the front surface of the blade.

14. When the preview of the fillet appears, set the Radius to 0.15 inches (Figure 8.42) and click OK to generate the feature.

15. Save your work.

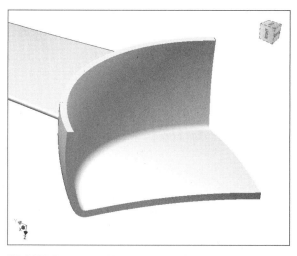

FIGURE 8.41 The hub after a Shell features is applied

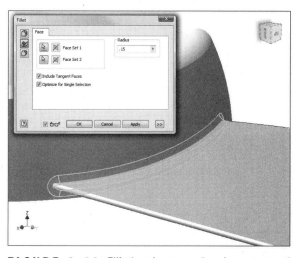

FIGURE 8.42 Filleting the two major elements together

Now that your part has the features that are common to the entire part, you can replicate those features.

In Chapter 4, "Working with Solid Models and Weldments," you used the Rectangular Pattern tool to create a pattern of Hole features. Some additional options are available for both the Rectangular Patter and Circular Pattern tools. Let's do a quick review of the Circular Pattern tool.

The Circular Pattern Tool

Circular patterns are very simple to create (see the dialog box in Figure 8.43), but it's also easy to overlook a couple of important options:

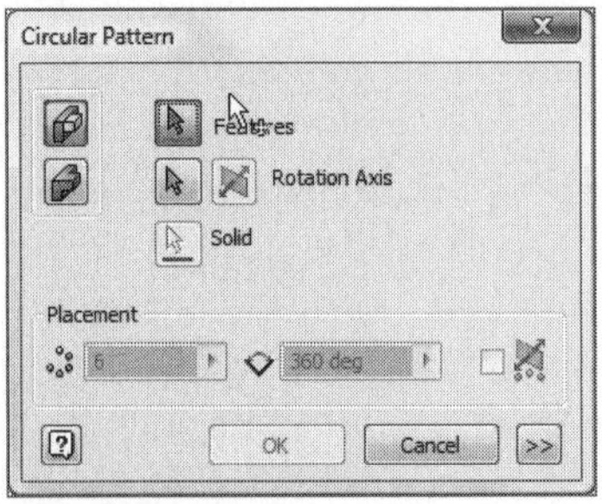

FIGURE 8.43 The Circular Pattern dialog box

Pattern the Entire Solid   Typically, you can select a few features that you want to pattern. The Pattern the Entire Solid option is great if you want to develop a part that has symmetry. This works for either rectangular or circular patterns as well as the Mirror tool. Whereas patterning individual features has Inventor calculate the new pattern members (instances), patterning the entire part calculates more quickly.

More   For the Circular Pattern tool, some important options are hidden under the More button:

> **Optimized**   The most important is the Optimized option. This option ignores feature calculations and replicates the body of the features rather than their values.
>
> **Incremental**   The default value for Positioning Method is Fitted. This applies the number of features evenly across the angle entered in the main part of the dialog. The Incremental option causes an angle value to be the angle between instances.

Let's complete the major portion of the component using a circular pattern.

Creating the Whole Body

When patterning complex shapes, I prefer to set up the model to pattern the entire solid. Duplicating features using complex calculations opens up the potential for a failed feature. So, I find it best not to do so when it's not necessary:

1. Start the Circular Pattern tool from the Pattern panel.

2. Set the type to Pattern the Entire Solid.

3. Set Origin Z Axis as the Rotation axis.

4. Set the Placement value to 5, as shown in Figure 8.44.

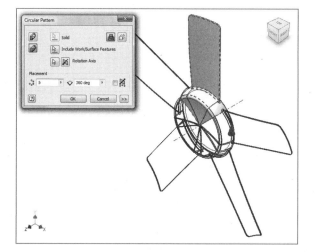

FIGURE 8.44 Creating the pattern of blades

5. Click OK to create the fan blade.

6. Rotate the view of the part so you can see the hollow back of the hub.

7. Create a new sketch on the XY plane.

8. Draw a 1.2-inch diameter circle.

9. Extrude using To Next Extents. On the More tab, include a 2-degree taper, as shown in Figure 8.45.

10. Click OK to create the boss.

11. Add a drilled hole with a diameter of 0.65 inches and a depth of 1 inch, concentric to the new extrusion. See Figure 8.46.

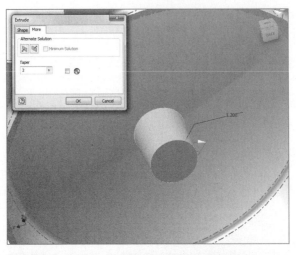

FIGURE 8.45 The Circular Pattern dialog box

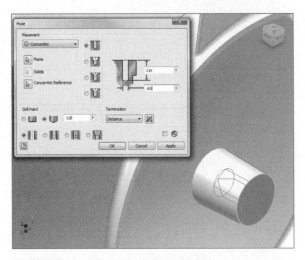

FIGURE 8.46 Add a hole to the boss.

12. Add a 0.3-inch fillet around the base of the boss.

13. Start a new sketch.

14. When placing, click the flat face at the top of the boss and drag into the part.

15. Set the offset of the new plane at −0.4 inches into the part, as shown in Figure 8.47.

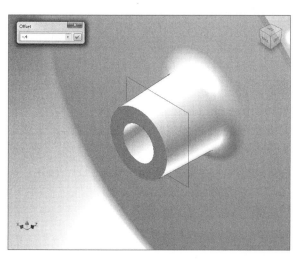

FIGURE 8.47 Creating a new sketch offset from a face

16. Pick the check mark in the dialog to create the work plane and start the new sketch.

17. In the sketch, draw a horizontal line in the space between the boss in the middle and the edge of the hub.

18. Add a Coincident constraint between the line and the sketch center-point. See Figure 8.48.

19. Finish the sketch, and save your work.

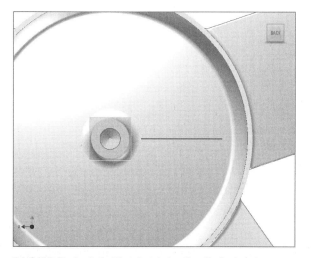

FIGURE 8.48 The sketch for the rib doesn't have to meet the edges of the model.

You have only one physical feature left to add to the part. It's a common feature, and without the right tool it can be difficult to add to a part like your fan blade.

The Rib and Web Tools

For plastic or cast-metal parts, reinforcement ribs are a common need. Drawing ribs individually can be very time-consuming, and creating the parametric relationships to maintain consistency across all the ribs can add a great deal of complexity to the part. Webs are similar to ribs. Unlike ribs, which typically terminate on a face and have their geometry blend into the part, webs begin on a plane but stop at a distance from that plane.

The process of creating both features is quite direct. Select the sketch elements you want to use, and then click the Direction button. Drag your mouse on the screen to determine the direction in which the ribs (or web) will be built. The dialog box also presents a few options:

Extents   This is where you select whether to create a rib or a web. If you select Web, a field appears below the Extents buttons so you can enter the depth of the web from the sketch plane.

Thickness   This option controls the width of the web or rib as it goes to its termination. Buttons below the value control whether the width is offset to one side or the other or split in the middle of the sketch element.

Extend Profile   When this is checked, a sketch element that isn't closed continues in its path until it finds a boundary on the existing geometry. If this isn't selected, the rib stops at the end of the sketch element.

Taper   This option adds a draft angle as the rib is created. Unlike when adding taper to an extrusion, you need not worry about a positive or negative angle.

Direction   If the preview of the rib or web isn't going in the proper direction, you can select this icon and, by moving your cursor in the Design window, reorient the direction of the preview.

By creating multiple lines, you can place several ribs at once.

Placing the Ribs

By sketching multiple lines, you can create a large number of ribs at once even when they intersect. For your model, you'll create one rib and then pattern it:

1. Start the Rib tool from the Create panel.

2. Because there is only one viable sketch, a preview should appear.

3. Set the Thickness value to **0.15** inches, set the Taper value to **2** degrees, and if necessary use the Direction tool to get your preview to look like Figure 8.49.

FIGURE 8.49 A preview of the rib shows the shape extending beyond the sketch.

4. Click OK to add the rib.

5. Turn off the visibility of the plane created for the rib sketch.
   The rib should extend to match the geometry in the hollow of the hub. It shouldn't penetrate the hole at the center or come out the side of the hub. That's the beauty of the Rib tool.

6. Create a circular pattern of eight ribs around the Z axis of the part.

7. Start a rule fillet. For the Feature selection, pick the rib and the pattern of the rib.

8. Set the Radius value to 0.2 inches, and keep the Rule value as Against Part. See Figure 8.50.

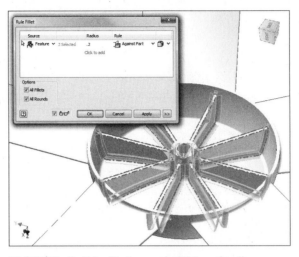

FIGURE 8.50 Placing a rule fillet on the ribs

9. Click OK to place the fillets.

10. Save your work.

11. Create a new work plane at –2 inches from the top of the boss, as shown in Figure 8.51.

12. Click the check mark to approve the new plane.

13. Rotate your view to see the new plane in front of the fan blade.

FIGURE 8.51 Defining a new work plane

You may have noticed that when you create work planes or have them visible, they appear to be one color from one point of view but change color when you see the other side of the plane.

You're not imagining things — that's really happening. Planes have a positive face and a negative face. For 2D sketches, it really doesn't matter which direction the plane's *normal* or positive direction is facing. For other elements, such as text, or when you're placing an image on a plane, it can have an effect.

On my screen, when I look at the front of the fan blade, the new plane appears blue. This means that in my color scheme, I'm looking at the back of the plane. You're about to create a sketch with an image in it, and having the plane face away from you will likely cause the image to be backward.

Let's fix this ahead of time:

14. Move your cursor near the new work plane. When it highlights; right-click, and select Flip Normal from the context menu.

15. Create a sketch on the work plane.
    Now you need to do a little work outside of Inventor.

16. In Windows Explorer, create a folder named C:\Data\Images.

17. Copy an image (.bmp, .jpg, .png, .tif, .gif, and so on) of your choice into this folder.

18. Return to Inventor, and select the Insert Image tool from the Insert panel of the Sketch tab. This brings up the Open dialog.

19. Navigate to the Images folder, and select the image file of your choice.

20. Click Open to place the image in your sketch.
    Depending on the size of your image, your preview will vary, but a boundary around the image will frame it. This lets you locate and size the image on the model — for example, if you have a scan of a safety sticker that is 3 inches wide, you can dimension the frame and it will scale to be 3 inches wide. This gives you a whole new way to deal with nomenclature on your designs.

21. Use the Horizontal and Vertical sketch constraints to center your image on the sketch centerpoint.

22. Apply a dimension to make the largest portion of your image 2.5 inches wide or tall.

23. Turn off the visibility of the work plane. See Figure 8.52.

24. Finish the sketch, and save the model.

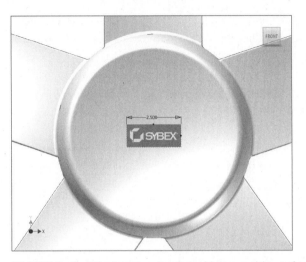

FIGURE 8.52 A centered and sized image waiting to be applied to the model

You have your image in your model file, but it's not "on" the model. Your fan blade is concave in the middle, and your images are flat. This isn't very realistic. Well, Inventor provides a fun tool for correcting it.

The Decal Tool

The Decal tool is essentially the Emboss tool, but it doesn't affect the volume of a component; it only stretches an image, document, or even a spreadsheet onto the faces of a component.

As you can see, the dialog offers few options, and some are available only in certain circumstances:

Wrap to Face   This option allows the image to be stretched to maintain its size when applied to the surface.

Chain Faces   If the image would overlap an adjacent face, having this option on allows the image to continue onto that face.

Let's add your decal to the face of the fan blade:

1. You can find the Decal tool by expanding the Create panel of the Model tab. It's the only hidden Create tool. Click the icon.

2. With Wrap to Face deselected, click the image file, and then pick the curved face behind it.

3. Click OK to create the decal, as shown in Figure 8.53.

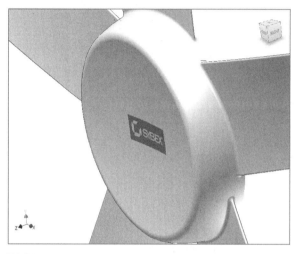

FIGURE 8.53 The decal applied to the fan blade

4. Save the file.

You're finished building your fan blade. Let's place it in the assembly.

5. In the Browser, right-click the icon for Fan Blade.ipt, and select Copy from the context menu.

6. Switch to the fan assembly.

7. In an open part of the Design window, right-click, and select Paste from the menu. This inserts an instance of the fan blade into the assembly.

8. Apply an Insert constraint between the bottom of the hole in the boss of the fan blade and the end of the shaft.

9. Apply an Angular constraint between the YZ plane of the fan blade and the right side of the housing, as shown in Figure 8.54.

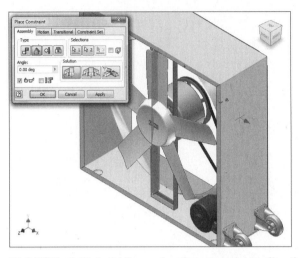

FIGURE 8.54 Adding an Angular constraint to align the fan blade

10. In the Browser, click twice slowly on the name of the Angular constraint you just created. When it lets you, rename the constraint **Fan Angle**.

11. Close the separate files for Bearing Cover.ipt, Bearing Cover.iam, and Fan Blade.ipt if they're still open. Accept saving any changes if prompted.

12. If the Update icon is active on the Quick Access Toolbar in the Fan.iam file, select it.

13. Save the assembly.

There was a time when to create a component like the fan blade, people looked to a system that was built around modeling surfaces.

Inventor is capable of creating extraordinarily complex components using a mixture of surfaces and solids. It isn't a matter of choosing one or the other but having the option of moving between tools that let you define elements until the part is whole.

N O T E   For the next exercises, you'll need to download the Grill.ipt and Power Knob.ipt files from www.sybex.com/go/inventor2010ner. Save the files to the C:\Data\Parts folder.

Downloading these files isn't about saving time as much as it's about focusing on some advanced tools rather than spending a lot of time using the sketching skills you already have. Trust me, you'll get plenty of practice with sketching as you start to translate your 2D models to 3D.

For the first exercise, you'll use a tool that is unique in its approach to using surfaces to develop a solid model.

The Sculpt Tool

In previous jobs, I've frequently worked with surface modeling tools. If you've never worked with a dedicated surface modeler, don't. Relatively few product types require it, and typically the workflow to create parts is considerably more complex than should be necessary. I wish I'd had access to Inventor's Sculpt tool years ago. It would've saved me many hours per week.

Using the tool is a straightforward process. First, you construct a collection of overlapping surfaces. Then, you start the Sculpt tool and click those surfaces (or planes); Sculpt finds the void between the surfaces and fills it with a solid model. There is only one primary option. When you select surfaces, a double-ended arrow appears, indicating the direction you want to favor. This can switch Inventor from ignoring a surface that passes through the body to using it to change the exterior boundary or create another void contour that acts like a part has been cut out. You can also use Sculpt to modify an existing solid body, similar to the Split tool but with more flexibility.

The Sculpt tool's dialog box is very simple. If you have an existing body, you can select whether you'll be adding or subtracting geometry as the default. You then select the planes and surfaces.

Expanding the dialog with the More button displays the list of selected surfaces so you can choose the surface direction in the dialog instead of clicking the arrows on the surfaces.

Now, you'll use the Sculpt tool to create the knob for your switch.

Sculpting the Power Knob

This quick exercise will give you a feel for the Sculpt tool and some practice with the Emboss tool:

   1. Open the Power Knob.ipt file from the Parts folder.

2. Start the Revolve tool. It should immediately pick up the outer surface sketch.

3. Click OK to create the outer surface.

4. Press the Enter key to start the Revolve tool again. This time, it detects the inner surface sketch.

5. Click OK to create the inner surface.

6. Save the file.

 7. Click the Sculpt tool in the Surface panel of the Model tab.

8. For Surfaces, pick the Origin XZ plane and then the inner and outer surfaces.

   The preview shows building a solid with no cavity.

9. Pick the top arrow, as shown in Figure 8.55. This tells Sculpt that the body is between the inner surface and the outer surface.

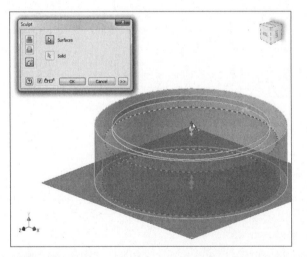

FIGURE 8.55 Telling Sculpt where the solid geometry should be formed

10. Click OK to create the solid.

11. Move the End of Part marker below Boss Sketch in the Browser.

12. Extrude the profile, as shown in Figure 8.56, using To Next Extents.

13. Move the End of Part marker to the bottom of the list of features.

Now that you've used Sculpt and Extrude to form the model, you'll embellish it with some text to indicate the state of power to the fan.

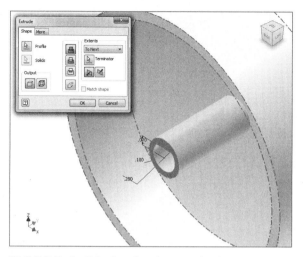

FIGURE 8.56 Creating the mounting boss

Adding the Text

Text as well as sketches can be formed to the part using the Emboss tool:

1. Edit the text sketch.

2. Start the Text tool.

3. Click and drag an expected text boundary (Figure 8.57) next to the rectangle that already exists.

4. When you're finished dragging the boundary, the Format Text dialog appears.

5. In the Format Text dialog, set the Center Justification option, choose Arial from the Font list, and pick .240 from the Size pull-down.

6. In the Text input window, type the capital letter I followed by three carriage returns (Enter key) and then the capital letter O.

7. If the letters appear to have different sizes, highlight them and reselect .240 in from the Size pull-down. See Figure 8.58 for reference.

8. Click OK to place the text into the sketch.

9. Press the Esc key to finish the Text tool.

10. Click and drag the corners of the text boundary to the corners of the sketched rectangle. It's only necessary to drag two opposite corners.

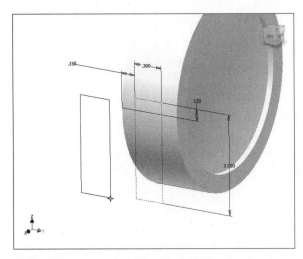

FIGURE 8.57 Roughing in a boundary for the text

FIGURE 8.58 Set your text values per this image of the Format Text dialog.

11. Finish the sketch.

12. Start the Emboss tool.

13. Select the text for the Profile value.

14. Set the Depth value to 0.03 inches.

15. Change the feature color by picking the Color icon and selecting Black. Click OK to accept the change in the Color dialog.

16. Pick the Wrap to Face check box, and select the outer cylindrical surface for the face. See Figure 8.59.

17. Click OK to create the embossed text.

18. Compare your model to Figure 8.60, and save it.

   The ability to add embossed (or engraved) text to your models is very useful if you're working with cast or plastic parts.

19. Save the file, and close it.

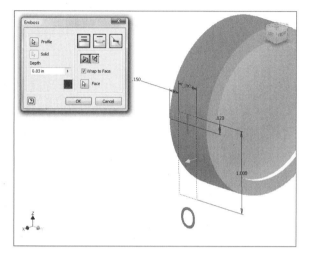

FIGURE 8.59 Setting up the Emboss feature

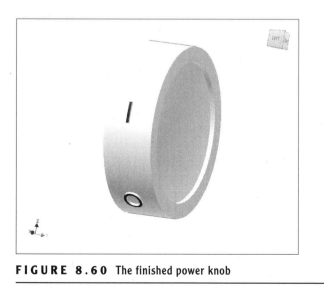

FIGURE 8.60 The finished power knob

Next, you'll add the power knob to your fan assembly.

Adding the Power Knob

A couple of quick constraints should lock everything in place:

1. Place the power knob into the assembly.

2. Place an Angular constraint between the edge of the flat face on the shaft of the switch and the edge of the flat face in the hole on the power knob, as shown in Figure 8.61. Set the Angle value to 180 degrees.

3. Click OK to place the constraint.

4. Place an Insert constraint (Figure 8.62) between the knob and the switch. Click OK to complete the step.

5. Save the assembly.

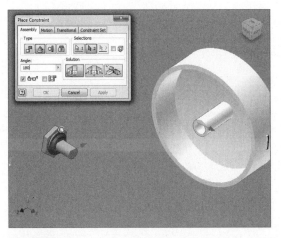

FIGURE 8.61 Mate the alignment flats just as they would be in a physical model.

Now you have one major component left, and your design will be complete. For the final component, the grill, you'll use the starter part you downloaded.

With the name *grill*, you probably have a good idea what the part is. The Grill tool that Inventor carries has a lot of tools within it for creating the mind-boggling geometry that is referred to as a *grill* on modern plastic parts. These features can be created using traditional modeling techniques, but doing so is a painful process at best.

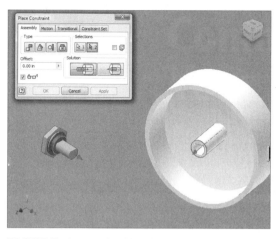

FIGURE 8.62 Locking the power knob into place

Let's do an overview of the Grill tool before you begin working on your model.

The Grill Tool

Because a Grill feature has so many options and dimensional controls that may need to be specified, the tool's dialog is segmented into tabs arranged by the types of subfeatures that may be used in the grill. On each tab are a number of input values to control the size of each of these elements.

Let's work through the dialog and attach some meaning to the parts of a grill.

The Boundary Tab

This tab is focused on picking the sketch that is used as the boundary for the grill and defining the geometry that is created on the perimeter.

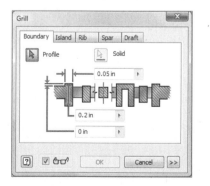

The Island Tab

An area that maintains the original surface geometry but is surrounded by grill elements is referred to as an *island*. In the Grill tool, you're allowed to establish a value for the wall thickness of the island. Where the top and bottom of the island are positioned is based on the values used for the boundary.

The Rib Tab

A rib is the most recognizable feature of a grill. The rib tends to follow the surface contour and be kept near that surface. In the Rib tab, you select the sketch elements that you want to apply the ribs to and then input the sizes for the width, depth, and offset from the top of the boundary.

The Spar Tab

The *spar* is the feature you often see recessed from the rib. It's primarily used to support the Rib feature. Its depth is set relative to the size of the rib.

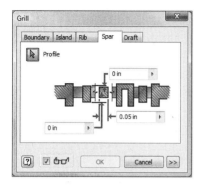

The Draft Tab

When parts need to be extracted from a mold, having a taper applied to the faces makes it easier to get the parts out. You set the angle of the draft on this tab. You can also pick the Parting Element check box to set a plane or face to establish where the draft begins.

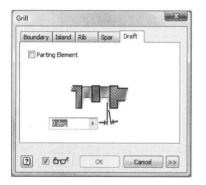

This is one of the most complex tools in Inventor, but the dialog makes it easy to use and understand what input is needed.

On all but one of the tabs, you need to select geometry to define an element of the grill. Let's set up the sketches that are needed to make the grill component a grill.

Editing the Sketch

In this exercise, you'll build the pattern of lines needed to place ribs in your part:

   1. Open the Grill.ipt file that you downloaded to the Parts folder.

   2. Double-click Sketch2 in the Browser to begin editing the sketch.

3. Set the view in the Design window to the front view.

   You need to pattern the lines in the sketch. To make things easier to see, I've colored the lines that you'll pattern. Rather than doing a simple input of numbers, I also wanted to use this opportunity to show a couple more examples of the power of parametric sketches.

4. Start the Rectangular Pattern tool from the Pattern panel of the Sketch tab.

5. For the Geometry, select the orange, vertical line.

6. Click the arrow icon for Direction 1, and pick a horizontal line in the sketch to establish the direction.

7. Highlight the value for the distance between instances of the pattern. Then, click the 1.500-inch dimension in the sketch to use its value.

   You've established the distance between the lines in the pattern. Now you'll create an equation in the dialog to set the number.

   To calculate the number of instances in the pattern you divide the length of the pattern by the distance between instances.

8. Highlight the value in the instances input.

9. Type a left parenthesis, and then select the 33-inch width dimension.

10. Add a slash, and then select the 1.5-inch dimension you selected for the distance.

11. Add a right parenthesis, a hyphen, and the number one.

    This equation says that you'll divide the width by the distance between the lines and then subtract one of the instances. See Figure 8.63. The reason for using an equation is to automatically adjust the pattern if you decide to change the spacing of the lines or change the width of what will be the boundary of your grill.

12. Click OK to create the pattern of lines.

13. Repeat the rectangular pattern for the red, horizontal lines, using the .500-inch spacing dimension and the 33-inch height dimension. See Figure 8.64 to verify the equation.

14. Click OK to create the pattern.

15. Finish the sketch, and save the part.

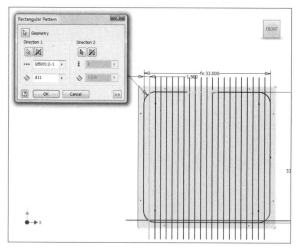

FIGURE 8.63 Building a pattern using an equation

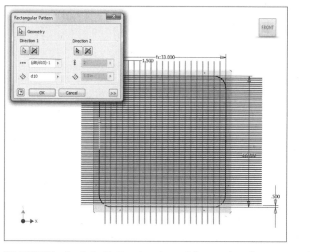

FIGURE 8.64 Patterning the red lines using the same technique

All that's left is to create your grill.

Adding the Grill

With the Grill feature's many capabilities, all you really need is the boundary and the ribs. Both your vertical and horizontal elements will be the same height and depth:

1. Start the Grill feature from the Plastic Part panel.

2. Select the square in the sketch for the boundary.

3. Set the width of the Boundary feature to be 0.05, the height to be 0.3, and the offset from the sketch face to be 0.05, as shown in Figure 8.65.

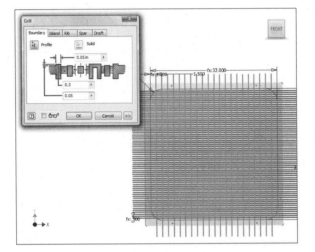

FIGURE 8.65 Setting the values for the boundary

4. Click the Rib tab.

5. Drag a crossing window (right to left) across only the orange and red lines.

6. Set the rib width to be 0.05, the height to be 0.25, and the offset to 0, as shown in Figure 8.66.

It's important that you verify that only the appropriate lines are selected for the rib.

7. Click OK to create the Grill feature in the part. The finished part should look like Figure 8.67.

8. Save the file, and close it.

You've now created all the components you need for your design. Next, you'll add the grill to the assembly and secure them in place.

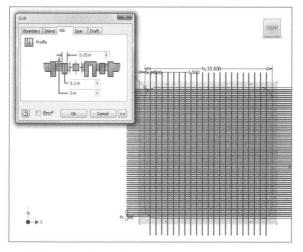

FIGURE 8.66 Selecting the lines for the ribs of the grill

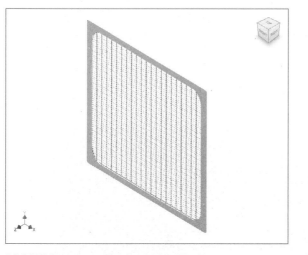

FIGURE 8.67 The finished grill part

Adding Grills to the Assembly

For the assembly, you need two grills. You need to attach them to the assembly using bolted connections; but on one side, the connection has to pass through an additional part. No problem:

1. Place one instance of the grill into the fan assembly.

2. Create a Mate constraint between the front of the housing and the back of the grill, as shown in Figure 8.68.

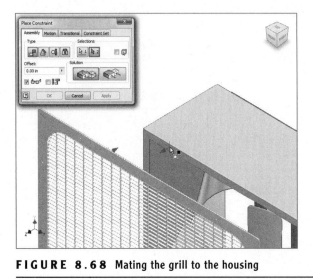

FIGURE 8.68 Mating the grill to the housing

3. Click Apply to create the constraint.

4. Create Mate constraints with Flush solutions between the YZ and XZ planes of the grill and the assembly. Doing so centers the grill on the assembly. See Figure 8.69.

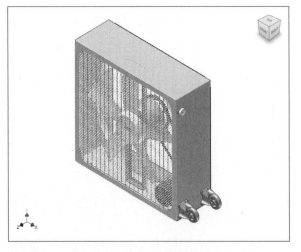

FIGURE 8.69 The grill constrained into place

5. Start the Place from Content Center tool.

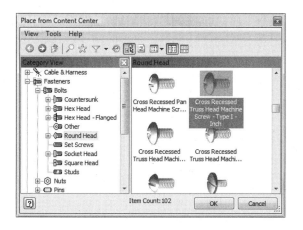

6. Locate the Cross Recessed Truss Head Machine Screw - Type I - Inch fastener. Using the context menu, add it to your favorites.

7. Drag the screw from the Favorites Browser, and place it on one of the holes in the grill.

8. When offered, select the Bolted Connection option from the toolbar.

9. When the Bolted Connection Component Generator dialog appears, set Termination to the back of the housing flange, as shown in Figure 8.70.

10. In the dialog, click the Click to Add a Fastener option at the bottom of the bolted connection on the right.
    This launches a dialog that initially shows applicable washers.

11. Change the Category option to Sheet Metal Nuts.

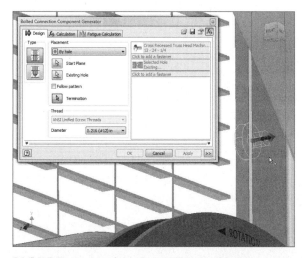

FIGURE 8.70 Selecting the Termination face

12. Select the PEM Self-Clinching Nuts S, SS, CLS, CLSS - Inch nut. This adds the nut to the bolted connection. See Figure 8.71.

FIGURE 8.71 Defining the bolted connection

13. Select the Follow Pattern option in the dialog, and click OK to create the bolted connections.

14. Save the file.

This particular bolted connection creates a hole in the housing large enough to press-fit the selected PEM fastener into. This is brilliant — Inventor even did it eight times for all the holes in the grill!

Now, you need to add an instance of the grill to the other side. You can use a Mirror tool because the duct is on the other side — the bolted connection has to pass through it, too.

15. Insert another instance of the grill part, and use Assembly constraints to place it using the same constraints as the first.

Double-check to make sure you're not putting the grill on backward. The larger boundary should go to the inside of the assembly.

16. Place the same bolted connection to the inside of the housing flange, and notice that the bolted connection tool creates a clearance hole for the bolt in the duct and the larger hole in the housing for the PEM nut. See Figure 8.72.

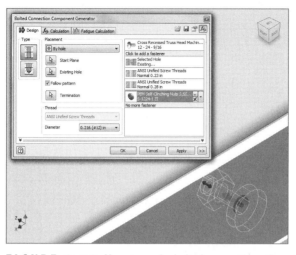

FIGURE 8.72 You can make bolted connections through more than two parts.

17. Click OK to place the new bolted connections.

18. Restore your home view, and save your work.

Look at the status bar at the bottom of the Inventor interface. In the course of these first eight chapters, you've created a 50-part assembly. Granted, you didn't model 50 components, but I think that's a good thing. Most people don't create products for which they fabricate every component.

If you buy things like bolts, screws, bearings, belts, casters, and motors, isn't it good that you don't have to model them to use them accurately?

In the next chapter, we'll focus on extending the use of this model beyond the typical scope of creating detail drawings of the individual parts and views of the assembly. You'll do some drawing, but you'll create the sorts of drawings that are difficult (at best) to do with a 2D CAD system. You'll also create exploded views and realistic renderings to help you sell your ideas to management and your customers.

In the world of digital prototyping, a model of your product is just the beginning of its usefulness (see Figure 8.73).

Congratulations on making the move to 3D!

FIGURE 8.73 The finished Fan assembly!

Are You Experienced?

Now you can...

- ☑ create an assembly from a single part
- ☑ add plastic features to a model
- ☑ loft a surface between sketches
- ☑ create a solid from surfaces
- ☑ easily model complex grills

CHAPTER 9

Communicating Your Design

- ▶ Building specialized drawing views

- ▶ Creating an exploded view of your assembly

- ▶ Adding balloons and a parts list to a drawing

- ▶ Creating a lightweight file for transmission

- ▶ Rendering your design

3D Is Just the Beginning

In Chapter 4, "Working with Solid Models and Weldments," you created a drawing of the bearing support assembly and a second drawing sheet of the plate. The tools you learned there will allow you to detail most of the components that many designers and engineers work with.

In this chapter, you'll work with a number of tools that, like traditional 2D drawings, are made to help you communicate your design with others. What is new in this age of creating digital prototypes is who you may need to communicate with and who may want to use your design data as the basis for a different form of communication.

You'll begin by addressing more traditional needs: creating descriptive drawing views that will be useful for manufacturing. Then, you'll repurpose some of that material to create communication materials that can be sent to a vendor or customer. Finally, you'll use your data to sell itself by creating images that can be used to promote your new product before you've built it.

Advanced Drawing Views

I hope you were impressed by Inventor's drafting capabilities in Chapter 4. Now, you'll add more artistic tools to your repertoire that will let you create drawing views you probably haven't used since you were on the drafting board.

Sketch-Derived Views

The advanced drawing views you'll be working with use sketching elements or require you to create sketches in order to define the construction of the views. Inventor allows you to add sketch elements to the drawing view for the sake of augmenting the view. All the sketching tools are the same as those used to define 3D models, so everything should be familiar.

Note that you can easily end up with unintended and undesirable results if you accidentally create sketch elements that aren't associated with the drawing view. It's important to make sure that the view you want to work with is highlighted before you start a sketch.

The first tool we'll discuss is the break-out view. The break-out view needs an existing drawing view to modify. Let's create a drawing to work with.

Creating a New Drawing

For this exercise you'll just add a single drawing view in a new file.

1. Create a new drawing file using the `Inventor NER.dwg` template.

2. Start the Base tool, and either select `Fan.iam` from the pull-down in the dialog or browse to it in the `C:\Data\Assemblies` folder.

3. In the dialog, set Level of Detail to Envelope Suppressed.

4. Set Orientation to Iso Top Right

5. Set Scale to .25 and Style to Shaded. See Figure 9.1.

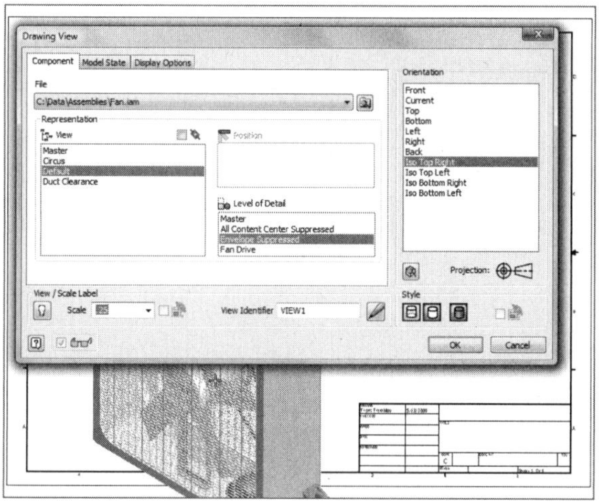

FIGURE 9.1 Creating a new base view

6. Select the Display Options tab in the dialog, and deselect the Tangent Edges check box.

7. Pick the drawing sheet to place the view.

   As you can see, the visible lines generated for the drawing make it difficult to see through the grill. To fix this you'll use your good old friend the layer.

8. After the view generates, move it onto the sheet.

9. Switch to the Annotate tab, and pick the Edit Layers tool from the Format panel.

10. In the dialog, pick the Line Weight value in the Visible (ANSI) layer row, and set the value to .001.

11. Click Done to close the dialog, and click Yes to approve saving the changes made to the layers.

12. After the dialog closes, you may not see the change immediately. If this is true, zoom or pan slightly in the Design window to update your view. It should closely resemble Figure 9.2.

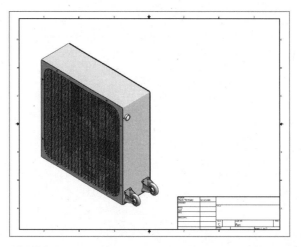

FIGURE 9.2 The view is updated using the thinner lines.

13. Save the new drawing to the Drawings folder as Fan.dwg.

Now you have the foundation needed for the Break Out tool to work.

The Break-Out View

The break-out view has a highly descriptive name: it allows you to "break out" part of a drawing. It's particularly useful with assemblies but can also be used in a single-part model to expose internal details.

The break-out view relies on a sketch for its definition. You can use any of the sketch tools as long as you create a closed loop for the sketch. To create visually appealing break-outs, many people use a spline to define the boundary.

The workflow is pretty simple. You create a sketch and then use that sketch to modify an existing view. However, the view that is modified can be either the view in which the sketch is defined or another view to which you apply the break-out.

The Break Out dialog box appears when you select the view to be edited. Let's look at each section:

Boundary Profile   You need to select a profile only if you've placed more than one closed loop into the view sketch.

Depth   The Depth fly-out has several options that define where the view stops passing through the part or assembly. Some options allow you to set a distance:

> **From Point**   After selecting a point in the view, you can set a depth from that point to cut. The point you select can be in the view with the cutting profile or another view. Setting a distance of zero stops the cut at the point you select. A positive number continues the cut past the point you select; a negative number stops the cut before it reaches the selected point.
>
> **To Sketch**   This option sets the cutting depth to match an open sketch in another drawing view.
>
> **To Hole**   In drafting, you commonly want to give a better view of how a part is constructed down to a major feature. Often, that feature is a hole or has a hole centered in it. The To Hole option allows you to use the center axis of a hole selected in the view that is cut or from another view to set the depth.
>
> **Through Part**   Using this option, you select the parts in the assembly view that you want to cut completely through to expose internal parts. Because no depth is specified for the cutting, the parts that are behind the selected parts remain intact.

Display   In a drawing view where the hidden lines are removed, it can be difficult to locate points or features that you want to select. This option causes hidden lines to appear in your selection view to make selection easier.

Section All Parts   Standard content elements such as bolts and shafts typically aren't sectioned. The Section All Parts check box sections through any part regardless of whether that part would normally be sectioned.

The break-out view should add a lot of clarity to your existing drawing view.

Creating the Break-Out View

First you'll add a sketch to your view then use it to remove some of the geometry.

1. Click the drawing view to highlight its border.

2. Click the Create Sketch tool in the Sketch panel.

3. Use the Spline tool to create a closed loop similar to the one in Figure 9.3.

FIGURE 9.3   Drawing a spline for the break-out boundary

4. Click the Finish Sketch tool when you're finished with the spline.

5. Select the Break Out tool from the Modify panel in the Place Views tab.

6. The dialog doesn't appear until you select the drawing view to modify. Pick the view of the assembly.

7. When the dialog opens, it has already selected the sketch. Set Depth to Through Part and pick Grill:1 in the Browser to edit that part.

8. Click OK to edit the view. This may take a few moments. See Figure 9.4 for the finished view.

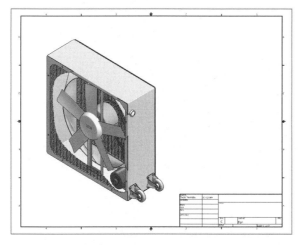

FIGURE 9.4 The assembly with the grill broken out

9. Save the drawing.

Having the grill broken out makes it easy to display interior detail. This isn't the type of view that people typically take the time to make using a 2D CAD system, yet it's very informational. It's really more of a technical illustration than a traditional drawing view.

Let's create another drawing.

Creating the Next Drawing

In this exercise, you want to create a drawing view on a sheet that you can print for a vendor:

1. Create a new drawing file using the `Inventor NER.dwg` template.

2. Right-click Sheet:1 in the Browser, and select Edit Sheet from the context menu.

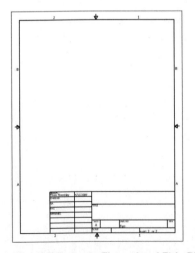

3. When the Edit Sheet dialog appears, change the Size value to A and Orientation to Portrait.

4. Click OK to change the drawing sheet.

As you can see, the title block doesn't fit quite right. Let's change it.

5. In the Browser, right-click NER Title Block under Sheet:1, and delete it.

6. Expand the Drawing Resources and Title Blocks folders.

7. Right-click ANSI A Title Block, and pick Insert. The new sheet should look like Figure 9.5.

8. Start the Base tool.

9. Navigate to C:\Data\Assemblies\Fan\Design Accelerator\, and pick Shaft1.iam.

FIGURE 9.5 The updated Title Block and border

10. Set Scale to 1 and Orientation to Top. See Figure 9.6.

11. Pick in the Design window to place the view.

12. Relocate the view as shown in Figure 9.7.

13. Save the drawing to the Drawings folder as Shaft.dwg.

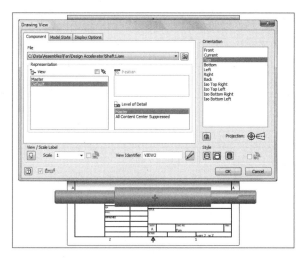

FIGURE 9.6 Preparing the new view

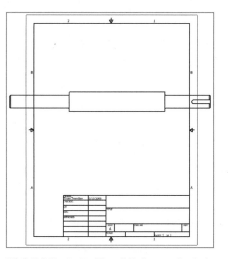

FIGURE 9.7 The slightly oversized view of the shaft

Right now, your drawing isn't looking so good. You need to shorten the display of the shaft, but you don't want inaccurate dimensions. You can do that.

The Break View

The Break tool is useful for creating views in which you need to see details at either end of an object but not what's in the middle. For example, you might use it to detail a long shaft, removing most of the length from the middle. To create the break, you define two points: the beginning and the endpoint of the portion of your part that will be removed from the view.

The Break dialog box allows you to define how the break appears. Similar to the Hole dialog box, it offers a preview that is representative of how the view will be generated:

Style   The Style buttons let you choose between the Structural style, which is a traditional border line with a single slash representing the break, and the Rectangular style, which creates a fractured look. The preview on the right changes to reflect your selected style.

Orientation   This option establishes whether the break lines are horizontal or vertical.

Display   The slide bar under the preview changes the size of the symbol at the point of the breaks.

Gap   The Gap value specifies how far apart the symbols and break lines are held from each other.

Symbols   This option box defines how many symbols appear on the line with the Structural break style.

Propagate to Parent View   This option is available only when the break is applied to a projected drawing view.

Let's break the view of the shaft:

1. Pick the Break tool from the Modify panel in the Place Views tab.

2. Select the drawing view of the shaft as the view to be modified.

3. Click a point near the left end of the large portion of the shaft, and then click another point near the right end, as shown in Figure 9.8.

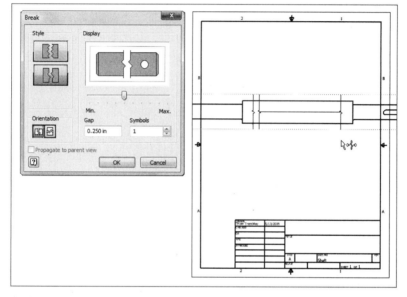

FIGURE 9.8 Selecting the portion of the shaft to be removed

When you pick the second point, the view updates to look like Figure 9.9.

4. Place another break on the left end of the shaft, and move the view to the left so it looks like Figure 9.10.

5. Save the drawing.

6. Create a projected view to the right of the shaft. Right-click, and select Create to generate the view.

7. Switch the Ribbon to the Annotate tab.

8. Pick the Baseline Set tool in the Dimension panel.

9. Pick the left edge of the large-diameter portion of the shaft, pick each end of the shaft, and then pick the other end of the large diameter.

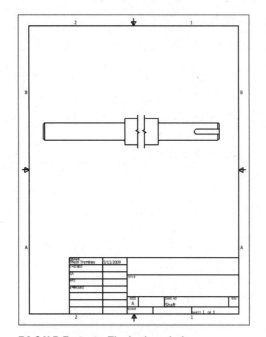

FIGURE 9.9 The broken shaft

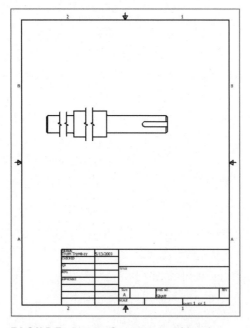

FIGURE 9.10 Create a second break

10. Right-click, and select Continue to get a preview of the dimension set.

11. Pick a location for the dimension, right-click, and pick Create to place them in the view. See Figure 9.11.

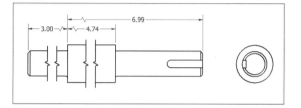

FIGURE 9.11 The dimensions show that they're on truncated geometry.

Note that the dimension lines show a jog that represents that the geometry isn't being displayed at its true length.

12. Save the drawing.

I encourage you to experiment with placing some other dimensions. I've added a few dimensions and center marks to Figure 9.12.

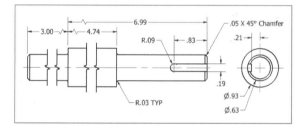

FIGURE 9.12 You've got to love Inventor's detailing tools.

I'd like you to create an exploded-view drawing, but the great thing about assembly constraints is that you can't just pull your assembly apart. Instead, you can create a special file that lets you make an exploded view without messing up the assembly.

Presentation Files

A presentation file creates an exploded version of the assembly so that you can animate the assembly process without harming the assembly file. This is primarily used for creating exploded drawing views.

The process is quite direct. You link an assembly to the presentation file and use tools to separate the parts and animate their rejoining. Because the process of setting up the exploded view is so interactive, we'll cover the dialogs when they come up.

Creating an Exploded View

In this exercise, you'll keep the scope limited to a few components and make changes to them to see their flexibility:

1. Open the New File dialog, and select the Standard (in).ipn template.

2. When the new presentation file is created, only one tool is available. Pick the Create View tool from the Create panel.

3. Locate or pick the fan assembly in the File list. Keep Explosion Method set to Manual.

   If you've created an assembly where parts are stacked directly on one another, the Automatic Explosion Method may work for you. After you select it, you can set the default distance by which the components are separated.

4. Click OK to place a representation of the assembly into the presentation file.

5. Save the new file to the Assemblies folder as Fan.ipn.

6. Change your view to see the Top, Right, and Back faces of the ViewCube.

7. Select the Tweak Components tool from the Create panel.

   Doing so opens the Tweak Component dialog. This dialog allows you to select what components are moved (or rotated), in what direction, and how far. A check-box option lets you generate trails that can be seen on the drawing.

The workflow is simple. Start the Tweak Components tool, set the direction, select the components, and establish how far those components move. You can click and drag the distance on the screen or type the value into the dialog, picking the check mark to update the position.

There's no Apply button, but you can make a tweak to components and then clear your selections to modify others without leaving the tool. Let's try it.

8. Pick the top of the housing. This displays a triad with the Z direction highlighted. You want to move the grill, so the Y direction is more appropriate.

9. Click the Y axis of the triad or the Y button in the dialog.

10. Pick the grill and the eight screws surrounding it.

11. When they're selected, click and drag in an empty area of the Design window, and move the grill and screws away from the assembly roughly three feet. You can watch the value in the dialog change as you drag. See Figure 9.13.

12. Release the mouse button when you've moved the components the desired distance.

13. Hold down the Shift or Ctrl key, and pick the grill again to remove it from the group of components being tweaked.

14. Click and drag the screws out another 20 inches or so, and release.

15. Pick the Clear button to reset your selections.

16. Place the triad for setting the direction as you did last time.

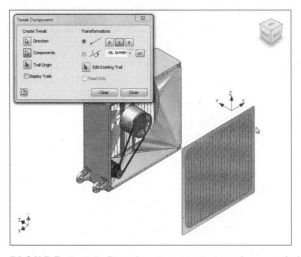

FIGURE 9.13 Dragging components to make an exploded view

17. Pick the two pulleys and the belt, and tweak them to around 9 inches.

18. Remove the two pulleys from the selected group, and tweak the belt another 10 inches by entering 10 in the dialog and clicking the check-mark icon.

19. Pick Close to stop tweaking components for now. The tweaked assembly should look like Figure 9.14.

20. In the Create panel, click the Animate tool.

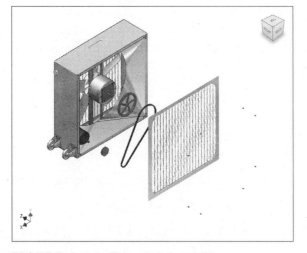

FIGURE 9.14 The exploded assembly

21. Pick the Play Forward icon, and see what happens.

22. When the animation is done, pick Cancel to close the dialog.

23. Save your work.

What was that? Could creating a basic assembly animation be that easy? Yes. Let's do some editing and make things even more interesting.

Editing the Presentation

By making some simple adjustments to timing and the view of the components, you can create a very compelling animation:

1. Open the Animate tool again.

2. Change the Interval value from 25 to 12, and click the Apply button.

3. Pick Play Forward to see the difference in the speed of the animation.

4. When the animation is complete, click the Play Reverse icon to see the assembly explode.

5. Click the Reset button to restore the presentation file.

6. Expand the dialog as shown in Figure 9.15.

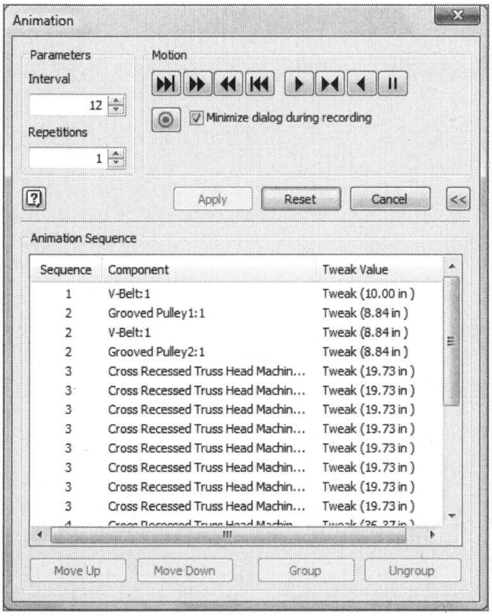

FIGURE 9.15 Each step of each component's movement is listed.

Every tweak to each component is recorded as a sequence. When you tweak multiple components in one step, those components are included in the same sequence. Sequences are numbered in reverse order; the highest-numbered one was done first.

What's great is that you can remove any component from a sequence and, if you like, add it to another sequence.

Let's make some modifications and see the effects.

7. Select the last tweak in the list, hold the Shift key, and click the first tweak listed in Sequence 3.

8. When all the tweaks are highlighted, pick the Group button that becomes available.

9. Click the Apply button.

10. Reduce the dialog, and pick the Play Forward button. Click Reset after the animation is finished.

    As you saw, the screws moved in one action with the grill. Let's make another change to the order.

11. Expand the Animation dialog again.

12. Hold the Ctrl key, pick the two sequences of the V-belt, and click Group.

13. Select the V-belts again, and click the Move Down button.

    Doing so reorders the steps so that the pulleys become the first components to assemble themselves.

14. Click Apply, minimize the dialog, and play the animation again. Click Reset when you're done.

15. Click the Cancel button to close the dialog.

16. Save the file.

N O T E   A really fun way of manipulating sequence groupings is to add a rotational tweak on a bolt and then group the rotational tweak and the translational tweak together to show the bolt turning into place.

Let's move on to changing the view of the sequences.

Editing the View of the Animation

You change the view in a very different way:

1. In the Browser, select the icon that looks like a funnel. Doing so opens a list of views.

2. Select the sequence view filter option from the pull down.

Doing so changes the Browser and adds the list of sequences you were working with in the Animation dialog.

3. Expand Sequence1 in the Browser.

   This lists the components that are attached to the sequence and the value of the tweak. You can also use the folder named Hidden to turn off the visibility of components for a particular sequence.

4. Reposition the view in the screen to match Figure 9.16.

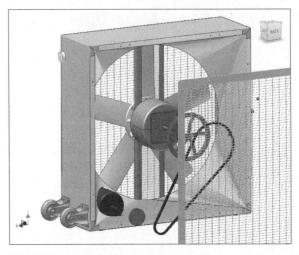

FIGURE 9.16 Change the screen view.

5. Double-click Sequence1 in the Browser. Doing so launches the Edit Task & Sequences dialog.

   This dialog has a lot of hidden potential. In it, you can play the animation of each sequence. You can also insert information that can be viewed by others. Earlier, you changed the Interval value and the speed of the animation; here, you can set an Interval value for each sequence.

   The Set Camera button attaches the present view to the sequence. In combination with the Hidden folder, it makes it very easy to create compelling animations.

6. Click the Set Camera button, and click OK to close the dialog.

7. In the Browser, use the Ctrl key to select Bolted Connection:2 and Grill:2, and drag them to the Hidden folder under Sequence1.

8. Change the view in the Design window to match Figure 9.17.

9. Double click Sequence2 in the Browser to reopen the dialog.

10. In the Text area under Sequence, add the words **Apply Belt Dressing before installation**.

11. Set the Interval to 8.

12. Click Set Camera, and then click the OK button.

13. Drag Bolted Connection:2 and Grill:2 under the Hidden folder beneath Sequence2.

14. Set the view in the Design window to look like Figure 9.18.

15. Use the Set Camera tool for Sequence3 to save this point of view.

16. Save your work.

17. Start the Animate tool, and pick Play Forward.

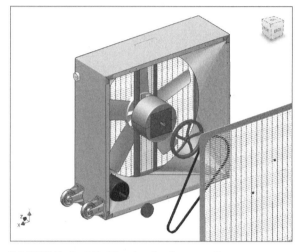

FIGURE 9.17 The view for Sequence2

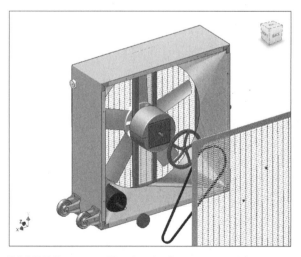

FIGURE 9.18 The view for Sequence3 and Sequence4

The view changes to the one you stored for Sequence1, and the grill and bolted connections disappear. The animation continues by changing the view and continuing the animation. I've been using this tool for years, and I'm still impressed at how easy it is to use.

Next, let's save your work to a file that anyone can view.

Creating an *.AVI* File

In this exercise, you'll generate a file to send to anyone who needs to know how you want to assemble your product:

1. Click reset to "rewind" the animation.

2. Click the Record button in the Animation dialog.
   This launches a Save As dialog for creating an animation file.

3. Set File to **Fan,** and change the file type to AVI. If you're offered a location for the new file to be placed, select one to your liking.

4. Click Save to close the dialog.

After a moment, Inventor brings up the Video Compression dialog so you can control the quality and compressor you want to use for your .AVI file. If you had selected a .WMV file, the dialog would look different but still ask for information about what the video will be used for (in order to set the quality).

5. Set Compressor to Microsoft Video 1, and click OK.

6. Click the Play Forward button to create the animation file.

7. When the Animation dialog reappears, click the Record button again to save the .AVI file to the disk.

8. Take a moment to replay the animation you've created.

9. Click Cancel to close the dialog.

You've begun to use your design to communicate information about how to assemble it in a new way. Don't you wish you could get a video of how to assemble your next project at home rather than the sometimes questionable instructions?

Now, you'll go back to a more traditional use for the exploded view.

Creating an Exploded-View Drawing

Let's add a new sheet to an existing drawing and add the exploded view:

    1. Open or activate Fan.dwg.

    2. Click the New Sheet icon on the Place Views tab.

    3. Start the Base tool.

    4. Set File to Fan.ipn.

    5. Pick the Change Orientation icon, and set the view to be the same as Figure 9.19.

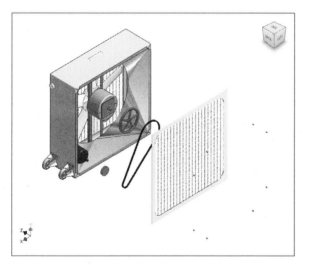

FIGURE 9.19 The view for the drawing

    6. Click the Finish Custom View tool to return to the Drawing View dialog.

    7. Set the view Scale to .15, set Style to Shaded, and click OK.

    8. Save your work. See Figure 9.20.

Next, let's focus on some additional annotations for the drawing.

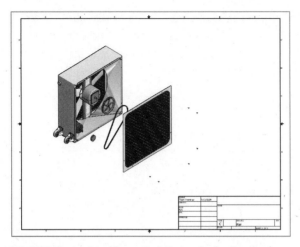

FIGURE 9.20 The exploded view in the drawing

Assembly Annotations

You can easily add dimensions, finish symbols, weld annotations, and many other types of information to drawings of parts and sometimes assemblies. Inventor has a few types of annotation that are almost exclusive to the assembly.

Annotations — such as the list of parts in an assembly and balloons to point out which part is being referred to in a drawing — are a must for most companies.

Parts List

Creating a parts list with AutoCAD or most other 2D systems involves a lot of typing and human interaction. With Inventor, the parts list is a representation of the Bill of Materials database that resides in the assembly file. Later in this chapter, you'll learn how to edit entries in this database, which is automatically generated as you add parts to the assembly.

Inserting a Parts List

Let's do a quick exercise to show you how easy it is to place a parts list in the drawing:

1. Continuing with Sheet:2 of Fan.dwg, activate the Annotate tab.

2. Pick the Parts List tool from the Table panel.

3. When the Parts List dialog appears, it asks you to pick a drawing view. Pick the exploded view.

You have the option of creating a parts list that shows all the individual parts or represents the structure of the assembly. The difference is, for example, that the fan support frame, which appears as a single component in a Structured parts list, will appear as 12 parts using the Parts Only BOM View option in the dialog.

4. Leave BOM View set to Structured, and pick OK. If you receive a BOM View Disabled dialog, click OK to enable.

A preview of the size of the parts list appears on the screen. Move to the upper-right corner of the drawing border; a glyph appears, showing that you can attach the parts list to the corner.

5. Pick the upper-right corner to attach the parts list to the drawing. The drawing looks like Figure 9.21 after you place the parts list.

6. Look at the parts list as placed, and save your work.

The parts list that is placed may not look exactly like the parts lists you generally create. You may use different columns, and so on; but using styles and standards, you can set the parts list to look like those you've been creating for the production people for years. You don't have to tell them that it now takes you only a second to create the list — and I won't tell either.

Now, let's include the balloons you need to clarify where components are located in the drawing view.

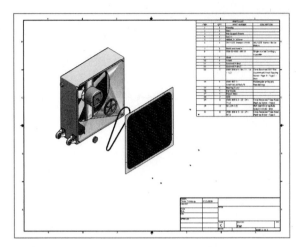

FIGURE 9.21 The parts list in the drawing

Balloon/Auto Balloon

Having a list of the parts that are included in the assembly is important, but it's also important for the person using the drawings to understand what the parts look like. The Balloon tool creates an annotation that maps parts in the drawing to their descriptions in the parts list. The appearance of this annotation is governed by a style, and like many other things, it has options that you can set to suit your needs.

Adding Balloons to the Drawing

You can place balloons either individually or as a group:

1. Locate the Balloon tool in the Table panel.

2. Expand the Balloon tool to expose the Auto Balloon tool, and select it.

3. As with the Parts List tool, select the exploded view to start.

4. When the view is selected, the Add or Remove Components icon activates. You can select components individually, but I'd like you to drag a crossing window (right to left) around all the components in the view.

5. Pick the Select Placement icon, and move your cursor back over the drawing to see a preview of the balloons.

   You can change the orientation of the balloons to wrap around the view or be vertical as well as the default horizontal.

6. Set the Offset Spacing value to .25, and place the balloons below the view by picking the drawing sheet.

7. Click OK to close the dialog. See Figure 9.22.

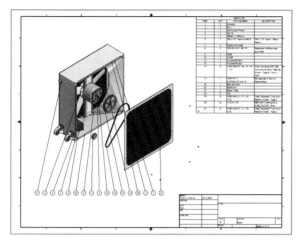

FIGURE 9.22 Placing all the balloons at once

8. In the parts list, find the shaft and the key (ANSI B17.1 0.1875x0.1875x0.75), and note their item numbers.

In my drawing, the shaft is 9 and the key is 14, so that is how I'll refer to them.

9. Find the balloon for the key. Select it in the Design window, and press the Delete key to remove it.

10. Find the balloon for the shaft, and right-click it.

11. From the context menu, pick Attach Balloon from List.

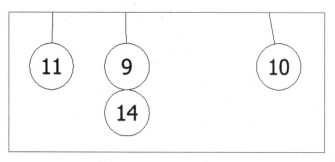

12. Pick the check box for the key, and click OK.

This gives you a preview of a second balloon attached to the shaft balloon. Moving your cursor around shows the balloon in different positions.

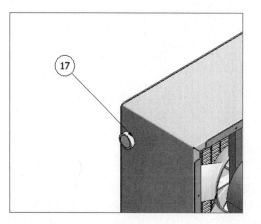

13. When the additional balloon appears below the shaft balloon, click to place it.

14. Click and drag the balloon pointing at the power knob above and to the left of the assembly.

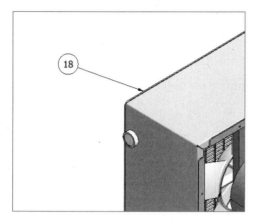

15. Click and drag the end of the arrow of that balloon so that the grill highlights. When it highlights, release the mouse button.

   The balloon changes item numbers to reflect that it's no longer referencing the power knob.

16. Use the Undo tool to revert the balloon back to the power knob.

17. Double-click the parts list to edit it.

18. Locate the item for the power knob in the parts list.

19. Double-click its value, and change it to **2010** as shown in Figure 9.23.

Parts List: Fan.iam

ITEM	QTY	PART NUMBER	DESCRIPTION
9	1	Shaft	
10	1	V-Belt	
11	1	Grooved Pulley1	
12	1	Grooved Pulley2	
13	3	ANSI B18.6.4 - No. 10 - 16 - 1/2	Cross Recessed 100° Flat Countersunk Head Tapping Screw - Type B - Type I - Inch
14	1	ANSI B17.1 - 0.1875x0.1875x0.75	Rectangular or Square Parallel Keys
15	1	Bearing Cover	
16	1	Fan Blade	
2010	1	Power Knob	
18	2	Grill	
19	8	ANSI B18.6.3 - 12 - 24 - 7/16	Cross Recessed Truss Head Machine Screw - Type I
20	16	S-1224-1 ZI	PEM Self-Clinching Nuts S,SS,CLS,CLSS - Inch
21	8	ANSI B18.6.3 - 12 - 24 - 9/16	Cross Recessed Truss Head Machine Screw - Type I

OK   Cancel   Apply

FIGURE 9.23 Editing the item number

20. Click OK to change the parts list.

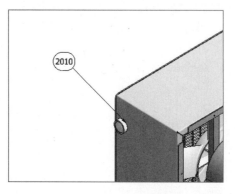

The balloon also updates to match the change to the item number in the parts list. You could have made this change at the balloon, and the parts list would've responded.

21. Save your work.

Adding an individual balloon is even simpler. You can also modify the balloon to change its shape. And instead of showing the item number, you can display the name of the component and even how many of it are in the assembly.

The balloon and parts list are merely representations of something that's far more important to the assembly: the Bill of Materials and the knowledge that Inventor automatically captures in it.

Bill of Materials

It's important that you understand that the Bill of Materials (BOM) isn't the same thing as a parts list.

You should think of the BOM as the master document that records what parts are in the assembly. Moreover, you can use it to alter the structure of the assembly without having to reorder how the assembly was built. If you edit the BOM from the drawing, you're actually changing the assembly as Inventor sees it.

A parts list is a representation of all or part of the BOM on a drawing. You can edit its appearance above and beyond the changes to the BOM, but it's critical that the BOM truly reflect the state of the assembly.

Within the BOM, you can structure a component several different ways:

Normal   Any part that you produce will most likely be regarded as a Normal component in the BOM.

Phantom   Sometimes the file structure of an Inventor assembly doesn't match how it will be built. For example, if you assemble several components into an assembly and then insert it as a subassembly into the top assembly, a Normal structure will show the subassembly in the BOM. If you change the subassembly to Phantom, the components within it are represented as being placed directly into the top-level assembly.

Reference   Any component that you don't want to appear in the BOM can be set as Reference. Its display in the drawing window is also affected. The geometry appears as phantom lines.

Purchased   A Purchased component can be a part or assembly, but it's treated as a single component. If you place a Parts Only parts list, it will still show the Purchased assembly as a single component.

Inseparable   This is a way to represent an assembly that you'll fabricate as a single line item in a Structured parts list.

Let's make a quick modification to the BOM and show that the parts list will respond:

1. Right-click over the drawing view (or parts list), and select Bill of Material from the context menu.

2. When the Bill of Material dialog appears, navigate to Fan Support Frame.

3. In the BOM Structure column, double-click the Normal status, and select Phantom as the new structure. See Figure 9.24.

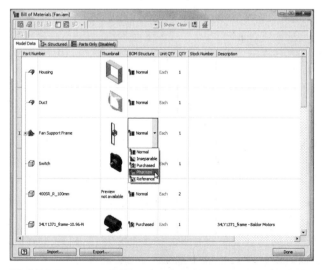

FIGURE 9.24 Editing the assembly structure in the BOM

4. Click Done to close the dialog and update the parts list, as shown in Figure 9.25.

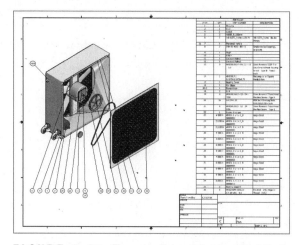

FIGURE 9.25 The parts list updates to reflect the new structure.

5. Save your work.

You can do more, but a lot of how you'll use balloons, parts lists, and a BOM will depend on your company.

Let's take some of this work and see how to make it available when someone needs more than an animation but you don't need to share live CAD data with them. You can use a special format: DWF.

DWF

The Design Web Format output option that is in most of Autodesk's products is something worth spending a minute on. Most people who've used an Autodesk CAD tool have probably created a .DWF file for simple, basic exchange because the original CAD file was too big to e-mail.

The format has a lot more to offer. Depending on the file from which you export it, you can not only create a secure document that can't be edited or completely reverse-engineered but also create a document that is a powerful communication tool.

In Inventor, you can use a .DWF file to capture the animation of a presentation file along with the assembly and parts it's based on. Just to make everything complete, you can also include the drawings.

Creating an All-Inclusive DWF

Let's do a quick exercise to show how easy it is to capture an enormous amount of information:

1. If it's not already, make Fan.dwg the active document.

2. Select the Application menu at upper left, and expand the Save As tool.

3. Select Save Copy As from the options.

4. Change the Save As type to DWF files (*.dwf).

5. Make sure that the file name is Fan.dwf and that it will be saved to the Drawings folder.

6. Click the Options button to open the dialog shown in Figure 9.26.

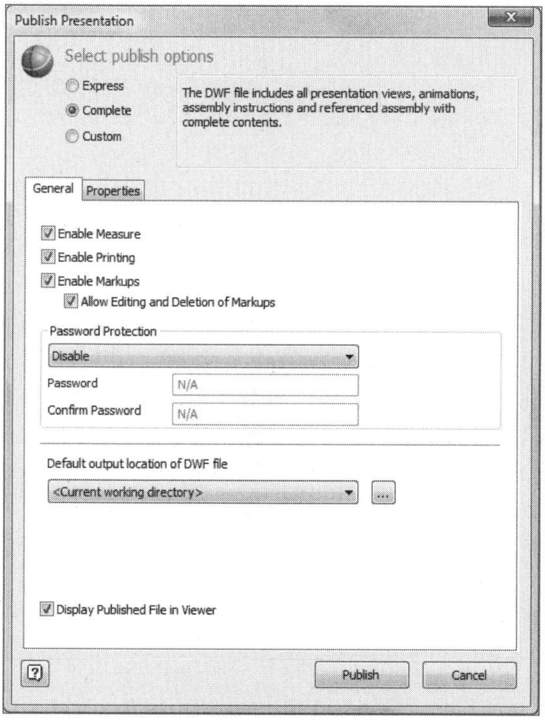

FIGURE 9.26 The Publish Presentation dialog

7. Click the Complete option near the top of the dialog.

8. Click Publish to generate the .DWF file. Then, Click Save.

After a few moments Autodesk Design Review opens with the new file active. See Figure 9.27.

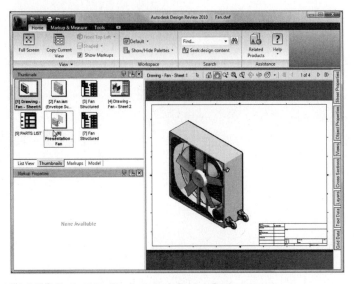

FIGURE 9.27 The Autodesk Design Review screen

At upper left are a number of thumbnails showing pages of the drawing, the assembly, the parts list, and the presentation file.

9. Click the presentation file, and watch the animation play.

10. Review the other included documents. Close Design Review when you're finished.

A vendor or customer who doesn't own Inventor or any other Autodesk product that includes Design Review can download the application for free at Autodesk's web site. There's even a version called Autodesk Freewheel that can be used by people who aren't allowed to download or install software.

As we explore the last category of communication tools, you'll create some fantastic renderings and an animation.

Inventor Studio Overview

The Inventor Studio tools aren't meant to replace dedicated, professional rendering systems like Autodesk 3ds Max or Maya, but they allow you to create great-looking renderings and animations of your parts and assemblies with relatively little work.

Using these tools, you can spend many hours experimenting with different lighting scenes, cameras, and so forth, but it's also possible to make attractive images in just a few seconds with only a couple of mouse clicks. In this section, we'll explore the basics of Inventor Studio, but we'll leave many great options for you and your imagination to explore.

Getting Started

Inventor Studio isn't just another tool that is used in the assembly or part file; it's actually a separate environment that runs in parallel with the part or assembly file.

To change your working environment to Inventor Studio, switch the Ribbon to the Environments tab, and select Inventor Studio from the Begin panel.

Entering the new environment doesn't just change the active Ribbon tab as you're now accustomed to; it also changes the Browser, similar to another environment — weldments. Having this environment inside the part and assembly files keeps it in line with any changes made to the model data. When you set up rendering conditions, any changes to the model are reflected in the rendering environment without the need to modify settings that you made previously.

Starting the Render Image tool opens the Render Image dialog box, which contains three tabs: General, Output, and Style. Along with the dialog box, a red rectangle appears in the Design window that shows the frame of the rendering that will be created.

The General Tab

You've probably noticed that in Inventor's tool dialog boxes, the basic and most important settings are typically on the first tab; the same holds true with Render Image dialog's General tab (Figure 9.28). This is where you tell Inventor Studio how to view, light, and surround the model as well as where you set the type of rendering and the resolution for the image:

Width and Height   You can enter values for the width and height of the rendered image individually, or you can select common screen resolutions from the pop-up menu that appears after you click the Select Output Size icon to the right.

The Lock Aspect Ratio check box allows you to enter either the width or height and have Inventor automatically calculate the other value to maintain the 4:3 ratio.

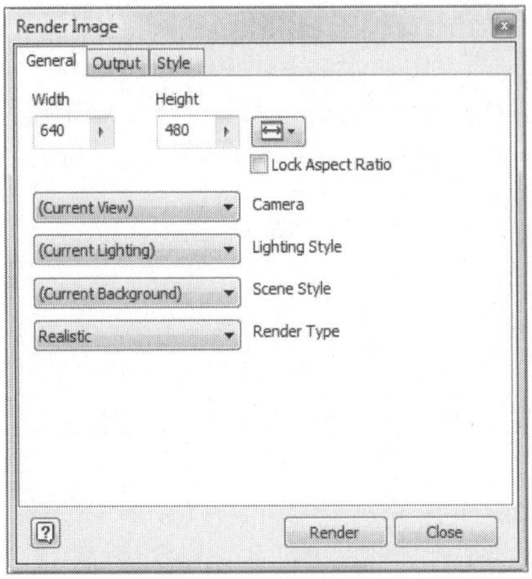

FIGURE 9.28 The Render Image dialog box's General tab

Camera   You can create a camera on the screen by clicking the Camera tool in the Panel bar and establishing a target and position. You can also copy an existing camera. My favorite technique is to establish a view in the Design window, right-click in the window, and select Create Camera from View from the context menu. After creating your cameras, you can select which one will be used for the rendering using the Camera pull-down list.

You can create a list of cameras, each of which saves a particular view position and size of the model. When you create a rendering, you can pick between cameras to quickly create a different look while reusing other elements like lighting and scene styles.

Lighting Style   Inventor comes with a collection of default lighting styles that you can use for the rendering or as templates for new styles. Use this pull-down list to select which style you want to use.

Scene Style   For a theatrical touch, Inventor Studio has the ability to change the surroundings your models are in. Scenes create an environment for the rendering by setting background colors or applying images to simulate a location for the model to be rendered in. Inventor comes with a few scenes, but you can create the greatest impact on your renderings with a good scene style.

Render Type   Inventor allows two types of rendering: Realistic and Illustration. Realistic rendering is the type that people most commonly want to create. The Illustration style creates renderings that are great for technical documentation and assembly instructions. This style has its own options, which you can modify on the Style tab.

The Output Tab

The quality of the image is controlled by the Output tab (Figure 9.29). Here's a look at its most important settings:

F I G U R E   9 . 2 9   The Output tab

Save Rendered Image   Selecting this check box launches the File Explorer dialog box, where you can define the name of the rendering that will be saved. You also can create your rendering and then define the file after the fact.

Antialiasing   Unless you're running at a very low-screen resolution, the rendering of your model will be at a lower resolution than the source model. In order to keep the edges smooth, Inventor Studio has to calculate a smooth edge. How this is done depends on the quality settings under Antialiasing. It's important to note that the higher the quality, the longer the rendering will take.

The Style Tab (Realistic Rendering)

On the Style tab, you set options controlling the way the model works with its environment. Figure 9.30 shows the Style tab when Realistic has been chosen as the Render Type on the General tab:

True Reflection   If this option is selected, the parts in a multiple-part rendering reflect off one another and other faces of the same part. Not selecting this option causes the parts to reflect the elements set in the scene style but not the other parts. Figures 9.31 and 9.32 illustrate the difference.

FIGURE 9.30 The Style tab options for Realistic rendering

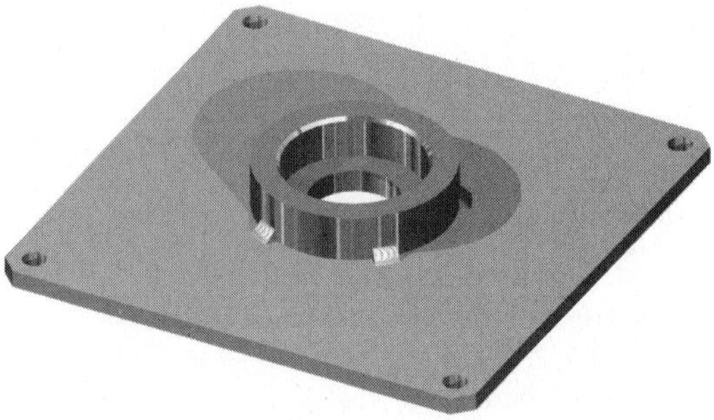

FIGURE 9.31 Rendering with True Reflection set to Off

FIGURE 9.32 Rendering with True Reflection set to On

The Style Tab (Illustration Rendering)

Many more options appear when you select Illustration as the Rendering Style (Figure 9.33).

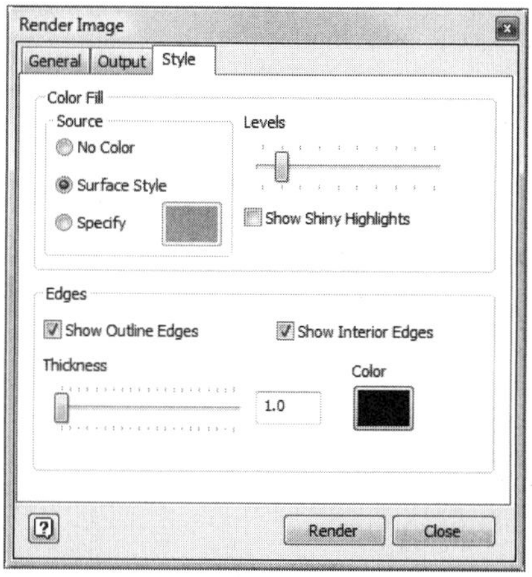

FIGURE 9.33 The Style tab options for Illustration rendering

Color Fill

Three source options are available for Color Fill; these determine what (if any) color is included in the rendering. There is also a slide bar for the quantity of colors in the rendering and an option to display highlights:

No Color   This option removes any reference to the part's color(s) in the rendering. The resulting appearance has a line-art quality.

Surface Style   Applying a surface style or color to your part can still have value in the Illustration rendering using this option. The Levels slide bar sets the number of colors from none, when the value is 1, to multiple color steps when set to 10.

Specify   Setting a color using Specify overrides the colors of all the parts in the rendering. The Levels slide bar sets the number of colors representing the curvature in the same way that it does with Surface Style selected.

Show Shiny Highlights   With this box selected, areas that would be highlighted in a realistic rendering still highlight to accentuate curvature.

Edges

Careful selection of how or whether to display edges in the rendering can create very dramatic results:

Show Outline Edges   This selection defines whether you want to calculate the profile edges of the model or just show a shape that is colored.

Show Interior Edges   Choose this option to display the tangent or other sharp edges of the model's interior.

Thickness   The Thickness value is a sliding scale that controls the thickness of the edges that are selected to be displayed. Although no specific width value is offered, the effect is very noticeable, and the range of line widths (thickness) is dramatic.

Color   Clicking the color sample brings up the Inventor color-selection dialog box, which lets you choose a color for the displayed edges.

Creating a Quick Rendering

Let's go ahead and make a quick rendering to use as a base to be able to see the effects of the changes you'll make along the way:

1. In the fan assembly, expand the V-Belt Transmission:1 component, right-click Grooved Pulley2, and pick Open to bring the pulley into a new window.

2. Switch to the View tab. In the Appearance panel, expand the Orthographic view, and switch to Perspective.
   Using a perspective view gives an additional level of realism because you see everything in perspective naturally.

3. Switch the Ribbon to the Environments tab, and pick the Inventor Studio icon.

4. Modify your view to resemble Figure 9.34.

5. Click the Render Image tool.

6. Change the Resolution to a minimum of 800×600 using the pull-down list to the right of the Width and Height input.

7. Without changing any other values, click the Render button.

8. Figure 9.35 shows the result. Note the reflections of faces on other faces.

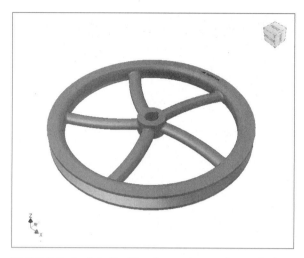

FIGURE 9.34 Position the component for rendering.

FIGURE 9.35 Even a quick rendering enhances the appearance of a component

9. Close the Render Output window.

10. In the dialog, set Scene Style to XY Ground Plane.

11. Click the Render button. The result looks like Figure 9.36.

12. Close the Render Output window.

13. Change the Scene Style to XY Reflective Ground Plane.

FIGURE 9.36 The rendering showing shadows on the ground plane

14. Run the Render tool again, and see the result in Figure 9.37.

FIGURE 9.37 Using a reflective ground plane shows the object reflected on the plane.

15. Close the Render Output window.

16. This time, use the Lighting Style pull-down to select Table Top.

17. Run the Render tool again, and compare your results to Figure 9.38.

18. Close the Render Output window.

FIGURE 9.38 A change to the lighting style can make a dramatic difference.

Before we explore modifying the styles, let's try the other kind of rendering.

Creating an Illustration Rendering

Sometimes, photorealism can be confusing or your communication medium doesn't allow the complexity. The Illustration rendering type offers a whole new set of options for those situations. In this exercise, you'll create a rendering using the Illustration style:

1. Change all the style settings in the Render Image dialog back to their default values.

2. Change the Rendering Type setting to Illustration.

3. Switch to the Style tab.

4. Set the value for the Source group to No Color.

5. Click Render. Figure 9.39 shows the result.

6. Close the Render Output window and the Render Image dialog.

Simply using the styles and options that are included with Inventor offers a great deal of potential in making your designs easy to present. Now, let's make a few changes and see how a handful of mouse clicks can really change things.

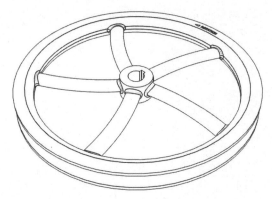

FIGURE 9.39 An Illustration rendering may be perfect for a maintenance document.

Scene Styles

An easy way to make a dramatic impact on a rendering is to customize the scene you're working in. You can open the Scene Styles dialog box (Figure 9.40) from the Inventor Studio Panel bar. This dialog box lets you modify existing styles or copy them to create something new.

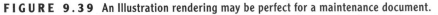

FIGURE 9.40 The Scene Styles dialog box with the Background tab active

The Scene Styles dialog box has a list of existing styles at upper left. Selecting one of the styles causes the preview at lower left to update, giving a general preview of how a rendering in the scene would appear. Above the list of styles are buttons that create, purge, update, or save styles to the library for use by others.

The dialog box has two tabs that control the properties of the scene style.

The Background Tab

This tab tells Inventor Studio what will be seen behind or around the model.

Use Application Options

Selecting the Use Application Options check box bypasses other background options in favor of using the settings in the Application Options Color tab that are used in your Design window.

Colors

Depending on the type of scene, you're able to click the color preview boxes and change what colors are present in the rendering through the standard Inventor color-selection dialog box.

Selecting one of the four types of scene quickly changes the look of the rendering:

Solid Color   This option uses a single color for the background of the scene and for the color of a plane that might pass around or through the part. When it's activated, there is only one color selection in the Colors group.

Color Gradient   In some of the renderings you've already created, the background transitions from black on the top to white at the bottom. The scene style you selected used a Color Gradient type and used the two colors defined in the Colors area. The box on top specifies the color at the top edge of the screen, and the lower color box is used to select the color at the bottom of the screen.

Image   Clicking the Image option launches an Open dialog box where you can select an image file to use as the background for the rendering scene. When an image is selected, additional options appear in the Image group that let you manage the appearance of the background.

Image Sphere   Similar to the Image type, Image Sphere wraps an image around the part rather than just applying an image behind the model. This enables the reflection of a different part of the environment on the front of the model than is shown behind the model. To use this option, I think it's necessary to use a spherical or hemispherical image. Resources are available on the Web for this type of image. Later in the chapter, you'll learn another technique that can simulate the result.

Image

When either of the Image types is selected, these tools become available:

Position   The options in this pull-down list work the same way as applying an image to your Windows Desktop. There are three options for the position of the image:

Centered   This option uses the image's true resolution to fill as much of the background as possible.

Tile   Tile repeats the image to fill the background. You can limit the number of repetitions using the Repeat options to the right of the Position pull-down list.

Stretch   This option allows the image to be distorted in order to fill the background of the rendering scene.

The Environment Tab

You control the position of the reflection plane relative to its origin in the model and how shadows and reflections are shown on it using the Environment tab (Figure 9.41).

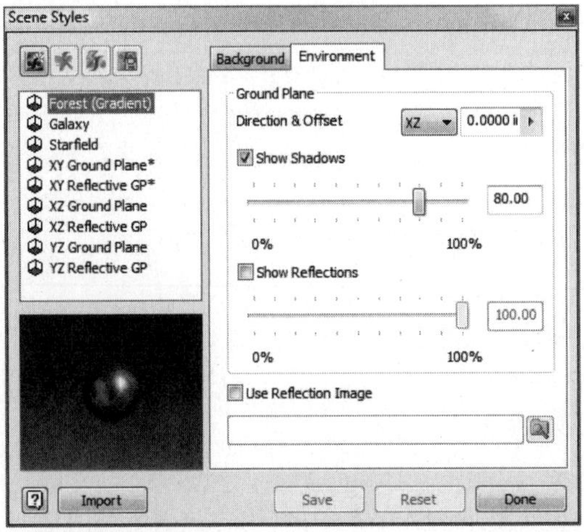

FIGURE 9.41 The Scene Styles dialog box's Environment tab

Ground Plane

If the ground plane passes through your model, it cuts off part of the model. You can change that effect using the options in the Ground Plane group:

Direction & Offset   Using the pull-down list, you can select the primary plane to use in the scene style and then enter positive or negative values to reposition the plane relative to its model source.

Show Shadows   This check box controls whether shadows are cast on the ground plane or other parts of the model. The slider beneath it lets you set the opacity of the shadow. Moving the bar all the way to the right or entering the value 100 creates a completely black shadow. A value of 30–60 is usually optimal.

Show Reflections   Show Reflections works like Show Shadows. Having the value at 100 makes the reflection appear to be very bright, almost luminous. A value of 30–60 is usually optimal.

Use Reflection Image   When you select the color scheme that you'll work in (using Application Options), you also select a reflection to appear in your model. This option allows you to select a different image to reflect in your part along with other components.

Let's get back to experimenting with the rendering by creating your own scene style.

Building a New Scene Style

You can easily construct scene styles from scratch, but I often build one based on an existing one. This not only saves a few clicks but also lets me quickly iterate from a style that I like to a new one that I can experiment with while keeping the last one intact:

1. Open the Scene Styles dialog box by click the Scene Styles tool in the Scene panel.

2. Right-click the XY Reflective GP style, and select Copy Scene Style.

3. A New Style Name dialog box appears. Type **Inventor NER - White** as the name, and click OK to create the new style.

4. On the Background tab, set the type to Solid Color. Make sure the color preview is white.

5. Click the Save button, and then pick Done to close the dialog.

6. Start the Render Image tool.

7. Set your Render Type back to Realistic, set Lighting Style to Table Top, and set Scene Style to Inventor NER - White.

8. Start the rendering, and watch the image in Figure 9.42 generate.

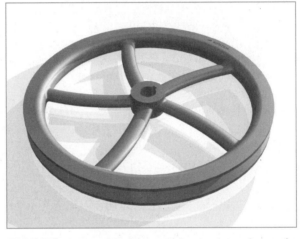

FIGURE 9.42 A new scene style can give an image character.

9. Close the Render Output window and the Render Image dialog.

The last major thing you can modify is the surface of the model you're rendering.

Surface Styles

Along with lighting, scene, and render styles, Inventor offers surface styles. Surface styles typically carry the same name as a color that you can select for your part from the Inventor Standard toolbar list. The difference is that you can modify the surface style to carry additional information and properties that control how the surface appears in the rendering. You can give a surface different reflection levels, change its opacity, apply a different texture, and even use a bump map to make the rendered version of the part appear to have an uneven surface texture.

In this introduction to Inventor Studio, we won't explore the full capabilities of surface styles. But one brief exercise will, I hope, pique your interest in learning more about them.

Rendering with a Surface Style

Some of the color selections that come with Inventor are already associated with surface styles that have a bump map enabled. In this exercise, you'll do a rendering with a bump map applied to see the difference.

The color that I chose for my pulley was Copper (Old/Polished), which has a smooth surface. Let's change that and see what the effect is:

1. Open the Surface Styles tool from the Scene panel.

   The Surface Styles dialog appears, with the part's color preselected and showing the properties inherent with it.

   The tabs of the Surface Styles dialog allow you to radically change the appearance of a component in the rendering from the way it appears in the model or assembly. One simple change should make an impression about just how powerful this style is.

2. Switch to the Bump Map tab.

3. Pick the check box next to Use Bump Image. This launches a dialog in which you can open an image file to use as a bump map.

   A bump map is just an image file. The program analyzes the contrast between portions of the image and uses that to replicate variations in the surface of the component when it's rendering.

4. Pick the first image, AlloySand2_bump.bmp, as the bump map, and click OK to load it into the surface style. See Figure 9.43.

5. Set the Scale slide bar to approximately 50 (%), or type the value 50 in the window to the right of the slide bar.

   The preview image at lower left updates with the change in scale.

6. Click Save and then Done to finish editing the surface style.

   Notice that the model's appearance in the Design window doesn't change. Applying a bump map only affects the rendered output.

7. Start the Render Image tool, and use the last settings to create the image shown in Figure 9.44.

8. Close the Render Output window and the Render Image dialog.

9. Save the file.

Creating a high-quality still rendering can make it much easier to explain an idea to someone who doesn't have experience in design and engineering. When delivering dimensional information isn't necessary, a rendering can tell the story effectively.

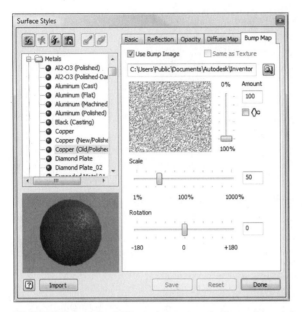

FIGURE 9.43 Adding a bump map to the surface style

FIGURE 9.44 Rendering with the bump map applied

Now let's move on to develop an animation of your assembly that can be generated as a fully rendered animation.

You can do animation in Inventor on a couple of different levels. Most assembly constraints can be driven through a range of motion. In the Inventor Studio environment, just about anything can be driven.

Working with Animation

Presentation files, which you explored in this chapter, are wonderful tools for creating technical documentation. When you need to go beyond that and build truly amazing animations, Inventor Studio is the place to be. You can build animations using combinations of a number of techniques. You can animate nearly anything in parts and assemblies. You can drive an assembly constraint (even showing acceleration), you can change the value of a parameter over time, and you can even control parts fading in and out.

After building the animation, you can apply the same rendering properties to components to create a great-looking movie of your work. By switching rendering styles, you can use the same animation steps to create materials for many different applications. The steps and activities within the animation are displayed on a timeline (see Figure 9.45), which makes editing easy.

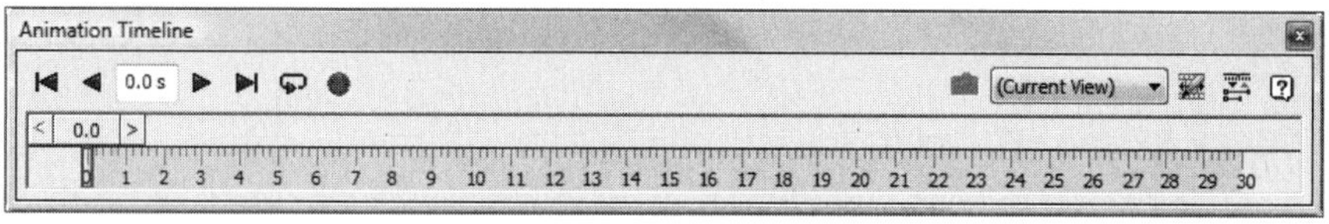

FIGURE 9.45 The Animation Timeline (collapsed)

In collapsed mode, all you see are the main controls and the timeline. In expanded mode, you see the individual actions that take place, with their positions and durations displayed as colored bars along the timeline.

Clicking and dragging the slider in the timeline moves you through the timeline. As you drag any animation, actions play out on the screen. This is a fantastic way to see your animation coming together.

Let's do some basic hands-on work to see a little of what is possible by animating in Inventor Studio. As you go through the exercise, you'll be introduced to the tools as needed.

Animating Visibility

In the first exercise, you'll fade a part's visibility:

1. Open or activate the Fan.iam file.

2. Set your view to look like Figure 9.46.

3. Click Inventor Studio in the Environments tab, and then click the Animate Timeline tool in the Animate panel of the Render tab. Confirm that you want to engage animation tools by clicking OK. The first step is to determine how long the animation will be.

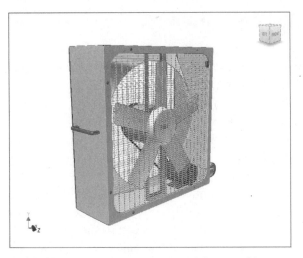

FIGURE 9.46 Setting the view of the assembly

4. Click the Animation Options tool in the Animation Timeline.

5. In the Animation Options dialog, set the Length value to 5 seconds.

6. Click OK to update the animation length.

7. In the Animate panel, select the Fade tool. This launches the Animate Fade dialog (Figure 9.47).

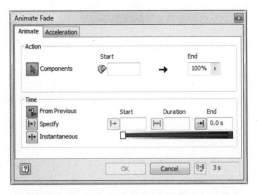

FIGURE 9.47 The Animate Fade dialog

8. Pick Grill:1 and Bolted Connection:1 from the Browser as your components.

9. Set the End value under Action to 5%.

10. Under Time pick the Specify icon, and set the Start time to 0.2 s and the End time to 1.0 s.

11. Click OK to set the values and close the dialog.

12. Pick the Play Forward button to see the result.

13. Pick and drag the slider slowly to the left back to the beginning of the animation, to see that you can observe the effects manually.

Now, let's add a twist by moving a component as part of the animation.

Animating a Constraint

Driving a constraint in the assembly moves a part. But in Inventor Studio, you can incorporate acceleration and deceleration:

1. Select the Animate Constraints tool from the Animate panel.

2. This dialog needs you to specify a constraint to animate. In the Browser, expand Fan Blade:1 and pick the Fan Angle constraint.

3. In the dialog, set the Start value to 0 and the End value to –720 (two full revolutions).

4. Pick the Specify icon, and set the Start value to .3 s and the End value to 4.8 s.

5. Pick the Acceleration tab in the dialog.

6. Select Specify Velocity, and set the first time percentage (Acceleration) to 10% and the last value (Deceleration) to 40%.
This gives the effect of the fan blade speeding up quickly and then gradually slowing.

7. Click OK to set the new values.

8. Play the animation and/or go through the timeline using the slider.

9. Click the Go to Start button.

Next, let's animate how you look at the assembly.

Animating the Camera

Cameras provide a lot of powerful options. But even a simple move can make your animation really shine:

1. Right-click in an open part of the Design window, and select Create Camera from View on the context menu.

This creates a new camera in the Browser, but that camera isn't automatically used by the animation.

2. In the Animation Timeline, use the pull-down at upper right to set the animation to use Camera1.

3. Use the slider to set the timeline to 3.5 seconds.

4. Rotate your view to the point of view shown in Figure 9.48.

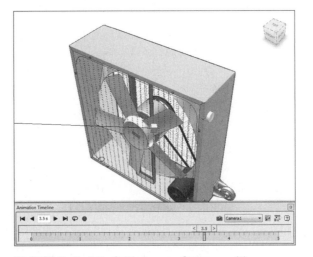

FIGURE 9.48 Setting a new Camera position

5. Click the Camera icon next to the Camera selection pull-down to set the position of Camera1 at the 3.5-second point on the timeline.

6. Pick the Go to Start button, and then click Play Forward to see the effect.

7. Pick the Go to Start button again, and save your work.

8. Click the Record Animation icon in the Animation Timeline.
   This launches the Render Animation dialog, which is very similar to the Render Image dialog. Most of the options are the same, although there are special settings for Animation.

9. Set the resolution to 800×600.

When you set the resolution, a red rectangle appears in the Design window. This is a preview of the portion of the screen that will be rendered.

To make sure your animation is captured, you can close the Render Animation window and use the Zoom tool to resize the assembly in the view.

10. In order to make the change effective, right-click Camera1 in the Browser, and choose Set Camera to View to reset the view.

11. Return to the Render Animation dialog.

12. Set Camera to Camera1.

13. Leave the Lighting and Scene Styles set to Current.

14. Set Render Type to Realistic.

15. On the Output tab, make sure the end of the time range is set to **5.0 s.**

    On the Output tab is a Preview: No Render option. This option allows you to create a test animation without taking the time to render each frame. This way, you can make sure the settings are right before you build the entire animation.

    Other options on the Output tab include the Frame Rate, which meters the smoothness of the animation; and the Format option, which has Inventor generate a series of images rather than a single animation file. These images can be combined by other video formats.

    You can save the animations as .AVI or .WMV files.

16. Select the Preview: No Render option, and set your Frame Rate to 10.

17. Click Render.

18. If prompted to save, save the file in C:\Data\, and name it Fan.avi. Click Save.

19. Set Compressor to Microsoft Video 1 or a format of your choice.

20. Click OK to create the animation preview.

21. Review the animation to see the results of the preview.

22. Close the Render Output dialog, and admire and save your work.

That's all we'll cover regarding renderings. I'll post a copy of the rendered animation to **www.sybex.com/go/inventor2010ner**.

I hope you've enjoyed building your fan and learning Autodesk Inventor along the way. By thinking about the needs of the design first, the tools you need to use will become self evident to an extent. If you've completed each of the exercises in this book, you've been exposed to the majority of tools that Autodesk Inventor has to offer.

I stress to people learning Inventor that they should *try things*. Try using a tool in different ways. The worst that can happen is that you'll have to use Undo. Enjoy your time with Autodesk Inventor. Thank you for making the effort to be more effective and better prepared in your career.

Are You Experienced?

Now you can...

☑ **create specialized views of the assembly**

☑ **place balloons in a drawing**

☑ **place parts lists**

☑ **modify the Bill of Materials**

☑ **generate a .DWF file to share with others**

☑ **create animations of an assembly**

☑ **render animations**

Keyboard
Shortcut Guide

have found Inventor's keyboard shortcuts to be priceless. Although I included the relevant shortcuts in the exercises, there are many more that weren't used but that you should know about.

This appendix lists the default shortcuts included with Inventor, but it's worth mentioning that you can also add or reassign shortcuts to whatever you like by using the Customize tool in the Options panel of the Tools tab; you can even export shortcuts to share with others. Before you do, take a look at the available shortcuts and be sure to keep in mind that the same keystroke can be used for different shortcuts based on the environment you're in. A few shortcuts can even change the environment. For example, pressing the S key in a sketch finishes the sketch; and pressing E automatically starts the Extrude tool if you're working in a new, unconsumed sketch.

If you decide to make changes, you may want to incrementally export the changes to allow you to restore them to a point. If you decide to abandon your changes, you can click the Reset All Keys button to restore Inventor's keyboard shortcuts to the defaults.

Tables A.1 through A.8 list Inventor's default keyboard shortcuts, sorted by the environment in which you access them.

TABLE A.1   Function Keys

Keystroke	Function
F1	Help Topics
F2	Pan
F3	Zoom
F4	Orbit
F5	Previous View
Shift+F5	Next View
F6	Home View
F7	Slice Graphics in Sketch
F8	Show All Constraints
Alt+F8	Open Macros Dialog Box
F9	Hide All Constraints

TABLE A.1 *(Continued)*

Keystroke	Function
F10	Unconsumed Sketch visibility toggle
Alt+F11	Open Visual Basic Editor

TABLE A.2 General Environment and Viewing Shortcuts

Keystroke	Function
Ctrl+C	Copy to Clipboard
Ctrl+Shift+E	Assembly Degrees of Freedom visibility toggle
M	Measure Distance
Ctrl+N	New File
Ctrl+O	Open File
Ctrl+P	Print
Ctrl+Shift+Q	iMate Glyph visibility toggle
Ctrl+S	Save File
Ctrl+V	Paste from Clipboard
Ctrl+W	SteeringWheels
Ctrl+Shift+W	Weld Symbols visibility toggle
Ctrl+X	Cut to Clipboard
Ctrl+Y	Redo
Z	Zoom Window
Ctrl+Z	Undo
Esc	Ends Active Command
Home	Zoom All

(Continued)

TABLE A.2   *(Continued)*

Keystroke	Function
Page Up	Look At
Delete	Delete selected object
End	Zoom Select
Ctrl+/	Origin Axes visibility toggle
Ctrl+]	Origin Planes visibility toggle
Ctrl+.	Origin Points visibility toggle
Alt+/	User Work Axes visibility toggle
Alt+]	User Work Planes visibility toggle
Alt+.	User Work Points visibility toggle

TABLE A.3   Drawing View Shortcut

Keystroke	Function
Ctrl+Shift+N	Create New Sheet

TABLE A.4   Drawing Annotation Shortcuts

Keystroke	Function
A	Baseline Dimension Set
B	Balloon
D	General Dimension
F	Feature Control Frame
O	Ordinate Dimension Set
T	Text
Ctrl+Shift+T	Leader Text

T A B L E A . 5   Sketching Shortcuts

Keystroke	Function
A	Center Point Arc
C	Center Point Circle
D	General Dimension
F	Fillet
H	Fill/Hatch Sketch Region
I	Vertical
L	Line
O	Offset
T	Text
X	Trim
=	Equal

T A B L E A . 6   Part-Modeling Shortcuts

Keystroke	Function	Feature Type
D	Face Draft	Placed
E	Extrude	Sketched
F	Fillet	Placed
H	Hole	Sketched
Ctrl+Shift+K	Chamfer	Placed
Ctrl+Shift+L	Loft	Sketched
Ctrl+Shift+M	Mirror	Placed
Ctrl+Shift+O	Circular Pattern	Placed
Q	Create iMate	Placed

(Continued)

TABLE A.6 *(Continued)*

Keystroke	Function	Feature Type
R	Revolve	Sketched
Ctrl+Shift+R	Rectangular Pattern	Placed
S	2D Sketch	Placed
Ctrl+Shift+S	Sweep	Sketched
;	Grounded Work Point	Work
/	Work Axis	Work
]	Work Plane	Work
.	Work Point	Work

TABLE A.7 Assembly-Modeling Shortcuts

Keystroke	Function
A	Analyze Interference
C	Constraint (Assembly)
Ctrl+Shift+E	Degrees of Freedom visibility toggle
G	Rotate Component
Ctrl+H	Replace
Ctrl+Shift+H	Replace All
N	Create Component in Assembly
P	Place Component in Assembly
V	Move Component
W	Fillet Weld (weldment environment)
Tab	Demote

TABLE A.7   *(Continued)*

Keystroke	Function
Shift+Tab	Promote
Ctrl+Enter	Return
/	Work Axis
]	Work Plane
.	Work Point
Ctrl+=	Parent
Ctrl+-	Top

TABLE A.8   Presentation Shortcut

Keystroke	Function
T	Tweak Components

Import and Export
File Formats

Inventor has the ability to communicate with many computer-aided design (CAD) and non-CAD software applications.

The reasons for exporting or importing data are widely varied. You may want to import an old AutoCAD file to convert to 3D, or you may need to export a file to a rapid prototyping and computer-aided manufacturing (CAM) application.

Regardless of the reason, you need flexibility. This appendix lists the available formats for exchange between other applications and Inventor.

Import File Formats

Inventor stores its data in several formats depending on the type of file you're creating. You can also import a number of neutral file formats as well as data directly from other 3D CAD systems. Here is a list of file extensions and the source the data can come from:

Format	Purpose
.idw	Inventor 2D drawing file
.dwg	Inventor and AutoCAD 2D drawing file
.ipt	Inventor part file
.iam	Inventor assembly file
.ipn	Inventor presentation file
.ide	Inventor library feature
.dwf, .dwfx	Autodesk Design Review Markup file
.dxf	Neutral 2D file
.wire	Autodesk Alias file
.sat	ACIS kernel-neutral exchange
.igs, .ige, iges	Neutral 3D surface file
.stp, .ste, .step	Neutral 3D solid file
.CATPart, .CATProduct	Dassault Catia V5 file
.x_b, .x_t	Parasolids binary and text-based exchange
.prt, .asm	Pro/ENGINEER part and assembly file
.g, .neu	Pro/ENGINEER kernel-based exchange
.prt, .sldprt, .asm, .sldasm	SolidWorks part and assembly
.prt	UGS NX part and assembly
.jt	Compressed-format file used by Siemens/PLM data-management applications

Export File Formats

Inventor can also share 2D and 3D data with many types of applications. Here is a list of the supported file types for export:

Format	Purpose
.idw	Inventor 2D drawing file
.dwg	Inventor and AutoCAD 2D drawing file
.ipt	Inventor part file
.iam	Inventor assembly file
.dxf, .dwfx	Neutral 2D file
.sat	ACIS kernel-neutral exchange
.igs, .ige, iges	Neutral 3D surface file
.stp, .ste, .step	Neutral 3D solid file
.stl	Stereolithography 3D-neutral
.x_b, .x_t	Parasolids binary and text-based exchange
.CATPart	Dassault Catia V5 file
.g, .neu	Pro/ENGINEER kernel-based exchange
.dwf	Autodesk 2D/3D Drawing Web
.pdf	Adobe Acrobat file
.png	Adobe Portable Network Graphics file
.jt	Compressed-format file used by Siemens/PLM data-management applications
.bmp	Windows bitmap file
.gif	Graphic Information file
.jpg	Common graphic file (Joint Photographic Experts Group)
.tif	Tagged image file
.xgl, zgl	Neutral 3D graphic viewing

INDEX

A

accelerators. *See* design accelerators
Add Member, 209
Additional Resources, 35, 49
advanced drawing views, 430-441
algebraic equations, 121
Allow Approximation option, 371
Aluminum, 20, 80, 123, 135, 275
Amber icon color, 33, 39
Angle constraint, 139
Angle option, 387, 396
angular constraint
    for bearing cover, *373*
    for fan blade, *410*
Animate Fade dialog box, 480
Animate tool, 444, 445, 449
Animation Options dialog box, 480
Animation Timeline, 479, 480, 482
animations. *See also* Inventor Studio
    fan assembly
        .AVI file and, 450-451
        camera and, 481-483
        constraint and, 481
        editing, 445-450
        exploded view, 442-445, *444*
        visibility and, 479-481
    Inventor Studio and, 462, 479-484
    presentation files and, 441-452, 479
Annotate tab, 178, 196, 200, 211, 431, 439, 452
annotations. *See* assembly annotations
ANSI standard, 151
Antialiasing, 465
Appearance panel, **22-24**
Application menu, 3-4, *4*
Application Options dialog box, 30-38, *31*, 33
    new work environment and, 38-40
    tabs in, 30-38
Apply button, 9, **237**
Area Loft, 386
Arrange (dimension editing), 209

assemblies, 52. *See also* fan assembly; *specific assemblies*
    components *v.*, 52
    editing components in, *147*
    Inventor and, 218
    Inventor LT and, 10, 15, 30
    leveraging, 218-222
    restructuring, 222-224
    sketches, 296-297
    3D models and, 135
assembly annotations, 452-462
    Balloon/Auto Balloon tool, 454-458
    BOM, 458-460
    DWF, 460-462
    parts list, 452-454
assembly constraints. *See* constraints
Assembly environment, 135, 248
assembly modeling
    concept, 135-137
    shortcuts, 490-491
Assembly tab, 38
associative dimensions, 70
associativity
    drawing view, 212-214
    principle of, 175, 212
Auto Balloon tool, 454-458
AutoCAD
    2000, 14
    command line and, 19
    drawings, Inventor templates and, 16
    Inventor interface and, 3
    Options control and, 14
Autodesk 3ds Max, 462. *See also* Inventor Studio
Autodesk AutoCAD. *See* AutoCAD
Autodesk Design Review screen, 462, *462*, 494
Autodesk Inventor 2010. *See* Inventor
Autodesk Manufacturing Community, 287
Autodesk Maya, 462. *See also* Inventor Studio
AutoDrop dialog box, 234, 236, **237**

Automatic Edge Chain option, 270
Automatic Face Chain option, 370
Autoproject Edges for Sketch Creation and Edit, 37, 39
Autoproject Part Origin on Sketch Create, 37, 39
.AVI file, fan assembly and, 450-451
axis, 396

B

Background option
    Colors tab, 32
    Display tab, 35
Background tab (Scene Styles dialog box), 473-474
Balloon tool, 454-458
base component, 52
base feature
    Contour Flange and, 81-83
    Revolve tool and, 396
Base tool, 182, 184, 186, 431, 436, 451
base views, 182-186
    bearing support and, 184-186
    creating, 182-184
Baseline Dimension tool, 204-205
bearing cover. *See also* fan assembly
    assembly creation and, 382-383
    Replace tool and, 383-384
    sketch
        angular constraint for, *373*
        building, 366-369
        extruding, 368, *369*
        fan support frame and, 367, *367*
        fillets and, 368, *369*
        rectangle in, 375, *375*
        shelling of, 371, *372*
        splitting, 372-375, *373*
    solid model
        bosses added to, 376-379
        Bottom, 373, 374, 376, 379
        finished, *381*
        lip and, 379-381
        Top, 373, 376, 379

Bearing Design, 311
Bearing Generator, 310-316
bearing holder, 156-159
 /bearing plate, assembling,
  168-170
 bearing support and. *See*
  bearing supports
 chain weld around, *173*
 changing color of, 169
 Extrude tool, 157-159
 sketch, 156, *157*
Bearing Life Calculation, 312
bearing plate
 /bearing holder, assembling,
  168-170
 bearing support and. *See*
  bearing supports
 building, 159-161
 Chamfer tool, 166-167
 work features and, 161-166
bearing supports, 168-169
 base view, 184-186
 bearing plate/bearing holder
  adding, 168-169, *169*
  welding together, 172-174
 bolted connections and, 234,
  240, 241
 bore in, *174*
 convert to weldment, 171-172
 fan support frame and, 232-233
bearings, fan assembly and, 312-316
Belt option, 322-323
Bend Intersection, 78
Bend Position, 84
Bend Radius, 77, 118
Bend Relief, 76
Bend tab, 76-77
Bend Transition, 77
beveled edge, 171
Bill of Materials (BOM), 458-460
 parts list *v.*, 452, 458
blue
 color theme, 33
 Dimension (ANSI) layer, 179
 fan blade and, 407
 pastel, 86
 Z axis, 19
Bodies dialog box, *383*
Body as Work Surface, 278
bolt stack, **238**, 239, 241
Bolted Connection button, 237

Bolted Connection Component
 Generator, 234, 237, 255,
 310, 425
Bolted Connection Component
 Generator dialog box, *237*,
 237-238
bolted connections, **234**. *See also*
 fan assembly
 bearing supports and, 234, 240,
  241
 fan assembly/grills and, 426-427
 fan support frame and, 234-243
 library of, 238
 template, reusing, 241-243
bore, 159, 173, 174. *See also* bearing
 supports
 in bearing support, *174*
 chamfer added to, *174*
Boss tool, **376**-379
bosses, bearing cover and, 376-379
Both (shell option), 370
Bottom bearing cover, 373, 374,
 376, 379
Boundary Profile, 433
Boundary tab, 417
box fan. *See* fan assembly
Break Out dialog box, 433-434
Break tool, 438-441
breaking view of shaft, 439-441
break-out view, 432-437
 creating, 434-435
 new drawings for, 431-432,
  435-437
Browse For Folder dialog box, 45
Browser bar, **17-18**, *18*
bump map, 476, 477, *478*
buttons, 9. *See also specific buttons*

C

CAD (computer-aided design)
 systems, 286, 330, 460, 494.
 See also AutoCAD
 3D, 494
 2D, 53, 62, 189, 296, 427, 435
calculating values, 121
Calculation tab
 Bearing Generator, 311
 Parallel Key Connection
  generator, 345
 Shaft Component Generator, 318
 V-Belts Component Generator, 323

CAM (computer-aided manufacturing)
 application, 494
Camera tool, 464
cameras, 463, 464
 fan assembly, animating, 481-483
Cancel (control), 14
Cancel button, 9
cast handle, 262-276
 basic shape, defining, 262-266
 draft and, 266-268
 fillets for, 270-274
 machined handled and, 277-286
 mirroring of, 274-276
casters, 288-292
Caster.stp, 258, 288
Center Line option, 386
Center Mark Only, 76
Center Mark tool, 196-198
Center Point, 70
Centered Pattern, 196
Centerline Bisector, 198-199
Centerline option, 70
Centerline tool, 198, 199
Chain Faces, 408
chain weld, bearing holder and, *173*
Chamfer tool, 166-167
Change Size, 237
Change View Orientation, 183
Check Calculation, 311
child view, 182
children features, 53
Chord Tolerance, 118
Circular Pattern dialog box, 400, *402*
Circular Pattern tool, 126, 400-404,
 489. *See also* hub
Circus (View representation), 253
clearance envelope, 354-355
Clearance Hole, 99, *363*
Click to Add function, 268, 272,
 323, 371, 393, 425
Closed Loop option, 386
Coincidence constraints, **59**, 60, 62,
 131, 219, 300, 388, 403
Collinear, 59
Color Fill, 467
Color Gradient, 473
Color Scheme option, 32
color schemes, 32, 38, 39, 407, 475.
 See also Presentation color
  scheme
Color Theme, 33, 39
Colors tab, 32-33

command line, 19
Commit and Move, 245
Component tab, 183
components. *See also specific components*
    assemblies *v.*, 52
    demoting, 222-224
    editing, in assemblies, *147*
    grounded, 136, 138
    instance, 136
    Make Components tool, 382-383
    parts *v.*, 251, 252
    physical properties, monitoring of, *85, 108*
    purchased, 150, 287. *See also* Content Center; Supplier Content Center
    Select Component Priority, 251
    suppressing, 248, 252. *See also* Envelope Suppressed
    Virtual Component option, 218
computer-aided design systems. *See* AutoCAD; CAD systems
computer-aided manufacturing (CAM) application, 494
Concentric, 59, 97
Conditions tab, 386-387
Constant tab, 268-269
Constrain panel, 58, 65, 66, 113
Constrain Sketch Plane to Selected Face or Plane (option), 219
Constrained Orbit tool, 28
constraining a sketch, 37
Constraint Audio Notification, 38
Constraint Inference, 60
Constraint Persistence, 60
Constraint Set tab, 142
constraints, 55. *See also specific constraints*
    angular
        for bearing cover, *373*
        for fan blade, *410*
    assembly, 137-142
        duct/housing and, 142-150
    dimension
        defined, 55
        dimensions and, 64-72
        sheet metal housing, 61-62
        sketch, 58-60
    fan assembly, animation of, 481
    geometric, *64*, 65
    housing and, 61-62

construction geometry, 70, 343, 391
Content Center, **150**. *See also* standard parts; Supplier Content Center
    dialog box, 159, *159*
    Frame Generator and, 224
    importance of, 150
    libraries, 32, 43
    limiting content, button for, 44
    Place from Content Center tool, 150, 153, 234, 236, 424, 425
    standard parts in, 150
context menus, 10
    drawing view, *187*
    Edit dimension, *208*
Contour Flange dialog box, *82*
Contour Flange tool, 81-83
contoured parts, 366-428
Convert to Weldment dialog box, 171, *171*, 172
Copy Object tool, 352-353
Copy Properties, 208
Corner Round tool, **125-126**
Corner tab, 77-78
Counterbore, 98, 173, 213
Countersink, 98
cowbell, 38, 142
Create 2D Sketch tool, 92, 120, 282, 355
Create Flat Pattern tool, 89, 128, 362
Create from the Component panel, 218
Create In-Place Component dialog box, 218, *218*, 223
Create New Folder icon, 12, 181
Cross Recessed Screw, 151, 235, 425
Curves tab, 386
custom libraries, 150
Customer Involvement Program, 2, 6
customization, Inventor, 30-40
Customize tool, 486. *See also* keyboard shortcuts
Cut option, 158
Cutout Shape, 194

D

dashed rectangular line, 188
data. *See also* file formats; files
    IGES, 286

    importing/exporting, 286, 494-495
    sharing, 494-495
    STEP, 286, 287, 288, 289
data management system. *See* Vault
decal, for fan blade, 409-410
Decal tool, 408-411. *See also* Emboss tool
Default Drawing File Type option, 36, 39
Degrees of Freedom (DOF), 62, 64. *See also* constraints
    assembly constraints and, 137
    geometric constraints and, *64*, 65
    motor, 293, *293*, 294
    six, 137, 292
Delete Member, 209
demoting components, 222-224
Depth (Break Out dialog box), 433-434
Derived Part dialog box, 277, *278*, 286
derived parts, 277-279
design
    building foundation of, 51-108
    communication of, 430-484
    functional, 224, 310. *See also* design accelerators
    Inventor and, 52, 310
design accelerators, 135, 310-363. *See also* Bearing Generator; bolted connections; Shaft Component Generator; Sweep tool; V-Belts Component Generator
Design Doctor, 20, 21
Design Review screen, 462, *462*, 494
Design tab
    Bearing Generator, 311
    Parallel Key Connection generator, 345
    Shaft Component Generator, 317
    V-Belts Component Generator, 322-323
Design Web Format. *See* DWF
Design window, **18-19**, 21-29
Detach Member, 209
detail views, 193-196
detailing tools, 196-199, 441. *See also* Center Mark tool; Centered Pattern; Centerline Bisector; Centerline tool

dialog boxes, **9-17**. *See also specific dialog boxes*
  design accelerator, 310
  resizing, 10
  sign-up (Customer Involvement Program), 2, 6
  tabs, 9-10
Die Formed, 117
digital prototypes, 296, 304, 316, 323, 427, 430
Dim Hidden Edges, 34, 39
dimension editing tools, 207-212
Dimension tool (sketches), 62, 66, 68, 114, 156
dimensioning tools, 199. *See also* Baseline Dimension tool; General Dimension tool; Hole/Thread Notes tool
dimensions, **62-63**. *See also specific dimensions*
  constraints and, 64-72
  housing and, 64-72
  reusing, 63
  shaft and, 441, *441*
Direction & Offset, 475
Direction condition (Conditions tab), 387
Direction icon (Rib/Web tools), 404
direction vector, 97
Display Full Boundary, 194
display modes. *See* 3D display modes
Display option
  Break Out dialog box, 434
  Break tool, 438
  Sketch tab, 37
Display Options tab, **183**, 431
Display tab, 34-35
Distance
  Chamfer tool, 166
  Hole feature, 98
Distance and Angle, 166
dividing parts, Split tool and, 372-375
Document tabs, 29
DOF. *See* Degrees of Freedom
Done option, 245
draft, cast handle and, 266-268
Draft tab, 419
drainage gutter, 81
Drawing Annotation shortcuts, 488
Drawing tab, **36**
drawing view associativity, 212-214
Drawing View dialog box, 182, *183*, 184, 451

Drawing View shortcut, 488
drawing views. *See also* detailing tools; *specific views*
  advanced, 430-441
  context menu, *187*
  relocating, *186*
  of shaft, 435-437, *437*
  2D, 175-181
drawings
  AutoCAD, Inventor templates and, 16
  2D, 175
Drilled, 98
driven dimensions, **70**, 71, 245, 300, 301, 302
duct, 112-135. *See also* fan assembly
  flat pattern of, *129*
  /housing
    combining and positioning, 142-153
    fan blade and, 142
    moving, 135-137
  motor and, 295
  mounting holes in, *133*
  sketches
    Corner Round tool, 125-126
    Face tool, 122-124
    finished, *132*
    Lofted Flange tool, 112-116, 118-122
    Rip tool, 127-135
  work plane modification, 133, *134*
Duct Clearance, 350
Duct.ipt, 114, 136
DWF (Design Web Format), 460-462
DWG files, 14, 36, 39, 175, 181, 185, 431, 432, 435, 437, 451, 452, 461, 494, 495

E

Edge Fillet, 268-269
Edge Select Mode, 84
Edges and Faces, Select, 252
Edges option (Style tab, Illustration rendering), 468
Edit Dimension context menu, *208*. *See also* dimension editing tools
Edit Dimension When Created option, 37
Edit Extent, 245

Edit Feature, 84
Edit Hole Note dialog box, 206, *207*
Edit Offset, 245
Edit option (dimension editing), 208-209
Edit Sheet, 435
Edit Sheet dialog box, 436
Edit Sheet Metal Rule, 74
editing fan support frame, 229-232
Education Community, 6
Emboss tool, 411. *See also* Decal tool
  Decal tool *v.*, 408
  power knob and, 413-415
Enable Enhanced Highlighting, 32, 253
Enable Optimized Selection option, 32
Enabled, 35, 39
enhanced highlighting, 32, **252-253**, 345
Envelope Suppressed, 246, 247, 251, 328, 350, 384, 431
Environment tab, *474*, 474-475
Equal constraint, 60
Explicit Reference Vector, 140
exploded view (fan assembly), 442-445, *444*
Explorer. *See* Windows Explorer
Export button, 30, 40
Export dialog box, 40
export file formats, **495**
exporting/importing data, 286, 494-495
Extend Profile, 404
extensions. *See* file formats
Extents group (Revolve tool), 396
Extents option (Rib/Web tools), 404
Extrude dialog box, *9*, 10, *157*
Extrude tool, 53, *157-159*, *221*
  Face tool *v.*, 122
extruding bearing cover sketch, 368, *369*

F

faces. *See specific faces*
Face dialog box, *123*
Face Draft, 53, 489
Face Extents, 127
Face Fillet, 269-270
Face tool, **122-124**. *See also* Extrude tool

Faces and Edges, Select, 252
Facet Angle, 118
Facet Control, 117-118
Facet Distance, 118
fan assembly. *See also* duct; grill;
 housing; hub; shaft
 animation
  .AVI file and, 450-451
  camera and, 481-483
  constraint and, 481
  editing, 445-450
  exploded view and, 442-445,
   444
  online posting of, 483
  visibility and, 479-481
 balloons and, 454-458
 bearing cover and, 383-384, *385*
 bearings and, 312-316
 casters and, 288-292
 50-part, 427
 finished, *428*
 grills added to, 423-427
  bolted connections, 426-427
 grills and
  broken-out, *435*
 nearly completed, *363*
 new base view, 431-432
 parts list and, 452-454
 power knob added to, 416-417
fan blade
 angular constraint for, *410*
 contour and, 385
 creating, 393-395
 decal for, 409-410
 duct/housing and, 142
 fillets and, 394-395
 hub, 397-400
 Inventor and, 410
 lofted features and, 385, 388-395
 ribs and, 405-408
 sketch, 388-393
 whole body, 401-404
Fan drive, 250, 251, 255, 318, 345,
 366
fan support frame
 bearing cover sketch on, 367, *367*
 bearing supports added to,
  232-233
 bolted connections added to,
  234-243
 building, 226-229
 changing size of, 243-248

 editing, 229-232
 frame envelope and, 226-229
 function of, 232
 Miter tool and, 229-230
 size, changing, 243-248
 updating, 241-243, *243*
Fan.iam
 creating, 135-137
 duct/housing
  combining, 142-153
  moving to space, 135-137
Favorites, 49, 234, *235*, 236, 425
features, 52-53. *See also specific*
 features
 placed, 52-53
 Select Feature Priority, 252
feet, housing and, *106*
Fence Shape, 194, 195
50-part fan assembly, 427. *See also*
 fan assembly
File Display Options, 13-14
File Explorer dialog box, 465
file formats, **494-495**. *See also* DWG
 files; *specific file formats*
 export, 495
 import, 494
 neutral, 286, 494
file list, *11*
 shortcuts and, 11-12
 Thumbnail view, 12, *13*
File Name (pull-down), 13
File Preview pane, 14
files. *See also* data
 opening, 15-16
 presentation, 441-452
Files of Type option, 12, *13*
Fillet tool, 268-274
fillets. *See also specific fillets*
 bearing cover and, 368, *369*
 cast handle and, 270-274
 creating, 268
 fan blade and, 394-395
 hub and, 398-399
 placing, 270
filters. *See* selection filters
Filters pull-down list, 20, 351
Find button, 14
Find File dialog box, 14, *15*
Finish Sketch tool, 58, 72, 159
Fix constraint, 59
Fixed Edge option, 267
Fixed Plane option, 267

Flange Angle, 84
Flange tool, **83-87**
flanges, 83, 85-88
 housing and, 85-88
 Mirror tool and, 89-90
flat patterns
 calculation methods and, 75-76
 Create Flat Pattern tool, 89,
  128, 362
 punch representation, 76
Folder Options area, 43
folders, **46**. *See also* Frequently Used
 Subfolders; *specific folders*
Follow Pattern, 237, 238, 242, 426
Format Text dialog, 177, 413, 414
formats. *See* file formats
Formed Punch Feature, 76
frame envelope component
 creating, 218-222
 demoting, 222-224
 fan support frame and, 226-229
Frame Generator, 224
 Content Center and, 224
 Insert dialog box, 224-225, *225*
Frame Member Selection, 225
frame members
 Orientation, 225
 Placement option, 225
 placing, 224-225
Free Condition, 387
Frequently Used Subfolders, 11,
 11, 43
 Housing.ipt, 135, 136
 line, 47
 Shock Absorber Front assembly,
  15, 41
 shortcuts, 11-12, 42, 43
From Point, 433
From Sketch, 97
From To (Revolve tool), 396
Full option (Revolve tool), 396
Full Round, 269
function keys, 486-487. *See also*
 keyboard shortcuts
functional design, 224, 310. *See*
 also design accelerators

G

Gap value, 438
General Dimension tool, 200-204
general environment/viewing
 shortcuts, 487-488

General tab
  Application Options dialog
    box, 32
  Render Image dialog box,
    463-464
geometric constraints, *64*, 65
geometry. *See specific geometry
  entries*
Geometry tab, 101, *101*
Geometry Text, 342-344
gesturing, 55, *56*, *67*
Get Started tab, *5*, 5-7, 15, 44
Go To Last Folder Visited, 12
graphical user interface (GUI). *See
  interface*
Graphs tab, 318
green
  arrows, 12
  Centerline (ANSI) layers, 179
  check mark, 69, 72, 122, 184
  circle, 243
  dots, 28
  Y axis, 19
grid lines, 36, 37, 39
grill. *See also* fan assembly
  fan assembly and, 423-427
    bolted connections, 426-427
    break-out view, *435*
  finished, *423*
  housing and, *425*
  ribs and, 418
  sketches for, 419-423
Grill tool, 375, **417-419**
  complexity of, 419
Grill.ipt file, 410, 419
grips. *See* 3D grips
Ground Plane, 475
Ground Shadow, 23
grounded component, 136, 138
grounding the point, 59
GUI (graphical user interface). *See
  interface*

H

Handle_Height, 302, 303, 304, 306,
  307
handles, 3D grips and, *244*
Hardware tab, 35
Height Datum, 84
Height Extents, 84
Help system, 49, 200

Hidden Edge display mode, 22,
  23, 35
Hidden Lines, 184
Hide Dimension Value, 208
highlighting, enhanced, 32, 252-
  253, 345
Hole feature, 96-99. *See also
  specific holes*
Hole/Thread Notes tool, 205-207
Home view, 29
Horizontal, 59
horizontal line segment, *54*
housing (sheet metal). *See also* fan
  assembly
  constraints and, 61-62
  creating, 52-53
  /duct
    combining and positioning,
      142-153
    fan blade and, 142
    moving, 135-137
  feet on housing, *106*
  grill and, *425*
  Mirror tool and, 89-91
  physical properties of, 85, *108*
  Punch tool and, 99-106
  sketch, 52-72
    constraints, 61-62
    dimensions, 64-72
  3D component
    base feature, 81-83
    flanges added, 85-88
    Mirror tool, 88-96
    Punch tool, 99-108
Housing.ipt, 58, 61, 85, 107, 135, 136
hub. *See also* fan assembly
  Circular Pattern tool and, 401-404
  creating
    portion, 397-400
    whole body, 401-404
  fillets and, 398-399
  rounding top edge of, *398*
  Shell features and, *399*
Hub Groove, 345
Hz (Minimum Frame Rate), 35

I

icons. *See specific icons*
IDW file format, 36, 494, 495. *See
  also* DWG files
IGES data, 286

illustration rendering, 464
  pulley, 471, *472*
  Style tab, 467-468
Image option, 473
Image Sphere, 473
iMate, 258-262
Import button, 30
import file formats, 494
importing/exporting data, 286,
  494-495
Incremental option, 400
inference lines, 192, *192*, 193
Infocenter, 49
Insert constraint, 140
Insert dialog box, 224-225, *225*
Insert Multiple, 237
Inside Shell, 370
instance, of component, 136
interface (graphical user interface/
  GUI), 2-49. *See also* Ribbon
  AutoCad and, 3
  parts of, *3*
Intersect option, 158
Intersection Curve tool, 355
Inventor (Autodesk Inventor 2010)
  assemblies and, 218
  command line and, 19
  Customer Involvement
    Program, 2, 6
  customizing, 30-40
  data sharing and, 494-495
  design and, 52, 310
  fan blade and, 410
  Help system, 49, 200
  Infocenter, 49
  interface, 2-49. *See also* Ribbon
Inventor LT, 10
  assemblies and, 10, 15, 30
  new work environment and, 38
  Transparency button and, 24
Inventor Studio, 462-484
  animations, 462, 479-484
  presentation files and, 479
  renderings, 427, 462-478
island, 418
Island tab, 418
Isolate, 250, 312, 314, 350, 366, 374
isolation, parts and, 252
isometric view, 187, 188, 189, 190, 191

J

Join option, 158

K

Key, 345. *See also* parallel key connection
keyboard shortcuts, **26**, **485-491**. *See also specific keyboard shortcuts*
    assembly modeling, 490-491
    Customize tool, 486
    Drawing Annotation, 488
    function keys, 486-487
    general environment/viewing, 487-488
    part modeling, 489-490
    Presentation, 491
    sketching, 489

L

Learn about Inventor panel, 6
Level of Detail (LOD)
    representations, 246, 247, **249-250**, 255, 318
leveraging assemblies, 218-222
libraries. *See also* Content Center
    of bolted connections, 238
    Content Center, 32, 43
    custom, 150
    Libraries setting, 43
    style, 48, 73
    Style Library, 80
    Use Style Library, 43, 48
Libraries setting, 43
Lighting Style, 464
Line tool, 54, 55, 56, 58, 262, 263, 264
Linear, 97
lip, bearing cover and, 379-381
Lip tool, **376**, **379-381**
Loads, 311
Location setting, 42
LOD representations. *See* Level of Detail representations
Loft tool, **385-388**
    fan blade
        shape, 388-393
        solid, 393-395
Loft Types, 386
lofted features, fan blade and, 385, 388-395
lofted flange, 385
Lofted Flange dialog box, *117*
Lofted Flange tool, **116-118**
    duct sketches, 112-116, 118-122

Look at Sketch Plane on Sketch Creation, 37, 39
Loop Select Mode, 84

M

machined handle, 277-286. *See also* cast handle
Maintain Each solid as a Solid Body, 278
Make Components tool, 382-383
Make Origin, 209
Manage tab, 121, 159, 180, 258, 259, 277, 287, 301, 306, 307, 382
manager buttons, project file, 44
Manufacturing Community, 287
Mastering Autodesk Inventor 2010 (Waguespack), 310
Mate constraints, 139, 424
Material (pull-down list), 75
Material Style, 74
Maya, 462. *See also* Inventor Studio
Mean option, 371
Measure Distance tool, 106, 351
Measure tool, *107*, 351
Merge option, 225
Merge Tangent Faces, 386
Messages, 312
metal frames. *See also* Frame Generator
    foundation, 218-222
metal shapes, 156, 224
Metric template, 17, 63, 175, 181
Microsoft Office 2007 Office button, 3, 4
Microsoft Windows Explorer. *See* Windows Explorer
middle-out, 52
Minimum Frame Rate (Hz), 35
Mirror tool, 88-96
    flanges and, 89-90
    housing and, 89-91
    Optimized option, 89
mirroring, cast handle, 274-276
"mistake," rectangle, 56, 57
Miter tool, 229-230
Model State, 183
Model tab, 96, 114, 117, 125
modeling. *See* assembly modeling; multibody modeling; part modeling; solid modeling
models. *See* part modeling; solid modeling; 3D models; *specific models*

More (»), 84
More button, 9, 89, 238, 269, 370, 400, 411
More tab, 10, 158, **371-372**, 401
Motion tab, 141
motor
    DOF, 293, *293*, 294
    duct and, 295
    in fan assembly, 292
    pulley and, 328-331
    simplifying, 295-296
    with suppressed features, *296*
    V-Belt and, 323-334
mounting boss, 413
mounting holes, 133, 282
Move to Expanded Panel, 7
multibody modeling, 278, 280, **366**, 381
    New Solid, 158, 386
    Split Solid, 280, 372
multibody part, 366, 371
multibody workflow, 280, 381
multiple users option, 42, 150, 180. *See also* Vault

N

named parameters, 300, 304-308
Navigate panel, **24-28**
navigation controls, **12**
Navigation Wheels, 24-25
negative face, of work planes, 407
NER Inventor 2010 project file, 45, 46, 47, 48, 53
neutral file formats, 286, 494
Never Too Thick, 371
Never Too Thin, 371
New File dialog box, **16-17**
    Default templates, *17*
    English tab, 53
    template creation and, 181
new project file wizard, 44, 46
New Solid, 158, 386. *See also* multibody modeling
normal geometry, 70
Normal option (BOM), 458
nuts. *See also* bolted connections; Content Center
    Content Center and, 44
    PEM Self-Clinching Nuts, 426, 427
    Sheet Metal Nuts, 425

O

Office button, 3, 4
Offset, 140-141. *See also* Thicken/
     Offset tool
OK button, 9
Oldversions directory, 43
On Point option, 97-98
Open (control), 14
Open dialog box, **10-16**
     file list, *11*
          shortcuts and, 11-12
Open Documents in Session, 19
opening files, **15-16**
Optimized option
     Circular Pattern tool, 400
     Mirror tool, 89
optimized shelling, 371
Options control, 14
Options group, 43
orange
     Hatch layer, 179
     vertical line, 418, 422
Orbit tool, 28. *See also* ViewCube
Orientation option
     Break tool, 438
     Drawing View dialog box, 183
     frame members, 225
     Sweep dialog box, 336
Origin planes, 64, 136, 162, 388
orthographic projections, 175, 187
Orthographic view, *22*, 468
Orthographic/Perspective button, 23
osnap options, 61. *See also* constraints
Output options (Lofted Flange
     dialog box), 117-118
Output tab, **465**
Outside Shell, 370
Overconstrained Dimensions
     option, 37
overrides, 69. *See also specific*
     overrides

P

Pan tool, 25
panels, 5. *See also specific panels*
panning, 25
Parallel, 59
Parallel constraint, 65, *66*
parallel key connection, 345-352
Parallel Key Connection Generator,
     344-352

parametric dimensions, 69, 70
parent features, 53
parent view, 182
parentheses, algebraic equations
     and, 121
part modeling, 200, 268, 277
part modeling shortcuts, 489-490
Part tab, 37
parts, **251**. *See also* components;
     contoured parts; plastic parts;
     sheet metal parts; standard
     parts; *specific parts*
     components *v.*, 251, 252
     derived, 277-279
     placing, 270
     purchased, 150, 287. *See also*
          Content Center; Supplier
          Content Center
     reusing, 258. *See also* cast
          handle; iMate
     Select Part Priority, 252
Parts folder, 47, 58, 114, 136, 159,
     160, 261, 265, 277, 279, 367,
     390, 411, 419
parts list, 452-454
     BOM *v.*, 452, 458
     fan assembly and, 452-454
Parts List dialog box, 453
Path, 335
Path & Guide Rail, 335
Path & Guide Surface, 335
Pattern panel, 89, 126, 165, 274,
     340, 401, 418
Pattern the Entire Solid, 400
Pattern tools, 126
PEM Self-Clinching Nuts, 426
Perpendicular, 59
Phantom, 458-459
physical properties, monitoring of,
     85, 108
Place button, 237
Place Component dialog box, 135, 261
Place Feature, 159, *159*
Place from Content Center tool,
     150, 153, 234, 236, 424, 425
placed features, 52-53
placeholder, 218
Placement
     Design tab, 317
     frame members, 225
     Hole dialog box, 97, 98
planes. *See specific planes*

Plastic (texture), 368
Plastic (White), 394
Plastic Part panel, 341, 375-376,
     379, 422. *See also* Boss tool;
          Grill tool; Lip tool; Rest tool;
          Rule Fillet; Snap Fit
plastic parts, 366-428
     basic part, 366-369
     multibody part, 366, 371
     working with, 366-369
Point to Point, 127
Position representations, 249
positive face, of work planes, 407
power knob, 411-417. *See also* fan
     assembly
     Emboss tool and, 415-416
     fan assembly and, 416-417
     finished, *415*
     mounting boss and, *413*
     text and, 413-415
Power Knob.ipt, 410, 411
Power Transmission pane, 323
Precision setting (dimension
     editing), 208
predefined metal shapes, 156, 224.
     See also Frame Generator
Predict Offset and Orientation, 138
Preparation and Machining panel, 173
Presentation color scheme, 38, 39
presentation files, 441-452. *See also*
     Inventor Studio
     animation and, 441-452, 479
     fan assembly and
          editing, 445-450
          exploded view, 442-445, *444*
     Inventor Studio and, 479
     purpose of, 441-442
Presentation shortcut, 491
Preserve All Features, 270
Press Break, 117, *119*
Preview option, *90*, 118, *119*
Process panel, 172, 173
profile, 396
progressive tooltips, 7, 32
Project File dialog box, 14, 15
Project File editor, 14, 41-42
Project File fly-out, 13-14
project files, **41-49**
     creating, 44-49
     defined, 41
     manager buttons, 44

NER Inventor 2010, 45, 46, 47, 48, 53
Samples.ipj, 41, 42
wizard, 44, 46
Project Geometry tool, 127, 147, 283, 297, 361
Projected tool, 187-188
projected views, 187-192
Projects dialog box, 46, 47
Propagate to Parent View, 438
Publish Presentation dialog box, *461*
pulley. *See also* spokes
Geometry Text and, 342-344
motor and, 328-331
rendering
illustration, 471, *472*
quick, 468-471
with surface style, 477-478
Rule Fillet and, 341-342
scene style and, 475-476, *476*
spoke and, 330
Pulleys group, 323
Punch tool, 99-106
PunchTool dialog box, *100, 101*
PunchTool Directory dialog box, 104
purchased components/parts, 150, 287. *See also* Content Center; Supplier Content Center

Q

Quarter Section View, 22
Quick Access Toolbar, *4*, 4-5, 19-20
Quick Launch, 14, 16
quilt, 354

R

RAD, 121
radians, 121
Rails, 386
Rails/Center Line/Placed Sections list, 386
realistic rendering, 464
Illustration rendering *v.*, 464
Show Shiny Highlights and, 467
Style tab, 465-466
Recover icon, 20
rectangle
on bearing cover (sketch), 375, *375*
"mistake," 56, 57
Rectangle feature, 160, 161, 163
Rectangle folder, 160

Rectangle tool, 94, 102, 262
rectangular line, dashed, 188
Rectangular Pattern tool, 160, 400
red
arrows, 9, 88, 140
cross, 213
error message and, 312
hidden-line font, 185
horizontal lines, 418, *421*, 422
layers, 179
line color, 299
Recover, 20
rectangle, 463, 483
X axis, 59
Redo, 4, 20, 487
Reflection Environment option, 33
Refold tool, 358-363
reinforcement ribs. *See* ribs
Relief Shape, 76
relocating drawing views, *186*
Render Animation dialog box, 482, 483
Render Image dialog box, 463-464
Render Type, 464
renderings, 427, 462-478. *See also* animations; Inventor Studio
illustration, 464
pulley, 471, *472*
Style tab options, 467-468
pulley, 468-471, 471, *472*
realistic, 464
Illustration rendering *v.*, 464
Show Shiny Highlights and, 467
Style tab options, 465-466
scene style and, 464
Replace tool, 383-385
representations, 248-251. *See also* *specific representations*
resizing dialog boxes, 10
Rest tool, 376
restructuring assemblies, 222-224
Reticle, 28, 288
Return button, 20
Revolve dialog box, *396*
Revolve tool, **396**-400
Rewind tool, 25
Rib tab, 418
Rib tool, **404**-408
Ribbon, 5
Ribbon Appearance, 7-8

ribs
fan blade and, 405-408
grill and, 418
rule fillet on, *406*
Webs *v.*, 404
right-click menus, **182**
Rip tool, **127**-135
Roll Along Sharp Edges, 269-270
Rolling Ball Where Possible option, 270
Rotatation-Translation, 141
Rotation constraint, 141
Round option, 77
rounding top edge, of hub, *398*
Rule Fillet, 340-344, 376, 406

S

Samples.ipj project file, 41, 42. *See also* project files
Save icon, 58
Save Rendered Image, 465
Save tool, 185, 383
Scale area, 194
Scene Style, 464
scene styles
building, pulley and, 475-476, *476*
Camera and, 464
properties, 473-475
renderings and, 464
Scene Styles dialog box, 472-476
scrubbing, 55, *56*
Sculpt tool, **411**-417
sculpting power knob, 411-417
Section All Parts, 434
section views, 192-193
Sections option, 386
Select Component Priority, 251
Select Faces and Edges, 252
Select Feature Priority, 252
Select Objects to Generate, 345
Select Part Priority, 252
Select Project pane, 42, 46
Select Sketch Features, 252
selection filters, 20, 151, **251-252**
defined, 20
Filters pull-down list, 20, 351
Selection option (General tab), 32
Selections group, 140
Self-Clinching Nuts, PEM, 426
sequence groupings, 446
Setbacks tab, 269

Shaded display modes, 22, 23, **35**, 39
shaft. *See also* fan assembly
    breaking view of, 439-441
    creating, 318-322
    dimensions added to, 441, *441*
    drawing view of, 435-437, *437*
    parallel key connection and. *See*
        parallel key connection
Shaft Component Generator, 316-322
Shaft Groove, 345
Shape tab, 10, 83-84
sharing data, 494-495
Sharp Point, 388
Sheet Formats folder, 214
Sheet group, 75
sheet metal defaults, 73
Sheet Metal Defaults dialog bog,
    73-74, *74*
sheet metal housing. *See* housing
Sheet Metal (in).ipt template, 53, 112
sheet metal parts, standard parts
    v., 54
sheet metal rules, **73**
    creating, 74, 78-81
    Sheet Metal Rule option, 74
sheet metal tools, **73**. *See also*
    Contour Flange tool; Flange
    tool; Lofted Flange tool
    advance capabilities, 112
Sheet tab, 75
Shell features, 370
    bearing cover and, 371, *372*
    hub and, 399
Shell tab, 370-371
Shell tool, 353, **369-372**, 398
Shell Types option, 370
shelling
    of bearing cover, 371, *372*
    optimized, 371
Shock Absorber Front assembly, 15,
    16, 19, 26, 35, 41, 44
    in Design window, *16*
    Rewind tool and, *25*
    transparency on, *24*
    work environment for, 38-40
    Zoom Window tool and, *27*
Shock Absorber Front.iam, 15, 19, 44
shortcut toolbar, 29
shortcuts, 43. *See also* keyboard
    shortcuts; *specific shortcuts*
    file list and, 11-12
    Help System, 49

Show All Constraints, 60, 486
Show Hidden Model Edges as
    Solid, 35
Show Reflections, 475
Show Shadows, 475
Show Shiny Highlights, 467
sign-up dialog box, Customer
    Involvement Program, 2, 6
Simple Hole, 98
Single Point, 127
Single Solid Body Merging Out Seams
    between Planar Faces, 278
Single User option, 42. *See also* Vault
six Degrees of Freedom, 137, 292.
    See also Degrees of Freedom
Size tab, 101, *101*
sketch constraints. *See* constraints
sketch dimensions. *See* dimensions
Sketch Features, Select, 252
Sketch on New Part Creation, 37
sketch override, 70
Sketch tab, *6*, 36-37
    modes of, *8*
sketch-derived views, 430. *See also*
    break-out view
sketched features, 52-53
sketches. *See also* 3D sketches;
    specific sketches
    assembly, 296-297
    axis and, 396
    Dimension tool, 62, 66, 68,
        114, 156
    profile and, 396
sketching shortcuts, 489
sketching tools, **52-58**
Smooth, 60, 388
Snap Fit, 376
Software Graphics option, 35
Solid Bodies folder, 366, 372
Solid Body Keep Seams between
    Planar Faces, 278
Solid Color, 473
solid modeling, 156-170. *See also*
    specific solid models
Solids option, 370
spar, 418
Spar tab, 418
specialized tooltip, 29
Specify Tolerance, 371
speed indicator, 92
Spine tool, 434
splines, 59, 60, 432, 434

Split Face, 280
Split Solid, 280, 372. *See also*
    multibody modeling
Split tool, **280-281**
    dividing parts with, 372-375
    splitting bearing cover, 372-375, *373*
spokes, 330. *See also* pulley
    building, 333-334
    path for, 332
    pulley and, 330
    Sweep tool and, 336-340
Spotface, 98
Standard (in).ipt template, 156,
    159, 219, 262, 277, 367, 388
standard parts, **150**
    in Content Center, 150
    sheet metal parts *v.*, 54
    working with, 150-153
start-up, 32
start-up action, 32
states, 183
status bar, 19
STEP data, 286, 287, 288, 289
Straight, 76
Style and Standard Editor dialog
    box, **75-81**
Style buttons, 438
Style group, 184, 189
style libraries, 48, 73. *See also*
    libraries
Style Library, 80
Style tab
    Illustration rendering, 467-468
    realistic rendering, 465-466
subassemblies, 156
subfolders. *See* Frequently Used
    Subfolders
Supplier Content Center, **286-287**
    modifying, 295-296
    using, 288-295
    vendors and, 286, 287
support frame. *See* fan support frame
suppressing components, 248,
    252, *296*. *See also* Envelope
    Suppressed
surface modeling tools, 411. *See*
    also Sculpt tool
surface styles
    defined, 476
    pulley rendering with, 477-478
    Surface Style option, 467
Sweep dialog box, 335-336

Sweep tool, 335-340

Symbols option box, 438

Symmetric, 60

T

tabs, 5-8. *See also specific tabs*
   Application Options dialog box,
      30-38
   dialog box, 9-10
Tangent (to Point), 388
Tangent constraint, 59, 140
Tangent option, 388
Tangent to Plane, 388
Taper option, 404
Taper Tapped, 99
Tapped Hole, 99
Tear option, 77
Template Description dialog box, 240
templates, 16. *See also specific*
      templates
   AutoCad drawings and, 16
   bolted connection, reusing,
      241-243
   creating, 181
   default, *17*
   drawing and, 175-181
   Metric, 17, 63, 175, 181
   Standard (in).ipt, 156, 159, 219,
      262, 277, 367, 388
Termination face, 241, 425
termination plane, *239*
text, power knob and, 413-415
Text function (dimension editing), 209
Thicken/Offset tool, 353-358, 393
Thickness option
   Rib/Web tools, 404
   Sheet group, 75
Thread group, 238
3 Bend Intersection, 78
3D CAD systems, 494
3D display modes, 22-23, *23*
   Hidden Edge display mode, 22,
      23, 35
   Shaded display modes, 22, 23,
      35, 39
   Wireframe, 22, 23, 34, 39, 243
3D grips, 243-248, 345, 346
   accessing, *244*
   controlling, 244-248
   handles and, *244*
   options, 245

3D Intersection Curve dialog box, 356
3D models. *See also* digital
      prototypes
   assemblies and, 135
   associativity principle and, 175,
      212, 297
   display modes and. *See* 3D
      display modes
   goal of, 296
   ViewCube and, 28-29
3D Navigation option, 35
3D sketches, 355-357
3ds Max, 462. *See also* Inventor
      Studio
Through All, 98
Through Part, 433
Thumbnail view, 12, *13*
Title Blocks folder, 176, 476
To Hole, 433
To Next (Revolve tool), 396
To option
   Hole feature, 98
   Revolve tool, 396
To Sketch, 433
Tolerance Method, 209, *210*
tolerance method, 302
tools. *See specific tools*
tooltips, 7, 236
   appearance options, 32
   progressive, 7, 32
   specialized, 29
Top bearing cover, 373, 376, 379
Total Occurrences in Active
      Document, 19
Transition tab, 388
Transitional tab, 141
Transparency button, 24
Transparency On, 24
Trim Solid, 280
True Reflection, 465, *466*
turning off visibility, 248
Tweak Components, 442, 443, 491
Two Distances, 166
2D CAD systems, 53, 62, 189, 296,
      427, 435
2D drawings, 175. *See also*
      drawing views
   associativity principle and, 175,
      212, 297
2D Sketch Rep and Center Mark, 76
2D Sketch Representation, 76

Type
   Assembly tab, 139-140
   Sweep dialog box, 335
Type of Strength Calculation, 311
Type option, 42

U

UCS (User Coordinate System), 142
Undo, 4, **20**, 25, 457, 484, 487
Undo Isolate, 314
Unfold Rule, 74, 75-76
Unfold tool, 358-363
Unique Face Thickness, 370-371
unitless value, 387
Up One Level, 12
Use Application Options, 473
Use Reflection Image, 475
Use Software Graphics option, 35
Use Style Library, 43, 48
Use Thickness from Rule, 74
User Coordinate System (UCS), 142
user interface. *See* interface
User Interface Overview panel, 6

V

Variable tab, 269
Vault, 14, **42**, 45, 150, 183
V-belts, 322
   editing, 327-328
   motor and, 323-334
V-Belts Component Generator,
      322-334
vectors
   direction, 97
   Explicit Reference, 140
vendors
   communication materials for,
      430, 435, 462
   Supplier Content Center and,
      286, 287
Vertical, 59
View Face tool, 26
View Identifier field, 184
View Menu, 12
View representations, **249**
   colors and, 253-255
   creating, 250-251
View tab, **22-28**
ViewCube, **28-29**
viewing/general environment
      shortcuts, 487-488

Virtual Component, 218
virtual pulley, 323
visibility
    fan, animation of, 479-481
    turning off, 248, 374

W

Waguespack, Curtis, 310
Web tool, 404-408
Webs, ribs *v.*, 404. *See also* ribs
Weight value, 387
Weld tab, 172
weldments, 171-175
Width and Height (Render Image
    dialog box), 463
Width Extents option, *90*
Windows Explorer, 10, 14, 48, 136,
    164, 407
Wireframe display mode, 22, 23, 34,
    39, 243

wizards
    Make Components tool, 382-383
    new project file, 44, 46
    Snap Fit, 376
work axis, 97, 161, **162**
work environment
    coloring, changing, 30
    creating, 38-40
    Inventor LT and, 38
    shock absorber and, 38-40
work features, 161-166
Work Features panel, 114, 162, 279,
    372
work planes, **161**. *See also* specific
    work planes
    modification, duct and, 133, *134*
    positive/negative face, 407
work point, 97, 161, **162**
Wrap to Face, 408

X

X axis
    Horizontal and, 59
    red, 19
X-Ray Shadow, 23

Y

Y axis
    green, 19
    Vertical and, 59

Z

Z axis, 19
Zoom Selected tool, 27
Zoom tool, 26
Zoom Window tool, 26-27, *27*